Religious Fundamentalisms and the Human Rights of Women

Edited by Courtney W. Howland

palgrave

First published in hardcover in 1999 by St. Martin's Press
First PALGRAVE™ edition: September 2001
175 Fifth Avenue, New York, N.Y. 10010 and
Houndmills, Basingstoke, England RG21 6XS
Companies and representatives throughout the world.

PALGRAVE is the new global publishing imprint of St. Martin's Press LLC Scholarly and Reference Division and Palgrave Publishers Ltd (formerly Macmillan Press Ltd).

ISBN 0–312–21897–4 hardcover
ISBN 0–312–29306–2 paperback

Library of Congress Cataloging-in-Publication Data
Howland, Courtney W.
Religious fundamentalisms and the human rights of women / edited by Courtney W. Howland
   p. cm.
  Includes index.
  ISBN 0–312–29306–2
  1. Women's rights. 2. International human rights law 3. Women and religion. 4. Religious fundamentalism I. Howland, Courtney W., 1954–

K3243.R45 1999
342'.0878—dc21   99–20549
                                                            CIP

A catalogue record for this book is available from the British Library.

Design by Letra Libre, Inc.

First paperback edition: September 2001
10 9 8 7 6 5 4 3 2 1

Printed in the United States of America

Contents

III
The Conflict between the Human Rights of Women and the Religious Freedom of Fundamentalists: The International Legal Framework

VII
Religious Challenges to Religious Fundamentalism

Foreword

This book grew out of a highly successful conference on religious fundamentalism and the human rights of women, organized by the International Rule of Law Center (IRLC) at the George Washington University Law School and co-sponsored with the Jacob Blaustein Institute for the Advancement of Human Rights. The conference was also supported by The John D. and Catherine T. MacArthur Foundation, The Shaler Adams Foundation, The Global Fund for Women, Catholics for a Free Choice, and The Ms. Foundation for Women. The conference was an important part of the IRLC's work of establishing respect for internationally recognized human rights as a fundamental manifestation of the rule of law. A number of the speakers, encouraged by their experience of the conference, have contributed to this excellent collection of essays.

One of the particular strengths of the conference, now reflected in the book, is that the topic is addressed by experts in a broad range of disciplines: education; health; social and political sciences; philosophy; theology; and national and international law, with particular emphasis on human rights law. This recognizes that human rights issues need input from many different disciplines to achieve the greatest level of credibility and legitimacy.

It is important that this subject also be addressed by individuals from a broad range of backgrounds and perspectives. The contributors to this volume include nonreligious and religious persons, with the latter coming from several different religions. Contributors come from both the North and the South; from both academic and activist backgrounds; and from both policy-making and grassroots-organizing perspectives. Their essays give us a base and structure from which to consider the challenges to women's rights posed by religious fundamentalism.

The primary goals of the conference were to increase knowledge about the worldwide phenomenon of religious fundamentalism and the particular legal and political problems it poses for women, and to develop legal and action-oriented strategies for dealing with these concerns. The conference was deeply enlightening on these issues. It was particularly important for advancing the discussion of religious fundamentalism and extremism to understand it not as just a diffuse collection of local or national issues, but as a worldwide phenomenon. The book further advances these goals and allows a wider audience to benefit from the insights of the contributors. The book also develops a broad range of strategies: intellectual strategies for ensuring the uniform application of international legal norms; political strategies for countering fundamentalist policies; and pragmatic strategies in a number of vital areas, including education and health care.

As we enter the twenty-first century, it is particularly crucial to establish women's rights at the heart of human rights jurisprudence, and this book is aimed at taking a step in that direction. This book focuses on one of the most difficult challenges facing human rights today. Progress in this area is key for guaranteeing the equality of women worldwide. We all hope to meet the challenge.

Thomas Buergenthal
Presiding Director, International Rule of Law Center
Lobingier Professor of Comparative Law and Jurisprudence,
George Washington University Law School
Member, United Nations Human Rights Committee

Acknowledgements

This book is a product of several years' work involving the issues raised by religious fundamentalisms and women's rights. Not surprisingly, there are therefore a good number of persons whom I would like to thank.

My thanks go first to all the contributors to this book, and to the participants in the May 1998 conference on religious fundamentalisms and the human rights of women, organized by the International Rule of Law Center (IRLC) at the George Washington University Law School and co-sponsored with the Jacob Blaustein Institute for the Advancement of Human Rights (JBI). This book was inspired by that conference. Although not all conference participants developed their texts into chapters for this book, the input of everyone at the conference was appreciated by all contributors to the book.

I wish to thank Jack H. Friedenthal who, as Dean of the George Washington University Law School, invited me there as a scholar in residence and gave me the support necessary to work on my project of religious fundamentalisms and women's rights. Likewise, I particularly wish to thank Thomas Buergenthal, who, as the Presiding Director of the IRLC, gave invaluable support to my work as a senior fellow at the IRLC. When the first part of my project was published, Tom suggested that the subject matter was appropriate for a conference, and he helped make sure that the conference took place. I also much appreciate the support of Louis B. Sohn, Director of Research and Studies at the IRLC, who always encouraged me and provided me with a range of information and texts that were most helpful.

I owe a considerable debt of gratitude to Rebecca Law, my research assistant at the George Washington University Law School. The book could not have been completed without her tireless and dedicated work. Her excellent work overall and her ability to track down sources used in the chapters surpass any I have previously encountered.

I would also like to thank Felice Gaer, Director of the JBI, and Frances Kissling, President of Catholics for a Free Choice, for their belief in the importance of the topic and their help in making the conference take place. I particularly would like to thank Mahnaz Afkhami, President of the Sisterhood Is Global Institute (SIGI), and Robin Morgan, a co-founder of SIGI, for their ongoing practical and moral support with respect to both the conference and the book. It is a pleasure now also to thank Susan Deller Ross, Director of the International Women's Human Rights Center at Georgetown University Law Center, for inviting me there as a visiting scholar in residence to finish this book and to continue my work in this area.

Finally, and most important, my greatest thanks go to Michael Singer, my husband and colleague, and formerly Executive Director of the IRLC, for his thoughtful intellectual support, patience, sense of humor, and moral support throughout the preparation of this book.

Courtney W. Howland

Introduction

Courtney W. Howland

This book explores the acute problems that religious fundamentalist movements around the world are posing for women's equality and liberty rights. The authors—religious and nonreligious individuals seeking common ground—address the challenge of religious fundamentalism from distinct but mutually reinforcing perspectives: first, an international human rights perspective that aims to strengthen women's rights throughout the world; second, a national law perspective that deals with issues and remedies in individual countries; third, a grassroots perspective that looks to nonlegal remedies and alternatives; and, fourth, a theological and philosophical perspective that offers alternatives to fundamentalist interpretations of religious doctrine. This fourth approach recognizes that many women will assert their legal rights only to the extent that they believe it consistent with their religious beliefs.

The book focuses attention on religious fundamentalism as a transnational movement linked to particular legal issues for women in international human rights law and national law. The contemporary rise of religious fundamentalism in all the major religions (including Buddhism, Christianity, Hinduism, Islam, and Judaism) has been accompanied by a vigorous promotion and enforcement of gender roles whose explicit intent entails the subordination of women. While recognizing that fundamentalism takes different forms within different religions, ethnic groups, and countries—hence the plural term "fundamentalisms"—the book nonetheless makes clear that these various movements share many features in terms of their detrimental effect on women's rights, and thus raise similar legal issues.

The authors take different approaches to the issue of whether religious fundamentalism is religion-based and should therefore be appropriately classified as "religion." Some prefer to regard religious fundamentalism (or, as some prefer to say, "religious extremism") as an abuse of religion—and therefore not really religion. Others prefer to regard religious fundamentalist movements as political or cultural movements that use religion as a cover. While others, myself included, prefer to regard religious fundamentalism as simply part of religion, because to determine as a legal matter what is "really" religion is not a task the law is competent to decide, nor is it a task that the law should be assigned, since the potential for abuse would be great. Instead, certain limitations may be imposed on religious activities (as we would impose on other activities) when the fundamentalisms of religion take its practice beyond the bounds of what is lawful behavior in the general society. Although these different approaches occasionally yield different results, there is nonetheless a surprising consistency in the urging of respect for women's rights, including women's right to religious freedom.

The diversity of the book's authors allows the book to have a broad frame of reference and great depth of perspective in which to consider these issues. The authors from the academic world represent a range of disciplines including law, sociology, anthropology, theology, philosophy, education, literature, and religious studies. The authors from outside academia bring to the book the important perspective of activists who come from a broad range of national and international organizations. While the authors have different theoretical and political orientations, they are all committed to increasing justice in the world for women.

The book also has great breadth in its geographic and political coverage with respect to legal issues in the context of religious fundamentalism. Geographically, the book looks at fundamentalist movements and religious issues and the problems they create for women in many countries including, inter alia, Afghanistan, Algeria, Belgium, Brazil, Egypt, India, Iran, Israel, Morocco, Pakistan, Sudan, Thailand, the United Kingdom, and the United States. In political terms, the focus of the book ranges from minority religious fundamentalist movements within countries to fundamentalist governments of countries.

The primary emphasis of the book is on human rights law and women's legal rights. One of the key aspects of religious fundamentalism, which I have noted elsewhere, is its tendency to take political action aimed at conforming a state's (a country's) law to religious doctrine, particularly in areas affecting women's rights.[1] For this reason, state laws have become a crucial battleground in this context.

Several themes recur throughout the book. Not surprisingly, a number of authors note that fundamentalists are particularly concerned with women's sexuality—as a danger and as a threat to society—and thus are keen to regulate and control women's sexuality and reproduction through a variety of measures. Controlling women's sexuality fits neatly into the religious fundamentalist promotion of the patriarchal family and the "proper" role for women as being in the home. A feature that fundamentalisms share is an emphasis on women's role being confined to that of wife and mother and the restriction of their role in the public world. Although controlling women's sexuality and reproduction is a theme throughout the book, it is of such importance that Section V is dedicated to dealing specifically with this issue.

A second theme throughout the book is the need not only for legal remedies at the international level or at the national level of an individual's country, but also for alternative approaches, including nonlegal approaches. Again, this is of such importance that Section VI is dedicated to looking at alternative remedies and strategies of resistance for women.

A third theme recurring throughout the book is how the West, particularly liberals in the West, through fear of being accused of racism or in the name of respect for another's culture or in the promotion of multiculturalism, have ended up colluding implicitly or explicitly with fundamentalists by failing to condemn violations of human rights, particularly women's human rights. Often such "respect" is in effect respect for a male elite's vision of the culture that prevents women's voices being heard or acted upon. Again, because the politics of difference and cultural relativism are of such importance overall to the subject, Section II is dedicated exclusively to this topic.

The first section of the book addresses the impact of religious fundamentalism on women from a social and political sciences perspective. The first major cross-cultural study of religious fundamentalism was the University of Chicago's five-volume study, The Fundamentalism Project, which in part addressed gender issues in one of its sections.[2] The link between religious fundamentalisms and gender has been furthered by the work of each of the contributors to this section. They now bring their expertise to this book.

John S. Hawley provides a comprehensive definition of religious fundamentalism that serves as a foundation for the book. He discusses the historical origin of the term, the academic development of the term, and the crucial role of gender in the language of fundamentalism. He gives examples from different religions and different countries. He also raises and analyzes the difficulties inherent in using the term.

Susan D. Rose specifically addresses the problems raised by Christian fundamentalism in the United States. The term "fundamentalism" was first used by, and of, U.S. Christian groups at the turn of the century. Rose links the earlier movement's patriarchy and anti-feminism to contemporary Christian fundamentalists. She explores the Christian political agenda in U.S. federal and state legislation, particularly the Christian Right's support for parents' rights over children's in the context of sex education. She links

Christian fundamentalists' "abstinence-only" approach to sex education to their desire to control women's sexuality.

Marie-Aimée Hélie-Lucas places Muslim fundamentalism in the context of other religious fundamentalisms (and fundamentalisms in general) that she recognizes as political movements of the extreme right. She notes that while women in Muslim countries and communities are oppressed in the name of religious interpretations that support patriarchy, there is no such thing as a uniform "Muslim world." Moreover, she notes that fundamentalist ideology that constructs an imaginary, ahistorical image of the "Muslim woman" ends up being strengthened from outside Muslim contexts by liberal—often well-meaning—collusion in the name of respect for the Other's culture and religion. Her examples include Algeria. She draws attention to the range of strategies, from entryism to internationalism, that, against a background of different political circumstances, women use in defense of their human rights.

Nira Yuval-Davis explores Jewish fundamentalism in the context of fundamentalist movements in general. She discusses Jewish fundamentalism in Israel and in the Diaspora, with particular focus on Jewish missionary movements. She reviews the reasons why women have joined the Lubavitch movement and explores the nature of the empowerment that *Khazara Bitshuva* (a "return," a conversion to ultra-Orthodox Judaism) is supposed to give to women. She argues that this "empowerment" must be understood in the overall context of these Jewish women's lives and that their sense of this empowerment is linked to and in turn affects the larger political agenda of Jewish fundamentalist movements.

The next section in the book addresses the cultural relativist argument in the specific context of religious fundamentalism, human rights, and international law. The authors in this section are eminent specialists in international human rights who come originally from different religious traditions (which they do not necessarily identify with now): Christianity, Hinduism, Islam, and Judaism. Their perspectives, coming from diverse backgrounds—Iran, Sri Lanka, and the United Kingdom—give real depth to the discussion.

Cultural relativism is based on the notion that there are no universal standards by which all cultures—or in this context all religions—may be judged, and thus comparative analyses of different cultural-religious systems are not possible. The cultural relativist arguments of religious fundamentalists are often accepted at face value, especially in the context of the role and treatment of women. Cultural relativist arguments are particularly problematic in the context of feminist political practice, which is aimed at identifying themes of gender and oppression across diverse situations. Since religious claims for cultural relativism enter at every stage of the analysis of fundamentalisms, it is particularly important to address this topic.

Michael Singer provides an introduction to this section on cultural relativism. He analyzes cultural relativism in the context of its anthropological, philosophical, and theoretical origins. He examines the cultural relativist claims of religious fundamentalists in the international human rights context and notes that these claims are often made by the elites of a group claiming to speak and act on behalf of the group as a whole. He argues that this is particularly suspect with respect to their representation of women in situations where women are denied the right to express their views publicly within or outside of the group, and may be denied education and liberty as well. He also demonstrates the theoretical inconsistencies of cultural relativist claims, and their reliance on simplistic notions of identity and static visions of "culture" in the face of the real complexity of identity and the continuous processes of change in cultures. He points out that there is no basis for claiming that cultural relativism can support a claim that any local culture is superior to the global culture of the international community, which has forged human rights as part of its identifying characteristics.

Christine Chinkin provides an introduction to the issues raised by cultural relativism in international law. She notes that public international law—including human rights law—makes a particular claim to universality in application, and that demands for priority to be given to diverse cultural or religious traditions undermine these claims, and even the utility of a rights-based discourse. She notes how religious extremists may further bolster their claims by appropriating human rights guarantees for religious freedom and nondiscrimination on the basis of religion, but that the potential contradiction between women's rights and religious freedom is only occasionally acknowledged in human rights instruments. She also discusses the complexity of the issue under international law, noting that religious freedom is at the interface between civil and political rights and economic, social, and cultural rights, and also between individual and group rights. She argues that legal strategies at both the international level and the national level should be pursued where possible, but that a confrontational posture of setting women's rights against religious rights may not necessarily be helpful because many women are strong adherents to their religion. She also stresses the need for nonlegal methodologies in this context.

Mahnaz Afkhami discusses the contemporary threat to women and their rights in the Muslim world from an Islamist resurgence that seeks to establish various degrees of gender apartheid in Muslim societies. She notes how the Islamist resurgence has corresponded with a general change in women's status, as Protestant fundamentalism also came into existence in response to the new visibility and mobility of women. She notes that neither Islam nor the cultures of Muslim peoples is per se an obstacle to women's achieving rights, but rather that Muslim women face patriarchal structures that certain men, in power or seeking political power, represent as religion and culture. She discusses how Islamists use the argument of cultural relativity, now in vogue in the West, to deny women's rights by introducing regimes of gender segregation. However, she points out that claims of relativity stem from very different foundations in the West and in Islamist circles: in the West, adherents to cultural relativism base it on an underlying claim to freedom of choice, particularly to choose elements of cultures different from white, Christian, European/American male culture, whereas Islamists insist that no rights may exist outside the cultural norms defined by their designated group.

Radhika Coomaraswamy regards cultural relativism and religious extremism as presenting the greatest challenges to international human rights, and finds that the deepest division between cultural relativists and human rights activists is the area of women's rights. She observes that human rights as constructed today are a product of the European Enlightenment, with the inclusion of human rights in treaties being aimed at creating an international social contract that binds states to human rights mandates. She reviews how this consent paradigm has often been challenged by non-European thinkers and, in contemporary times, by heads of government, particularly in defense of "Asian values," which they argue are more communitarian in nature than the individualistic approach of human rights. She discusses and evaluates three different approaches to bridge the gap between the concept of universal human rights and cultural relativism: a principled approach that she suggests is appropriate at the international level; a balancing approach that she finds to be more sensitive to the issues but unworkable in practice; and a multicultural dialogue that emphasizes health and education initiatives that she considers may be successful at actually eradicating cultural practices harmful to women.

The next section serves as an introduction to the issues raised in the international legal framework by religious fundamentalism and women's human rights. As I have noted, one of the key concerns is the move by religious fundamentalists to make the law of states conform to religious laws. Since many religious norms, at least as interpreted by fundamentalists, are highly discriminatory against women, this raises serious issues about the legality of laws based on those norms under the international legal system. This section gives a sampling of the issues raised under the major human rights treaties (the International Covenant on Civil and Political Rights; the Convention on the Elimination of All Forms of Discrimination

Against Women; the Convention on the Rights of the Child) by authors specializing in these areas.

In my chapter, I discuss issues raised by religious fundamentalist restrictions concerning women's freedom under the International Covenant on Civil and Political Rights. I note that this treaty offers much more potential for ensuring women's rights than has sometimes been acknowledged, and suggest that a spirit of democracy, implicit and explicit in the treaty text, is within the core "object and purpose" of the treaty and must be taken into account in interpreting it. First, I argue with respect to states that have enacted religious "family" laws that discriminate against women and may have made reservations to the treaty for "family" laws on the basis of religious freedom, that such laws violate women's core rights safeguarded by the "political" articles of the treaty. These include the rights to opinion, to freedom of expression, to assembly, to vote, and to associate with others. Moreover, state reservations with regard to "family" laws do not prevent finding violations under the "political" articles of the treaty. Second, I argue that with respect to certain discriminatory religious laws that have not been enacted into state law, the state has an affirmative obligation to provide effective legal remedies for women abused under these laws and to protect its citizens against certain actions that have heretofore been characterized as "private." Such state action is the only way to guarantee women's political freedoms such that they can be fully effective citizens in a democratic polity.

Ann Elizabeth Mayer discusses the religious reservations that Muslim countries have entered to the Convention on the Elimination of All Forms of Discrimination Against Women—reservations that reject central provisions of the treaty such as requiring the elimination of discrimination against women in all matters relating to marriage and family relations. She questions whether these reservations are ever truly "religious," and argues that evolving political contingencies, not Islamic beliefs, are the determinative factor in making these reservations. She demonstrates the political nature of these reservations using the examples of Morocco, Kuwait, Pakistan, and Algeria. She also examines how Western legal scholarship has contributed to the misconception that religious beliefs underlie Muslim countries' reservations. She argues that some authors, extrapolating from the fact that the U.S. government is bound to respect the religious beliefs of minority communities, come to the unwarranted conclusion that Muslim countries who have entered reservations are aiming to uphold the religious freedom of their citizenry. She demonstrates that this is not the case because in almost all the countries involved, Islam is the state religion and the official Islamic law is applied to all citizens regardless of their religious beliefs, and moreover dissent from the official version of Islam is treated as political opposition, often with dire consequences.

Bahia G. Tahzib-Lie discusses the right to freedom of religion or belief that is found in most human rights treaties and what this right means for women. She finds that no global human rights treaty has specifically articulated women's equal entitlement with men to the right to freedom of religion or belief. She notes that this is surprising, given the specific articulation of a range of rights for women. However, she argues that since this right is given to "everyone" in treaties and that the treaties also forbid discrimination on the basis of sex, women do have an equal right to freedom of religion or belief. She reviews under international law what the content of this right means, and discusses both the freedom of religion and belief and the freedom to manifest religion and belief.

Geraldine Van Bueren and Deirdre Fottrell discuss a girl's right to education under international law and how so many children are denied education throughout the world as a result of the interplay of socioeconomic and cultural factors, including religion. They note that the right to education is important because its denial can amount to the exclusion of girls from society and can contribute to their subordination for the rest of their lives. They review how international human rights law protects a girl's right to education and what the nature of that right is. They discuss the intersection of the child's right to education and the child's rights to freedom of thought, conscience, and religion, as well as the parent's role regarding each of these rights.

The fourth section of the book offers examples of the types of issues raised in national contexts by religious fundamentalist agendas for women or by claims of legal autonomy by large religious groups within an individual country. One of the key issues in this context is what law is to be applied to different religious or secular groups living within the same country. Should the same law be applied to everyone or should it be so only as long as it is nonreligious or secular law? If only religious law governs, what of those persons who do not want to be governed by religious law? If the state only allows religious law, then is each religious community entitled to its own laws? Should a state have some persons governed under religious law and some under secular law? May an individual chose the system of law by which she wants to be governed? For example, the laws of India and Israel (like those of a number of states) provide that the religious law of each separate religious community governs certain issues of marriage, family, and personal status. In the book, these issues are addressed by lawyers and academics who have dealt with these matters in their own countries.

Ratna Kapur discusses Hindu fundamentalism and women's rights in the context of the rise of the Hindu Right in India. She explores the way in which secularism and equality have been deployed by the Hindu Right. She explains that secularism in India has never meant the separation of religion from the state, but rather equal respect for all religions within both the public and private spheres. She argues that the Hindu Right has been trying to cast itself as the true promoters of this secular tradition and that its promotion of formal equality for all religions results in the Hindu majority being the norm against which all other religions are to be judged. She argues that the Hindu Right's claims that it supports women's rights (by, for example, proposing a Uniform Civil Code based on progressive practices from all traditions) must be viewed and assessed in light of its broader political program of cultural nationalism.

Frances Raday discusses how religion, subcultures, and the family share a common element as to how they are regarded in legal systems: private, and deserving of autonomy such that they are free from political and legal regulation. She notes that this element combines with the fact that they all share patriarchal norms to result in women being denied equality under the law and being legally subjected to patriarchal norms in the family. She argues that the demand for cultural and religious subgroup autonomy is antithetical to the universality of the principle of equality between the sexes. She gives the Israeli legal system as an example of the institutionalization of legal inequality for women in the situation where the state delegates autonomy to different religious groups. The deference given to Jewish, Christian, and Muslim religious values has resulted in patriarchal norms being enshrined into law. She reviews how women are discriminated against under the family laws of these three religious communities, with particular emphasis on the fact that belonging to one of the communities is not a question of religious choice but one of birth status.

Marie-Claire Foblets discusses the extent to which a family court in Europe is obliged under choice-of-law rules to recognize (that is, to rely on in order to decide the case) family laws of the foreign jurisdiction of an immigrant community when such laws do not meet the host country's standards of gender equality and nondiscrimination. She focuses on the legal impact on Muslim women in this debate. Under current choice-of-law rules in Belgium, and in other European civil law states, the court has traditionally looked to the family law of the person's nationality of origin if he or she has retained it, even if the case has no direct connection with the country of origin and even if the country of origin is no longer the domicile of the parties. Because this would result in the enforcement of discriminatory provisions against women, courts have started to try to find other legal theories to deal with this issue. After being asked by the Belgian Minister of Justice to investigate this matter, Foblets interviewed a number of Moroccan Muslim women and men, law practitioners, judges, and others, and proposed that Belgium no longer maintain the choice-of-law rule of nationality, but instead adopt the choice-of-law rule of domicile (the law of the person's permanent place of residence), except for those couples who, at the time of their marriage, explicitly express the wish to be governed by the law of their nationality of origin.

The fifth section of the book examines the impact of an already noted key feature of religious fundamentalisms: the desire to control and regulate women's bodies, sexuality, and reproduction. Under religious fundamentalisms, women's sexuality is regarded as potentially evil and destructive of men, and thus a number of norms are aimed at making sure that women's sexuality is controlled—not by women, but by men. The authors in this section are both academics and activists who have long specialized in these issues in the international sphere.

Lynn Freedman introduces this section by discussing how women's bodies and their reproductive capacities and sexualities are the symbolic and real currency used by virtually all fundamentalist movements in their aim to change the world. She notes that fundamentalist groups have colluded with each other and have expertly co-opted concepts and language normally associated with progressive movements, with the result that mainstream organizations find themselves giving legitimacy to fundamentalist political projects (often anti-democratic) and that the natural opponents of fundamentalists lose their footing as their language is taken and redeployed in a destructive way. She discusses the reproductive health paradigm that emerged at the International Conference on Population and Development as an example of bringing together issues of the politics of women's bodies with the issues of the politics of social and economic development. Yet, she argues that this paradigm's link between reproductive health and social justice is threatened by fundamentalists. The paradigm's concept of "choice" has been redeployed by fundamentalists who characterize it as selfish, crass, and immoral and regard it as destructive of families and communities—a form of Western cultural imperialism. She notes how important it is for women to strengthen their commitment to the paradigm with its vision of reproductive freedom and social justice, even in the face of fundamentalist co-option and opposition.

Frances Kissling discusses how the Roman Catholic Church (Church) meets commonly accepted definitions of fundamentalism and serves as an obstacle to women's well-being and autonomy. She discusses the religious basis of Roman Catholic fundamentalism and the Church's opposition to abortion, contraception, sterilization, and fertility treatments. She argues that the Church's deep-seated hostility to the concepts of the plural and secular state and to any separation between church and state is a profoundly religious stance and is crucial to understanding the

Church's position as regarding itself as both a religion and a state. It is against this background that the Church's political activity in national and international lobbying against laws permitting contraception and abortion and its lobbying in the United States for exemptions for Catholic hospitals from providing reproductive health care must be evaluated. She also argues that the Church's opposition to abortion may be rooted in a hostility and fear of women rather than on its teaching that human life must be absolutely protected, since its teaching on this is inconsistent. She also notes that while the Church may posture as a supporter of women's rights, it in fact regards women's role as primarily one of being a mother.

Asma M. Abdel Halim discusses how the status of Muslim women has been articulated by traditional interpretations of the shari'ah (Islamic law). She notes that these interpretations have focused on sex and sexuality as key determining factors of a woman's rights and obligations. She argues that Muslim fundamentalists oppose the concept of gender for the very reason that it delinks the status of women from their sexuality. She discusses how women have been regarded as lustful creatures whose sexuality is obstructive to the performance of men's duties, and potentially destructive. As examples of rules regarding women's sexuality and their impact on women, she considers: interpretations of *hejab* (segregation of women and men, and the requirement of women covering in public); interpretations concerning *zina* (fornication); interpretations concerning the status of women in marriage; adoption of female circumcision by certain Muslim societies as mandated by Islam despite the lack of religious foundation for it; and interpretations of Paradise in which sexual pleasures are given only to men.

Lucinda Joy Peach discusses the role of Buddhist culture in Thailand in preventing the recognition and enforcement of women's human rights, especially with respect to the trafficking of women for prostitution. She discusses how women, often teenagers, from Thailand and Burma are encouraged, coerced, or even sold into the sex trade in Thailand. Forced into a system of debt bondage, the women are virtually imprisoned, physically abused, underpaid, and deprived of basic rights to liberty and medical treatment. She argues that both traditional Buddhist concepts of women as inferior and as sexual temptresses associated with the nonspiritual world and Buddhist practice under the Sangha in Thailand (the male monastic establishment) provide an atmosphere in which trafficking is allowed to flourish and increase the difficulties of using international human rights law to protect women.

The sixth section of the book explores two related aspects of women challenging religious fundamentalisms: how women resist in fundamentalist contexts, and what alternative remedies or possibilities exist for women. As can be seen from early chapters in the book, education of girls and women is a constant theme in the context of religious fundamentalism. Education is crucial to the girl's sense of self, ability to negotiate the world, and capacity to evaluate her own context and, if she so decides, to resist her parents, her community, and her government. For all these reasons, education serves as one of the battlegrounds in the fight between religious fundamentalists and supporters of women's and girl's human rights. The issues involving education at the most basic level are: will girls receive an education at all (for example, the Taliban in Afghanistan and fundamentalists in Bangladesh oppose education for girls)?; and, if so, what is to be the content of the education (for example, Christian fundamentalists fight hard to control the content of education in U.S. schools)? We can see how two women have dealt with these issues from an activist perspective. In this section, we can also see that even when women are highly oppressed, they nonetheless use the space available to them to manifest their resistance, as in the case of Iran. This section also provides a discussion of the option open to women who wish to exit their country and possibly even their community as well: seeking asylum in another country.

Sakena Yacoobi discusses her founding of the Afghan Institute of Learning (AIL), which she started for Afghan refugee children in Pakistan. She discusses how the AIL believes that the education of girls is the best investment for the future growth and development of Afghanistan. She discusses how the AIL trains teachers to provide innovative teaching in very difficult economic and material conditions. She also reviews the type of curriculum that is taught to children, including not only traditional subjects such as reading, mathematics, science, and social studies, but also basic health education for young children and more advanced health education for the educators so that they can deal with the issues of disease prevention and illness in the refugee camps.

Cecile Richards discusses how the Religious Right movement in the United States has had a significant impact on public policy and has instituted a backlash against women's rights. She regards the Religious Right as a far right movement that misuses religion in order to promote a political agenda and achieve political power. She discusses, with examples of activities of Christian fundamentalists, how the Religious Right has denigrated feminism and set about redefining what women's equality means. In response, she formed the Texas Freedom Network, a nonpartisan grassroots organization of religious and community leaders, to provide an alternative to the Religious Right in Texas. Her organization engages in a wide range of activities: monitoring the activities of the Religious Right; training leadership in how to stand up to the Religious

Right; educating the media and providing a balance of coverage on issues, particularly with respect to public education; and advocating for rational public policy at the state and local level.

Paul Nejelski discusses his experiences as an U.S. immigration judge with respect to cases involving gender-based asylum and women fleeing the hardships of religious fundamentalist persecution. He reviews U.S. immigration law and the standards for political asylum, noting that U.S. law conforms to international legal standards. He recounts how he has granted asylum to women from Sudan, Pakistan, Iran, Afghanistan, and certain countries of Latin America. He also discusses how he has recognized that a woman's opposition to the subservient role imposed on her by her husband and societal religious norms is an expression of political belief, and that mandating her to conform to that role is repression of her political belief, and that it is attributable to the state. He also argues that in granting relief in these cases he did not give special treatment to women but rather recognized that these claims justified asylum regardless of the sex of the applicant.

Azar Nafisi discusses how Iranian women resist the religious fundamentalist regime of the Islamic Republic of Iran. She notes that the Islamic regime has put forth the argument that the Islamic Revolution served to rid the country of Western imperialists and their domestic agents—such as women fighting for their rights. She demonstrates that contrary to this story, Iranian women have been fighting for their rights and freedom of choice, not as domestic agents of imperialists, but for themselves and their country, and have been doing so for a century and a half. She discusses how women started to resist wearing the "veil" (a black, body-length garment that covers a woman's hair and head, down to her toes) in the early part of the nineteenth century and continued to do so until Reza Shah prohibited the wearing of the veil. In response to Ayatollah Khomeini's order mandating that women wear the veil she notes that, contrary to what some in the West have claimed, 100,000 women marched in the street in protest. She notes that women in Iran are still resisting the veil in the space left to them, in a range of ways.

The final section of the book addresses religious challenges to religious fundamentalism. The authors in this section discuss how so many women find their religion to be an important and positive part of their lives, and because they recognize the patriarchy that infuses traditional interpretations, they are unwilling to leave the interpretation of their religion to fundamentalists or traditionalists. Each of the authors, with much experience in the theological and historical traditions of her religion, either reviews how women have provided alternative interpretations to fundamentalist or traditional interpretations or provides such an interpretation herself.

Paula Hyman discusses feminist strategies in response to patriarchy and fundamentalism in Judaism. She reviews how Jewish feminists in the United States and Israel have argued that patriarchy and the consequent subordination of women are not essential parts of Judaism. She notes how Jewish women have asserted the equality of women in Judaism and introduced egalitarianism as a communal value. She discusses the range of activities of Jewish feminists in creating egalitarian communities, including: scholarly writing that reinterprets classical Jewish texts; creating new ceremonies for girls in cases where there were only ceremonies for boys; and increasing Jewish education for girls. She also reviews feminist strategies that have been used in Israel, where they receive less communal support than in the United States.

Suwanna Satha-Anand discusses how the issue of women's equality in Buddhist societies, such as Thailand, has been linked to the issue of how women are regarded in Buddhism with respect to the sanghas (the orders of monks and nuns). She argues that the Buddhist canonical text describing Buddha's reluctance to establish a women's order, together with the fact that he seemed to subordinate the nun order under the monk order, should not be regarded as a mere compromise with his already existing monk order, but rather should be understood as the universality of Buddhist truth over the truth of convention, which would have disallowed the nuns' order entirely. She argues that since the Buddha did allow female ordination, he was in fact respecting the rights of women to religious practice. She also argues that permitting women's ordination confirmed that convention was overruled in support of women's rights, and that this principle of truth over convention should serve as a philosophical basis for women's rights in Buddhism.

Maria José Rosado Nunes discusses Roman Catholicism's difficulty in accepting the notion of individual autonomy that underpins the concept of human rights, particularly with respect to women. She discusses the conflict between the liberal conception of human rights and the "natural law" of Catholic theology. She reviews how Latin American women have reformulated a liberal concept of human rights for women such that women's rights are integrated into collective rights and include social rights and reproductive rights. She discusses how this vision of rights is also in conflict with Catholicism. She gives Brazil as an example of that conflict in action. She gives examples of the Brazilian Church engaging in fundamentalist political action with respect to reproductive rights in its aim to make Brazil's laws correspond to traditional Catholic doctrine.

Ghazala Anwar discusses how, in addition to fundamentalist (Islamist) movements that have been interpreting the shari'ah, a variety of Muslim reformers have been attempting to reform the shari'ah by making use of a wide variety of Islamic jurisprudential and hermeneutical concepts. She notes, however, that these approaches are of limited efficacy in achieving the goals of articulating gender equity and universal human rights, primarily because they share too many basic premises with the fundamentalists. She finds that reformers particularly fail to articulate a theological basis for a secular state, and that it is an imperative that this be done. She argues that it is necessary to rethink the Qur'an and the Sunnah (the sayings and exemplary customs and habits of Muhammad drawn from the Qur'an and the hadith literature). She discusses the historical critical method in the context of the hadith literature and the Qur'an, arguing that such critique transforms the hadith from a representation of the actual word or deed of the Prophet into a representation of the voice of the communal wisdom of the past community along with other voices seeking political and social power, and also transforms the written word (*mushaf*) of the Qur'an such that it need not be taken as the literal word of God. This interpretation allows Muslims to reaffirm their sense of justice and belief in human rights, but at the same time allows them space for religious life since the possibility of revelation, which is the foundational belief for Muslims, is maintained through the retention of the pre-revelatory and oral-recitation elements of the Qur'an.

NOTE TO READER

To help the general reader in locating sources, please note that footnote citations have generally followed the standard U.S. legal citation style of the *Bluebook*.[3] Some useful information has been added to standard *Bluebook* form, in particular the name of the publisher and the place of publication of books.

NOTES

1. *See* Courtney W. Howland, *The Challenge of Religious Fundamentalism to the Liberty and Equality Rights of Women: An Analysis under the United Nations Charter*, 35 COLUM. J. TRANSNAT'L L. 271, 277–78, 280–81, 288–89 (Buddhism), 294–96 (Christianity), 304–04 (Hinduism), 311–16 (Islam), 322–24 (Judaism) (1997).
2. *See* 2 THE FUNDAMENTALISM PROJECT, FUNDAMENTALISMS AND SOCIETY 129–310 (Martin E. Marty & R. Scott Appleby, eds.) (Chicago/London: University of Chicago Press, 1993).
3. THE BLUEBOOK: A UNIFORM SYSTEM OF CITATION (compiled by editors of Columbia Law Review, Harvard Law Review, University of Pennsylvania Law Review & Yale Law Journal) (Cambridge, MA: Harvard Law Review Association, 16th ed., 1996).

I

Social and Political Sciences Perspectives on the Impact of Religious Fundamentalism on Women

Chapter 1 ❧

Fundamentalism[1]

John Stratton Hawley

"Fundamentalism" is an embattled term. It arose in the United States in about 1920 as a term of self-reference adopted by a group of Protestant Christians who rallied behind a series of pamphlets called *The Fundamentals* (1910–1915). These writings deplored the evils of modernism—especially scientific naturalism, an "uncritical" use of higher criticism of the Bible, and perceived lapses in moral values. They favored returning to "the fundamentals" of Christian belief and practice, eternal pillars of an idealized past. In time, liberal Christians and modernists of a more secular hue began to use the term "fundamentalist" in a rather broader sense, to designate groups they saw as naive enough to believe they could reverse the course of history in favor of a mythic, dogmatically and socially homogeneous Christian past.[2]

In the 1980s, this pejorative usage became a staple in journalistic analyses of political debates about the Equal Rights Amendment (ERA), abortion, and prayer in the schools, indicating positions articulated by conservative Christian groups, especially evangelical Protestants. It was also employed by extension to designate the stances of religious groups around the world, especially Muslims, who took political action to reject Western secular modernism in its various forms. The Islamic revolution in Iran in 1979 put the term into wide use for the first time. Before long it also came to designate Hindus, Sikhs, Buddhists, and others. Many people so designated understandably came to resent the term's superior overtones—its suggestion of atavism and a narrow, rigid mentality. Not without justice, Muslims in particular have often seen it as cultural imperialism of a specifically Judeo-Christian variety.

In the 1990s, scholars sensitive to this problem have suggested a series of alternate terms to designate conservative, neotraditionalist, and often militant religious groups whose ideas and actions they continue to see as parallel, and which have on occasion made common cause across religious boundaries. One such term, favored by writers such as Peter van der Veer and Mark Juergensmeyer, is "religious nationalism."[3] Nikki Keddie, implicitly questioning whether nationalism is always the main focus of such efforts, has proposed "the new religious politics."[4] The large "Fundamentalism Project," organized by Martin Marty and R. Scott Appleby and funded by the MacArthur Foundation through the American Academy of Arts and Sciences, rejected the idea that there was a single global enemy of an enlightened, pluralist approach to religion-state relations, instead recognizing a plurality of "fundamentalisms."[5] Yet the organizers retained as proper the sense that the groups being so described would insist on seeing themselves as standing for a cohesive religious world view that focused on "the fundamentals."[6]

Until recently, it has been insufficiently appreciated—even on the part of the wide-ranging Fundamentalism Project—that issues of gender play a crucial role in the language of fundamentalism. While some thinkers continue to emphasize the appeal to inerrant scripture as a principal defining feature of fundamentalist groups,[7] others—myself included— have focused on the centrality of an appeal not to scriptural fundamentalism but to a certain "social fundamentalism."[8] We have noted that shared fears about enlarged domains of relative autonomy for women are a major focus of attention, even in groups that represent themselves as being concerned first and foremost about submission to inerrant scriptural revelation (the Torah, the Bible, the Qur'an, the Guru Granth Sahib) or about the wounded dignity of a particular national culture (*Hindutva* in India or Sinhalese Buddhism in Sri Lanka). In this, American fundamentalist struggles to defeat the ERA and reverse court rulings about a woman's right to choose abortion are hardly exceptional. What is being championed is a divinely sanctioned vision of natural differences between the sexes that make it appropriate for women to live within boundaries that would be restrictive for men—and to live under men's protection and even surveillance.

The abortion debate is particularly instructive in this regard. Opponents of abortion clearly regard a woman's proper space as delineated within the reproductive sphere of family. Anti-abortion rhetoric seems to project this space onto the womb, and provides for it a threatening opponent: the woman who seeks to destroy the safe space within which a child should dwell. The debate is about whose space that is: hers ("right to choose") or its ("right to life"). If "its," the uterine space stands for the prelapsarian purity of God's creation. The fetus's space is literally the woman herself; but by the same token the woman's space is firmly circumscribed by the in-

fant, who represents and guarantees the mother's embeddedness in patriarchal family structures.

Controversies about women's legal rights and women's visibility in
public space have been notable in the sorts of discourse we might call fundamentalist. For example, two interrelated disputes captured wide attention in India in the late 1980s. One had to do with whether Shah Bano, a
Muslim woman divorced against her will, should be restricted to the legal
rights defined by Muslim personal law, as the Indian Constitution allows,
or should have access to India's universal civil code.[9] The other dispute
concerned whether a young Hindu women called Roop Kanwar had the
religious right to immolate herself on the pyre of her recently deceased
husband, according to the little-practiced and long-outlawed custom of
sati.[10] (Whether she acted by her own volition was a separate question—
extremely dubious from the evidence available, but never entirely resolved.[11]) Both cases became occasions when conservative communities,
captained principally by men, disputed the right of the secular state to intervene in matters they considered religious, and both became instances in
which one religious community portrayed another as the covert enemy.
Muslims arguing for their autonomy in the Shah Bano case depicted their
opponents as intolerant Hindus. Pro-*sati* activists in the Roop Kanwar affair suggested there was bias in granting Muslims a degree of religious freedom denied to Hindus, as in the Shah Bano affair.

It is tempting to argue that in both cases the aggrieved conservatives
saw a woman—and perhaps womanhood in general—as the primary sign
of the dignity, integrity, and autonomy of their religious community.
Such symbology is also present in the desire to place restrictions on a
woman's dress and freedom of movement, a theme that emerges with
great frequency in fundamentalist rhetoric. Press reports about the self-
proclaimedly Islamic actions of Taliban militants in Afghanistan have repeatedly stressed this dimension.[12] It also figures, for example, in dress
codes for women that were stipulated by Sikh militants agitating for an
independent Khalistan in the late 1980s[13] and in statements of the Vishva
Hindu Parishad (World Hindu Council), a group closely associated with
the Hindu nationalist contingent of the Bharatiya Janata Party (BJP).[14]

Feminists around the world have launched a series of efforts to stop the
victimization of women by groups such as these. Yet it is important to recognize that women themselves are often vocal and active in organizations
one might characterize as fundamentalist. Phyllis Schlafly's efforts to block
the ERA and Uma Bharati's anti-Muslim tirades on behalf of the BJP
come instantly to mind.[15] Feminist scholars in particular have been eager
to account for this apparent anomaly,[16] and have observed that in certain
situations, some of the most effective avenues open to women desirous of

escaping the confinements of domestic space may be precisely those offered by religious or religio-political organizations that can make special use of what is often called "a woman's voice." Not only that, in the upheavals occasioned by rapid social change, "traditional" domestic roles sanctioned by religion do sometimes promise women power and protection more effectively than the available "secular" or "modernist" alternatives.

Hence the debate about "women and fundamentalism" is not a single controversy easily framed as "women vs. fundamentalism," but a complicated series of overlapping debates that involve often very different local cultures, histories, and constituencies. Yet certain patterns recur on the boundaries between women's lives and politically active neotraditionalist religious groups. Women regularly serve as the "Othered" body upon which struggles with the cosmopolitan, modernist "Other" are enacted— even when women themselves are speaking. Women easily represent nostalgia for an authoritatively organized childhood now felt to have been lost. And women justify a certain "religious machismo" on the part of the men who would protect them. Such continuities would seem to support the continued use of a single term for comparative analysis.

But should that term be "fundamentalism"? There are two significant objections. First, it is regarded as pejorative by many whose profile it seeks to describe. The term "fundamentalism" may not carry so intrinsic a negative judgment as words like "religious extremism" and "religious fanaticism," yet we must realize that even in the world of conservative Christianity, only a limited group would today choose to identify themselves as fundamentalists. Many more would prefer the word "evangelical." That term, however, possesses such distinctly Christian overtones as to bar it from comparative use. Moreover, the enthusiasm it connotes is not quite the well-planned zealotry that has animated the history of Protestant fundamentalism in the United States—a zealotry that seems so comparable to "fundamentalist" movements elsewhere.

A second objection to the term "fundamentalism" is that it carries inescapable historical, cultural, and sectarian baggage by virtue of its American Protestant origins. Members of other religious communities therefore feel easily misunderstood. To avoid this problem, scholars of the Muslim world have coined the term "Islamist," which is intriguing from a comparative point of view precisely because it resists comparative use. One would have to resort to a word like "religionist" to pursue in a general way the effort to distinguish true religion from its political caricature. That term would display clearly the value judgment that is involved: the modern Western notion that religion is individual, not communal, and belongs exclusively in the private sphere. One way to escape these difficulties is to fall back on the old political distinction between left and right. This has the advantage of highlighting the existence of a spectrum of religio-political behavior, even though many in the "Religious Right" would deny its legitimacy. The problem is that the polarizing of left and right provides little help in thinking about religious alliances such as those we see between the Neturei Karta (left) and *haredim* (ultra-Orthodox) (right) in contemporary Israel.

Clearly we must be aware of the difficulties that this search for words displays. No one term is really adequate for comparative usage. But in my view, at least, that muddy reality suggests there is good reason for continuing to use the word "fundamentalism." By contrast to many of the alternatives, it keeps to the fore the sense shared by many militantly conservative religious groups that their cause is a principled one focusing on a restoration of divinely sanctioned core values—fundamentals—that have been attacked, obscured, or overridden by the forces of modernity, often in colonial or imperial guise. Not only that, it leads one to ask comparatively which are the most fundamental of these fundamental values. Time and again we discover that however widely the other "fundamentals" may vary, there persists a basic concern to keep women in their "proper place."

NOTES

1. Many parts of this essay were first framed as a contribution to the ENCYCLOPEDIA OF WOMEN AND WORLD RELIGION (Serinity Young, ed.) (New York: Macmillan, 1999).

2. For a lengthier discussion of Christian and comparative uses of the term "fundamentalism," with bibliographical apparatus, see John Stratton Hawley and Wayne Proudfoot, *Introduction, in* FUNDAMENTALISM AND GENDER 3–44 (John Stratton Hawley, ed.) (New York/Oxford: Oxford University Press, 1994).

3. PETER VAN DER VEER, RELIGIOUS NATIONALISM: HINDUS AND MUSLIMS IN INDIA ix–xiv (Berkeley: University of California Press, 1994); MARK JUERGENSMEYER, THE NEW COLD WAR? RELIGIOUS NATIONALISM CONFRONTS THE SECULAR STATE 1–8 (Berkeley: University of California Press, 1993).

4. Nikki Keddie, *The New Religious Politics: Where, Why, and When do Fundamentalisms Appear?, in* 40 COMP. STUDIES IN SOC'Y & HIST.—(forthcoming).

5. *See* Martin E. Marty & R. Scott Appleby, *Introduction: The Fundamentalism Project: A User's Guide, in* 1 THE FUNDAMENTALISM PROJECT, FUNDAMENTALISMS OBSERVED vii, viii–ix (Martin E. Marty & R. Scott Appleby, eds.) (Chicago/London: The University of Chicago Press, 1991).

6. *See* Martin E. Marty & R. Scott Appleby, *Introduction, in* 4 THE FUNDAMENTALISM PROJECT, ACCOUNTING FOR FUNDAMENTALISMS 1, 1 (Martin E. Marty & R. Scott Appleby, eds.) (Chicago/London: The University of Chicago Press, 1994).

7. *See, e.g.,* BRUCE B. LAWRENCE, DEFENDERS OF GOD: THE FUNDAMENTAL-IST REVOLT AGAINST THE MODERN AGE 1–8, 14–16 (Columbus, SC: University of South Carolina Press, 1995).

8. BETTY A. DeBERG, UNGODLY WOMEN: GENDER AND THE FIRST WAVE OF AMERICAN FUNDAMENTALISM 1–12 (Minneapolis: Fortress Press, 1990); *See, e.g.,* Gita Sahgal & Nira Yuval-Davis, *Introduction: Fundamentalism, Multiculturalism and Women in Britain,* in REFUSING HOLY ORDERS: WOMEN AND FUNDAMENTALISM IN BRITAIN 1, 1–11 (Gita Sahgal & Nira Yuval-Davis, eds.) (London: Virago Press Limited, 1992); Hawley & Proudfoot, *supra* note 2, at 3–4, 16–35; Joan Menscher, *Introduction,* in MIXED BLESSINGS: GENDER AND RELIGIOUS FUNDAMENTALISM CROSS CULTURALLY (Judy Brink & Joan Menscher, eds.) (New York/London: Routledge, 1997); Nikki Keddie, *The New Religious Politics and Women Worldwide: A Comparative Study,* 10 J. WOMEN'S HIST.—(Winter 1999, forthcoming) (Special Issue: Women and Religious Politics in the Twentieth Century: Beyond Fundamentalism) (Nikki R. Keddie & Jasamin Rostam Kolayi, eds.).

9. *See* Peter J. Awn, *Indian Islam: The Shah Bano Affair,* in FUNDAMENTALISM AND GENDER, *supra* note 2, at 63–78.

10. John Stratton Hawley, *Hinduism:* Sati *and its Defenders,* in FUNDAMENTAL-ISM AND GENDER, *supra* note 2, at 79–110.

11. *See* Veena Talwar Oldenburg, *The Roop Kanwar Case: Feminist Responses,* in SATI, THE BLESSING AND THE CURSE: THE BURNING OF WIVES IN INDIA 101–130 (John Stratton Hawley, ed.) (New York/ Oxford: Oxford University Press, 1994).

12. *See* PHYSICIANS FOR HUMAN RIGHTS, THE TALIBAN'S WAR ON WOMEN: A HEALTH AND HUMAN RIGHTS CRISIS 30 (U.S.A.: Physicians for Human Rights, 1998).

13. *See* Harjot Oberoi, *Sikh Fundamentalism: Translating History into Theory,* in 3 THE FUNDAMENTALISM PROJECT, FUNDAMENTALISMS AND THE STATE 256, 272 (Martin E. Marty & R. Scott Appleby, eds.) (Chicago: University of Chicago Press, 1993).

14. *See* Hawley & Proudfoot, *supra* note 2, at 4, 35 n.3.

15. *See* Amrita Basu, *Feminism Inverted: The Gendered Imagery and Real Women of Hindu Nationalism,* in WOMEN & RIGHT-WING MOVEMENTS: INDIAN EX-PERIENCES 158, 158–180 (Tanika Sarkar and Urvashi Butalia, eds.) (London/New Jersey: Zed Books Ltd. 1995) (discussing Uma Bharati).

16. *See, e.g.,* Amrita Basu, *Feminism Inverted: The Real Women and Gendered Imagery of Hindu Nationalism,* 25 BULLETIN OF CONCERNED ASIAN SCHOL-ARS 25 (Amrita Basu, guest ed.) (1993) [hereinafter ASIAN SCHOLARS]; Tanika Sarkar, *The Women of the Hindutva Brigade,* in ASIAN SCHOLARS, *supra,* at 16; Paola Bacchetta, *All Our Goddesses Are Armed: Religion, Resistance, and Revenge in the Life of a Militant Hindu Nationalist Woman,* in ASIAN SCHOLARS, *supra,* at 38; *see* Basu, *supra* note 15, at 158–180; Keddie, *supra* note 8.

Chapter 2

Christian Fundamentalism: Patriarchy, Sexuality, and Human Rights

Susan D. Rose

I. INTRODUCTION

The Universal Declaration of Human Rights (Universal Declaration) adopted by the United Nations (UN) proclaims that "[a]ll human beings are born free and equal in dignity and rights,"[1] yet women's freedom, dignity, and equality are persistently compromised by law, custom, and religious tradition in ways that men's are not. This chapter will focus on Christian fundamentalism and patriarchy, and how they interactively help shape and rationalize both cultural views and social policy related to gender, sexuality, health, reproductive choice, and violence against women and girls.

The reinforcement of patriarchy is the trait that Christian fundamentalism most clearly shares with the other forms of religious belief that have also been called "fundamentalist." This characteristic is most evident across the Abrahamic tradition of the three major monotheistic religions—among fundamentalist Israeli Jews, within both Sunni and Shi'ite Muslim communities in various countries, and within the current revival of evangelical Protestantism emanating from the United States—but is also evident in fundamentalist Hindu and Buddhist movements.[2] All seek to control women and the expression of sexuality. Fundamentalists argue that men and women are by divine design "essentially" different, and they aim to preserve the separation between public and private, male and female, spheres of action and influence.[3] As Charlotte Bunch notes:

The distinction between private and public is a dichotomy largely used to justify female subordination and to exclude human rights abuses in the home from public scrutiny. . . . When women are denied democracy and human rights in private, their human rights in the public sphere also suffer, since what occurs in "private" shapes their ability to participate fully in the public arena.[4]

The most common rationale given for denial of human rights to women is the preservation of family and culture. While article 16 of the Convention on the Elimination of All Forms of Discrimination Against Women (CEAFDAW) requires state parties to take "all appropriate measures" to ensure the equality of women and men in marriage and in parental rights and responsibilities,[5] fundamentalists across these traditions maintain that women are the keepers of the heart and hearth, whereas men are the keepers of the mind and marketplace.

The struggle for women's and children's rights as human rights poses a fundamental threat to "traditional" cultural orders and social structures, and especially to "secondary-level male elites."[6] When "secondary-level male elites" are struggling to maintain male dominance in the middling areas of society where jobs are increasingly contested by women, they find that they can reassert themselves in the family, school, and church, which are the social institutions most accessible to them.[7] In contrast, the first-level male elite, who control the major financial institutions and/or manage the corporate structures, are not so concerned with this kind of patriarchal restoration.[8]

II. MAKING MEN, SUBDUING WOMEN IN LATE-TWENTIETH-CENTURY AMERICA

In the early twentieth century, the original, U.S. Christian fundamentalist movement explicitly stated that reining in women was essential to maintaining social cohesion.[9] Fundamentalists were also aware that although religion remained important to women, its appeal was declining among men.[10] In addition, the shift from an agrarian to an industrial society made it more difficult for men to live out "traditional" notions of masculinity.[11] As a result, concerns about the feminization of men and of Christianity developed into a kind of militant, virile masculinity that became the hallmark of the Christian warrior, and the movement's literature became "rife with strident anti-feminist pronouncements, some of them bordering on outright misogyny."[12]

This is no less true today. As Martin Riesebrodt argues, fundamentalism is primarily a "radical patriarchalism" that represents a protest movement against the increasing egalitarianism between the sexes.[13] Within the vast majority of fundamentalist, Pentecostal, neo-Pentecostal, and charismatic Protestant churches (which I refer to under the umbrella terms "evangelical" or "fundamentalist")[14] spreading both within and beyond the United States, the downward lines of authority of the nuclear, patriarchal family are still being firmly reinforced: children are to be obedient to their parents, wives to their husbands, and husbands to their God.[15]

One of the most prominent evangelical groups today to promote a modernized form of patriarchy is the "Promise Keepers." Founded in 1990 by Bill McCartney, head coach of the University of Colorado football team, the Promise Keepers (and their female counterpart, the Promise Reapers) has embraced the goal of motivating men toward Christlike masculinity. For example, Pastor Tony Evans, in *Seven Promises of a Promise Keeper,* argues that the primary cause of (our) national crisis—the decline of family structure—is "[t]he Feminization of Men," and he urges men to take back their male leadership role: "Unfortunately, however, there can be no compromise here. . . . Treat the lady gently and lovingly. But *lead!*"[16]

The Promise Keepers are promoting good old-fashioned patriarchy with a new twist. They are encouraging men to become more involved in family life, and more responsible to and for their children, but their approach would not meet the obligations of equality under article 16 of CEAFDAW—which they would be bound to oppose in any event. Rather than working toward greater equality for both men and women, leaders reassure men that they will *gain* rather than lose power and authority within the family. Within the fundamentalist framework, family life continues to be gendered along patriarchal lines, and while men are called back to the private sphere, gender apartheid is still maintained. This has significant consequences for social policy that affects the lives and choices of all citizens, particularly in the arenas of reproductive choice and health.

III. LEGISLATING THE CHRISTIAN PATRIARCHAL AGENDA

The pro-family political platform of the contemporary Christian Right in the United States unabashedly supports patriarchy, and privileges men's rights over women's rights, and parents' rights over children's and states' rights. This approach is particularly pernicious given that studies of domestic violence indicate that wife and child abuse is more common among families that adhere to traditional, patriarchal sex role norms.[17]

Over the past several years, conservative groups such as the Christian Coalition, Focus on the Family, the Eagle Forum, and Of the People have campaigned for "parental-rights" legislation at the federal level and in more than 25 states. These various attempts have included the "Pupil Protection Act," also known as the Hatch Amendment of 1978, which requires parental consent when a federally funded program in a school calls for a student to submit to a survey or evaluation that may reveal information concerning, among other things: political affiliations; mental and psychological problems potentially embarrassing to the student or his family; sex behavior and attitudes; and illegal, anti-social, self-incriminating, and demeaning behavior.[18] The Christian Religious Right used the Hatch Amendment to attack the curricula of public education and to prohibit curricula dealing with: health issues of suicide, drug and alcohol abuse, and sex education; globalism and world issues such as information on the Holocaust and news reporting from worldwide magazines (*Time* and *Newsweek*); diversity issues, including exposing children to books by African American and homosexual authors; and general programs concerning political participation, including mock elections.[19] The breadth and depth of the attack on the integrity of a free public education was so great that even Senator Orrin Hatch, the sponsor of the bill, called for "the rule of commonsense [to] prevail."[20]

The patriarchal approach of the Christian Right is also apparent in the recently proposed "Parental Rights and Responsibilities Act of 1995," which prohibits any government from interfering with or usurping the right of the parent in the upbringing of the child in such areas as education, health, discipline (including corporal punishment), and religious teachings.[21] Such a bill would, among other things, have an obvious "chilling" effect on intervention in child-abuse cases.[22]

The Christian Right's support for parents' rights over children's rights and its attacks on public education demonstrate the clear conflict of interest between, on the one hand, the rights of children to an informed education (including their health) and the duty of all states to provide informed education and, on the other hand, the extent of the parental right to socialize and educate their children within the parameters of their religious faith. It is also important to note that the strongest impact will be on girls because the Christian Right educational agenda includes the promotion of patriarchy and thus unequal roles for men and women. It is hard to imagine how girls can take away from such education the Universal Declaration's proclamation that "[a]ll human beings are born free and equal in dignity and rights."[23]

The most recent victory for the conservative crusaders in their influence on public school education was their successful lobbying of Congress, in 1996, to pass welfare reform that included a provision to promote teen sexual abstinence programs in public schools. The federal government had previously funded similar programs and had been sued for providing public funding to those programs that promoted specific religious teachings.[24] Although the settlement in the case included a requirement that funded programs be medically accurate and free of religious teachings,[25] it is unclear that this standard is being met under the newly funded programs.

IV. THE SEXUAL POLITICS OF ABSTINENCE

Contemporary evangelicals have concerns about sex and sexuality that focus on issues regarding social order and control—especially over women's bodies and desires. Within the evangelical framework, lack of control over sex and the desires of the body are thought to threaten the integrity of the soul.

Exposure to information about sex, many evangelical leaders argue, leads to sex. Therefore, the political platform of the Religious Right aims to curtail sex education in the schools, and severely limit contraceptive research and dissemination at large. With the United States holding the record for the highest rate of teenage (ages 15 to 19) pregnancies and abortions in the industrialized world,[26] these issues have become all the more critical. Rightfully concerned about the high rates of teenage pregnancy, abortion, sexually transmitted diseases, and AIDS, evangelicals are active in trying to influence public policy. Although the U.S. teenage pregnancy rate has actually fallen to its lowest level in 20 years,[27] teenage pregnancy *is* still a problem—but when, where, how, and why it became constructed as a social problem is important to examine. For example, cross-national data indicate that the countries that have low teen pregnancy rates tend to have more open attitudes toward sexuality and sex education, access to contraceptives and a national health care system, and greater socioeconomic equality.[28] But rather than dealing with the complex problems associated with high rates of teenage pregnancy, including the fact that the United States has one of the highest rates of child poverty, child death, and infant mortality in the industrialized world, and that young teens often become pregnant as a result of rape or incest,[29] abstinence-only advocates simply advise young people to "just say no." Abstinence-only advocates have "just said no" to substantial and well-documented empirical data that show that the degree to which an effect of comprehensive sexuality education has been identifiable in studies, it has *postponed* initiation of sexual intercourse.[30]

A. "Just Say No"

Sex education has always been a point of conflict between public educators and conservative religious groups. Since the 1960s, Religious Right political groups have opposed the teaching of comprehensive sexuality education in public schools. By the 1980s, however, it was clear that the Religious Right was having little success in removing sex education from the schools because the general American public favors comprehensive sex education.[31] As a result, Religious Right groups, including the Eagle Forum, Concerned Women for America, Focus on the Family, and Citizens for Excellence in Education have all devoted major resources to promoting "abstinence-only" curricula in the public schools as a substitute for comprehensive sex education programs. As noted, in 1996, bowing to the Religious Right, Congress allocated fifty million dollars annually for abstinence-only education programs.[32] The provision funds programs to teach children that "sexual activity outside of the context of marriage is likely to have harmful psychological and physical effects."[33]

Religious Right groups use sophisticated, fear-based tactics in their abstinence-only programs: "Just say no or die."[34] For example, the video, *No Second Chance,* juxtaposes images of men dying from AIDS with an evangelical sex educator interacting with a classroom of teenagers. She compares having sex outside of marriage with playing Russian roulette: "every time you have sex, it's like pulling the trigger." When one teenage boy asks, "[w]hat if I do have sex before I get married?" She responds, "I guess you'll just have to be prepared to die."[35]

Leslie Kantor, the former director of the Sexuality, Information, and Education Council of the United States (SIECUS) Community Advocacy Project, conducted an extensive content analysis of abstinence-only sex education programs produced and promoted by Christian Right groups and that are used in public schools. She concluded that these programs omit the most fundamental information on contraception and disease prevention, perpetuate medical misinformation, and rely on religious doctrine and images of fear and shame in discouraging sexual activity.[36]

B. Holding Girls Responsible

When reading through these Christian abstinence materials, one becomes aware of an old, traditional message: the cautionary story of sex as one of male predators and female prey. On the one hand, from an evangelical perspective, humans are not animals (which is at the crux of the evolution-creation debate), rather they stand only a little lower than angels. Yet, beyond a certain point, humans—especially men—are regarded as not being able to control their sexual urges. In fact, according to the sexual arousal time line in *Sexual Common Sense: Affirming Adolescent Abstinence,* "the prolonged kiss" is pinpointed as the "beginning of danger:"[37]

KNOW the Progression of Sexual Feeling with Increased Physical Intimacy

Sexual Arousal

Being Together	Hand Holding	Simple Good Night Kiss	Prolonged Kiss	Necking	Petting	Heavy Petting	Mutual Sex Play	Sexual Intercourse	End of Relationship in its Present Form
No genital feeling aroused			beginning of danger	Male Genital feeling aroused	Female Genital feeling aroused	Female Genital feeling aroused			

*Coleen Kelly Mast, *Sex Respect: The Option of True Sexual Feeling–Student Handbook 7*, 90 (Bradley, IL: Respect Incorporated, rev. ed. 1997) *reprinting chart from* Patricia B. Driscoll & Mary Rose Osborn, *Sexual Common Sense: Affirming Adolescent Abstinence* (Walnut Creek, CA: Womanity Publications, 1982).

After this point of "danger," there is no turning back from sexual arousal. The sexual arousal time line also indicates that while females too have sexual instincts, they take longer to become aroused. Therefore, they hold greater responsibility in exercising constraint. Women are considered to be less controlled by their sexuality and more responsible not only for their own sexual behavior but for the sexual behavior of men. Evangelist James Robison, whose book *Sex is Not Love* sold over half a million copies, warns that "[s]ex before marriage . . . develops sensual drives that can never be satisfied and may cause a man to behave like an animal."[38] He states that "[s]ome girls become that way, too . . . but most of them don't. When they do, it's the most awful thing that can happen to humanity."[39]

However, it would appear that there are more awful things that can happen: the use of tax dollars to support abstinence-only programs that provide medical misinformation and promote fear and ignorance, and the failure to provide support to implement effective social policy that could effectively curb teenage pregnancy and provide better economic, educational, and health opportunities for all young people.

V. WHOSE RIGHTS?

Central to the sex education debate is the Religious Right's attempt to preserve men's rights over women's rights, and parental rights over children's rights. The Family Research Council in 1995 critiqued the Fourth World Conference on Women, stating that the conference reflected "a radical feminist agenda" that "denigrate[d] motherhood and the traditional family" by noting that there were "unequal power relations" in the family.[40] Radical? Yes, writes evangelical psychologist James Dobson, who heads up the largest Christian Right Organization in the United States, Focus on the Family. He warns that the UN Conference on Women represents "the most radical, atheistic, anti-family crusade in the history of the world"[41] and that "[t]he Agency for International Development will channel hundreds of millions of dollars to support women's reproductive and sexual rights and family planning services. The only hope for derailing this train is the Christian church."[42]

As we enter the new millennium, family planning, reproductive and sexual health, and economic well-being are vital concerns for individuals, communities, and nations. Rates of pregnancy, and AIDS and other sexually transmitted diseases, remain alarmingly high among America's youth, yet opponents of sexuality education are trying to censor vital, life-saving information that has proven effective in dealing with these problems. Instead, the Religious Right continues to blame the "fallen girl/woman" and the feminization of men for the ills of our society rather than economic and structural forces that perpetuate inequality between men and women, and between the very wealthy and the middle and impoverished classes. In the battle over sexuality and choice and education, it's girls' and women's bodies, lives, and livelihoods that are all too often sacrificed.

With respect to girls' rights in education, it is important to remember that the International Covenant on Civil and Political Rights (ICCPR)—to which the United States is a party—prohibits discrimination against women or girls.[43] The Human Rights Committee, the monitoring body of the ICCPR, has interpreted ICCPR provisions as allowing parents to ensure that their children receive a religious and moral education but that public schools are limited to teaching the general history of religion in a nondiscriminatory manner and only if it is given "in a neutral and objective manner" because the "instruction in a particular religion or belief is inconsistent" with the ICCPR.[44] Does the Christian Right educational agenda meet this standard?

While evangelicals represent only 25 percent of the U.S. population, their influence on social policy regarding sexuality education, sexual orientation, teen pregnancy, reproduction, family planning, and economic equity has been significant, though less in establishing their agenda than in putting the brakes on research, education, and funding that could reduce the rates of teen pregnancy, abortion, and violence against women and children; increase the equality between women and men; and better protect and prepare children for healthy, active, responsible lives in the twenty-first century. Their impact is also felt beyond the borders of the United States. Today North American evangelicals are the largest group of missionaries moving across the globe on mission quests.[45] They are effective in establishing churches, schools, and health clinics in various places around the world. What kind of messages will they be disseminating? What kinds of influence may evangelical "sex experts" have as they fund programs and advise people and political leaders, not only in the United States, but around the world about gender, family planning, sex, contraception, violence—about life and death?

NOTES

1. *See* Universal Declaration of Human Rights, *adopted* Dec. 10, 1948, G.A. Res. 217A (III), U.N. GAOR, 3d Sess., pt. 1, 183d plen. mtg., at 71, art. 1, U.N. Doc. A/810 (1948) [hereinafter Universal Declaration].

2. *See* STEVE BROUWER, PAUL GIFFORD, & SUSAN ROSE, EXPORTING THE AMERICAN GOSPEL: GLOBAL CHRISTIAN FUNDAMENTALISM 218–26 (New York/London: Routledge, 1996) [hereinafter BROUWER, EXPORTING]; Helen Hardacre, *The Impact of Fundamentalism on Women, the Family, and*

Interpersonal Relations, in 2 THE FUNDAMENTALISM PROJECT, FUNDAMEN-
TALISMS AND SOCIETY 129, 131–47 (Martin E. Marty & R. Scott Appleby,
eds.) (Chicago/London: The University of Chicago Press, 1993)[here-
inafter FUNDAMENTALISMS AND SOCIETY]; John S. Hawley, *Hinduism: Sati
and Its Defenders, in* FUNDAMENTALISM AND GENDER 79, 93–103 (John
Stratton Hawley, ed.) (New York/Oxford: Oxford University Press, 1994);
see also JAN GOODWIN, PRICE OF HONOR: MUSLIM WOMEN LIFT THE VEIL
OF SILENCE ON THE ISLAMIC WORLD (New York/Boston/Toronto/Lon-
don: Little, Brown, and Company, 1994). For a further discussion of "fundamentalism" across religions, see John Stratton Hawley, Fundamentalism,
in this volume.

3. *See* Courtney W. Howland, *The Challenge of Religious Fundamentalism to
the Liberty and Equality Rights of Women: An Analysis under the United Nations Charter*, 35 COLUM. J. TRANSNAT'L L. 271, 283–85 (1997).

4. Charlotte Bunch, *Transforming Human Rights from a Feminist Perspective, in*
WOMEN'S RIGHTS, HUMAN RIGHTS: INTERNATIONAL FEMINIST PERSPEC-
TIVES 11, 14 (Julie Peters & Andrea Wolper, eds.) (New York/London:
Routledge, 1995).

5. *See* Convention on the Elimination of All Forms of Discrimination Against
Women, *adopted* Dec. 18, 1979, G.A. Res. 34/180, U.N. GAOR, 34th Sess.,
Supp. No. 46, at 193, 196, art. 16 (1), U.N. Doc. A/34/46 (1979), 1249
U.N.T.S. 13, 20.

6. BRUCE B. LAWRENCE, DEFENDERS OF GOD: THE FUNDAMENTALIST RE-
VOLT AGAINST THE MODERN AGE 100 (Columbia, SC: University of South
Carolina Press, 1989).

7. *See* SUSAN D. ROSE, KEEPING THEM OUT OF THE HANDS OF SATAN: EVAN-
GELICAL SCHOOLING IN AMERICA 1–10 (New York/London: Routledge,
1988).

8. *See* BROUWER, EXPORTING, *supra* note 2, at 219 & n.19.

9. *See* BROUWER, EXPORTING, *supra* note 2, at 219–20.

10. *See* MARGARET LAMBERTS BENDROTH, FUNDAMENTALISM AND GENDER,
1875 TO THE PRESENT 13, 17 (New Haven/London: Yale University Press,
1993).

11. *Id.* at 17; BROUWER, EXPORTING, *supra* note 2, at 219–20.

12. *See* BENDROTH, *supra* note 10, at 31.

13. MARTIN RIESEBRODT, PIOUS PASSION: THE EMERGENCE OF MODERN
FUNDAMENTALISM IN IRAN AND THE UNITED STATES 176–208 (Berke-
ley/Los Angeles/London: University of California Press, 1993).

14. For a more detailed discussion of these different groups and terminology,
including the use of the umbrella term "evangelical," see BROUWER, EX-
PORTING, *supra* note 2, at 263–71; Nancy T. Ammerman, *North American
Protestant Fundamentalism, in* 1 THE FUNDAMENTALISM PROJECT: FUNDA-
MENTALISMS OBSERVED 1, 2–5 (Chicago/London: the University of
Chicago Press, 1991); Laurence R. Innaccone, *Heirs to the Protestant Ethic?
The Economies of American Fundamentalists, in* 3 THE FUNDAMENTALISM

PROJECT: FUNDAMENTALISMS AND THE STATE 342, 343–44 (Chicago/London: The University of Chicago Press, 1993).

15. *See, e.g.*, Dr. Edward Hindson, former Director of Counseling at Jerry Falwell's Thomas Road Baptist Ministries, *quoted in* ROSE, *supra* note 7, at xvii ("The Bible clearly states that the wife is to submit to her husband's leadership.").

16. Tony Evans, *Spiritual Purity, in* SEVEN PROMISES OF A PROMISE KEEPER 73, 80 (Al Janssen & Larry K. Weeden, eds.) (Colorado Springs, CO: Focus on the Family Publishing, 1994).

17. *See* GENDER VIOLENCE: INTERDISCIPLINARY PERSPECTIVES (Laura L. O'Toole & Jessica R. Schiffman, eds.) (New York/London: New York University Press, 1997); JAMES ALSDURF & PHYLLIS ALSDURF, BATTERED INTO SUBMISSION: THE TRAGEDY OF WIFE ABUSE IN THE CHRISTIAN HOME 10, 16–18 (Downers Grove, IL; InterVarsity Press, 1989).

18. Protection of pupil rights, 20 U.S.C. §1232h (1994). The Hatch Amendment itself was amended in 1994, but the key provisions remain intact. The current regulations are those that were written before the 1994 amendments. *See* Student Rights in Research, Experimental Programs, and Testing, 34 C.F.R. §98 (1996); *see generally* Anne C. Lewis, Little-Used Amendment Becomes Divisive, Disruptive Issue, PHI DELTA KAPPAN, June 1985, at 667.

19. *See* Susan Rose, *Christian Fundamentalism and Education in the United States, in* FUNDAMENTALISMS AND SOCIETY, *supra note* 2, at 452, 467–473.

20. Pupil Protection Rights Regulations, 131 CONG. REC. 2449, 2451 (1985).

21. *See* H.R. 1946, 104th Cong. (1995); S. 984, 104th Cong. (1995).

22. The Alan Guttmacher Institute, *Supremacy of Parental Authority New Battlecry For Conservative Activists,* WASHINGTON MEMO, Dec. 21, 1995, at 4.

23. For a discussion of how international human rights law can protect the girl child's right to education, see Deirdre Fottrell & Geraldine Van Bueren, *The Potential of International Law to Combat Discrimination Against Girls in Education,* in this volume.

24. *See* Brown v. Kendrick, 487 U.S. 589 (1988) (remanded for trial).

25. *See* Leslie M. Kantor, *Attacks on Public School Sexuality Education Programs: 1993–94 School Year,* 22 SIECUS REPORT, Aug./Sept. 1994, at 11, 11.

26. *See* ANDREW L. SHAPIRO, WE'RE NUMBER ONE! WHERE AMERICA STANDS—AND FALLS—IN THE NEW WORLD ORDER 11–16 (New York: Vintage Books, 1992); SEX AND AMERICA'S TEENAGERS 40–43 (New York/Washington, D.C.: The Alan Guttmacher Institute, 1994); ELISE F. JONES ET AL., TEENAGE PREGNANCY IN INDUSTRIALIZED NATIONS 1 (New Haven/London: Yale University Press, 1986).

27. *See* Patricia Donovan, *Falling Teen Pregnancy, Birthrates: What's Behind the Decline?,* THE GUTTMACHER REPORT: ON PUBLIC POLICY, Oct. 1998, at 6, 6.

28. JONES ET AL., *supra* note 26, at 216–27.

29. *See* Debra Boyer & David Fine, *Sexual Abuse as a Factor in Adolescent Pregnancy and Child Maltreatment,* 24 FAM. PLAN. PERSP. 4 (1992); PATRICK A.

LANGAN, PH.D. & CAROLINE WOLF HARLOW, PH.D., CHILD RAPE VICTIMS, 1992 (Washington, D.C.: U.S. Department of Justice, 1994).

30. *See* PEOPLE FOR THE AMERICAN WAY, TEACHING FEAR: THE RELIGIOUS RIGHT'S CAMPAIGN AGAINST SEXUALITY EDUCATION 22–26 (Washington, DC: People for the American Way, 1994) [hereinafter TEACHING FEAR].

31. *See* THE BEST INTENTIONS: UNINTENDED PREGNANCY AND THE WELL-BEING OF CHILDREN AND FAMILIES 132 (Sarah Brown & Leon Eisenberg, eds.) (Washington, D.C.: National Academy Press, 1995).

32. Maternal and Child Health Services Block Grant, Pub. L. 104–193, 110 Stat. 2353 (1996), 42 U.S.C.A. §710 (Supp. 1998).

33. The Alan Guttmacher Institute, *Snapshot Welfare Reform Law,* WASHINGTON MEMO, Oct. 8, 1996, at 5.

34. *See* TEACHING FEAR, *supra* note 30, at 6; Kantor, *supra* note 25, at 11–12; *see, e.g., Sex, Lies, and the Truth,* video distributed by James Dobson's organization, Focus on the Family.

35. *See* TEACHING FEAR, *supra* note 30, at 8 (quoting *No Second Chance,* film used for Sex Respect programs developed by the Committee on the Status of Women, an anti-choice organization founded by Phyllis Schafly).

36. Leslie M. Kantor, *Scared Chaste? Fear-Based Educational Curricula,* 21 SIECUS REPORT, Dec. 1992/Jan. 1993, at 1, 1–15; *see also Sexuality Education Around the World,* 24 SIECUS REPORT, Feb./Mar. 1996, at 1.

37. COLEEN KELLY MAST, SEX RESPECT: THE OPTION OF TRUE SEXUAL FEEL-ING-STUDENT HANDBOOK 7, 90 (Bradley, IL: Respect Incorporated, rev. ed., 1997) *reprinting chart from* PATRICIA B. DRISCOLL & MARY ROSE OS-BORN, SEXUAL COMMON SENSE: AFFIRMING ADOLESCENT ABSTINENCE (Walnut Creek, CA: Womanity Publications, 1982).

38. William Martin, *God's Angry Man,* TEXAS MONTHLY, April 1981, at 153, 223.

39. *Id.* (quoting James Robison).

40. Family Research Council, *UN: Bound for Beijing,* 6 WASHINGTON WATCH: SPECIAL REPORT, Aug. 24, 1995, at 1.

41. James Dobson, *The Family Under Fire By the United Nations,* FOCUS ON THE FAMILY NEWSLETTER, August 1995, at 1.

42. Letter from James Dobson, President, Focus on the Family, mass mailing to members, 6 (Oct. 1995) (footnote omitted).

43. *See* International Covenant on Civil and Political Rights, *adopted* Dec. 16, 1966, G.A. Res. 2200 (XXI), U.N. GAOR, 21st Sess., Supp. No. 16, at 52, arts. 2(1), 3, 23(4), 24(1), 26 U.N. Doc. A/6316, 999 U.N.T.S. 171, 6 I.L.M. 368 (1967) [hereinafter ICCPR].

44. Human Rights Committee, General Comments Adopted under Article 40, Paragraph 4, of the ICCPR: General Comment No. 22 (48) (art. 18), U.N. Doc. A/48/40 (Pt. I) 208, para. 6, at 209 (1993).

45. *See generally* BROUWER, EXPORTING, *supra* note 2, at 182–86.

Chapter 3

What Is Your Tribe?: Women's Struggles and the Construction of Muslimness

Marie-Aimée Hélie-Lucas

I. INTRODUCTION

The first part of the strange title of this article originates in a personal experience. In 1962, after a seven-year bloody war with two million victims, Algeria became independent from French colonization. Shortly after independence, some of us were being introduced, as Algerians, to some Left intellectuals in Paris who had been in favor of our liberation movement. To my utter surprise, they insisted on knowing not only our religion (although all of them without exception were atheists, but somehow we were not supposed to fail to profess a religion), but also, in their own words, our "tribe of origin." It was a shock and a revelation to me that, for those intellectuals, Third World people could not do with just citizenship: we had to bear the marks of exoticism. Our sameness was deeply disturbing to them. Moreover, it was, in their views, challenging our very identity—a recently acquired national identity that we had fought for, for so many years.

The second part of my title refers to the dangerously growing trend of precisely constructing exoticism and Otherness in the political, thus reinforcing the ideology as well as the power and legitimacy of extreme right political forces, both within and outside Muslim contexts.

II. FUNDAMENTALISM IN CONTEXT

There are many forms and varieties of fundamentalism, and for that reason I would rather speak of fundamentalisms. However, they have common characteristics. In particular, one key element of their politics is the control of women. This is true of all religious fundamentalisms, including, inter alia: the Christian Right in the United States, promoting their views of morality by assassinating medical doctors who perform abortions; Muslim fundamentalists, promoting gender apartheid in Iran, Sudan, Algeria and Afghanistan; and the Hindu Right in India, promoting *sati* (burning of wives alive on the pyre of their deceased husbands). There is a long list of other religious fundamentalists' anti-women stances manifesting their hatred of women. Indeed, in a context of Islam-bashing and racism, it is important to remember that Muslim fundamentalism, despite being specifically singled out in the international media, is no different in that respect from other religious fundamentalisms.

Moreover, religious fundamentalisms cannot be isolated from other forms of fundamentalism that do not focus on religion, but do create ideological and political alliances with each other, such as fundamentalisms based on ethnicity and culture. For religious fundamentalism is not a religious movement, as it pretends to be. Religious pretexts, as in Ireland, inevitably cover up much deeper infrastructural conflicts. These are political movements, aiming at seizing political power, by force if not otherwise.

For example, it has been reported that Ali Belhadj, one of the main Algerian fundamentalist leaders and co-founder of the FIS party (Islamic Salvation Front), stated long before elections were cancelled in Algeria: "I do not respect either the laws or the political parties which do not have the Qur'an. I throw them under my feet and I trample them. These parties must leave the country. They must be suppressed."[1] He further stated about democracy: "[b]eware of those who pretend that the concept of democracy exists in Islam. . . . Democracy is kofr [blasphemy]."[2] "There is no democracy because the sole source of power is Allah, through the Qur'an, and not the people. If people vote against the law of God, this is nothing but blasphemy. In this case, one must kill these unbelievers for the good reason that they want to substitute their authority to the authority of God."[3] Abhorrent of democracy, Algerian fundamentalist leaders, such as Anouar Haddam, who was the representative of the FIS in Washington, inevitably advocate violence against democrats in the form of *jihad* (holy war), and has been reported as stating: "If the Islamic state in Algeria is not brought to power by dialogue, this will be done by the jihad."[4]

Claiming that they represent, if not the holy people chosen by God, then the purest and most excellent race, or the most ancient and elaborate culture, these movements, when they rise to power, impose their rules, codes of conducts, beliefs, and principles on "subhuman" races, "inferior" religions and cultures. Fundamentalisms are political movements of the extreme right, which, in a context of globalization, i.e., forceful international economic exploitation and free-for-all capitalism, manipulate religion, culture or ethnicity, in order to achieve their political aims. Fundamentalism is the form that fascism takes today. Like Nazism in Germany, it emerges in a context of economic crisis and pauperization, builds itself on the discontent of the people, manipulates the poorer sections of the populations, exalts their moral values and their culture (Aryanism for Nazi Germany), covers itself with the blessing of their God (the Nazi SS had inscribed on their belts "Gott mit uns" [God is with us]), wants to convert or submit the world, and eliminates and eradicates their political opponents as well as the "untermensch" (subhumans). Far from being obscurantists and economically backwards, fundamentalists are modernists and capitalists.

It is in this context that I shall discuss Muslim fundamentalists, women, and human rights. This particular form of extreme right movement and its specific oppression of women should not be analyzed outside a global political frame such as the one I have indicated here.

III. THE MYTH OF A HOMOGENEOUS MUSLIM WORLD

Women in Muslim countries and communities are indeed oppressed, in the name of religious interpretations that sustain and support patriarchy.[5] However, there is no such thing as a uniform Muslim world, nor a unique shari'ah (body of Islamic law) applied everywhere. Women in Muslim societies lead very different lives, suffer different degrees of oppression, and enjoy different rights.[6]

This diversity in itself is sufficient to counter the fundamentalist ideology of Muslimness, as a belief, a way of life, a code of conduct, a "culture"[7] that is supposed to characterize the life of so-called Muslims all over the world. Like all totalizations, it ignores differences of cultures, political regimes, classes, and the like, and proposes the oppressive vision of an unchallengeable, unchangeable, divinely defined homogeneity. However, by insistently suggesting its existence, fundamentalists have managed to convince many Muslims and non-Muslims of its virtual reality.[8] In fact, many well-meaning people, outside as well as inside Muslim contexts, in good faith, play into the game of fundamentalists and their identity politics. But a homogeneous Muslim world exists nowhere else than in their imagination.

Differences in Muslim societies are due to three main factors. First of all, Islam has spread, over centuries, in many different cultures across all continents and it has absorbed local traditions. For example, female genital mutilation (FGM), although practiced by animists and Christians too in the concerned areas, is considered and promoted as Islamic in certain parts of Africa while unheard of in Islamic communities elsewhere, and the caste system, originally Hindu, functions in Muslim communities as well in the Indian subcontinent.

Secondly, the Qur'an and hadith have been interpreted throughout the centuries, by different schools of thought, and ongoing reinterpretation is still an option for many Muslims. Like all holy books, one can find in the Qur'an both the God of Love and the God of Wrath, as well as many historically connoted positions. A historical analysis can be and, indeed, is applied by many Muslims today to the injunctions concerning women. For example, an Algerian Muslim scholar's analysis has concluded that the function of the veil at the time of Muhammad was to protect women, and thus the veil's most appropriate modern equivalent is education and schooling that in our times gives the most protection to a woman.[9]

Third, it is clear that political powers using culture and religion choose to emphasize different elements or interpretations in both culture and religion, according to circumstantial needs.

I would therefore make an essential distinction between two concepts: Islam and Muslims.[10] Islam, as a religion, an ideology, and a utopia, can be analyzed from the point of view of theology or of philosophy. "Islam," in this sense, does not exist anywhere in the material world. Muslims are those who attempt to materialize their interpretation of these ideas—both the men and women who define themselves as religious beings, or followers of Islam, and the political forces that monopolize the reading of the text and use it as a major strategy for accessing or keeping political power. Analysis of these political forces belongs to the fields of sociology and political sciences. It follows suit that not all that is done by Muslims is Islamic and that which is Islamic is subject to debate, and, indeed, is debated among Muslims. Muslimness is man-made, not God given.

This important conceptual distinction should allow one to defend human rights in Muslim countries without fear of being seen as anti-Islam. It is an important distinction, too, for women inside Muslim contexts who fight for their human rights. Hence I will not refer to Islam, but to Muslims and so-called Muslims since it is assumed by many that all persons born and raised in Muslim families or countries are automatically Muslim believers. Freedom of faith or belief is automatically assumed not to be of interest to persons born in such contexts, and, as such, is denied. No one would dream of defining a French man or a Swiss woman first as "a Christian" rather than as "a Frenchman" or as "a Swiss." While we, Algerians, Nigerians, Pakistanis, Fijians, Canadians, or British alike, believers and non-believers alike, atheists and free thinkers alike, are labeled "Muslims." Are we really talking of faith?

Muslimness is becoming a transnational identity—much to the delight of fundamentalists. It is becoming an "original sin"—impossible to expurgate—a stamp on the skin and soul of persons whose accidental location of birth made them "Muslims." This extension of the sense of the term "Muslim" operates as an insult to true believers for whom faith is a deeply important choice in life, and to the notion of freedom of religion or belief. It is, as well, an insult to the personal integrity of those who have not chosen religion as a marker of their identity. Moreover, such political labeling is very dangerous, as "Jews," believers and nonbelievers alike, would confirm.

IV. THE DIVERSITY OF WOMEN'S STRUGGLES AND STRATEGIES

Women themselves are organizing their struggles for human rights on all of these fronts simultaneously. Their strategies range from working within the framework of religion by reinterpreting the Qur'an from a feminist perspective to working from an entirely secular, international approach toward human rights.[11]

Interpretation of the Qur'an has long been monopolized by male scholars. But, for the last couple of decades, feminist theologians and women's human rights Muslim scholars have begun to challenge this monopoly.[12] These scholars focus on reform from within the religious framework of those laws and practices that originated in obscurantist interpretations of religion. They have successfully initiated a dialogue on *ijtihad* (reinterpretation), which was dormant for centuries. With their entryist strategy, they have deeply modified the field of Islamic theological research.

Initially, such an approach of religious reform was regarded by nonreligious human rights advocates as hardly distinguishable from, or even as colluding with, Muslim fundamentalists' forceful attempts—now unfortunately more and more successful—to infiltrate the human rights domain. Yet, there is an important distinction between these two very different movements. Religiously inclined women human rights advocates do not try to monopolize the field of human rights. Rather they ally with secularists, using a combination of approaches. The fundamentalists' approach, however, excludes and violently combats any other strategy.

At the other end of the spectrum, other women—be they believers or atheists—may incorporate the pioneering work of new feminist theologians, but they do not see religious debate as a main strategy for social change. Instead, using their anthropologically grounded awareness of the fact that there is no such thing as a homogeneous Muslim world and far less a transnational Muslim culture, they have successfully pointed to the diversity of situations in which women live in Muslim countries and communities around the world. Criticizing conservative or even inhuman laws and practices, they condemn violations of women's human rights regardless of the fact that such violations may be justified—locally, nationally, or internationally—by reference to religion.[13] They have also identified the various good laws and practices that exist in different Muslim contexts and argued for their adoption in other Muslim contexts—without the promoters of cultural purity and nationalist isolationism arguing that such laws are the importation of foreign (non-Muslim) mores.[14]

This strategy could not exist without a strong international linkage between women from Muslim countries and communities worldwide, and without the raised consciousness about our commonalities and diversity.[15] It would not exist without the clear internationalist understanding that the rights that women gain in one place are bound to affect positively women elsewhere, and that the rights women lose in one place may affect negatively women elsewhere. At the global level, the 1994 United Nations International Conference on Population and Development, held in Cairo, gave a formidable example of the unholy alliance between the Vatican and El-Azhar University (the first Islamic University and a source for *fatwas* [religious opinions]) that tried to stop women's demands for reproductive rights, contraception, and abortion.[16] It quickly became clear that the curtailing of reproductive rights that women had faced in Poland and in the ex-Democratic Republic of Germany were indeed part of a concerted effort toward depriving women in Muslim contexts, and globally, of the same rights.[17]

This is why internationalist women strongly advocate universal human rights. Although universalism, as it exists today, is generally criticized for its implicit ethnocentrism and leaning toward so-called Western values, most women nevertheless recognize the need for, support the principle of, and work toward a new definition of universality in human rights. The massive presence of autonomous women's rights organizations from Muslim countries and communities at the United Nations Fourth World Conference on Women, held in Beijing, attests to the fact that women see the urgent need not only for linkages within Muslim contexts but also with the global women's movement.

What is most impressive about women's various strategies against fundamentalist forces is their integration, interpenetration, and cross-fertilization, and the reciprocal reinforcement and mutual support that exists.[18] In most instances, far from being contradictory or oppositional, these approaches are often complementary, or at the very least nonantagonistic.[19]

V. THE CONSTRUCTION OF MUSLIMNESS

This vision of the world is a far cry from the unilateral one-sided vision of fundamentalists, for whom "Islam" is the only possible solution, and their interpretation of it is the only one to be enforced, *volens nolens,* upon the world. For them, all struggles for women's human rights, be they from within the frame of religion or from a secular perspective, are equally seen as betrayal. Betrayal of one's religion: the monolithic Islam. Betrayal of one's culture: the imaginary transnational Muslim culture. Betrayal of one's community: the *ummah* (community of the believers). Women's struggles for human rights are seen as dangerously divisive of the "Muslim world."

However, if one can expect such an analysis from fundamentalists, the collusion of well-meaning liberals and human rights advocates with fundamentalists' ideology comes as a surprise. It is particularly notable that of these different but complementary strategies of women, only one—the strategy of religious interpretation—is artificially isolated and receives the most attention, funding, and recognition. It is regarded as the only authentic strategy—the best for "Muslims." Those from outside Muslim contexts, in the name of respect for the Other's culture and religion, or for fear of being accused of racism, as well as those within Muslim contexts who have internalized the notion of betrayal, are unduly reluctant to name and condemn violations of human rights, and particularly women's human rights, in Muslim countries and communities. In short, not only racists, but enlightened people and women's allies, too, align themselves with the most "Muslim" strategy, excluding all other possibilities as alien to them. By selecting one strategy, an imaginary, ahistorical, immutable image of the "Muslim woman" is retained, supporting fundamentalist ideology and essentializing the Other.[20] This most "Muslim" strategy sends us back to the image of exoticism that is so often attached to the so-called Muslim woman. Yet such an image limits the choice and imposes/denies a "Muslim" identity to women who in their own context and at a specific historical moment in time may choose other strategies.

Why is this construction of the so-called Muslim woman so well-received and accepted by such different sections of the political spectrum, indeed, by almost everyone? The notion of difference can be manipulated from several points of view: racist, fundamentalist, Muslim immigrant, liberal, and human rights. For what is difference? Differences are produced by specific historical, geographical, and political circumstances. However, when isolated from their context, when essentialized, referred to as "natural"— ahistorical and unchangeable—under whatever disguise, difference feeds into the ideology of racism. The promotion of difference has always been at the heart of a racist agenda.[21] Not surprisingly, in times when extreme right political forces are on the rise, there is an upsurge of arguments based on "nature" and biology, including in feminist theory and in science. There has developed a cult of difference, rather than integration. "Communalization" (the South Asian concept of separate communities) is promoted and becomes the buzzword of human rights advocates, rather than the "melting pot" concept (indeed so often a failure and a disillusion in practice). I am not advocating the eradication of cultural differences, but I do wish to note the consequences that the present political construction of a "natural" Otherness, especially for so-called Muslims, have for women and for their human rights.

"Difference" presently benefits from a conjunction of interests that give it a dangerous prominence. Failure to achieve equality leads to exaltation and fantastication of difference; witness the politics of nostalgia of immigrants bound together by being confronted with the same racism. For racists, social differences are seen as the inevitable product of natural differences and thus justify exclusion. Various social and political scientists elaborate on the "common sense" understanding of difference, giving it academic legitimacy.[22] Hand in hand with racists and extreme right political parties, exploiting the inadequacy of social scientists' methodologies and the naiveté of liberals, fundamentalists exploit the momentum to further their agenda.

Within the prevalent discourse of multiculturalism and multi-ethnicism in Europe and North America, Muslims are seen as sharing a religion that has also been dubbed a culture despite the many differences between "Muslims" that I have already noted. Culturalist Islamism assumes a dead culture—a culture impenetrable to others' culture, to historical developments, and unchangeable overtime—that bears no resemblance to the stunning diversity of social reality.

Liberals and too many human rights advocates follow this ideological line. In the name of respect of the Other, respect of the Other's culture, they promote cultural relativism. They want to redefine equality so that it fits difference. In the name of difference, they justify practices that, for themselves, would be considered barbaric. Faced with concerned persons, particularly women, who are challenging violations of human rights in this imaginary culture, they are not even sure whether they should defend the victims, or, hand in hand with fundamentalists, defend the supposedly betrayed culture.

One cannot help suggesting a few epistemological questions: Who defines culture? Are women entitled to do so? Is citizenship restricted to men, elders, representatives of the community, and vocal fundamentalists? Is culture immutable, and in that case, in which century are we deciding that it stopped evolving?[23] Are human rights today so totally depoliticized?

The point is that all opinions and all practices are not equally valid and respectable. Fundamentalism and fascism do not each just represent another opinion. It is not "tolerable"—tolerance nowadays seems to be regarded as a cardinal virtue and the epitome of human rights—that: Nazis physically eliminated "unfits," communists, gypsies, homosexuals, and Jews; Hindu fundamentalists sell audiocassettes by the millions calling for the murder of Muslims; the Afghani Taliban regime imposes gender apartheid; Algerian fundamentalists cut the throats, the breasts, and the genitals of women and invoke Islam to rape them, impregnate them, and force them to bear and produce "good" Muslims; Serbs impregnated Bosnian women to force them to bear and produce the "superior" race.

For these crimes are not accidental casualties of war; they are the logical consequences of ideologies that clearly, in the name of purity of the race or of the holy creed, intend to commit these crimes and justify the intention of committing them. These opinions and ideologies are not just another view of life. Should these ideologies be voiced and given space by human rights organizations in the name of freedom of speech and freedom of opinion? For example, since the fundamentalist war against civilians started in Algeria,[24] well-established human rights organizations have given a platform to fundamentalists, painting them exclusively as victims of repression by the state and deliberately ignoring that the fundamentalists' main role in Algeria has been as perpetrators of crimes and ignoring the magnitude of those crimes, particularly against women.[25] For example, we fear that Anouar Haddam, the Algerian fundamentalist leader whose justification of *jihad* was quoted at the beginning of this chapter, may be granted asylum in the United States.

Moreover, human rights organizations ignore the fact that fundamentalists' ideology justifies all these crimes on the basis of their (religious?) principles. The wonderful principle of freedom of speech was not meant to help propagate hatred, support calls to murder, and give power to those who wish to destroy democracy and negate any concept of human rights, including the right to freedom of speech. This support of fundamentalists, in the name of freedom of thought, freedom of speech, and democracy—to the benefit of theocracy—is based on a frightful confusion between ends and formal means and will lead to the subsequent access to political power of the new Hitlers of our time.

At the end of a century that sees the reemergence of old religions and new sects, as well as spirituality, in societies that have lost faith in transformation toward social justice, deceived and hopeless people turn to gods and values that many of us thought dead. At the end of a century that sees economic and political globalization threaten the very lives of people, one witnesses an unforeseen outcome of globalization: atomized, interchangeable individuals fearing for their lives, instinctively regrouping with their kin in order to support each other. A North African saying summarizes this reaction to precariousness: "Me against my brother. Me and my brothers against my cousin. Me, my brothers and my cousins against my tribe. Me, my brothers, my cousins, my tribe against the other tribe in the next village. . . ." This is the situation that fundamentalisms build on and exploit. But is it not what all fascisms have always built on? Human rights, with their counter goal of universalism, have to identify fundamentalisms as the greatest threat of our time.

NOTES

1. RASSEMBLEMENT ALGERIN DES FEMMES DEMOCRATES: RAFD, CE QUE DECLARENT LES FOSSOYEURS DE L'ALGERIE! (Algeria: RAFD, n.d.) (no page numbering) [hereinafter RAFD], *quoting* Ali Belhadj, ALGER RÉPUBLICAIN, Apr. 5, 1991 (author's translation).

2. RAFD, *supra* note 1, *quoting* Ali Belhadj, LE MATIN, Oct. 29, 1989 (author's translation).

3. RAFD, *supra* note 1, *quoting* Ali Belhaj, HORIZONS, Feb. 29, 1989 (author's translation); *see also* RAFD, *supra* note 1, *quoting* Abassi Madani, ALGÉRIE ACTUALITÉ, Dec. 24, 1989 (author's translation).

4. MAHL, ALGERIA: A WAR AGAINST CIVILIANS (Grabels, France: WLUML, forthcoming 1999), *quoting* Anouar Haddam, ENNAHAR, Nov. 1994, (Beirut, Lebanon) (author's translation); *see* RAFD *supra* note 1, *quoting* Ali Belhadj, Open letter to *Mudjahidin* [fighters of the faith], Oct. 2, 1994 (author's translation).

5. *See* Women Living Under Muslim Laws [hereinafter WLUML], *Declarations and Statements, Muslim Thinkers' Plea to Rulers,* WLUML, DOSSIER 19, at 153 (excerpted from *New India Times,* Oct. 17, 1997, at 4) (Statement by 15 Muslim Scholars from India, Iran, Pakistan, Bangladesh, Morocco, the Sudan, Palestine, Syria, and Turkey) (Marie-Aimée Hélie-Lucas & Harsh Kapoor, eds.) (Grabels, France: WLUML, 1997).

6. *See* WLUML, PLAN OF ACTION (1986), ARAMON FRANCE 3–4 (Grabels, France: WLUML, 1986) (on file with editor).

7. *See* Aziz Al-Azmeh, *Muslim "Culture" and the European Tribe, in* AZIZ AL-AZMEH, ISLAMS AND MODERNITIES 1 (Prologue) (London: Verso, 1995), *reprinted in* WLUML, DOSSIER 19, *supra* note 5, at 7.

8. *See* Marie-Aimée Hélie-Lucas, *The Preferential Symbol For Islamic Identity: Women In Muslim Personal Laws,* WLUML, DOSSIER 11/12/13, at 5, 8 (Marie-Aimée Hélie-Lucas, ed.) (Grabels, France: WLUML, 1993).

9. *See* SOHEIB BENCHEIKH, MARIANE ET LE PROPHÈTE: L'ISLAM DANS LA FRANCE LAÏQUE [THE REPUBLIC AND THE PROPHET: ISLAM IN SECULAR FRANCE] 142–45 (Paris: Éditions Grasset & Fasquelle, 1998).

10. *See* Hélie-Lucas, *supra* note 8, at 6–8.

11. *See* Marie-Aimée Hélie-Lucas, *Women's Struggles and Strategies in the Rise of Fundamentalism in the Muslim World: From Entryism to Internationalism, in* WOMEN IN THE MIDDLE EAST: PERCEPTIONS, REALITIES AND STRUGGLES FOR LIBERATION 206 (Haleh Afshar, ed.) (New York: St. Martin's Press, 1993).

12. *See, e.g.,* Ghazala Anwar, *Reclaiming the Religious Center from a Muslim Perspective: Theological Alternatives to Religious Fundamentalism,* in this volume; Riffat Hassan, *An Islamic Perspective, in* WOMEN, RELIGION AND SEXUALITY 93 (Jeanne Becher ed., First Trinity Press Int'l 1991) (1990).

13. *See, e.g.,* WLUML Statement on Reproductive Rights/NGO Forum/ICPD, Cairo Sept. '94, WLUML, WOMEN'S REPRODUCTIVE RIGHTS IN MUSLIM COUNTRIES AND COMMUNITIES: ISSUES AND RESOURCES 3 (1994).

14. *See* Marie-Aimée Hélie-Lucas, *Women Living Under Muslim Laws, in* OURS BY RIGHT: WOMEN'S RIGHTS AS HUMAN RIGHTS 52, 58–59 (Joanna Kerr, ed.) (London: Zed Books in Association with The North-South Institute, 1993).

15. Marie-Aimée Hélie Lucas, *L'Internationalisme dans le mouvement des femmes: les réseaux internationaux de femmes, [Internationalism in the Women's Movement: the International Network of Women],* WLUML Occasional Paper No 4., at 14 (Grabels, France: WLUML, 1994).

16. *See* Mark Nicholson, *Fears of Violence Stalk Cairo Conference,* FIN. TIMES, Sept. 1, 1994, at 4.

17. *See* Lynn P. Freedman, *The Challenge of Fundamentalisms,* 8 REPROD. HEALTH MATTERS 55 (1996).

18. *See* Farida Shaheed, *Controled* [sic] *or Autonomous: Identity and the Experience of the Network Women Living Under Muslim Laws,* 19 SIGNS, no. 4 (Summer 1994), *reprinted in* WLUML Occasional Papers Series No. 5, 1994, at 5–11.

19. On the concepts of complementarity and reciprocity in international solidarity, see Marieme Hélie-Lucas, *WLUML "Heart and Soul,"* transcribed from Plan of Action, Dhaka '97, at 4–7 (n.p., 1997) (on file with editor); PETER WATERMAN, GLOBALIZATION, SOCIAL MOVEMENTS AND THE NEW INTERNATIONALISTS 162 (London/Washington: Mansell Publishing Ltd., 1998).

20. *See* Kenan Malik, *The Perils of Pluralism,* Index on Censorship, No. 3/97, May 1997, *reprinted in* WLUML, DOSSIER 20, at 138, 141 (Marie-Aimée Hélie-Lucas & Harsh Kapoor, eds.) (Grabels, France: WLUML, 1997).

20. *See* Al-Azmeh, *supra* note 7, *in* WLUML, DOSSIER 19, at 12–13.

22. *See* PIERRE BOURDIEU, THE LOGIC OF PRACTICE 135–41 (Richard Nice, trans.) (Stanford: Stanford University Press, 1990)/PIERRE BOURDIEU, LE SENS PRATIQUE 233–44 (Paris: Les Editions de Minuit, 1980).

23. *See* Mahnaz Afkhami, *Gender Apartheid and the Discourse of Relativity of Rights in Muslim Societies,* in this volume; Michael Singer, *Relativism, Culture, Religion, and Identity,* in this volume.

24. *See* MAHL, *supra* note 4.

25. *See* Marieme Hélie-Lucas, *Fundamentalism and Femicide, in* COMMON GROUNDS: VIOLENCE AGAINST WOMEN IN WAR AND ARMED CONFLICT SITUATIONS 108, 112–20 (Indai Lourdes Sajor, ed.) (Quezon City, Philippines: Asian Center for Women's Human Rights, 1998).

Chapter 4

The Personal Is Political: Jewish Fundamentalism and Women's Empowerment

Nira Yuval-Davis

I. INTRODUCTION

Fundamentalism is probably the most important—and dangerous—social movement of our times.[1] One of the most difficult political tasks we are facing today is how to fight and resist fundamentalist movements without allowing such a resistance to become a cover for racist attacks on the demonized "Other."

In this chapter,[2] I am going to look at some of the reasons fundamentalist movements have arisen in general and in the Jewish context in particular. I shall then look at the nature of the empowerment that *Khazara Bitshuva* (a "return," a conversion to an ultra-Orthodox version of Judaism) is supposed to give to women. My argument is, first, that such a sense of "empowerment" has to be seen within the overall context of these Jewish women's lives, and second, that personal empowerment cannot be seen as an ultimate political goal without looking at the ways such personal sense of empowerment is linked to and affects the larger political project of Jewish fundamentalist movements.

Despite their differences, fundamentalist movements all over the world "are basically political movements which have a religious or ethnic imperative and seek in various ways in widely differing circumstances to harness modern state and media powers to the service of their gospel. This gospel, which can be based on certain sacred texts or evangelical experiential moment linked to a charismatic leader, is presented as the only valid form of the religion, the ethnic culture, and the truth."[3]

An important part of fighting against fundamentalism is, therefore, resisting fundamentalist movements' definitions of religions and cultures. Cultural and religious traditions are not fixed or homogenous. They are rich resources that are used selectively by different social agents in various social and political projects within specific power relations in and outside the collectivity.[4] When states and nongovernmental organizations accept religious fundamentalist leaderships' definitions of the "genuine" essence of a specific religion or culture, they reinforce their specific political projects vis-à-vis those of other, more marginalized and disadvantaged sections within the collectivity.

The recent rise of fundamentalism is linked to the crisis of modernity. Both communism and capitalism have proved unable to fulfill people's material, emotional, and spiritual needs.[5] A genuine sense of despair and disorientation has opened people to religion, giving them a sense of stability and meaning, as well as a coherent identity.[6] In the Third World and among Third World minorities in the West, the rise of fundamentalism is also intimately linked with the failure of nationalist and socialist movements to bring about successful liberation from oppression, exploitation, and poverty.

Fundamentalist movements, therefore, can align themselves with different political trends in different countries and manifest themselves in many forms.[7] They can appear as a form of orthodoxy, maintaining "traditional values," or as a revivalist radical phenomena, dismissing impure and corrupt forms of their religion. Fundamentalist movements fall into two categories: first, those of dominant majorities within states, which look for universal domination in the society, such as Christian fundamentalists in the United States or Khomeini's fundamentalist group in Iran; and, second, those of minorities, who use state and media powers and resources to promote and impose their gospel primarily within their specific constituencies, which are usually defined in ethnic terms.[8]

Finally, fundamentalist movements generally make the control of women and the promotion of the patriarchal family central to their agenda.[9] This is true of Jewish fundamentalist movements as well.

II. JEWISH FUNDAMENTALISM

Due to the specific history of Jewish people, Jewish fundamentalist movements (and the position of women inside them) embrace both forms of religious fundamentalism: in Israel, fundamentalists are of the majority and seek domination of the state; and in the Diaspora, Jews consist of minorities in countries and thus Jewish fundamentalists share features with other fundamentalist movements of minorities.

The rise of Jewish fundamentalist movements is connected specifically with crises both within Judaism and Zionism. Since the Jewish emancipation and the breakup of classical Judaism in eighteenth-century Europe, the question of "who" or "what" is a Jew has become a major debate. Is Judaism a religion, a nationality, a culture, or a race? A variety of movements and ideologies, developed by both Jews and non-Jews, have attempted to answer this question.[10]

The delegitimization of open anti-Semitism after World War II has enabled assimilation on a much wider scale, but the sense of being different and "the Other" has continued. Jews who are not Israelis or religious often feel that their identity has boundaries but no content. Ultra-Orthodox Judaism is understood to refer to the fundamentalist or radical element of the Orthodox, where "Orthodox" refers to Jews who observe all the religious commandments, and interpret those commandments to require a traditional life strictly attached to religious ritual.[11] Ultra-Orthodox Judaism offers the illusion of authenticity, homogeneity, and an ahistoric, unchanging Judaism, at least until the arrival of the Messiah. The rise of Orthodox missionary fundamentalist movements has supplied the necessary bridges to enable Jews who have not grown up in Orthodox homes to join radical Orthodox Jewish communities and to feel that they know who they are. For example, the primary reason many of the *Khozrim Bitshuva* (both men and women) who I interviewed have given for their return to Judaism has been that "at last, I know who I am. I know what it is to be a Jew."[12]

Jewish fundamentalism in Israel basically takes two forms: a right-wing Zionism, led by the settlers in the Occupied Territories, in which the actual establishment of the Israeli state is a positive religious act;[13] and the *haredim* (ultra-Orthodox) movements that have been non- or even anti-Zionist, but in recent years have become increasingly Zionist, who regard the state as a convenient source of political and economic support for their own projects.[14] Zionism originally presented itself as a modern alternative to Orthodox Jewishness. However, the two were never completely separated.[15] The Zionist movement needed the legitimization of Orthodox Judaism for its claim on the country and for its claim to represent the Jewish people as a whole.

The Messianic element is central to Zionist fundamentalist movements, both in Israel and in the Diaspora. Although often the individual motivation of people who become *Khozrim Bitshuva* is totally subjective and personal, Judaism is a communal religion. The general political message of these movements as a whole is Messianic and therefore "the Promised Land"—Israel and the Occupied Territories—is central to them. In all versions, the ultimate aim is constructed in terms of the coming of the Messiah. The coming of the Messiah means that differences among Jews would fade away so that the people of Israel would be in the land and state of Israel with the Messiah as their ruler. Although most Orthodox rabbis treat suspiciously Jewish Messianic movements and reject as false all those who declare themselves to be Messiahs, the active role of promoting the coming of the Messiah has nonetheless been found to be a major mobilizing power among Zionist fundamentalists.

Gush Emunim (the Bloc of the Faithful) is an example of a Zionist fundamentalist group. They initiated a project, which was initially illegal, of Jewish settlement in the Occupied Territories, especially near the Jewish holy places. In their actions, the settlers, many of whom were the product of the Israeli state religious educational system, combined Zionist pioneering myths with religious practice, and produced a new mode of Jewish religion in which the "Land of Israel" gained a cardinal importance; its control and settlement by Jews became a precondition for the arrival of the Messiah.[16] Their vision is total, and there is no space in it for any recognition of the national aspirations of the Palestinians, nor any compromise or negotiated peace with the Arabs. Its most extreme wings, however, turned themselves into paramilitary units terrorizing and counterterrorizing the Palestinians, as well as threatening to resist by force any attempt by Israel to withdraw from the Occupied Territories.

The other major Jewish fundamentalist group are the *haredim,* which consist of a vastly heterogeneous body of various rabbis and their followers, both Hasidim and Misnagdim. The attitude of the *haredim* to the Israeli state has traditionally been suspicious—although only a small proportion of them have been actively anti-Zionist. Some of them, however, have always been actively Zionist. Their political and economic power has increased dramatically in recent years because they are of crucial importance in the Israeli electoral system—they hold the balance of power between the two major political parties. Generally, the *haredim* use the Israeli state both to gain more resources for their institutions and to impose as many religious practices on Israeli society as possible. A central feature of the *haredim* agenda is to retain the Israeli personal law system, which delegates the control of marriage, divorce, and personal status to the religious courts and thus enables the *haredim* to retain control of women's position and status in society.[17] As the *haredim's* power has increased in Israel, their political project appears to be increasingly fundamentalist. Rather than merely using the state for resources, it is now been argued that they are more interested in taking over the state as well.[18]

However, as Foucault has observed, power creates its own resistance,[19] and with other social, economic, and political developments in Israel, more and more secular Jews have come to resent the growing powers of the Religious Right. This resistance became stronger after the murder of Israeli Prime Minister Itzkhak Rabin by a religious zealot.

III. THE JEWISH MISSIONARY MOVEMENT OF THE LUBAVITCH AND WOMEN

Unlike Christianity, the Lubavitch and other Jewish missionary movements of the *haredim* are not interested in any outside converts, but only those they define as Jews—those who were born to Jewish mothers. From their perspective, the notion of collective responsibility, which is linked to being self-defined as "the chosen people," dictates that all Jews be made to see the light and start keeping the *mitzvoth* (religious commandments). It is only when this occurs that they believe that the Messiah will come. For this purpose, the Lubavitch movement sends emissaries all over the world. They not only take over synagogues and build Jewish community centers, but they also stand on street corners and in train stations proselytizing. They have even developed "*mitzvoth* tanks" to go into Jewish neighborhoods and persuade people to pray and to keep religious commandments. They have carefully managed to insinuate themselves into the mainstream and thus are active in mainstream Jewish schools and synagogues, such as United Synagogues. At the same time, they also keep separate organizational and financial structures in order to keep control over their movement. They use sophisticated modern communication techniques, like satellites and the internet, to spread the message.

The Lubavitch Women's Organization published a book aimed at women, particularly trying to convince single American Jewish women that they should return to Judaism.[20] As the *mitzvoth* that women have to practice in Judaism all relate to their roles as wives and mothers (single girls do not even have to cover their hair), and as early arranged marriage is the normal practice among the ultra-Orthodox, the task of targeting single women is not as simple as it would have been had Judaism been aimed at individual (gender neutral) redemption. The argument used in the book at once emphasizes the collective nature and collective responsibility of the Jewish people, which transcends gender differences, while at the same time maintaining the different construction of men and women in Judaism.[21] The different-than-men roles for women are emphasized in the book by the fact that the majority of the articles deal with women as being solely Jewish wives and mothers. Significantly, only the first chapter of the book assumes that women might also have a career.

The position of women in Judaism depends, of course, not only on the particular religious ideology within which they are operating, but also on their class position and other sociological determinants. Although all ultra-Orthodox would claim that there is an inherent Jewish position on women, women's degree of freedom and empowerment varies from one community to another, a function of the different interpretations that are given to religious laws held in common. The difference between a middle-class professional American woman, and a poor housewife in a development town in Israel is immense, even if both are ultra-Orthodox, married, and have four or five children.

However, there are some basic inequalities in the position of men and women in Orthodox Judaism that cut across these differences.[22] Women are not counted as part of a *minyan* (the quorum necessary for prayer or the Jewish "public"); they are not allowed to lead prayers, to become rabbis, *dayanim* (judges), or hold any other public religious position; their evidence is not acceptable in court; and, they cannot, unlike men, obtain a divorce against their husbands' will, even if their case is conceded to be just. In fact, there is recognition within the prayers of Judaism itself of women's unequal and undesirable position in Judaism since each Jewish man, in his daily morning prayer, thanks God for not having made him a woman, whereas each Jewish woman thanks God for having made her according to His will.[23]

The Jewish missionaries, however, claim that women's position is not inferior but different, and as important as that of the men. Since the rise of the feminist movement, a lot of energy has had to be spent to show that the Jewish woman's position is "really" even more important and powerful than the man's. These arguments appear rather suspicious given the overall approach of the movement toward women.

A close look at the *mitzvoth* for women give a better idea of what is, in fact, expected of women. As Rachel Adler points out, a woman's specific *mitzvoth* are done by her as wife, housewife, and mother for the sake of her family—husband and children—whereas a man's specific *mitzvoth* are done by him as a separate, individual Jew (not in any particular role defined by others) or as part of the Jewish public.[24] Women, therefore, are constructed as the guardians of the Jewish home, which is regarded as the foundation of the Jewish people.

IV. EMPOWERMENT FOR WOMEN?

The construction of women as wives and mothers, and the drudgery of domestic labor, have been at the base of the feminist rebellion of the 1970s and 1980s. At the same time, the emphasis in Jewish fundamentalist movements is on the "natural" differences between men and women. The argument is that women were created differently and thus have different religious duties and life careers. How have Jewish women who have joined the Lubavitch movement been able to reconcile their feminist past (for those who had one) with their "return" to a Judaism that constructs them only as wives and mothers? One woman I interviewed said,

> In every other society I think it is not fair. But in my society it is fair that when both the man and the woman work out all day, the woman comes home and does all the cooking and cleaning. Because my husband doesn't come home and watch the Telly—he studies the Torah. And we were taught that that's what gives eternity for women—that you encourage the men to learn and you remove the petty worries in their life.

In addition to containment and clarity of gender roles, the lifestyle of the ultra-Orthodox often offers to its *Khozrim Bitshuva* an escape from loneliness. Many of the women (and men) I interviewed described the feeling of warmth that encompassed them when they first started to spend their Sabbath with an ultra-Orthodox family. They were treated as part of the (usually large) family, and they participated in the Sabbath meal, the ritual, the festivity, and the general togetherness of the family. Lonely single women who become *Khozroth Bitshuva* also gain a chance to have families of their own. As the Jewish family is "the unit of Jewish existence,"[25] a lot of energy is spent in the ultra-Orthodox community in arranging marriages. A woman I interviewed commented that "[b]efore I 'returned' I never met any men who were not afraid of commitment."

The sense of community and mutual help and support goes beyond the family cells. Because ultra-Orthodox Jews need to live within walking distance of their synagogues, there are always other ultra-Orthodox families close by who provide vital networks of mutual support. Since one of the religious duties is to give away 10 percent of income (and many also interpret this as 10 percent of one's time) to charity work, there is always somebody to help when a baby is born, when somebody is ill or in any other crisis, even when there are no other members of their family around.

The naturalization of the sexual division of labor, in terms of religious duties, in the family and in the community, creates a very strong separate women's community. Moreover, because of the system of arranged marriage and the fact that husbands and wives spend very little time together as a rule—other than on the Sabbath and holidays—much of the emotional bonding occurs between women. However, although Debra Kaufman has pointed out a similarity between the sense of empowerment of Jewish women fundamentalists and that of radical feminists,[26] such a view confuses the crucial difference between the form of a separate women's community and its purpose. Separateness in radical feminism is not the same as mandatory segregation of women, where women's separate community is in fact a space defined by men. It is easy to talk about women's empowerment as emanating from women's difference as long as it is done without relating it to the actual reality of women's lives.

The actual reality is not all warmth and happiness. Social workers who work among the *haredim,* as well as the ultra-Orthodox women with whom I talked, reported many cases of physical and mental exhaustion and extreme postnatal depression among ultra-Orthodox women who bore many children in conditions of serious overcrowding and inadequate housing.

Moreover, the other side of the warmth and support of the community is the harshness the community directs toward any "deviant" who does not adhere to the very strict rules of internal authority and who does not close ranks against the outside world. Family conflicts, for example, are usually handled by the rabbi, who attempts to reestablish domestic peace. Battered women who may wish help beyond the reestablishment of domestic peace would not fit neatly into the role envisioned for them by the community.

The ultimate goal of so many contemporary identity-politics movements is empowerment.[27] It has been argued that the feminist movement, by differentiating between "power of" and "power over," has resolved any problematic aspect of women claiming power.[28] However, such a differentiation is often impossible to make in relation to personal lives. The notion of empowerment in the context of women who have joined Jewish religious fundamentalist groups is particularly problematic.

Minority women often face the dilemma that the same particularistic collective identity that they seek to defend against racism and subordination, and from which they gain their empowerment to resist dominant oppressive systems and cultures, also oppresses them as women and can include many reactionary and exclusionary elements. In the Jewish case, the picture is even more complicated, because the same collective identity that constructed them as a persecuted minority is also the one which, via the hegemony of Zionism and Israel, links them to a collective identity that is racist and exploitative of others. This is true even in most contemporary Jewish identities that do not see themselves as Zionist. The search of the women of the Lubavitch *Khozroth Bitshuva* for a secure identity not only raises pertinent questions about the kinds and limits of any empowerment that they could get in man-made spaces, but also puts them in a position that supports the kind of fundamentalist Messianism that is racist and expansionist. This is so, even if they never move to Israel (which these days they often do) and even if they never make this political connection themselves. Yet, God, the religious laws, and Israel are all connected in Jewish ultra-Orthodoxy and are definitely linked in its contemporary fundamentalist versions. The reproduction of the Jewish fundamentalist system depends on women, their cooperation, and their hard work.[29]

One of the most important insights the feminist movement has brought into social and political theory has been the realization that "the personal is political." In the Jewish fundamentalist context, such a recognition is a must.

NOTES

1. *See* NIRA YUVAL-DAVIS, GENDER AND NATION 61 (London/Thousand Oaks/New Delhi: Sage Publications, 1997).
2. This chapter is an updated and shortened version of my article, *Jewish Fundamentalism and Women's Empowerment,* which first appeared in REFUSING HOLY ORDERS: WOMEN AND FUNDAMENTALISM IN BRITAIN 198 (Gita Sahgal & Nira Yuval-Davis, eds.) (London: Virago Press, 1992) [hereinafter Yuval-Davis, *Jewish Fundamentalism*].
3. YUVAL-DAVIS, *supra* note 1, at 61.
4. *See id.* at 39–67.
5. *See id.* at 62.
6. *See id.*
7. *See id.*
8. *See id.*
9. *See id.* For a further definition of fundamentalism, see John Stratton Hawley, *Fundamentalism,* in this volume.
10. Nira Yuval-Davis, *The Jewish Collectivity and National Reproduction in Israel, in* WOMEN IN THE MIDDLE EAST 60 (Khamsin series) (N.J./London: Zed Books, 1987) [hereinafter Yuval-Davis, *Jewish Collectivity*]; BOAS EVRON, HA-ÒHESHBON HA-LEUMI [A NATIONAL RECKONING] (Tel-Aviv: Devir Publishing House, 1988) (Hebrew).
11. *See* Samuel C. Heilman & Menachem Friedman, *Religious Fundamentalism and Religious Jews: The Case of the Haredim, in* 1 THE FUNDAMENTALISM PROJECT: FUNDAMENTALISMS OBSERVED 197, 197–99 (Martin E. Marty & R. Scott Appleby, eds.) (Chicago/London: The University of Chicago Press, paperback ed. 1994) (1991).
12. Yuval-Davis, *Jewish Fundamentalism, supra* note 2, at 198.
13. According to the ideological leader of this doctrine, Rabbi Kook, the secular Zionists who built the state of Israel are like the Messiah's donkey—helping to bring the Messiah without knowing it. *See* SEFI RACHLEVSKY, ÒHAMORO SHEL MASHIAÒH [THE MESSIAH'S DONKEY] (Tel-Aviv: Yediot aòharonot, 1998).
14. YUVAL-DAVIS, *supra* note 1, at 62.
15. *See* Yuval-Davis, *Jewish Collectivity, supra* note 10, at 65–66.
16. IAN S. LUSTICK, FOR THE LAND AND THE LORD—JEWISH FUNDAMENTALISM IN ISRAEL (New York: Council on Foreign Relations, 1988).
17. *See* Nira Yuval-Davis, *The Bearers of the Collective: Women and Religious Legislation in Israel,* FEMINIST REV., no.4, at 15, 20–21 (1980). For a further discussion of this issue, see Paula Hyman, *A Feminist Perspective on Jewish*

Fundamentalism, in this volume, and Frances Raday, *Religion and Patriarchal Politics: The Israeli Experience,* in this volume.

18. *See* Galia Golan, *Movement Toward Equality for Women in Israel,* 2 TIKKUN 19, 19–20 (1987).

19. *See* MICHEL FOUCAULT, POWER/KNOWLEDGE: SELECTED INTERVIEWS AND OTHER WRITINGS, 1972–1977, 134–45 (Colin Gordon, trans. & ed.) (Brighton, U.K.: Harvester Press, 1980).

20. LUBAVITCH WOMEN'S ORGANIZATION, THE MODERN JEWISH WOMAN: A UNIQUE PERSPECTIVE (Brooklyn, NY: Lubavitch Educational Foundation for Jewish Marriage Enrichment, 1981).

21. *E.g.,* Dr. Shaina Sara Handelman, *On Being Single & Jewish, in* THE MODERN JEWISH WOMAN: A UNIQUE PERSPECTIVE, *supra* note 20, at 3; Abstract of *Changing Careers,* Chapter two, Table of Contents, *in* THE MODERN JEWISH WOMAN: A UNIQUE PERSPECTIVE, *supra* note 20, at v.

22. *See* Hyman, *supra* note 17; Raday, *supra* note 17.

23. *Tefilath Shakharith* [the morning prayer] in the *Sidur* [daily prayer book] (from author's translation).

24. Rachel Adler, *I've Had Nothing Yet So I Can't Take More,* 8 MOMENT, no.8, September, 1983, at 22, 23.

25. MOSHE MEISELMAN, JEWISH WOMAN IN JEWISH LAW 16 (New York: Ktav Publications House, 1978).

26. Debra Renee Kaufman, *Paradoxical Politics: Gender Politics among Newly Orthodox Jewish Women in the United States, in* IDENTITY POLITICS AND WOMEN: CULTURAL REASSERTIONS AND FEMINISMS IN INTERNATIONAL PERSPECTIVE 349, 357–60 (Valentine M. Moghadam, ed.) (Boulder: Westview Press, Inc., 1994).

27. For a general discussion of empowerment, women, and ethnicity, see YUVAL-DAVIS, *supra* note 1, at 116–33.

28. *See, e.g.,* WOMEN AND THE POLITICS OF EMPOWERMENT (Ann Bookman & Sandra Morgan, eds.) (Philadelphia: Temple University Press, 1988).

29. Nira Yuval-Davis, *National Reproduction and 'The Demographic Race' in Israel, in* WOMAN-NATION-STATE 92, 100–05 (Nira Yuval-Davis & Floya Anthias, eds.; Jo Campling, consulting ed.) (Houndmills/Basingstoke/Hampshire: Macmillan, 1989; New York: St. Martin's Press, 1989).

II

Responses to Religious Fundamentalist Assertions of Cultural Relativism

Chapter 5

Relativism, Culture, Religion, and Identity

Michael Singer

I. RELATIVISM AND CULTURE

Human beings in many places and at many times have searched for a universal sense of truth, values, ethics, morality, and justice. Relativism is the view that this search is hopeless and futile because the concepts of truth and falsehood, right and wrong, rights and duties, can exist and be valid only within a specific context that defines them and gives them meaning, and consequently they can have no universal validity.[1] Relativism rejects any claim of universal human rights based on natural law, and equally rejects any universal process for interpreting treaties that could support universal human rights standards.

A relativist claim provokes the question: "Relative to what?"[2] What is the specific, type of context, that defines truth, values, and so forth? One response is that each individual defines his or her own sense of truth and values, in which case relativism is effectively reduced to subjectivism.[3] A different and relatively recent response is that the defining context is "culture"; this approach is then called cultural relativism.[4]

Cultural relativism is in fact a hybrid doctrine derived from relativism, with empirical and normative input from anthropology,[5] and developed initially in reaction against Western assertions of cultural superiority. Anthropologists study the commonalities of groups of human beings sharing a culture. They define the culture of the group in various ways, but generally in terms of a supposedly shared group process by which meaning is assigned to behavior, social action is articulated, and social modes for guiding and governing behavior are developed.[6] The term "culture" or "society" is often used to denote the group that shares, and is defined by sharing, a common culture.

Culture shapes the development of each individual's normative sense. Cultural relativism asserts that all values and norms are culturally produced. From this it follows that culture is the appropriate context for defining values and norms, and that there can be no universally valid norms.[7] Indeed, the most radical form of cultural relativism denies the possibility of meaningful discussion of norms between cultures, since meaning is defined only within a cultural context.[8]

An immediate problem with the cultural relativist position is that it gives no guidance for relations between cultures.[9] If your culture gives you a right to suppress my culture, I have no normative basis for argument with you. *My* normative sense does not grant you any such right, but my normative sense is a product of my culture and valid only within my culture; it is irrelevant to your culture. It might be nice to have a universal principle that cultures should respect each other; but because you and I are from different cultures, by definition we do not share a normative context within which we could develop such a principle.

Consequently, cultural relativism creates its own universal norm, declaring that there is one, and only one, principle of universal validity: cultures must respect each other's autonomy. This moral position has been called "prescriptive relativism,"[10] and is based on both empirical and normative reasons. The empirical basis is that since we cannot even discuss norms together it is futile to try to impose norms on one another. The normative basis is that it is wrong to undermine the values of a culture, since this will rob the members of the culture of their sense of meaning and worth, and thus of their identity.[11]

II. CULTURAL RELATIVIST CLAIMS

Within the international community, prescriptive relativism has been invoked to support claims that international human rights provisions should not apply, or should apply only with a special interpretation, to certain groups because the provisions in their normal form of application are alien to the groups in question.[12] These claims are sometimes made within the context of international law, in which case they argue that cultural relativism is, or should be, in some fashion part of international law. At other times the claim is made that cultural values, particularly when based on religious values,[13] enjoy supremacy over international law.

Regardless of how the claim is stated, it is generally made by an elite of a group claiming to speak and act on behalf of the group as a whole. Thus, the first question facing the international community is whether the facts

Cultural Relativism

HORIZON PRINTING

Carroll's Hill P.O. Box 1417
Southwest Harbor, ME 04679
244-9066 — Fax 244-9933

Trisha,

Please cancel

Contemporary World

Issues from

ABC-CLIO

Thanks.

Marcia

of the case are as the elite has presented them. Is the elite describing the group's culture (or religion) exactly as it is, or rather as what the elite would like it to be or is trying to force it to be? The international community has the responsibility to satisfy itself on this question.

Such concerns arise, for example, when fundamentalists take power and try to establish the cultural forms (based on religious norms) that existed, or that they imagine existed, in some idealized place or time, but do not exist in the group here and now.[14] This threatens to destroy the cultural (and religious) values and sense of identity of nonfundamentalist members of the group, and in many cases has been particularly destructive to the cultural (and religious) identity of women. Cultural relativism is not relevant in such a setting because cultural relativism advocates respect for a culture as it is, with a view to safeguarding the sense of worth and identity of present members of the culture. It grants no privileges to an attempt to re-model a culture, regardless of the underlying motives or justifications.[15]

This is particularly relevant to groups that in the name of culture (or religion) deny women the right to express their views publicly, within or outside the group, or deny women the opportunity to form and develop their views by denying them education and liberty. In such cases the international community should assume that if these women were given a full and free opportunity to form their views and declare them, they would reject the group elite's version of their culture (or religion). When a party silences a potential witness, it is reasonable to assume that the testimony of the witness would not have supported the position of that party.[16]

Particular care is needed when the elite is a government, because no government can be trusted to state the facts completely and honestly on any matter that will affect the extent of its own powers. Thus, a cultural relativist claim coming from a government should be closely examined and adjudged, with the burden of proof on the government that the culture is indeed as the government describes it.

III. CULTURAL IDENTITIES

After clarifying the facts, the international community should next determine whether cultural relativism is even relevant to the situation. Cultural relativism is relevant only to protecting and maintaining a cultural context in which human beings are forming their sense of worth and identity. However, claims of cultural relativism are often made when it is not clear whether a culture is trying to maintain its own identity or rather trying to dominate or suppress another culture living near to or within it.

This raises the problem of how to decide whether a group constitutes a single culture, or several cultures living in proximity, or one or more cultural groups that are subgroups of another cultural group. The international community has inherited this problem from anthropology. At one extreme, if a culture is defined as consisting of all persons who share precisely the same sense of meanings and values in all matters, then every individual constitutes a culture, since no two people agree precisely on every issue of meanings and values. The term "culture" would then lose any independent meaning. Anthropology rescued the concept of culture from this fate by making empirical and normative simplifying assessments of cultural identity. These assessments have entered the discourse of international human rights with damaging effect, particularly as this discourse relates to women.

As a preliminary simplification, anthropology privileges ethnic (or at least endogamous) groups as cultural entities.[17] As further, and related, simplification, anthropology privileges men in the assessment of cultural identity. It draws cultural boundaries largely by reference to a common sense of identity and values among a group of men living in proximity. Thus, for example, Clifford Geertz claims that the Balinese cockfight "as a popular obsession of consuming power . . . is at least as important a revelation of what being a Balinese 'is really like'" as are Balinese "mythology, art, ritual, social organization, patterns of child rearing, [and] forms of law."[18] Since the Balinese cockfight is (unlike the other social activities listed) an exclusively male activity,[19] Geertz is effectively claiming that Balinese men epitomize all Balinese, but adduces no evidence in support of this.

Having drawn cultural boundaries by reference to the men, anthropology simply assigns the women living within the same physical environment to the same culture, often without scrutiny of *their* sense of identity and values, and indeed even when it is explicitly recognized that this sense diverges sharply from that of the men. In many cultures, women live within their own structural forms and derive their normative sense from them. The international community, following anthropology, has tended to ignore such lines of separation even when the separation reaches the level of segregation. But if women and men in such a group develop discernibly different senses of meaning and norms, then we might just as well identify two cultures within the group,[20] with, in many cases, one culture at least in part dominating the other.

In general, it is an oversimplification to assume that an individual's culture consists of one identifiable group, usually taken to be the individual's ethnic or religious group. This may be more or less valid for small, isolated groups (and then only if the issue of gender is ignored), but such groups now make up a very small proportion of the human race. For most people, cultural identity is not such a simple, single-group identification. Speaking for my own most obvious cultural identifiers, I am English, Jewish, male, of Middle-European ancestry, partly American, and a scholar; I have put these in alphabetical order. If my culture is defined as the intersection of all of these identifiers, then according to cultural relativism I am unable even to have a meaningful discussion about values with any other contributor to this volume, because none of them shares all these identifiers. Certainly we can reach no normative agreement on anything other than to leave each other alone. This of course is nonsense.

It may be more true to say that I have a number of cultural homes, one within each of these several cultures, and can therefore communicate meaningfully within all of them. But this also makes nonsense of the oversimplified view of cultural identity, because in this sense every human being has more than one cultural home. Everyone has at least one ethnic-group identity as well as a gender identity and a class identity. Cultures, including those based on ethnic and religious identities, interact with one another all the time, through travel, television, the telephone, e-mail, and the internet, and in this process their members extend their cultural boundaries to include a variety of affiliations that then become part of their sense of values and identity.

Moreover, there is no basis for a group elite to claim that some aspects of their members' culture are more essential or important than others. No authority is in a position to conclude that my Jewishness has been corrupted by contact with English values, or vice versa. All aspects of my cultural identity simply *are*,[21] and have helped to shape my sense of meaning, values, and identity. An authority may nevertheless wish to cut selected pieces out of my cultural identity in order to bring me into conformity with its sense of what my culture and my identity ought to be. However, it cannot claim exemption from international norms for its endeavors on the basis of cultural relativism, because this would undermine the respect for all cultures (including mine) that cultural relativism is intended to promote.

Thus, an assessment of cultural identity should take into account relationships among interacting cultural groups. In addition, it should take into account the existence of culturally identifiable subgroups within a group, as well as the existence of larger affiliations of which the group is a part. An example of this is the relationship between the culture of the town, the culture of the nation, and perhaps even the culture of a supranational grouping. The main focus of people's cultural identification may shift over time from town to nation to supranational grouping, and back again. Any attempt by an elite to gain ascendancy for the culture at one level is thereby an attempt to suppress the cultures at the other levels.[22] Consequently, such an attempt cannot rely on cultural relativism for an exemption from human rights standards.

IV. CULTURAL DEVELOPMENT

Cultures interact with other cultures, and in the process they change. Some relativists claim "absence of change" as itself a value within the culture, and thus try to reject the entire process of interaction and change on the basis of cultural relativism. But there is nothing relative about this. In every culture there are persons who fear and dislike the continuing processes of cultural interaction and change. These persons are particularly found within the elite, because cultural interaction leads to changes that the elite cannot control, and the elite generally has much to lose from cultural changes that lie beyond its control. The elite may endeavor to suppress the cultural development of those who are open to external values in order to safeguard the cultural (or religious) purity of those who are closed off. But the elite cannot claim exemption from international standards for these endeavors on the basis of cultural relativism, because its culture is, in respect of its elite's distaste for change, not qualitatively different from any other culture.[23] Cultural relativism claims respect for cultural difference, but it cannot offer a guarantee of cultural stability and permanence in our volatile and uncertain world.

V. GLOBAL CULTURE

Taking into account the real complexity of cultural identity and the inevitability of change eliminates many claims based on cultural relativism. The only remaining cases are those where a culturally uniform and homogeneous group demands exemption from international norms as uniformly interpreted for practices that maintain the existing culture in its present form. These cases may involve the kind of practice that Isabelle Gunning elegantly describes as "culturally challenging,"[24] or may involve the process of acculturation of children into the group.[25]

Even in these cases cultural identity is not a single fixed point. Every culturally identifiable group, even a uniform and homogeneous group, is part of a larger culturally identifiable affiliation: the global culture of the international community that was forged in the aftermath of the Second World War. This culture has its own culturally identifying texts, valued to many and even sacred to some: the Charter of the United Nations, the Universal Declaration of Human Rights,[26] and the international human rights covenants.[27] Global culture is of recent origin, but so also are many cultures—especially national cultures—that strongly assert their identities and are accorded respect. Within global culture, people from all parts of the world and of all languages discuss values and norms and reach accord. Any attempt to suppress global culture cannot claim exemption from international norms on the basis of cultural relativism, because cultural relativism cannot support a claim that any local culture is superior to global culture.[28]

Global culture may be less relevant if all members of the group uniformly reject all its norms, although children may lack the capacity to reject their global cultural heritage. But it is even improbable that all adult members of the group will utterly reject global culture. Some members of the group may, for example, value dialogue with nonmembers of the group. Dialogue is valued in global culture, and consequently the elite of the group may not assert cultural relativism as a basis for suppressing dialogue. The international community may then use dialogue to press for reconsideration of culturally challenging practices and their speedy eradication.

The cases where dialogue is ineffective are the most difficult, and require sensitive contextual approaches. Other chapters in this volume focus on these difficulties and guide us toward their resolution. However, in the process of resolution it should never be forgotten that cultural relativism itself requires sensitivity and respect for both the local and the global cultural values involved.

NOTES

1. *See* RICHARD J. BERNSTEIN, BEYOND OBJECTIVISM AND RELATIVISM 2–20 (Philadelphia: University of Pennsylvania Press, 1983); PLATO, THEAETETUS *161c-e (presenting Socrates as ascribing relativism to Protagoras and ridiculing the position).

    A distinction is often drawn between *moral relativism* (the view that values, ethics, and morality are contextually dependent) and *cognitive relativism* (the view that, furthermore, reason, truth, and the very reality of the world are contextually dependent). *See, e.g.,* Martin Hollis & Steven Lukes, *Introduction* to RATIONALITY AND RELATIVISM 1, 5–11 (Martin Hollis & Steven Lukes, eds.) (Cambridge: MIT Press, 1982). Cognitive relativism has been regarded as the most radical form of relativism, and there have been attempts to reject cognitive relativism while embracing moral relativism. *See* BERNSTEIN, *supra,* at 13. For doubts regarding this compromise position, see Hollis & Lukes, *supra,* at 6. The concerns of international human rights law usually focus on moral rather than cognitive issues of relativism.

2. Hollis & Lukes, *supra* note 1, at 11.

3. Bernstein denies that relativism provides support for subjectivism. BERNSTEIN, *supra* note 1, at 11–13. However, his arguments are of limited relevance within the relativist universe, because a relativist has no basis for dismissing the values of another person as mere subjectivism and devoid of reason. In that person's conceptual and normative framework (which may be unique to him) his reasons may be entirely valid. The relativist can claim

no broader context in which to adjudicate a dispute over valid reasoning or norms between the other person's framework and her own.

4. Cultural relativism depends on the ethnographic concept of culture that developed in nineteenth-century anthropology. For development of the term "culture," see DAVID LLOYD & PAUL THOMAS, CULTURE AND THE STATE 2 n.2 (New York/London: Routledge, 1998).

   Other possible responses are, for example, that the defining context is gender, or class. Note that the response to the question "relative to what?" does not predetermine the issue of how much of the world view (from normative to cognitive) is seen as relative. Thus, for example, the view that the physical world is objective, but values are relative to cultural context, embraces cultural moral relativism but rejects cognitive relativism of any kind. The term "cultural relativism" is commonly used without regard to the extent of the relativist claim.

5. For development of cultural relativism within twentieth-century anthropology, see Hollis & Lukes, *supra* note 1, at 2. An example of normative input from anthropology is the warning of the executive board of the American Anthropological Association that the Universal Declaration of Human Rights could suppress cultural differences. *Statement on Human Rights,* 49 AM. ANTHROPOLOGIST 539–43 (1947).

6. *See, e.g.,* CLIFFORD GEERTZ, THE INTERPRETATION OF CULTURES 4–5 (New York: Basic Books, Inc., 1973).

7. *See, e.g.,* Barry Barnes & David Bloor, *Relativism, Rationalism and the Sociology of Knowledge, in* RATIONALITY AND RELATIVISM, *supra* note 1, 21, 26–28. For discussion of various forms of cultural moral relativism, see JAMES W. NICKEL, MAKING SENSE OF HUMAN RIGHTS: PHILOSOPHICAL REFLECTIONS ON THE UNIVERSAL DECLARATION OF HUMAN RIGHTS 68–79 (Berkeley/Los Angeles/London: University of California Press, 1987).

8. *See, e.g.,* WILLARD VAN ORMAN QUINE, FROM A LOGICAL POINT OF VIEW 61 (New York/Evanston/San Francisco/London: Harper & Row, Publishers, 2d. ed., 1961).

9. This, of course, applies equally to any groups asserting relativist claims.

10. NICKEL, *supra* note 7, at 74–75.

11. The first reason has limited validity. The second reason is better. Culture does indeed give people much of their sense of identity and worth, and abrupt shifts in cultural forms can be destructive.

12. For example, within some religious groups it has been claimed that the human rights provision requiring equality between spouses in marriage should accept the exchange of a husband's duty to protect his wife for a wife's duty to obey her husband as equality, because this is how the group regards it. *See* Courtney W. Howland, *The Challenge of Religious Fundamentalism to the Liberty and Equality Rights of Women: An Analysis under the United Nations Charter,* 35 COLUM. J. TRANSNAT'L L. 271, 282–324 (1997).

13. Solely for purposes of discussion I allow that religion may make a cultural relativist claim. I do not consider in this chapter whether religion may

claim exemption from or mitigation of human rights norms on the basis of norms of religious freedom.

14. *See* Azar Nafisi, *Tales of Subversion: Women Challenging Fundamentalism in the Islamic Republic of Iran,* in this volume.

15. Remodeling a group's culture, or religion, may indeed be part of the business of the group leadership, but this process is subject to the normal rules of the international community, uniformly interpreted and applied, and deserves no special privileges or exemptions.

16. For example, U.S. courts deny a party the right to introduce certain out-of-court statements of an absent witness into evidence when the party has procured the absence of the witness for the purpose of preventing the witness from attending or testifying. FED. R. EVID. 804(a)(1)(5), (b).

17. Using the term "ethnography" to define what anthropologists do, *see* GEERTZ, *supra* note 6, at 5, in practice generally narrows the primary focus of anthropology rather than broadens the sense of the term "ethnic." Some studies of non-ethnic groups virtually apologize for treating the group as a "culture" or "society." *See, e.g.,* Hilary Callan, *The Premiss of Dedication: Notes towards an Ethnography of Diplomats' Wives, in* PERCEIVING WOMEN 87, 87 nn.1, 2 (Shirley Ardener, ed.) (New York: John Wiley & Sons, 1975).

18. GEERTZ, *supra* note 6, at 417.

19. *Id.* at 417 n.4.

20. "A society in which . . . [a certain sense of common terms of reference] was lacking would not be a society in the normal sense of the term, but several." Charles Taylor, *Interpretation and the Sciences of Man, in* INTERPRETIVE SOCIAL SCIENCE: A SECOND LOOK 33, 57 (Paul Rabinow & William M. Sullivan, eds.) (Berkeley/Los Angeles/London: University of California Press, 1987). Anthropologists generally simply ignore this principle in relation to women and men within an endogamous group.

    Many groups have regarded women as capable of shifting readily (often under compulsion) from one culture to another upon marriage. *See* Lisa C. Stratton, Note, *The Right to Have Rights: Gender Discrimination in Nationality Laws,* 77 MINN. L. REV.195, 203–04 (1992); Lovelace v. Canada (adopted 30 July 1981, 13th Sess.), Communication No. R.6/24, Report of the Human Rights Committee, U.N. GAOR, 36th Sess., Supp. No. 40, Annex XVIII, at 166, U.N. Doc. A/36/40 (1981).

21. Franck claims that identity today is made up of "multilayered loyalty references" that each individual *chooses.* This may be an exaggerated claim for the role of choice in identity formation. Notably, while Franck includes "state, ethnic group, race, religion, city, business firm or professional association and family" among loyalty references, he makes no mention of sex, gender, sexual identity, or class. Thomas M. Franck, *Clan and Superclan: Loyalty, Identity and Community in Law and Practice,* 90 AM. J. INT'L L. 359, 376–77 (1996).

22. This was illustrated in the dispute regarding whether the four Comoro Islands should become independent from France as a single unity, or whether the island of Mayotte, with a mainly Christian population, should

achieve a separate independence from the other three islands, whose population is mainly Muslim. *See* FREDERIC L. KIRGIS, JR., INTERNATIONAL ORGANIZATIONS IN THEIR LEGAL SETTING 195–96 (St. Paul, Minn: West Publishing Co., 2d. ed., 1993).

The development of European cultural identity has brought about changes in the national cultural identities of states within the European Union. *See, e.g.,* David O'Connor, *Limiting "Public Morality" Exceptions to Free Movement in Europe: Ireland's Role in a Changing European Union,* 22 BROOK. J. INT'L L. 695, 711 n.74 ("[the popular vote] to adopt a . . . constitutional amendment to end the ban on divorce . . . is yet another example of the profound social changes in Ireland as a direct result of Ireland's membership in the more socially liberal European Union").

23. "Those who sit astride the status quo have always opposed change and have always ended, sooner or later, in defeat." Nawal El Saadawi, *Women, Religion and Literature: Bridging the cultural gap, in* THE NAWAL EL SAADAWI READER 134, 142 (London/New York: Zed Books, 1997).

24. Isabelle R. Gunning, *Arrogant Perception, World-Travelling and Multicultural Feminism: The Case of Female Genital Surgeries,* 23 COLUM. HUM. RTS. L. REV. 189, 191 n.8 (1992).

25. I do not consider in this chapter the legal and moral issues regarding a child's acculturation into its family's society.

26. Universal Declaration of Human Rights, *adopted* Dec. 10, 1948, G.A. Res. 217A (III), U.N. GAOR, 3d Sess., pt. 1, 183d plen. mtg., at 71, U.N. Doc. A/810 (1948).

27. *E.g.,* International Covenant on Civil and Political Rights, *adopted* Dec. 16, 1966, G.A. Res. 2200 (XXI), U.N. GAOR, 21st Sess., Supp. No. 16, at 52, U.N. Doc. A/6316, 999 U.N.T.S. 171, 6 I.L.M. 368 (1967).

28. El Saadawi denounces global culture as a form of capitalist-inspired imperialism that "aims at expanding, homogenizing and unifying the world into one market. . . ." Nawal El Saadawi, *Why Keep Asking Me About My Identity?, in* THE NAWAL EL SAADAWI READER, *supra* note 23, at 117, 121. She views adherence to "the 'internationalization' process" of global cultural development as "false consciousness," caused by the "deadly poison" of "[c]ultural imperialism." Nawal El Saadawi, *Democracy, Creativity and African Literature, in* THE NAWAL EL SAADAWI READER, *supra* note 23, at 188, 199. Plainly, any local culture (together with its adherents) is vulnerable to disparagement—on these grounds or others—especially from the standpoint of a culture that forms a subgroup of it. *See, e.g.,* Maria Luisa Nunes, BECOMING TRUE TO OURSELVES: CULTURAL DECOLONIZATION AND NATIONAL IDENTITY IN THE LITERATURE OF THE PORTUGUESE-SPEAKING WORLD 19, 24–25 (New York/Westport, Connecticut/London: Greenwood Press, 1987) (considering women within Portuguese society as a cultural group colonized by men). Cultural relativism cannot support a claim for supremacy of local culture on the ground that global culture is distasteful, intrusive, or aggressive, just as it could not support the converse claim.

Chapter 6

Cultural Relativism and International Law

Christine Chinkin

I. INTRODUCTION

Public international law makes a particular claim to universality in application, if not in origin, and central to this claim is the universality of the human rights standards articulated under the auspices of the United Nations (UN). While international human rights instruments, from the 1948 Universal Declaration of Human Rights[1] onward, derive substantially from Western intellectual, philosophical, and spiritual traditions, they have nonetheless today acquired widespread international commitment. There are, for example, over 160 state parties, representing every geographic region and espousing all religions, to the 1979 UN Convention on the Elimination of All Forms of Discrimination Against Women (CEAFDAW)[2] and 191 state parties to the 1989 UN Convention on the Rights of the Child.[3] UN member states' adoption by consensus of General Assembly resolutions, such as the 1993 Declaration on the Elimination of Violence against Women,[4] has meant that formally there are no dissentient voices to the view that gender-specific violence constitutes a direct denial of human rights and prevents women's enjoyment of all rights.

Such notions of universal application are, however, undermined by demands for priority to be accorded to diverse cultural and religious traditions.[5] The international human rights standard of legal and social equality between women and men has been denied in situations where religious leaders, or fanatics, present it as contrary to religious doctrine. This chapter will briefly outline the tensions generated within international human rights law by cultural relativist claims that purport to justify the continued subordination of women, and some of the dilemmas these tensions present to advocates for women's rights. It will finally discuss strategies for moving beyond these tensions and dilemmas.

II. RELIGIOUS RIGHTS AND WOMEN'S RIGHTS

The confrontation between claims for the enjoyment by women of the panoply of internationally guaranteed human rights and those for observance of religious tenets are frequently presented in terms of universality versus cultural relativism.[6] The force attributed to culture in maintaining social cohesion bestows upon cultural claims a resonance that is cloaked with legal authority by their invocation of the UN Charter provision that excludes matters within the domestic jurisdiction of the state from international regulation.[7] Under such a relativist perspective, claims for universality can accordingly be rejected as imperialistic and as a form of conspiracy that uses human rights to uphold Western economic interests to the detriment of developing states. Although this debate is typically cast in terms of cultural rather than religious relativism, claims for deviance from human rights standards founded upon religious grounds share some of these underpinnings. However, religious claims are regarded as having a particularly strong appeal, based as they are upon practices purportedly required by sacred doctrine that determines the relationship between a people and their God. Religious extremists further bolster and legitimate their claims by appropriating for their cause human rights guarantees for religious freedom and nondiscrimination on the basis of religion.[8]

Relativist claims in the name of religious imperatives do not fit easily within the traditional parameters of human rights law and are manipulable in ways that challenge not only the affirmation of universality, but even the utility of a rights-based discourse. Enhancement of the human rights of women must be considered in these contexts.

First, the right to religious freedom lies both at the interface between civil and political rights (for example, freedom of association and expression) and economic, social, and cultural rights (for example, access to education, health and employment) and that between individual rights and group rights. The right to freedom of thought, conscience, and religion accords to all individuals the right to manifest their religious beliefs through "worship, observance, practice and teaching."[9] However, the right of economic, social, and cultural development, which might be thought to encompass the freedom to observe one's religion alongside others, is, rather, part of the right to self-determination, and as such a group right.[10]

The inclusion of group rights within a catalogue of human rights creates conceptual confusion, particularly in situations where assertions of individual liberty do not conform with those of the group to a collective identity, including a religious identity. For example, article 18 of the International Covenant on Civil and Political Rights provides individuals the right to manifest religious belief "individually or in community with others,"[11] but says nothing about an individual's right to be free from the imposition of the teachings and practices that a community might espouse as essential to religious conformity.

The issue of women's individual rights in the context of her group's religious identity is yet more complex. Cultural and religious groups are often identified by the role and behavior that they designate to women. Thus, demands for women's advancement may be regarded as threatening societal and familial coherence. Where the existence of a group is under threat, the rights of women become even more ambiguous. On the one hand, the targeting of women of one group by another group in order to cause actual and psychological harm to the identity of the opposing group has long been a common, if historically unremarked, concomitant of conflict.[12] The systematic and widespread rapes and other sexual abuse of Muslim women in Bosnia and Herzegovina is a recent manifestation of this reality. At the same time, women may be required to adhere even more strictly to religious and cultural norms to preserve a threatened group's separate existence.[13]

Thus, the particular place allotted to women in maintaining group coherence means that the factors that might ensure their true self-determination (free determination of their political and social status) and their equality within the group have not been regarded as requiring separate consideration from more general issues in struggles for a group's self-determination. This is true even in cases of national liberation or liberation from an oppressive government, situations that frequently incorporate demands for respect for religious autonomy.

The right to self-determination has also been linked to that of democratic entitlement,[14] but the formal processes of Western democracy assumed to be part of democratic entitlement typically deliver less freedom to women than to men.[15] It has been suggested that rather than focus upon the narrow issue of cultural relativism, international lawyers should promote different models of democratic self-determination that embrace economic and political freedom, thereby facilitating rejection of nondemocratic, extremist demands and enhancing women's equality.[16] The dialogue on universality and relativism needs to bring the lens of gender to bear on the construction of new, more genuinely participatory models of democratic social ordering.[17]

Second, claims based on religion often have a trumping effect on other claims. The threat to the societal status quo that is inherent in demands for women's equality allows such trumping to occur, even in the face of destabilizing and violent tactics by religious extremists. For example, there is the lack of serious, sustained objections by state parties to, or analysis of, the substantive reservations on religious grounds to CEAFDAW and the Convention on the Rights of the Child.[18] Failure by state parties to object to reservations that subordinate the treaty obligations to imprecise and indeterminate religious priorities allows the latter to assume legitimacy and to be asserted by those acting in the name of religion.

Third, claims based on religion confront the scope of human rights protection. Traditionally, states have been able to avoid intervening in situations involving wrongs committed by private individuals because human rights law has been focused on the actions of the state vis-à-vis the individual.[19] Advocates of women's human rights have especially argued for the expansion of the arena of human rights guarantees to encompass acts of private individuals, notably those of family and community members.[20] However, in the context of religion and women's human rights, this potential for intervention may prove to be a doubled-edged sword. For example, where the state has been co-opted by religious demands, state intervention in family relationships may reinforce certain limited roles for women thereby denying women the protection that is normally associated with state scrutiny.[21] Where this is not the case, women's rights to freedom, equality, and nonviolence may be met by claims by other family members for privacy in practicing their religion.

Only occasionally is the potential contradiction between individual women's rights and religious freedom explicitly acknowledged within human rights instruments, let alone resolved in favor of women. In 1987, there were calls within the UN Economic and Social Council and the General Assembly, (prompted by a request of the Committee on the Elimination of Discrimination Against Women) for a study of the compatibility of CEAFDAW (which makes no reference to the problem) with the teachings of Islam, but these were successfully opposed.[22] Such general resistance within the institutional framework legitimates and fuels more fundamentalist demands. In 1993, the World Conference on Human Rights called for "the eradication of any conflicts which may arise between the rights of women and the harmful effects of certain traditional or customary practices, cultural prejudices and religious extremism,"[23] without specifying which way the conflict should be resolved. However, shortly thereafter, the Declaration on the Elimination of Violence Against Women asserted that: "[s]tates should condemn violence against women and should not invoke any custom, tradition or religious consideration to avoid their obligations with respect to its elimination."[24]

While important, this stronger assertion is limited to the elimination of violence against women and does not extend to the broader guarantee of all women's rights.

However, the state is responsible for ensuring human rights to all individuals within its territory. This entails a positive obligation upon state agencies to act in conformity with the international obligations incurred, including those for women's rights. Where the state has adopted religious demands, there is nonetheless legal responsibility for any ensuing violations of human rights obligations, although this is rarely acknowledged. Subversion of international law by the instrumentalities of the state negates for women the usefulness of recourse to law and leaves them with only political avenues available, where they may be unable to mobilize adequate support. Indeed, the manipulative use of religious codes by states in defiance of international norms has been described as a new manifestation of the postcolonial state.[25] Even where this has not occurred, there is a duty upon the state to act with due diligence to ensure respect for human rights within its territory.[26] Article 4 (c) of the Declaration on the Elimination of Violence Against Women explicitly requires this standard "whether those acts are perpetrated by the State or by private persons."[27] Nevertheless, where religious forces threaten or cause public disorder in the face of the enforcement of secular law, or where religious extremists exercise effective local control, the state may be unwilling or unable to comply with its international obligations.

Human rights discourse has given insufficient attention both to the resolution of conflicting rights and to the challenge of ensuring adequate protection against abuses committed by nonstate actors. Since both are essential components of ensuring women's human rights against the demands of religious extremism, these deficiencies seriously weaken the effectiveness of human rights legal discourse for the protection of women.

III. STRATEGIES

A. Legal Remedies and Their Limitations

Despite these weaknesses in international human rights law, appeals to its standards should not be abandoned. Nondiscrimination on the basis of sex is given equal validity with other prohibitions of discrimination in all legal instruments, including the UN Charter.[28] This includes the right of all women to act in accordance with their own conscience and beliefs and not to be forced into subordination in accordance with other people's beliefs. It is an abdication of responsibility to give way to extremist demands in the name of freedom of religion. Thus, such legal arguments must be made in UN and regional human rights arenas.

In addition, domestic courts and agencies are also important forums for advancing such legal arguments. States are obliged to ensure that domestic law conforms with their international obligations, and thus primary responsibility for the enforcement of human rights obligations must come through domestic agencies. The growing number of cases brought by women in domestic courts reflects this fact, and such litigation also provides a means of ending the silence that traditionally enshrouds the violation of women's rights.

Nevertheless, it is not always successful or possible to pursue legal remedies: women may not be able to access courts; courts may not be willing to apply legal norms in the face of extremist demands; or state agencies may resist implementation of legal standards. The confrontational posture entailed in setting the problem in terms of women's rights against those of religious teachings may not be helpful.

In addition, emphasis upon enforcement of legally protected rights is itself culturally based. It also assumes a polarization of rights that fails to take into account the multiplicities of women's own identities. Many women are strong adherents to the tenets of their own religion, while claiming the right to human dignity and choice within it. More pragmatically, it is apparent that human rights implementation will always be impeded where there is dissonance between legally articulated standards and deeply rooted customs and beliefs. The degree of genuine compliance with human rights standards depends upon how much a society feels such standards are its own.

These realities present particular dilemmas for advocates of women's rights. There is an evident need for understanding and mutual cooperation between women from all cultures and religions in fighting the denial of women's human rights presented by fundamentalist demands. However, such solidarity is not easy to achieve. Southern women and women of color have claimed that too often Northern women see the issue of women's rights myopically, through their own cultural lenses, and thus fail to engage with the former's realities. Northern feminists too readily discount the historical roots of other feminisms, including, for example, women contesting injustices in the contexts of slavery and colonialism. Many women's concern with gendered subordination has been played out in the wider context of struggles for national or racial liberation.[29] Such struggles result in a different understanding of what it is to be female from that of Northern, white women, and may create loyalty to, and identification with, members of a woman's own religious, political, or social group. Factors of class, history, economic well-being, nationality, ethnic origin, and culture all identify and construct a person and her understanding of rights, as well as gender and religion.[30]

Entwined with these varying perceptions of feminist struggles are different national perspectives of modernity. Geraldine Heng has argued that an ambivalence to modernity that pervades socioeconomic relations is another factor with which feminist claims to rights in many countries must contend.[31] Even as modernization and economic development are actively pursued, national identity through national culture and religion are sought.[32] An antipathy to Western culture is encapsulated in rejection of demands for women's rights, which are also usefully seen as antithetical to economic advancement.

How can these dilemmas be resolved? Clearly, assessing the usefulness of particular strategies requires consideration of context and participants. There can be no consistently right way of addressing the question. Instead, different approaches will be appropriate in different contexts.

B. Other Strategies

Nonlegal methodologies should be pursued alongside legal claims within national and international arenas. The Vienna Declaration and Beijing Platform for Action reinforce this commonsense approach through their commitment to employing law to eradicate violative laws and practices in conjunction with international cooperation in such fields as economic and social development, education, health care, and social support.[33] Various authors have described different techniques for enhancing constructive communication and understanding in attempts to negotiate a common language of women's needs in the face of women's diversity.[34] It must always be remembered that while theory and dialogue seek to be responsive to diversity, they must transcend "the relativistic tendencies that ultimately support the status quo."[35]

Constructive dialogue techniques can be engaged at the international level through the state reporting system of the human rights treaty bodies and UN state and thematic rapporteurs. For dialogue to lead to effective change, participants must receive training in self-awareness, gender, cultural, and religious sensitivity, and in providing the space for all involved to express their needs and interests freely. Within international institutional arenas, it is important to include the voices of those who have suffered abuse justified by reference to religion. Women from all religious backgrounds must be accorded opportunities to express their own understanding of the position of women within their own particular society. Little advance will be made if views are consistently mediated through representatives of a dominant culture, elites of a society, men, or representatives of intergovernmental organizations or nongovernmental organizations. All women, including women from all religions, must be represented, and their voices made to matter, within mainstream UN policy and decision-making bodies, regional bodies, and human rights groups and commit-tees,[36] and not merely be relegated to the ghetto of CEAFDAW.

Outside the formal institutional structures, constructive dialogue tech-niques are also being developed through women's transborder networks and support groups. These operate through cooperation between women working at all levels, including those working at grassroots organizations. The importance of such initiatives must also be recognized and supported, although not appropriated, by official agencies.

Greater inclusion of all women's voices will inevitably create a multi-plicity of voices, and may promote disharmony and lead to the formation of new elites claiming a legitimacy that they do not necessarily possess. Such disharmony is necessary if human rights law is to evolve to encom-pass those previously silenced. Similarly, denying the force of religious ar-guments will not achieve equality for women. Rather, attempting to engage with those making such arguments may ultimately be instrumen-tal in promoting change. The debate can be understood as encompassing other debates: between short-term and long-term solutions; between em-powerment and subordination; and between seeing those who are ad-versely affected by denial of human rights as objects in need of assistance and giving effect to their status as subjects of human rights law.

However, strategies based upon communication and dialogue will not be effective where there is no good faith attempt to achieve such under-standing. Where state, military, and economic forces are either used to con-tinue the subordination of women or are powerless in the face of extremist movements, other strategies must be engaged. For example, with respect to the Taliban in Afghanistan, members of the international community, states, and intergovernmental organizations must choose either to affirm human rights standards or to allow the principle of nonintervention into matters of domestic jurisdiction to control, thereby subjecting women to unconstrained denial of their rights, including the right to life. The inter-national community must also decide whether to work with such regimes in order to induce change or to subject them to international isolation. The Security Council imposed sanctions on the racist apartheid regimes in South Africa and Southern Rhodesia,[37] and has the ability to impose such sanctions in the context of gender apartheid. The increased use of sanctions by the Security Council since the early 1990s has led to greater sophistication in their design and implementation. They can include such measures as nonrecognition of the regime, withdrawal or denial of all eco-nomic and other aid, and suspension of air traffic. Ultimately, the military option is available. In Somalia in 1992, the Security Council for the first time used its powers under Chapter VII of the UN Charter on humanitarian grounds to authorize "all necessary means" to deliver assistance to the Somali people.[38] The institutional powers exist at the international and regional levels to respond to gross denials of human rights, whether committed directly by states or by nonstate actors. What is needed is the political will for their execution and far greater analysis, including gender analysis. The effects of such measures must also be monitored to ensure that they do not exacerbate the position of those they are intended to benefit, both in terms of economic deprivation and in causing further marginalization within their own society. International response to the denial of women's human rights caused by fundamentalist demands must encompass all such options, from education and dialogue to sanctions and coercion.

NOTES

1. Universal Declaration of Human Rights, *adopted* Dec. 10, 1948, G.A. Res. 217A (III), U.N. GAOR, 3d Sess., pt. 1, 183d plen. mtg., at 71, U.N. Doc. A/810 (1948) [hereinafter Universal Declaration].
2. Convention on the Elimination of All Forms of Discrimination Against Women, *adopted* Dec. 18, 1979, G.A. Res. 34/180, U.N. GAOR, 34th Sess., Supp. No. 46, at 193, U.N. Doc. A/34/46 (1979), 1249 U.N.T.S. 13 [hereinafter CEAFDAW].
3. Convention on the Rights of the Child, *adopted* Nov. 20, 1989, G.A. Res. 44/25, U.N. GAOR, 44th Sess., Supp. No. 49, at 166, U.N. Doc. A/44/49 (1989), 28 I.L.M. 1448 (1989), *corrected at* 29 I.L.M. 1340 (1990).
4. Declaration on the Elimination of Violence Against Women, *adopted* Dec. 20, 1993, G.A. Res. 48/104, U.N. GAOR, 48th Sess., 85th plen. mtg., Supp. No. 49, at 217, U.N. Doc. A/48/49 (1993), 33 I.L.M. 1049 (1994).
5. *See* Christine Chinkin, *Women's Human Rights: Guaranteed by Universal Standards or Discounted by Cultural Bias?*, *in* 5 COLLECTED COURSES OF THE ACADEMY OF EUROPEAN LAW 11 (European University Institute, ed.) (The Hague/Boston/London: Martinus Nijhoff Publishers, 1997).
6. *See* Fernando R. Tesón, *International Human Rights and Cultural Relativism*, 25 VA. J. INT'L L. 869, 875–84 (1985).
7. U.N. CHARTER art. 2, para. 7.
8. For examples of human rights guarantees of religious freedom and nondiscrimination in human rights treaties and declarations, see U. N. CHARTER art. 1, para. 3; Universal Declaration, *supra* note 1, art. 2; International Covenant on Civil and Political Rights, *adopted* Dec. 16, 1966, art. 2, 26, G.A. Res. 2200 (XXI), U.N. GAOR, 21st Sess., Supp. No. 16, at 52, U.N. Doc. A/6316, 999 U.N.T.S. 171, 173–4, 179, 6 I.L.M. 368, 369, 375 (1967) [hereinafter ICCPR].
9. ICCPR, *supra* note 8, art. 18, 999 U.N.T.S. at 178.
10. *See, e.g.,* ICCPR, *supra* note 8, art. 1, 999 U.N.T.S. at 173; International Covenant on Economic, Social and Cultural Rights, *adopted* Dec. 16, 1966,

art. 1, G.A. Res. 2200 (XXI), U.N. GAOR, 21st Sess., Supp. No. 16, at 49, U.N. Doc. A/6316, 993 U.N.T.S. 3, 6 I.L.M. 360, 360 (1967).

11. ICCPR, *supra* note 8, art. 18, 999 U.N.T.S. at 178.

12. RADHIKA COOMARASWAMY, *Of Kali Born: Women, Violence and the Law in Sri Lanka, in* FREEDOM FROM VIOLENCE: WOMEN'S STRATEGIES FROM AROUND THE WORLD 49, 50 (Margaret Schuler, ed.) (New York: UNIFEM, 1992).

13. For example, after the initial phase, Palestinian women were prevented from public participation in the Intifada. *See* Christine Chinkin, *The Potential and Pitfalls of the Right to Self-Determination for Women, in* HUMAN RIGHTS, SELF-DETERMINATION AND POLITICAL CHANGE IN THE OCCUPIED PALESTINIAN TERRITORIES 93, 104 (Stephen Bowen, ed.) (The Hague/Boston/London: Martinus Nijhoff Publishers, 1997).

14. *See* Thomas M. Franck, *The Emerging Right to Democratic Governance,* 86 AM. J. INT'L L. 46, 52 (1992).

15. For a discussion of the underrepresentation of women in government despite democratization in most countries, see Beijing Declaration and Platform for Action adopted by Fourth World Conference on Women, *adopted* Sept. 15, 1995, paras. 181–95, at 82–87 (Annex II: Platform for Action), U.N. Doc. A/CONF. 177/20 (preliminary version), 35 I.L.M. 401, 445–47 (1996) [hereinafter Beijing Platform].

16. *WILIG Panel Discussion on Ethnicity, Culture, and International Law,* 6 Women in International Law Interest Group: Washington Steering Committee Newsletter, Sept. 1994, at 1–2 (referring to remarks of Azizah al-Hibri).

17. *See* Karen Knop, *Re/Statements: Feminism and State Sovereignty in International Law,* 3 TRANSNAT'L L. & CONTEMP. PROBS. 293 (1993) (arguing that reconceptualizing state sovereignty and its role in international law would increase women's direct participation in international law making).

18. *See* Christine Chinkin, *Reservations and Objections to the Convention on the Elimination of All Forms of Discrimination Against Women, in* HUMAN RIGHTS AS GENERAL NORMS AND A STATE'S RIGHT TO OPT OUT: RESERVATIONS AND OBJECTIONS TO HUMAN RIGHTS CONVENTIONS 64, 75–82 (J.P. Gardner, ed.) (London: British Institute of International and Comparative Law, 1997) [hereinafter OPT OUT]; Jenny Kuper, *Reservations, Declarations and Objections to the 1989 Convention on the Rights of the Child, in* OPT OUT, *supra,* at 104. For further analysis and critique of the religious reservations to CEAFDAW, see Ann Elizabeth Mayer, *Religious Reservations to the Convention on the Elimination of All Forms of Discrimination Against Women: What Do They Really Mean?, in* this volume.

19. *See* Hilary Charlesworth & Christine Chinkin, *The Gender of* Jus Cogens, 15 HUM. RTS. Q. 63, 72 (1993).

20. *See* Hilary Charlesworth, *What are "Women's International Human Rights"?, in* HUMAN RIGHTS OF WOMEN: NATIONAL AND INTERNATIONAL PERSPECTIVES 58, 68–73 (Rebecca J. Cook, ed.) (Philadelphia: University of Pennsylvania Press, 1994).

21. For a discussion of the effect of the public/private dichotomy in the context of the religious freedom guarantees of the ICCPR, see Courtney W. Howland, *Safeguarding Women's Political Freedoms under the International Covenant on Civil and Political Rights in the Face of Religious Fundamentalism,* in this volume.

22. *See, e.g.,* G.A. Res. 42/60, Nov. 30, 1987, U.N. GAOR, 42d Sess., 85th plen. mtg., at 188, U.N. Doc. A/RES/42/60 (1987); *see* ANDREW BYRNES, REPORT ON THE SEVENTH SESSION OF THE COMMITTEE ON THE ELIMINATION OF DISCRIMINATION AGAINST WOMEN AND THE FOURTH MEETING OF STATES PARTIES TO THE CONVENTION ON THE ELIMINATION OF ALL FORMS OF DISCRIMINATION AGAINST WOMEN 6–7 (International Women's Rights Action Watch: 7th cedaw/iwraw report, 1988).

23. Vienna Declaration and Programme of Action: adopted by The World Conference on Human Rights, *adopted* June 25, 1993, para. 38, at 19, U.N. Doc. A/CONF. 157/23, pt. II, B.3, 32 I.L.M. 1661, 1678 (1993) [hereinafter Vienna Declaration].

24. Declaration on the Elimination of Violence Against Women, *supra* note 4, art. 4, 33 I.L.M. at 1052.

25. Radhika Coomaraswamy, *To Bellow Like a Cow: Women, Ethnicity, and the Discourse of Rights, in* HUMAN RIGHTS OF WOMEN: NATIONAL AND INTERNATIONAL PERSPECTIVES, *supra* note 20, at 39, 51.

26. *See* Velásquez Rodriguez Case, I.-A. Court H.R., Judgment of July 29, 1988, Series C: Decisions and Judgments, No. 4 (1988), 28 I.L.M. 294 (1989).

27. Declaration on the Elimination of Violence Against Women, *supra* note 4, art. 4, 33 I.L.M. at 1053.

28. Courtney W. Howland, *The Challenge of Religious Fundamentalism to the Liberty and Equality Rights of Women: An Analysis Under the United Nations Charter,* 35 COLUM. J. TRANSNAT'L L. 271, 331 (1997).

29. *See generally* FEMINIST GENEALOGIES, COLONIAL LEGACIES, DEMOCRATIC FUTURES (M. Jacqui Alexander & Chandra Talpade Mohanty, eds.) (New York/London: Routledge, 1997).

30. *See* Angela P. Harris, *Race and Essentialism in Feminist Legal Theory,* 42 STAN. L. REV. 581 (1990).

31. Geraldine Heng, *A Great Way to Fly: Nationalism, the State, and the Varieties of Third-World Feminism, in* FEMINIST GENEALOGIES, COLONIAL LEGACIES, DEMOCRATIC FUTURES, *supra* note 29, at 30, 33.

32. Lama Abu-Odeh, *Post-Colonial Feminism and the Veil: Considering the Differences,* 26 NEW ENG. L. REV. 1527, 1528–29 (1992).

33. *See generally* Vienna Declaration, *supra* note 23; Beijing Platform, *supra* note 15.

34. *See* Karen Engle, *Female Subjects of Public International Law: Human Rights and the Exotic Other Female,* 26 NEW ENG. L. REV. 1509 (1992) (discussing doctrinalist, institutionalist, and external critique techniques); Isabelle R. Gunning, *Arrogant Perception, World-Travelling and Multicultural Feminism: The*

Case of Female Genital Surgeries, 23 COLUM. HUM. RTS. L. REV. 189 (1992) (discussing world-travelling technique); NIRA YUVAL-DAVIS, GENDER AND NATION 129–30 (London: Sage Publications, 1997) (discussing "rooting and shifting" technique developed by Italian feminists).

35. *WILIG Panel Discussion on Ethnicity, Culture, and International Law, supra* note 16, at 1 (referring to remarks of Cecile Romany).

36. *See* Beijing Platform, *supra* note 15, para. 231.

37. *See, e.g.,* Security Council Resolution 253, May 29, 1968, U.N. SCOR, 23d Sess., 1428th mtg., Resolutions and Decisions of the Security Council 1968, at 5 (1970) (Southern Rhodesia: economic sanctions); Security Council Resolution 418, Nov. 4, 1977, U.N. SCOR, 32d Sess., 2046th mtg., Resolutions and Decisions of the Security Council 1977, at 5 (1978) (South Africa: arms embargo).

38. Security Council Resolution 794, Dec. 3, 1992, U.N. SCOR, 47th Sess., 3145th mtg., Resolutions and Decisions of the Security Council 1992, at 63, 64 (1993).

Chapter 7

Gender Apartheid and the Discourse of Relativity of Rights in Muslim Societies

Mahnaz Afkhami

I. INTRODUCTION

In modern times, women have moved from the margins to the center of history, playing increasingly important roles in families, communities, and states across the world. As women became increasingly aware and assertive, their demands for equality, participation, and access elicited reactions that ranged from curtailing their right to the privacy of their bodies and minds to policies denying them experiences that are essential to their ability to compete in society. The infringement of women's rights is usually exercised in the name of tradition, religion, social cohesion, morality, or some complex of transcendent values. Always, it is justified in the name of culture.

It is important to note that women's status in society—socially, politically, legally, economically—has been fundamentally the same across history for a majority of the world's population. Except for surface differences in manner and style, the basic arrangements for division of labor and power between men and women have been the same across the world. A woman's right over major decisions about her children's future, place of residence, marriage, inheritance, employment, and the like, have been severely curtailed in most of the world during most of human history.[1] Until the beginning of the twentieth century, when New Zealand became the first country to give women the right to vote, there was no place on earth where women shared in the political process. Nor did they have the same chance to train for a job, get a job, or, once having gotten it, receive equal pay. Indeed, in some of these areas, especially in the area of ownership of land, Muslim women fared better than their sisters in the West.[2] The first fundamentalist movement started in the United States at the beginning of the twentieth century.[3] Protestant fundamentalism came into existence very much in response to the modern age, and especially the new visibility and mobility of women. Everywhere, a change in women's status has meant a change in the culture of patriarchy. In other words, cultural change is both a byproduct of, and requisite for, change in women's status.

The contemporary threat to women and their rights in the Muslim world springs mainly from a resurgence of radical Islamist thought and politics in the last quarter of the twentieth century. There are many reasons for the recent salience of Islamism, ranging from failure of sociopolitical and economic structures at home to neocolonial pressures. It is important to understand the reasons for each case of Islamist resurgence in order to devise appropriate strategies for improving women's rights and status. However, whatever justifications are given for causing economic despondency, religious revival, or nationalist fervor, they may not be validly used to justify the subjugation of women. My purpose in this chapter is to show that neither Islam nor the culture of Muslim peoples is per se an obstacle to women's achieving rights. Rather, Muslim women face patriarchal structures that certain men, in power or seeking political power, misrepresent as religion and culture. The function of this misrepresentation is to keep women where they best serve patriarchal priorities. Where civil society has already somewhat developed, as for example in Iran, the Islamist establishment seeks to force women back to conditions that women have long since surpassed and, therefore, find unacceptable.

The resulting tension between the Islamist attempt at establishing various degrees of gender apartheid in Muslim societies and women's determination to secure and preserve their human rights has led in recent years to widespread and continuous violence. In Afghanistan, the Taliban has in fact forced women into total segregation, denying them any right or venue to participate in the affairs of society.[4] In Algeria, a veritable war of attrition is raging, in which women are the primary victims.[5] In Iran, the Majlis (the Islamic Consultative Assembly) passed a bill that makes it illegal for newspapers and magazines to publish pictures of women, even when veiled, on their front pages.[6] The same Assembly has just passed a bill that will segregate hospitals, and thus prohibit male physicians from attending female patients.[7] All this is justified in the name of religion and culture.

The Islamist revival has succeeded in turning its representation of Islam into a dominant discourse not only in most Muslim societies but also in the West. The Islamist discourse seeks to establish a particular rendition of

Muslim religion as the true image of Muslim societies as they "actually" exist. This presumed image is then presented as the actual culture of the Muslim people. All "rights" then, including Muslim women's, are regarded as naturally flowing from this culture. The Islamists present a cohesive, logical, and harmonious concept of women's place in society with predetermined answers to women's economic, social, ethical, and psychological needs. Gender apartheid is clearly defined in all laws and regulations pertaining to the role of women within the private and public spheres. Inheritance, dowry, guardianship, personal and professional boundaries, and other rules that limit women's spaces and movements are all worked out so that women's dependent and separate sphere is justified, protected, and perpetuated. Within this construct, women do not have rights as defined in the international documents of rights; rather, they have privileges that issue from the Qur'an, the shari'ah, and the hadith, and are supported by folklore and myth.[8]

This vision is supported by the Western Orientalist understanding of Islam that tends to identify an Islamic ideal type—inherently different from the West—and then insist that such a type actually exists within the real world.[9] The Orientalist construct plays into the hands of the Islamists insofar as the latter pretend that Islam is both ontologically and epistemologically different from other religions. Islamists argue that Muslim societies are fundamentally different from Jewish, Christian, or other societies. Muslim societies, unlike the others, remain religiously authentic despite the West's political hegemony and cultural onslaught. The non-Islamic traits in Muslim societies are regarded as aberrations resulting from colonial intrusion, and need to be eradicated.[10]

Statements by Muslim religious leaders about women's rights, however, are rarely clear because of the ambiguity of meaning when words are used in different contexts. Terms such as freedom, equality, equity, justice, authenticity, humanity, legitimacy, law, law-abiding, and the like, are complex, and change meaning depending on who utters them, where they are uttered, and why. It is therefore essential to a fair understanding of them always to contexualize them. For example, to grasp the implications of Ayatollah Khomeini's *Islamic Government*[11] one must not only read it in its entirety but also place it within his world view. Only then does one begin to understand from where the authority for arranging the affairs of society issues, who is competent to interpret this authority, and why it is one's obligation to obey the rule of the *faqih* (a competent Muslim jurist). Furthermore, that understanding is reflected in the Constitution of the Islamic Republic of Iran (Constitution), which, on the one hand, clearly sets forth the structures and rules that are to implement it, and, on the other hand, is replete with phrases about civic rights that seem to be taken verbatim from any modern social democratic document.[12] The so-called moderate Muslim leaders usually speak with even less clarity or, because listeners tend to understand utterances in terms of their own frames of reference, are not easily understood. When Iran's President Mohammad Khatami speaks of *qanunmandi* (the rule of law), most observers assume that the concept denotes the commonly understood concept in secular law, when, in fact, he means, as he himself has insisted, the law as contained in, and derived from, the Constitution.[13] The confusion, resulting partly from contextual difference, partly from deliberate subterfuge, and partly from the receiver's wishful thinking, however, is not always a handicap, because it creates room for dialogue.

II. THE RELATIVIST DISCOURSE

The argument from relativity is based on two sets of assumptions. The first has to do with our understanding of culture. Webster's dictionary defines culture as "the training and refining of the mind, emotions, manners, taste, etc.; the concepts, habits, skills, arts, instruments, institutions, etc. of a given people in a given period; civilization."[14] There are two distinct strings of meaning in these definitions. The first suggests the best in the arts, manners, literature, music, philosophy, science, and all the other refined attributes that a civilization has achieved. This meaning of culture is common to all societies. It is also the reason why people everywhere always have been sensitive to the word itself.

The emotional attachment to this meaning of culture often creates misunderstanding when the second meaning is intended. The second set of meanings, namely, the concepts, habits, skills, arts, instruments, etc., constitutes the more modern meaning attached to the term and is originally an invention of the Western social scientists who studied primitive societies in modern times.[15] These societies exhibited social habits that had remained substantially unchanged over time. The societies were then understood to be easily recognizable and categorizable based on particular characteristics; ideal types that nevertheless existed in actuality. The idea of culture derived from these societies was then extended to the study of so-called traditional societies, which, in essence, were societies of non-Western peoples. A curious result of this process is the similarity that exists between the Orientalists' reports of traditional Islamic societies and contemporary Islamists' descriptions of Muslim societies before Western corruption that are used to bolster their claims of legitimacy.

This interpretation of culture is inapplicable to contemporary Muslim societies. There are over a billion Muslims in the world, living under different laws and vastly different customs. It is, of course, true that they are all Muslims. It is also true that they do not all understand or practice Islam in the same way. What is perhaps common to all is variety and contradiction resulting from uneven development. One must make a deliberate effort not to see the profound differences that exist—that have always existed—between the majority of Muslims who live in South and South East Asia and others who live in the Middle East, Central Asia, and Africa. Furthermore, all of these societies have undergone significant social, economic, and cultural change in this century. More important, each of these societies has experienced change unevenly. Consequently, in any Muslim society different social types hold different mixes of indigenous and imported values. Often, these mixes create new forms, which are neither Western nor traditional. One might say they are modern in the sense of contemporary. The modern Muslim society is a mix of values, mores, and emotional responses. This is why any system of government that wishes to force uniformity on this dynamic variety will necessarily have to use considerable violence. The Islamist world view is defined mostly by its treatment of women and thus wherever Islamism has assumed power or otherwise become politically active women have born the brunt of the violence.

The second error in the argument from relativity emerges from the difference in the foundations of the argument in the West and in the Islamist or other authoritarian circles. The relativity argument has been in vogue for some time in the Western academe. Its adherents base it on a claim to freedom of choice, particularly freedom to choose elements of cultures different from those of the white, Christian, European/American male. The claim assumes that the individual has the right to choose but that governments or social forces are stifling this right. The moral force of the argument derives from a universalist conception of individual freedom and human rights.

The Islamist position is quite the opposite. It says essentially that there exist no rights outside the cultural norms as defined by a designated group of "experts" to which individuals may appeal. This position denies that there is such a thing as universal rights. Rather, it insists that all rights are derivatives of Islam as interpreted by a select group of men. Most Muslim women object to this rendition of Islam or their rights. The Islamists use the confusion resulting from the similarity in terminology to advance their position by introducing the idea of cultural imperialism—a politically and emotionally potent subject that is nevertheless irrelevant to the argument. By suggesting that the West has invented the idea of universality of rights in order to impose its way of life on others, the Islamists attempt to disparage the validity of the argument for rights in the eyes of their peoples, including women. In this, they have been assisted by other authoritarian leaders, ranging from the Chinese and Malaysian leaders to those in the Vatican.[16]

The central point in women's human rights is simple. The Islamists always posit the question of women's rights within an Islamist frame of reference. That frame of reference determines the boundaries of my existence as a Muslim woman. The questions I ask are: Why should I, as a mature Muslim woman, not have the right to determine how to organize my personal life? What gives another person the right to interfere in my personal life? Why is it that a Muslim cleric arrogates to himself the right to place me forcibly in a preordained framework? Does he derive his authority from God? Does he derive it from the text? Does he derive it from tradition? I reject all of these claims for his authority. I argue that as a Muslim woman I know in principle as well as any man what God ordains or what the text says. I argue that tradition is no longer a valid source of authority because societies change, cultures change, I change, and I am both willing and able to discuss these points with him. Before we begin this discussion, I grant him every right to be who he wants to be; to do what he wants to do; and to preach what he wants to preach. I only demand that he does not force me to do what he wants me to do against my wishes, in the same way that I do not force him to do what I wish; this is my frame of reference.

This frame of reference has nothing to do with the East, West, South, or North. It has nothing to do with color, creed, race, sex, or religion. There was a time when Christians burned women at the stake as witches because their behavior did not conform to the prevailing norms. Those who committed the murder justified their action by reference to Christian principles. Slavery was once the norm everywhere. Women were kept out of social and political decision making across the world. But times have changed. Christians have changed. Jews have changed. Muslims have changed. To the extent that this change has made me aware of my person as having a specific identity that I recognize independently of my race, creed, nationality, or religion, I resent and reject being forced to do things that I do not wish to do by reference to any of these characteristics. Indeed, any act of forcing me to do something against my will is an act of violence. My frame of reference, therefore, has to do with acceptance of the reality of change. It has to do with the fact that there exists no longer a monolithic Islam—if there ever was one. Therefore, to justify acts of violence by an appeal to Islam is disingenuous.

Clearly, this is not simply a question of law—religious or secular. Secular law may be as repressive as religious law. Rather, it has to do with the historical development of a kind of individual consciousness that defines the meaning of the concept of right. History moves from law to right; that is, from norms that have been given before the fact to norms that are established by participation and by dialogue among free individuals. Rights, therefore, can not be severed from freedom.

Considered in this light, rights are not only attributes of the relationship between government and individual, but, more important, construct an individual's space within the social system. The notion of right encompasses the ability of a woman to speak, to move, to work, and to choose freely. Millions of Muslim women in Muslim societies demand but are denied this space by their governments or by the more powerful members of their male-dominated societies.

The concept of right is also related to the concept of obligation, morally and instrumentally. This is the most central point to the concept of right; namely, that in order to demand it for yourself you must defend it for others. This mutuality is an important aspect of the frame of reference of right. The statement is sometimes made that, in contemporary times, rights—as opposed to obligations—are stressed whereas historically the emphasis was the reverse. However, this is a confusing statement and needs clarification. To the extent that obligation represents legitimacy, obligation is never diminished because one also has rights. Rights, in fact, create obligations, because they are always intertwined with legitimacy. Simply put, we cannot have rights without obligations because we cannot have rights that are not reciprocal. But, we can be forced to perform tasks under threats that are disguised as obligation—obligation that is not legitimate and not connected to the concept of right. This is precisely what many women in contemporary Muslim societies are forced to suffer, and valiantly object to.

Muslim women who strive for recognition of the concept of right are not oblivious to history. They realize that cultures do not change uniformly, and therefore there are others in Muslim societies, men and women, who see the truth differently than they do. This fact of cultural multiplicity, important as it is politically, nevertheless does not alter the moral foundation of their position—the frame of reference that rejects force and violence in religion and that respects the identity, privacy, freedom, and integrity of the human individual. This position recognizes that religious experience is a personal experience, and that enforced religion is essentially not religion, but a political act of violence perpetrated by one group of people on another. The basic principle, therefore, that "I" as a human being have the right to choose is, by definition, a universal principle—it is morally true whether I live in New York, Beijing, Katmandu, or Tehran. The fact that in practice I may not be able to exercise it everywhere is a matter for political and social analysis and action.

This point leads us to the relativity of means, which is a matter essentially of politics and implementation. There are many different ways to promote human rights across the world. The efficiency of approach usually is geared to the prevailing cultural and political conditions. Clearly, all of us must seek dialogue. Not only because we need to communicate if we are to effect change, but, perhaps also for a more fundamental reason. The concept of right is not a property of any particular culture. It is a product of the evolution of human consciousness and the demands' that the process produces. If so, then the concept of right has more to do with the possibility of individual choice than the choice itself. Thus, each culture may produce its system of rights, provided that the frame of reference, the universality of the possibility of choice and freedom, is maintained.

III. CONCLUSION

The international community now recognizes that women's rights are human rights and human rights are women's rights. These positions are recorded in several international documents,[17] and are encapsulated by the Mission Statement to the Platform for Action of the United Nations Fourth World Conference on Women, held in Beijing, 1995:

> The Platform for Action is an agenda for women's empowerment. . . . This means that the principle of shared power and responsibility should be established between women and men at home, in the workplace and in the wider national and international communities. Equality between women and men is a matter of human rights and a condition for social justice and is also a necessary and fundamental prerequisite for equality, development and peace. A transformed partnership based on equality between women and men is a condition for people-centered sustainable development. A sustained and long-term commitment is essential, so that women and men can work together for themselves, for their children and for society to meet the challenges of the twenty-first century.[18]

This world view has been reinforced in recent times by the changes that have occurred throughout the world—changes that constitute the reality of our time. The argument and symbolism now advanced by Islamist patriarchs under the guise of religion is very similar to the argument and symbolism advanced nearly a century ago by the fundamentalists in the West. The English and American suffragettes faced the same opposition, vilification, ridicule, and attacks on their morality as do contemporary Muslim feminists. The crass infringement of women's rights we see in the Muslim world has more to do with power, patriarchy, and misuse of religion as political weapon than with religion properly understood as individual faith. The Islamists draw on the discourse of relativity, now in vogue in the West, to deny or infringe women's rights by introducing or perpetuating a regime of gender segregation. This, we must oppose.

On the occasion of the fiftieth anniversary of the Universal Declaration of Human Rights, United Nations Secretary General Kofi Annan stressed the fundamental bond that ties human rights to human nature. He said human rights did not belong to any government, nor were they limited to any continent. Rather, they belong to everyone. He emphasized that "the next century must be the age of prevention. . . . Let this be the year in which the world once again looks to the Universal Declaration of Human Rights, as it did 50 years ago—for a common standard of humanity for all of humanity."[19]

In this, I believe, he should receive our support.

NOTES

1. *See generally* WOMEN, RELIGION AND SOCIAL CHANGE (Yvonne Yazbeck Haddad & Ellison Banks Fiendly, eds.) (Albany: State University of New York Press, 1985).

2. For example, until the mid-nineteenth century, at common law in the United States, once a woman married, her personal property became her husband's property and her real property became subject to his control for the duration of the marriage. *See* CORNELIUS J. MOYNIHAN, INTRODUCTION TO THE LAW OF REAL PROPERTY 52–54 (St. Paul, Minn.: West Publishing Co., 1962). In contrast, the Qur'anic legal system of centuries before gave a woman the right to own and manage property herself, and to keep possession of it after marriage. *See* JOHN L. ESPOSITO, WOMEN IN MUSLIM FAMILY LAW 24 (Syracuse, N.Y.: Syracuse University Press, 1982).

3. *See* Nancy T. Ammerman, *North American Protestant Fundamentalism, in* 1 THE FUNDAMENTALISM PROJECT: FUNDAMENTALISMS OBSERVED 1, 2 (Martin E. Marty & R. Scott Appleby, eds.) (Chicago and London: The University of Chicago Press, 1991).

4. For a description of the restrictions on women in public and private life, see PHYSICIANS FOR HUMAN RIGHTS, THE TALIBAN'S WAR ON WOMEN: A HEALTH AND HUMAN RIGHTS CRISIS IN AFGHANISTAN 30–34, 113–19 (Appendices A,B,C) (U.S.A: Physicians for Human Rights, 1998).

5. *See* Karima Bennoune, *S.O.S. Algeria: Women's Human Rights Under Siege, in* FAITH AND FREEDOM: WOMEN'S HUMAN RIGHTS IN THE MUSLIM WORLD 184 (Mahnaz Afkhami, ed.) (London and New York: I.B. Tauris & Co. Ltd., 1995).

6. *See* The Islamic Republic News Agency (visited Mar. 17, 1998) <http://www.netiran.com/dailynews.html> (English version).

7. *See* Dawn Corbett, *Women Around the Globe Face Threats to Human Rights,* Fall 1998, National NOW Times, at 11. This bill was rejected by the Council of Guardians, a higher legislative body, on the grounds that there were

not enough funds to cover implementation, and it was sent back to the Majlis. *See Segregated health services' [sic] bill rejected in Iran,* Deutsche Presse-Agentur, Oct. 14, 1998, *available in* LEXIS, World Library, Allwld file; *Iranian authority rejects hospital segregation bill,* Agence France Presse, Oct. 14, 1998, *available in* LEXIS, World Library, Allwld file.

8. *See* Mahnaz Afkhami, *Introduction, in* FAITH AND FREEDOM: WOMEN'S HUMAN RIGHTS IN THE MUSLIM WORLD, *supra* note 5, at 1–15.

9. The early European travelers to the Islamic Middle East called it the Orient, and thus they are generally referred to as the Orientalists. For a critique of Orientalist texts, see EDWARD SAID, ORIENTALISM (New York: Pantheon Books, 1978), who argues that Western scholarship on the Orient is based on racist assumptions and "ineradicable distinctions between the West and the Orient." *See* ANN ELIZABETH MAYER, ISLAM AND HUMAN RIGHTS: TRADITION AND POLITICS 6 (Boulder/Oxford: Westview Press, 3d ed., 1999).

10. The present leaders of the Islamic Republic of Iran make a point of regularly emphasizing the perils of the West's cultural invasion of all Muslim countries. They differ on how to face the challenge. For ongoing examples of the leaders making such presentations, see The Friday Sermons at Tehran University, which are translated and published by The Islamic Republic's News Agency, <http://www.irna.com/headlines>.

11. *See* AYATOLLAH RUHOLLAH KHOMEINI, ISLAMIC GOVERNMENT (trans. Joint Publications Research Service) (New York: Manor Books, 1979).

12. *Compare* art. 4 ("All civil, penal, financial, economic, administrative, cultural, military, political, and other laws and regulations must be based on Islamic criteria.") *with* art. 3 (14) ("securing the multifarious rights of all citizens, both women and men, and providing legal protection for all, as well as the equality of all before the law") of the CONSTITUTION OF THE ISLAMIC REPUBLIC OF IRAN OF 24 OCTOBER 1979 AS AMENDED TO 28 JULY 1989, *reprinted in* CONSTITUTIONS OF THE COUNTRIES OF THE WORLD 18 (Albert P. Blaustein & Gisbert H. Flanz, eds.) (Dobbs Ferry, N.Y.: Oceana Publications, Inc., 1992), excerpts *reprinted in* MAYER, *supra* note 9, at 193–201 (Appendix A).

13. *See CNN Special Event: Iran: A New Opening,* CNN television broadcast, Jan. 7, 1998, *available in* LEXIS, News Library, Script File (Interview with Pres. Khatami).

14. WEBSTER'S NEW TWENTIETH CENTURY DICTIONARY OF THE ENGLISH LANGUAGE, UNABRIDGED 444 (n.p.: William Collins + World Publishing Co., Inc., 2d. ed.,1975).

15. *See, e.g.,* BRONISLAW MALINOWSKI, A SCIENTIFIC THEORY OF CULTURE AND OTHER ESSAYS 1 (Chapel Hill: University of North Carolina Press, 1944). For a comparison of various theories of culture, see CHRIS JENKS, CULTURE (London: Routledge, 1993).

16. For example, the Vatican joined Islamists to protest the 1994 Conference on Population and Development, in Cairo, and its Programme of Action.

See Mark Nicholson, *Fears of Violence Stalk Cairo Conference,* FIN. TIMES, Sept. 1, 1994, at 4.

17. *See, e.g.,* Universal Declaration of Human Rights, *adopted* Dec. 10, 1948, G.A. Res. 217A (III), U.N. GAOR, 3d Sess., pt. 1, 183d plen. mtg., at 71, U.N. Doc. A/810 (1948); Convention on the Elimination of All Forms of Discrimination Against Women, *adopted* Dec. 18, 1979, G.A. Res. 34/180, U.N. GAOR, 34th Sess., Supp. No. 46, at 193, U.N. Doc. A/34/46 (1979), 1249 U.N.T.S. 13.

18. Beijing Declaration and Platform for Action adopted by Fourth World Conference on Women, *adopted* Sept. 15, 1995, annex II, chap. 1, para. 1, at 10, U.N. Doc. A/CONF. 177/20 (preliminary version), 35 I.L.M. 401, 409 (1996).

19. *See Hamshahri,* Iranian Daily, (Persian version) <http://www.neda.net/hamshahri/770713/siasi.htm>.

Chapter 8

Different but Free: Cultural Relativism and Women's Rights as Human Rights

Radhika Coomaraswamy

"Torture is not Culture"

—Alice Walker[1]

"Conceptions of human dignity tend to be indeterminate and contingent, and what may appeal to one school as torture, may be absolved and approved of by another as culture."

—L. Amede Obiora[2]

In the latter half of the twentieth century, the greatest challenge to international human rights comes from cultural relativism and religious extremism. In fact, it could be argued that there are *two* mutually antagonistic discourses that challenge the international human rights framework as it is constructed today. The first is feminism, and the second is cultural relativism. Both argue that their voices have not been recognized by the dominant paradigm of human rights. Though feminism attempts to strengthen the human rights framework by making it apply to a larger segment of the population, cultural relativism seeks the opposite. It often challenges the very substance and basis of human rights as a Eurocentric world view that ignores the diversity of the world's cultures.[3]

Human rights as they are articulated and constructed today are the product of the European Enlightenment. Though the sentiments expressed in human rights documents may be discovered in religious and cultural writings in all of the world's cultures, the structure and content of human rights is a direct trajectory from the Enlightenment. The Enlightenment notion of man, unfettered and equal, is central to the vision of human rights as it is described in international human rights documents. Many have argued that it is the modern version of natural law that is embodied in the *jus cogens* of nations.[4]

The inclusion of human rights in treaties, conventions, and covenants is aimed at creating an international social contract that binds all states, as well as, in some cases, nonstate actors, to human rights mandates. According to this social contract theory, all states who are signatories to the United Nations Charter (Charter)—and thus also bound to the Universal Declaration of Human Rights (Universal Declaration) as an "authoritative interpretation" of the human rights in the Charter[5]—and to the human rights instruments, have consented to the international regime of human rights. This consent theory, along with notions of *jus cogens,* argues that all states are bound by these universal norms and that their internal practices must conform to international human rights provisions. Cultural practices that violate human rights may be exposed, and if in violation of international human rights norms, may receive the censure of the international community.

This consent paradigm has a history of being challenged by cultural relativist theories of non-European scholars and thinkers.[6] In recent times, their ideas are being articulated by heads of government.[7] Eva Brems in a recent article outlines the different positions taken by cultural relativists.[8] The most radical approach is to reject human rights in totality as inappropriate to non-Western cultures. But more often cultural relativists contest only certain rights as being human rights. They also may question the interpretation that attaches to certain human rights. This is particularly true when it comes to women's human rights. The classic cases involve the situation where many Islamic countries signed and ratified the Convention on the Elimination of All Forms of Discrimination Against Women (CEAFDAW), but made their ratifications subject to the restriction that the interpretation must conform to the shari'ah.[9]

The critique of international human rights has been recently articulated by Asian scholars and leaders in what has been coined the "Asian values" debate.[10] The argument, generally couched in terms of non-Western values, is that Enlightenment-based human rights privilege the notion of autonomous individuals while non-Western societies are more communitarian in character.[11] They argue that non-Western cultures emphasize duty and responsibility over rights, and resolve conflict through consensus and not through law and litigation. The Asian challengers argue that they concentrate on human needs and the economic and social rights of individuals over divisive civil and political rights.[12] In this context, non-Western men criticize Third World feminists for using the tools of cultural imperialism in their fights against male domination.

The terrain on which cultural relativists and human rights activists have their deepest division is in the area of women's rights. This is particularly true with regard to religion-based cultures. Control over women's position in society is seen as an important marker of cultural autonomy. Women are exalted as the custodians of culture, the spiritual center of the nation.[13] This role for women, as spiritual guardians and symbols of cultural autonomy, has made the women's issue particularly contentious. As a result, every international conference sees the battle lines being drawn between feminists and cultural relativists. This was true at the 1993 World Conference on Human Rights, held in Vienna, the 1994 Conference on Population and Development, held in Cairo, and the 1995 Women's Conference, held in Beijing.[14]

It is generally accepted that feminists have won most of the international battles and that the international human rights framework is increasingly responsive to the human rights of women. But the battle is not over, and in recent times, the demand by the Malaysian Prime Minister that on the fiftieth anniversary of the Universal Declaration we should consider revising the Declaration to take into consideration "Asian Values"[15] has sent shock waves through the human rights community at the national and international levels.

The problem of cultural relativism and women's rights raises the many dilemmas associated with the confluence of nation, ethnicity, class, and gender. Partha Chatterjee, in a study of Indian nationalism, analyses how the "women's question" was constructed in the " 'inner' space of the [Indian] middle-class home."[16] He shows that although nationalism allowed women's emancipation in terms of giving them access to education, it also brought with it a whole set of controls; "[t]he new woman . . . was subjected to a *new* patriarchy . . . contrasted not only with that of modern Western society; it was explicitly distinguished from the patriarchy of indigenous tradition. . . ."[17] Women were central to the definition of the cultural identity of a nation, and represented the spiritual sphere of the nation, away from colonial life and the public sphere. Thus, the resulting public/private dichotomy—where the inner space of private family life is linked to the spiritual, the home, and the feminine, and the public space is linked to the material, the world, and the masculine—has particularly important legal ramifications for women of different ethnic groups and religious denominations.

Although public life was penetrated by Western colonial ideas and notions from the Enlightenment, private life remained immune and was constructed and reinvented so that women's position became tied up with the cultural symbolism of the nation or ethnic group. As a result, while most of the laws of public life changed to accommodate more recent thinking, laws governing private life and family relations remained moribund. Women's position in the home under various personal laws remained unchanged since the medieval era. Needless to say, their content was in sharp contrast to the international standards with regard to women's rights contained in CEAFDAW. Cultural relativism theory is particularly used in this context to screen personal and family laws from international standards. Thus, it has increasingly come to mean the right of cultures to regulate the private lifestyles of their women, especially with respect to matters of sexuality, family, and the marital home.

The issue of gender and cultural relativism raises the question of how important secularism is to the human rights paradigm. Courtney Howland describes how in drafting the Universal Declaration there were attempts to bring in references to a deity, especially in the preamble.[18] The deliberate decision of the drafters to reject any reference to deities leads one to believe that secularism, and separation of state and religion, are essential to the human rights paradigm. This supposition creates a major dilemma for countries that base their legal system on religious codes, or where state religions predominate. In addition, article 18 of the Universal Declaration is interpreted to ensure freedom of choice with regard to religious belief, thereby challenging state-sponsored religion.[19] States that have a religious foundation are bound to argue that there is a natural law order, or a moral system of belief, that supersedes human rights, and that if there is a conflict between human rights and the religious order, then the latter must prevail. This raises serious problems about the interpretation and implementation of human rights in religion-based states.

Further, article 5 of CEAFDAW imposes a positive duty on state parties to transform customs, attitudes, and practices that discriminate against women.[20] CEAFDAW not only mandates that the state should not discriminate, but obligates the state to intervene actively in society to transform value systems. State parties that sign CEAFDAW must therefore agree to change their cultural practices so that they conform with these international standards. In essence, states are called upon to accept the fact that their cultural regime is subordinate to international norms and must be transformed in their light. This is one of the reasons why many states make reservations to article 5 since they do not wish to make the concession that their cultural norms must conform to universal human rights standards.

The other dilemma facing those who wish to close the gap between cultural relativism and international human rights is what is often termed the law versus anthropology debate. Although many lawyers view cultural practices as violating specific international norms and therefore request governments to outlaw the practice and criminalize the offense, anthropologists are more wary of passing judgment. Even practices like female genital mutilation and *sati* (a widow's being burned to death on her husband's funeral pyre) have their defenders. While lawyers and human rights activists give graphic accounts of the pain and suffering endured by women, often accompanied with photographs, many anthropologists highlight the fact that these practices are community rituals and celebrations, involving joy, love, and affection. They are viewed not as classic abusive situations, but as moments of celebration. Veena Das, for example, argues that *sati* is integrally linked to a community's notion of heroic death.[21] These radically different perspectives transform these debates into vicious ideological confrontations. In this free-for-all we forget that what we are speaking about are often the most fundamental of human rights—the right to life and the right to physical integrity.

The fact that women are often perpetrators of violence against other women in certain cultural contexts adds another dimension to the dilemma. It has been reported that mothers, grandmothers, and mothers-in-law are often more involved in perpetuating cultural rituals that are violent to women than the men in the family.[22] These women are outraged when feminists construct them as abusive parents. For them these cultural rituals are part of the socialization of women and rites of passage that will ensure that their daughters will marry well and be sexually restrained. These embedded systems of socialization pose a major challenge to law-based strategies of change. The setting of legal standards is an important measure, but unless it is accompanied by other processes cultural practices are unlikely to be eliminated.

Most of the cultural practices that appear to violate women's human rights relate to the control of female sexuality.[23] Female genital mutilation is perhaps the best known example. Human rights instruments drafted by men are silent on the issue of sexuality and reproductive rights. Feminist legal scholars have attempted to read these rights into the penumbra of other rights so that a woman's physical integrity is respected with regard to her reproductive organs.[24] Many of the cultural practices regarding women will disappear only if the international community accepts a woman's right to control her sexuality and her reproductive capacity. Until this is recognized as a universal right superior to cultural norms, many of the practices related to women's subordination will continue.

While women may have won the international battles, many people are concerned that they are losing the battles within nation-states, especially in light of radical movements of religious extremism. In this context, it is important to recognize the political economy of religious extremism. In many societies in Asia and Africa, religious extremism has become the major vehicle of dissent against oppressive establishments because alternative ideologies either do not exist or have not struck a responsive chord among the vast majority of the people. Therefore, ideologies that appeal to cultural and religious symbols receive support, especially when they are regarded as a means to eject despotic and corrupt rulers. It is thus important that groups who work for human rights and women's rights in civil society engage in these ideological battles, and present an alternative framework for dissent against oppressive political and economic structures. In the end, the success of human rights in Asian and African societies will depend upon the success of such campaigns.

In discussing these issues, it is important to make the distinction between culture and religion. Culture is the broader term, but practices rooted in religious interpretation are more difficult to eradicate. Most of the world's religions have sacred texts that form the basis of their religious world. These texts place an outer limit on reform. In societies where these religions are dominant, human rights will only be successful if they are interpreted in light of these texts. Although spiritual texts themselves do not pose much of a problem, the law codes and ritual practices that have evolved through the centuries in conjunction with these texts are often in flagrant violation of modern international human rights. For this reason, scholars like Abdullahi An-Na'im have argued that we must separate the sacred texts of Islam from man-made law and legal constructions that developed as responses to concrete realities of life in previous centuries.[25] This division is relevant for all the world's religions. It is essential to argue that the spirit of all the world's religions is supportive of human rights and that it is only man-made practices that result in the violation and abuse of human rights.

Another aspect of the cultural relativism debate centers around the question of rights versus development. In many states and communities, there is agreement that certain cultural practices should be eradicated through health and education strategies as part of the development process. These same interest groups resist any attempt to frame the question in terms of human rights because they regard such an approach as based on imperialist arrogance. For example, to characterize female genital mutilation as a violation of human rights turns parents into abusers and neighbors into accomplices. This same debate occurs not only at the community and state level, but also in the United Nations Human Rights

Commission itself. The refusal to accept the framework of rights is reflective of the refusal to see women and girls as autonomous beings with the right to bodily integrity. Instead, development from the top down, directed by the state, is seen as acceptable since it operates within a less threatening framework.

Those involved in the cultural relativist debate are very sensitive to the nuances of language. Language itself becomes a site of contestation. Whether a cultural practice is termed torture, mutilation, or murder becomes a matter of enormous importance, and the use of a term may alienate many a constituency. The word "rights" is also a coded term, and is, in fact, the most threatening term when it comes to institutions of the state. Even those who may wish to eradicate certain practices are divided on the terms to be used, and enter into heated debates on the proper language of respect for cultural differences.

If cultural relativism is the greatest challenge to universal human rights and women's rights in particular, how do we attempt to bridge the gap? Different scholars have provided us with different methodologies and insights. In her article analyzing religious fundamentalism under the Charter,[26] Howland adopts what I may term a principled approach. She argues that states, by joining the United Nations, have agreed to be bound by the Charter, and therefore this consent warrants that they accept their obligations. She further argues that the Charter requires that race, sex, and religious discrimination be treated equally and that state religious laws cannot therefore trump women's international rights. Universal human rights as adopted by the Charter are more important than local cultural and religious practices. These practices have to be brought in line with universal standards. This approach is particularly attractive because of its clarity and its unabashed acceptance of the supremacy and universality of human rights. The international texts must prevail over actual practices.

Donna Sullivan has another approach.[27] She argues in favor of balancing various rights. She states that the central contradiction is that the instruments of human rights protect the right to religious freedom on the one hand, while, on the other hand, argue for gender equality. She states that a balancing approach may help resolve the tension in a more acceptable manner. The questions she feels should be asked are: How important is the issue for gender equality?; How important is the issue for religion?; How does one infringe on the other?; and, Are international human rights implicated? Asking these questions may lead many to see that the issues relating to gender equality are not really an integral part of religious doctrine. Further, the balancing approach may be regarded as addressing the problems in a more sensitive way than the clear, unbridled, principled approach.

Isabelle Gunning, in the context of female genital mutilation, has put forward one of the most influential positions with regard to the resolution of the conflict between cultural relativism and universal human rights.[28] She argues against approaching culturally challenging practices as an "arrogant perceiver . . . [one who] sees himself as the center of the world."[29] She aims to develop a method of understanding that would preserve the sense of respect for, and equality of, various cultures. Her solution is a multicultural dialogue and a search for shared areas of concern. She claims that legal approaches are not only arrogant but that they are weak in enforcement when it comes to issues of cultural practices that have existed over a long period of time.

Gunning has a very specific methodology. She argues that before we condemn other practices we must first understand our own cultural context. For example, she suggests that Western feminists first look to examples of genital surgeries that took place in Western history. This ensures a more sober and less arrogant attitude toward "the Other." She then argues that one must move on to see how "the Other" perceives you, your context, and the historical and social interactions between you that have been culturally insensitive in the past. It is then important to analyze "the Other" in her own context, and the nature of the cultural practice—where it came from and what role it plays in the society. This gives the reformer a sense of context and a historical understanding of the social forces that govern a cultural practice. It is also necessary to evaluate whether law and rights discourse will be effective at eradicating the practice. This evaluation requires a look to past history to review the success of any previous attempts at legal reform. If the law and human rights approach has failed, then it is important to look to other strategies, including health and education initiatives. For example, with regard to female genital mutilation, calling it a "humanitarian" problem may produce greater results. Gunning argues that this cautious, culturally sensitive approach is probably more successful for the actual eradication of cultural practices that are violent toward women.

In evaluating these methods, it has to be pointed out that the Howland method must be the one that prevails at the international level. To rely on balancing as a method would be to vest so much discretion in the hands of the judiciary—which will remain predominantly male for many years to come—that it will work against the development of coherent and clear jurisprudence at the international level. Balancing as a methodology requires a particular kind of judiciary, one that is accustomed to constitutional nuances, and the vast majority of the world's judiciaries are not equipped to adopt this methodology. International standards should be clear and easy to implement. It is therefore important that the jurisprudence rest on a positivist premise; governments consent to and are bound by human rights norms when they become members of the international community. Without that clarity, any effort at validating human rights at the international level will fail.

However, in a particular cultural context, the world-traveller approach is also useful. Individuals from international agencies who go to work in other cultures and who are expected to abide by human rights norms are well-advised to adopt Gunning's approach if they hope to be successful in their campaigns. Law enforcement is weak in many societies, and the work of aid and development agencies play an important role in eradicating negative cultural practices. For these agencies, the world-traveller approach encourages a degree of cultural sensitivity that would make the local population more responsive to human rights concerns.

Cultural relativism and religious fundamentalism are important challenges to international human rights and particularly women's rights. What is needed to combat them is a mixture of "arrogance," and in Gunning's words, "playfulness." Arrogance? Yes; the arrogance is the communal arrogance of the international community. International standards must be articulated and imposed on recalcitrant states. The accountability of states is essential and requires the legal framework. Playfulness? Yes; we must engage societies at the human level, with cultural understanding and open-mindedness. This playfulness will bring down boundaries, create networks, and allow individuals to bond across cultures. As a result, human rights will not only exist as an ideal in international textual law, but will be part of the everyday life of individuals. A combination of strategies, which clearly sets out norms but that also respects the dignity of the world's peoples, is the only method that will bring us the results we desire.

NOTES

1. David Kaplan et al., *Is it Torture or Tradition?,* NEWSWEEK, Dec. 20, 1993, at 124 (quoting Alice Walker).
2. L. Amede Obiora, *Bridges and Barricades: Rethinking Polemics and Intransigence in the Campaign Against Female Circumcision,* 47 CASE W. RES. L. REV. 275, 277 (1997).
3. *See* Eva Brems, *Enemies or Allies? Feminism and Cultural Relativism as Dissident Voices in Human Rights Discourse,* 19 HUM. RTS. Q. 136, 142–44 (discussing cultural relativist critiques) (1997).
4. *See, e.g.,* MALCOLM N. SHAW, INTERNATIONAL LAW: FOURTH EDITION 97 (Cambridge: Grotius Publication/Cambridge University Press, 1997); MARK W. JANIS, AN INTRODUCTION TO INTERNATIONAL LAW 63–64 (Boston/New York/Toronto/London: Little, Brown and Company, 2d

ed., 1993). *Jus cogens,* or peremptory norms, are those norms accepted and recognized by the international community from which no derogation is permissible and that may only be modified by subsequent norms of the same fundamental character. States may not contract out of these norms. These peremptory norms mainly address actions that shock the conscience of the international community, and prohibit, among other things, genocide, slavery, and torture.

5. Louis B. Sohn, *The New International Law: Protection of the Rights of Individuals Rather than States,* 32 AM. U. L. REV. 1, 16–17 (1982); *see* Universal Declaration of Human Rights, *adopted* Dec. 10, 1948, G.A. Res. 217A (III), U.N. GAOR, 3d Sess., pt. 1, 183d plen. mtg., at 71, U.N. Doc. A/810 (1948) [hereinafter Universal Declaration].

6. *See, e.g.,* Josiah A. M. Cobbah, *African Values and the Human Rights Debate: An African Perspective,* 9 HUM. RTS. Q. 309 (1987); James C. Hsiung, *Human Rights in an East Asian Perspective, in* HUMAN RIGHTS IN EAST ASIA, A CULTURAL PERSPECTIVE 1 (James C. Hsiung, ed.) (New York: Paragon House Publishers, 1985); Ashis Nandy, *The Making and Unmaking of Political Cultures in India, in* AT THE EDGE OF PSYCHOLOGY: ESSAYS IN POLITICS AND CULTURE 47 (Ashis Nandy, ed.) (Delhi: Oxford University Press, 1980); *but see, e.g.,* Mahnaz Afkhami and Erika Friedl, *Introduction, in* IN THE EYE OF THE STORM: WOMEN IN POST-REVOLUTIONARY IRAN 1, 17–18 (Mahnaz Afkhami and Erika Friedl, eds.) (Syracuse, N.Y.: Syracuse University Press, 1994).

7. *See infra* note 15; Kishore Mahbubami, Deputy Secretary of the Ministry of Foreign Affairs of the Republic of Singapore, *quoted in,* The World Conference on Human Rights, 4th Sess., Agenda Item 5, U.N. Doc. A/CONF.157/PC/63/Add. 28 (1993).

8. *See* Brems, *supra* note 3, at 142–47.

9. *See* Convention on the Elimination of All Forms of Discrimination Against Women, *adopted* Dec. 18, 1979, G.A. Res. 34/180, U.N. GAOR, 34th Sess., Supp. No. 46, at 193, U.N. Doc. A/34/46 (1979), 1249 U.N.T.S. 13 [hereinafter CEAFDAW]. For examples of state reservations, see U.N. Doc. CEDAW/SP/1998/2, Feb. 6, 1998, at 20–21, 24, 28 (reservations of Egypt, Iraq, and Libya respectively), MULTILATERAL TREATIES DEPOSITED WITH THE SECRETARY-GENERAL: STATUS AS OF 31 DECEMBER 1997, at 173, 174, 175, U.N. Doc. ST/LEG/SER.E/16, U.N. Sales No. E.98.V.2 (1998). For a discussion of these reservations, see Ann Elizabeth Mayer, *Religious Reservations to the Convention on the Elimination of All Forms of Discrimination Against Women: What Do They Really Mean?,* in this volume.

10. *See* Nikhil Aziz, *The Human Rights Debate in an Era of Globalization: Hegemony of Discourse,* 27 BULL. CONCERNED ASIAN SCHOLARS 9, 16, 19, 20–21 (1995). For an early exploration of this topic, see ASIAN PERSPECTIVES ON HUMAN RIGHTS (Claude E. Welch, Jr. & Virginia A. Leary, eds.) (Boulder, Co./Oxford: Westview Press, Inc., 1990).

11. *See* Brems, *supra* note 3, at 145 & n.45.

12. *See, e.g.,* Chandra Muzaffar, *From Human Rights to Human Dignity,* 27 BULL. CONCERNED ASIAN SCHOLARS 6, 8 (1995) (slightly modified version of address at the International Conference on Rethinking Human Rights, Kuala Lumpur, Malaysia, Dec. 6–7, 1994).

13. For an excellent description of this in India, see PARTHA CHATTERJEE, THE NATION AND ITS FRAGMENTS: COLONIAL AND POSTCOLONIAL HISTORIES 116–34 (Princeton, N.J.: Princeton University Press, 1993).

14. *See* Vienna Declaration and Programme of Action: adopted by The World Conference on Human Rights, *adopted* June 25, 1993, U.N. Doc. A/CONF. 157/23, 32 I.L.M. 1661 (1993) [hereinafter Vienna Declaration]; Programme of Action of the International Conference on Population and Development, *adopted* Sept. 13, 1994, U.N. Doc. A/CONF. 171/13 (preliminary version) (1994); Beijing Declaration and Platform for Action adopted by Fourth World Conference on Women, *adopted* Sept. 15, 1995, U.N. Doc. A/CONF. 177/20 (preliminary version), 35 I.L.M. 401 (1996) [hereinafter Beijing Declaration].

15. *See* Richard Bourne, *Bullies Must be Cast Out,* THE GUARDIAN, Oct. 21, 1997, at 13; Lynette Clemetson & Sheila McNulty, *Malaysia's Moment,* NEWSWEEK, Sept. 1, 1997, Atlantic ed., at 25; *Nations Must Speak Out on Human Rights Abuses,* THE FIN. POST (Toronto), July 31, 1997, at 8.

16. *See* CHATTERJEE, *supra* note 13, at 137.

17. *See* CHATTERJEE, *supra* note 13, at 127, 126–32.

18. *See* Courtney W. Howland, *The Challenge of Religious Fundamentalism to the Liberty and Equality Rights of Women: An Analysis under the United Nations Charter,* 35 COLUM. J. TRANSNAT'L L. 271, 341 (1997).

19. *See* Universal Declaration, *supra* note 5, art. 18; Howland, *supra* note 18, at 342.

20. *See* CEAFDAW, *supra* note 9, art. 5.

21. VEENA DAS, CRITICAL EVENTS: AN ANTHROPOLOGICAL PERSPECTIVE ON CONTEMPORARY INDIA 107–117 (New Delhi: Oxford University Press, 1995). For a different perspective on *sati* and the Roop Kanwar case in India, see Radhika Coomaraswamy, *To Bellow Like a Cow: Women, Ethnicity, and the Discourse of Rights, in* HUMAN RIGHTS OF WOMEN: NATIONAL AND INTERNATIONAL PERSPECTIVES 39, 48–50 (Rebecca J. Cook, ed.) (Philadelphia: University of Pennsylvania Press, 1994).

22. *See* Isabelle R. Gunning, *Arrogant Perception, World-Travelling and Multicultural Feminism: The Case of Female Genital Surgeries,* 23 COLUM. HUM. RTS. L. REV. 189, 220–23, 229 (1992).

23. *See Preliminary report submitted by the Special Rapporteur on violence against women, its causes and consequences, Ms. Radhika Coomaraswamy, in accordance with Commission on Human Rights resolution 1994/45,* United Nations Economic and Social Council, Commission on Human Rights, 50th Sess., Agenda item 11 (a) of the provisional agenda, at 14, U.N. Doc. E/CN.4/1995/42 (1994).

24. *See, e.g.,* Rebecca Cook, *Human Rights and Reproductive Self-Determination,* 44 AM. U. L. REV. 975 (1995).

25. *See* ABDULLAHI AHMED AN-NA 'IM, TOWARD AN ISLAMIC REFORMATION: CIVIL LIBERTIES, HUMAN RIGHTS, AND INTERNATIONAL LAW 34–35, 52–68 (Syracuse, N.Y.: Syracuse University Press, 1990).

26. *See* Howland, *supra* note 18, at 324–74.

27. *See* Donna J. Sullivan, *Gender Equality and Religious Freedom: Toward a Framework for Conflict Resolution*, 24 N.Y.U. J. INT'L L. & POL. 795 (1992).

28. *See* Gunning, *supra* note 22.

29. *Id*. at 198.

III

The Conflict between the Human Rights of Women and the Religious Freedom of Fundamentalists: The International Legal Framework

Chapter 9

Safeguarding Women's Political Freedoms under the International Covenant on Civil and Political Rights in the Face of Religious Fundamentalism

Courtney W. Howland

I. INTRODUCTION

Civil and political freedoms have long been regarded as at the core of democracy and forming the foundation for an individual's liberty within a democracy. In international law, these freedoms are embodied in human rights treaties, and failure to comply with these treaties constitutes a breach of international law. The doctrine of state responsibility in international law holds a state accountable for breaches of international obligations to the extent that they derive from acts or omissions committed by or attributable to the state.[1] International law is thus primarily addressed to the activities of states, and a state is generally regarded as not responsible for the private acts of its nationals.[2]

Some feminist scholars have argued that the public/private dichotomy that exists in most countries and cultures, where women are more or less constricted to the private sphere while men predominate in the public, has correspondingly led to a deep gender bias in major human rights treaties.[3] The International Covenant on Civil and Political Rights (ICCPR)[4] is one of the major human rights treaties, with 140 state parties. Yet, some scholars have regarded this treaty as an example of this gender bias on the ground of its being primarily aimed at protecting civil and political rights (public rights) from interference by the state, rather than protecting rights in the family (private sphere), where women often suffer harm and violence by private actors (such as a battering husband).[5] The core of this critique is therefore that the ICCPR focuses on limiting the impact on the individual of state or public power rather than private power, and women, who suffer many of their greatest harms within the private sphere,[6] are thus not adequately protected by these civil and political rights.

However, I would argue that the ICCPR has much more to offer women than is suggested by the above public/private dichotomy critique. Rather than critique the ICCPR as too limited for ensuring women's rights in this context, I would suggest a two-part approach to the ICCPR that takes into account the spirit of democracy that is at the core of the ICCPR while respecting international law's principles of state responsibility.

First, it is important to recognize that many of the women's rights at stake in this context are core civil and political rights rather than simply issues of gender equality within the family. Religious fundamentalists have structured the dialogue to make the dispute appear to be about women's rights within the family or about private issues of religious belief. Feminist arguments that identify the lack of protection afforded to women within the family as due to human rights law not reaching the acts of private actors actually reinforce fundamentalist characterizations of these issues as involving "private" matters or actions by "private" individuals. There has been little focus on recognizing these so-called private rights and wrongs within the family as political public rights.

Instances of inequality within the home do not only reflect lack of gender equality and imbalances of general political power, but rather operate effectively as repression of core political rights, such as the right to opinion, to freedom of expression, to assembly, to vote, and to associate with others. The loss of basic civil and political liberties is of essential concern in traditional human rights discourse, and so remedying the loss of these rights by women should be a high priority even within traditional discourse. Moreover, because the repression of political rights is at issue, states should be prevented from claiming that these matters are covered by reservations that they may have made to articles such as article 23, which requires equality between men and women in marriage and dissolution laws.[7]

The second part of my approach is to recognize that the political articles of the ICCPR and its spirit of democracy require an interpretation of the ICCPR that recognizes the breadth of a state's affirmative obligations under the treaty—without expanding the doctrine of state responsibility. A state should be obligated to protect its citizens against certain actions that have heretofore been characterized as "private." As a result, women's political freedoms will be more adequately protected.

II. RELIGIOUS FUNDAMENTALISMS AND THE ICCPR

Although there have been modest developments in human rights law recognizing that certain practices inflicting harm on women violate international human rights law, the development of religious fundamentalism in different religions and in different countries threatens even these developments.[8]

Under religious fundamentalism, the notion of a claim for religious freedom, free from state interference, has in recent years expanded in at least two ways. First, there are states whose governments make overt claims for religious freedom as justification for discriminatory policies against women, in an attempt to make their entire legal system exempt from equality requirements. The state has turned what is essentially an individual's or a particular community's right to religious freedom into a right by the state to pass religious laws as the representative of a particular religious group. The result is that broad, vague notions of religious freedom and representation serve as the justification for the state controlling an ever-enlarging public sphere that may well encompass every aspect of public and private life.

Second, other states are becoming increasingly sympathetic to broadening claims of religious freedom by religious groups within the state, with the result that religious groups are accorded large autonomous zones of so-called privacy within which women's rights may be severely limited. In this type of situation, states try to avoid responsibility for the discriminatory practices of these private actors, even though such actors are not really private because they could not function without the approval of the state.[9] Thus, broadening claims of religious freedom are in effect trumping women's rights by allowing claims of religious freedom to transform parts of the public world into the "private." Since religious freedom is one of the core political rights protected by the ICCPR, it becomes immediately evident that claims of religious freedom may help to turn the ICCPR into a weapon against women despite its guarantees of equality for women.

My two-part approach, which focuses on the democratic principles underpinning the ICCPR, aims to meet the challenge that these religious-freedom claims pose to women's rights.

III. ASSUMPTIONS ABOUT DEMOCRACY AND CITIZENSHIP UNDERPINNING THE ICCPR

Democracy implies equal and free participation by all citizens in the polity. A democratic society also implies not merely rule by the majoritarian political will of the people but also that such rule must be tempered by the protection of individual liberties that moderate the authority of the state.[10] The tension between majoritarian will and individual liberties, and how this relates to judging the legitimacy of a government, has been endlessly theorized. The assumption made in liberal-democracy theory is that a government is legitimate if, and only if, its citizens have the ability to reflect on their own interests and on the public good and then act together to govern. There is evidence supporting this broad notion of democracy in the history of the ICCPR,[11] but, more important, the ICCPR text[12] supports this notion in the substantive rights that it protects and in the mention of a "democratic society" in some of its articles.

All of the rights in the ICCPR are arguably aimed at supporting democratic society. However, there are particular rights specifically aimed at protecting political freedoms. These political rights include article 18's protection of the right to freedom of thought, conscience, and religion.[13] The language protects freedom of thought without limitation, thus including nontheistic or atheistic beliefs and political and social thought, and without giving priority to religious belief.[14] Coercion is impermissible with respect to adoption of religion or belief.[15] Article 19 guarantees the right to hold opinions without interference, and the right to freedom of expression.[16] This freedom includes the right to seek, receive, and impart information and ideas of all kinds through any media of choice.[17] Article 21 guarantees the right of peaceful assembly and article 22 recognizes the right of freedom of association with others.[18] The right of association includes the right to come together with one or more other persons for social, cultural, economic, or political reasons.[19]

In the context of the rights of peaceful assembly and rights of freedom of association, the ICCPR makes specific references to a "democratic society." These two rights—of assembly and of association—may not be subject to any restrictions unless such restrictions are "necessary in a democratic society."[20] So even where the ICCPR is willing to accept restrictions on these rights, the restrictions have to *further* a democratic society. Finally, article 25 guarantees every citizen "the right and opportunity" to take part in public affairs, including the right to vote, to be elected, and to have access to public service.[21] It would be fair to conclude that within the core "object and purpose" of the ICCPR is its support for democratic society and that this may not be undermined by any state.[22]

The rights encompassed in these political articles are premised on a broad concept of democracy that envisions all citizens[23] being able to participate meaningfully in the choice and running of a democratic government. These rights envision protecting the individual in the development of her intellectual, social, political, and moral personalities.[24] The traditional interpretative approach to the political rights in the ICCPR makes the underlying assumption that the individual, if free from certain politically relevant constraints, will function as a politically effective citizen.

There is thus an assumption that the individual is free and able to define his own ends; has the capacity to reflect on his own interests and on the public good; and to act with others, as necessary, to govern.[25] The participation of free and equal citizens in the polity is essential to preserving the notion of their consent to be governed and thus the legitimacy of the government of the polity.[26] The politically relevant constraints in the ICCPR context refer to those constraints imposed pursuant to the state's power. And the state is responsible for constraints that it imposes in the performance of its executive, legislative, or judicial functions, whether by acts or omissions.[27]

However, these theoretical assumptions regarding the free, self-defining individual underestimate the impact of structural, systematic inequalities created by private power on women and thereby on women's participation in democratic governance and in the public world. My emphasis here is not that women suffer a lack of protection in the "private" sphere from "private" actors,[28] but rather that these systematic inequalities created by private power impact on women as political beings and limit women's participation in the polity as fully effective political citizens. Consequently, the lack of women's full political participation undermines the legitimacy of democratic institutions. Since any interpretation of the ICCPR text with respect to state power must fulfill the object and purpose of the ICCPR, any such interpretation must therefore aim to bolster democratic institutions and their legitimacy, and thus must work to ensure women's effective political participation.

A. Religious Fundamentalist Laws Evaluated under the ICCPR

The first part of my approach is to evaluate religious fundamentalist laws under the political articles of the ICCPR. I will focus on two particular religious fundamentalist norms that tend to hold true in Buddhism, Christianity, Hinduism, Islam, and Judaism.[29] The first is what I call the obedience rule. This states that a wife is required to submit to the authority of her husband—to be obedient to her husband.[30] This submission often gives the husband an explicit or implicit right to discipline his wife—in other words, to batter her. There are few limitations on what the husband may require under the obedience rule.[31] The second norm is what I call the modesty code, which requires a woman to be modest in matters of behavior and dress. Modesty codes can have wide-ranging effects.[32] They often require segregation of the sexes in education, health, and employment. They may prohibit women from moving outside their home or country; prohibit women from meeting with others in public places; prohibit women from raising their voices; and mandate particular covering dress for women in public, including prohibiting women from showing their faces.[33]

Under traditional interpretations of the doctrine of state responsibility, state laws (regardless of whether they are based on religious laws or norms) are clearly attributable to the state. A number of states do have such laws regarding women's obedience and modesty.[34] Evaluating these laws under international human rights law has been hampered by the general acceptance of the religious fundamentalist characterization of these laws as dealing exclusively with family, personal status, and private issues of religious freedom. This has obscured the fact that the laws constitute a violation of the *political* articles of the ICCPR that is not in any way excused by a state's reservations to the *family law* articles of the ICCPR or by a state's assertion of different interpretations of equality under the family law articles.

Thus, a state law requiring wives to be obedient to their husbands and to comply with certain modesty rules interferes directly with their political rights associated with participation in a democratic society and therefore violates the ICCPR. Such laws directly impinge on the right to freedom of belief without coercion (article 18(2)), the right to hold opinion without interference, and the right to freedom of expression (article 19), since a woman may not seek, receive, or impart information without her husband's permission. They also directly impinge on the rights to freedom of peaceful assembly (article 21) and association (article 22), since a woman may not join any assembly, including political rallies, without her husband's permission, and may also be subject to modesty code penalties if she joins a public assembly. Modesty code requirements also violate her right of association by disallowing her to associate with others (specifically, men) in public or in private and may also interfere with her right to freedom of expression since she may even be unable to communicate through facial expression. Plainly, religious fundamentalist laws of modesty and obedience as state laws that restrict women's voting rights are a direct infringement of article 25 rights.[35] In addition, obedience rules operate as restrictions on rights in that they would entitle a husband to require his wife to vote a certain way, forbid her to run for election, and even to obtain information about political parties. Even if a wife obtains her husband's permission to run for election, the modesty code prohibitions on her appearing and speaking in public may make this impossible in practice.[36]

The result is that she has no public place to express her political opinion and belief and no forum in which to exchange ideas. Moreover, the constant threat of violence that accompanies the obedience rule effectively dampens her political freedoms. Thus, a woman's participation in the democratic process of society is foreclosed because she has no opportunity to lobby or work for the change of the very laws that repress her political rights.[37]

So it is clear that under traditional interpretations of state responsibility, states that have enacted laws that require the obedience of wives to husbands, or enforce such laws through their jurisdictional delegation to religious courts, are contravening the political articles of the ICCPR. What remains is to remedy these political violations with the same rigor that political violations are remedied in other contexts.

B. Understanding State Obligations in Light of the Spirit of Democracy in the ICCPR

With respect to religious fundamentalist obedience and modesty laws that have *not* been enacted into state law, the concept of the politically developing individual, already at the core of the ICCPR, needs to be fully implemented. This concept has the potential to help correct the structural systematic inequalities created by private power by recognizing that the state must not undermine democracy and must support democratic legitimacy and the full participation of all its citizens. This concept effectively imposes an affirmative obligation on the state to ensure that women's political rights are protected from systemic private interferences.

The text of the ICCPR provides the foundation for interpreting the political articles as imposing an affirmative obligation on states. Article 2(1) provides that each state party has a twofold legal obligation. First, a state is required "to respect" all of the rights recognized in the Covenant,[38] which requires that it not violate these rights by imposing direct constraints on them, as I have already discussed. Second, each state has the legal obligation "to ensure" these rights. This obligation goes beyond the obligation "to respect," in that, as Thomas Buergenthal has noted, it "implies an affirmative obligation by the state. . . . [I]t may perhaps require the state to adopt laws and other measures against private interference with enjoyment of the rights, for example against interference with the exercise of the right to vote and other political rights."[39] State responsibility for rights thus appears to increase the closer the right is to the core of those political rights that are crucial for a functioning democracy.

Thus states have an affirmative obligation to ensure that women enjoy their political freedoms free from interference. An affirmative obligation requires states to provide effective protection and effective remedies to women who are abused under the obedience laws of religious fundamentalist communities. The state's affirmative duty may require it to provide effective legal remedies for physical assault and to inform women about such remedies in such a way as to insure that women are not subject to reprisals in the community that may chill the exercise of their political rights. The state's duty may require it to make information about equality and political freedoms available to women through various means, including the media. A state would also be permitted, and indeed may have a duty, to outlaw religious practices that are systemically violative of women's political rights.[40] Under this approach, it is arguable that states may have a duty to pass laws prohibiting the practice of requiring wives to be obedient because it is inevitable that political rights, such as expression, association, and assembly are undermined by a rule of obedience.[41]

By understanding wrongs against women in the home as violations of core political rights under the ICCPR and by determining state obligation under the ICCPR in light of this treaty's object and purpose to uphold the spirit of democracy, women's rights to political freedoms, and thus women's rights overall, will be more fully ensured. Assuring women's political freedoms allows them to be fully effective citizens in the polity and protects the legitimacy of democratic institutions.

NOTES

1. *See* Report of the International Law Commission on the work of its forty-eighth session 6 May–26 July 1996, U.N. GAOR, 51st Sess., Supp. No. 10, arts. 3, 11, at 6, 7–8, U.N. Doc. A/51/10 (1996) (Draft Articles on State Responsibility).

2. *See* Case Concerning United States Diplomatic and Consular Staff in Tehran (U.S. v. Iran), 1980 I.C.J. 3, 29 (May 24).

3. *See* Hilary Charlesworth & Christine Chinkin, *The Gender of* Jus Cogens, 15 HUM. RTS. Q. 63, 69–74 (1993); Rebecca Cook, *State Responsibility for Violations of Women's Human Rights,* 7 HARV. HUM. RTS. J. 123, 130–34 (1994).

4. International Covenant on Civil and Political Rights, *adopted* Dec. 16, 1966, G.A. Res. 2200 (XXI), U.N. GAOR, 21st Sess., Supp. No. 16, at 52, U.N. Doc. A/6316, 999 U.N.T.S. 171, 6 I.L.M. 368 (1967) [hereinafter ICCPR].

5. *E.g.,* Charlesworth & Chinkin, *supra* note 3, at 70–71; *see* Cook, *supra* note 3, at 156–57.

6. *See* Charlesworth & Chinkin, *supra* note 3, at 69–70, 72–73.

7. For example, Israel has made a reservation to article 23 of the ICCPR (equality in marriage) and "any other provision thereof to which present reservation may be relevant, matters of personal status are governed in Israel by the religious law of parties concerned. To the extent that such law is inconsistent with its obligations under the Covenant, Israel reserves

right to apply that law." *See* MULTILATERAL TREATIES DEPOSITED WITH THE SECRETARY-GENERAL AS OF 31 DECEMBER 1997, at 125, U.N. Doc. ST/LEG/SER.E/16, U.N. Sales No. E.98.V2 (1998) [hereinafter MULTI-LATERAL TREATIES]. Yet Israel has not reserved with respect to the political articles, and a reservation to these articles, the core of the ICCPR, would surely be unacceptable as against the object and purpose of the treaty. *See infra* note 22.

8. For a review of the rise of religious fundamentalisms in Buddhism, Christianity, Hinduism, Islam, and Judaism in the context of international law, see Courtney W. Howland, *The Challenge of Religious Fundamentalism to the Liberty and Equality Rights of Women: An Analysis under the United Nations Charter,* 35 COLUM. J. TRANSNAT'L L. 271, 282–324 (1997).

9. *See* Deborah Rhode, *Feminism and the State,* 107 HARV. L. REV. 1181, 1187 (1994).

10. *See* Alexandre Charles Kiss, *Permissible Limitations on Rights, in* THE INTERNATIONAL BILL OF RIGHTS: THE COVENANT ON CIVIL AND POLITICAL RIGHTS 290, 307 (Louis Henkin, ed., 1981)[hereinafter "THE INTERNATIONAL BILL OF RIGHTS"].

11. *See id.* at 305–08; Karl Josef Partsch, *Freedom of Conscience and Expression, in* THE INTERNATIONAL BILL OF RIGHTS, *supra* note 10, at 208, 230–32.

12. Analysis of international treaties must be based squarely on text. Vienna Convention on the Law of Treaties, *adopted* May 22, 1969, by the U.N. Conference on the Law of Treaties, art. 31, U.N. Doc. A/Conf. 39/27, at 289 (1969), 1155 U.N.T.S. 331, 341, 8 I.L.M. 679, 691–92 (1969) (hereinafter Vienna Convention).

13. ICCPR, *supra* note 4, art. 18(1).

14. *Id.; see also* Partsch, *supra* note 11, at 213–14.

15. ICCPR, *supra* note 4, art. 18(2).

16. ICCPR, *supra* note 4, art. 19(1),(2).

17. ICCPR, *supra* note 4, art. 19(2).

18. ICCPR, *supra* note 4, art. 22(1).

19. Partsch, *supra* note 11, at 235.

20. ICCPR, *supra* note 4, arts. 21, 22(2). The text of both articles 21 and 22(2) limits restrictions to those "which are necessary in a democratic society in the interests of national security or public safety, public order (*ordre public*), the protection of public health or morals or the protection of the rights and freedoms of others." *Id.; see also* Partsch, *supra* note 11, at 232; Kiss, *supra* note 10, at 305–08.

21. ICCPR, *supra* note 4, art. 25. Note that these rights are accorded to all citizens without distinction of any kind, including race, sex, religion, and political or other opinion. *Id.* art. 25 & art. 2 (2).

22. A state must not undermine the "object and purpose" of a treaty. Vienna Convention, *supra* note 12, art. 31(1), 1155 U.N.T.S. at 341, 8 I.L.M. at 691.

23. These articles, except for article 25, may apply more broadly than merely to citizens of the state.

24. *See* Partsch, *supra* note 11, at 209.

25. For a similar discussion in the context of U.S. constitutionalism, see Tracy E. Higgins, *Democracy and Feminism,* 110 HARV. L. REV. 1657, 1664–65 (1997).

26. *See id.*

27. *See* IAN BROWNLIE, PRINCIPLES OF PUBLIC INTERNATIONAL LAW 446–52 (Oxford: Clarendon Press, 4th ed., 1990). A state is responsible for the religious fundamentalist laws it passes and also for enforcement of religious fundamentalist laws through its delegation to religious courts. Howland, *supra* note 8, at 366–71.

28. *See generally* Cook, *supra* note 3; Charlesworth & Chinkin, *supra* note 3.

29. *See* Howland, *supra* note 8, at 282–324.

30. *See id.*

31. The only substantial limitation is that, in some cases, a husband may not demand that his wife do something that would violate other strong norms of the religion. *See* Howland, *supra* note 8, at 353 n.350 (1997).

32. *See id.* at 288 & n.54 (Buddhism), 293 & n.87 (Christianity), 301 & n.133 (*purdah* in Hinduism), 309–11 (*hejab* in Islam), 321–22 (Judaism).

33. *See id.*

34. For example, Afghanistan, Algeria, Iran, Iraq, Sudan, India, and Israel have such laws. *See* Howland, *supra* note 8, at 367–68. These are all member states of the ICCPR. *See* MULTILATERAL TREATIES, *supra* note 7, at 121.

35. Article 25 gives everyone the right to take part in government, directly or through freely chosen representatives, the right of equal access to public service, and the right to vote in periodic elections. ICCPR, *supra* note 4, art. 25; *see* Howland, *supra* note 8, at 316 & n.201(discussing limits on women's right to vote in Kuwait and Algeria).

36. *See, e.g.,* SAFIA IQBAL, WOMAN AND ISLAMIC LAW 115–19 (rev. ed. 1991) (arguing that under Islamic law, modesty codes prohibit women from running for public office).

37. "Women who claim that they support laws of obedience and modesty codes call into question the reliability of their own position. There is no way that an outside observer can evaluate whether or not this political position is her own since she is subject to obedience rules and corresponding coercive violent sanctions. The very existence of the rules undermines the credibility of a woman who supports such rules while subject to them." Howland, *supra* note 8, at 357 n.364.

38. ICCPR, *supra* note 4, art. 2(1). Article 2 also requires that all the rights in the Covenant are to be guaranteed "without distinction of any kind, such as race, colour, sex, language, religion, political or other opinion. . . ." The underlying premise of this nondistinction language is that human rights are not dependent upon any particular religion; the provisions in favor of religion are extensions of the principle of nondistinction, and thus no particular religion alone may determine the parameters of these rights. *See also* Howland, *supra* note 8, at 329–30 (arguing that U.N. Charter nondistinc-

tion language implies that human rights are not dependent upon any particular religion). The guarantees of nondistinctions based on religion and on sex are of equal importance.

39. Thomas Buergenthal, *To Respect and to Ensure: State Obligations and Permissible Derogations, in* THE INTERNATIONAL BILL OF HUMAN RIGHTS, *supra* note 10, at 72, 77–78; THOMAS BUERGENTHAL, INTERNATIONAL HUMAN RIGHTS IN A NUTSHELL 43 (2d. ed., 1995); *see also* Human Rights Committee, General Comments 3 and 4, Compilation of General Comments and General Recommendations Adopted by Human Rights Treaty Bodies, at 4, 5, U.N. Doc. HRI/GEN/1/Rev. 3 (1997).

40. *See* Howland, *supra* note 8, at 357 n.364 (discussing how India has attempted to deal with Hindu fundamentalism by enacting civil laws of marriage and divorce that do not discriminate—or discriminate much less than traditional and fundamentalist Hindu norms—and legislation specifically banning certain discriminatory Hindu religious practices such as *sati,* dowry deaths, and the prohibition of widow remarriage).

41. The approach is similar to that of India in enacting a law that outlawed the Hindu prohibition on widow remarriage. *See supra* note 40.

Chapter 10

Religious Reservations to the Convention on the Elimination of All Forms of Discrimination against Women: What Do They Really Mean?

Ann Elizabeth Mayer

I. INTRODUCTION

Many governments of Muslim countries that have ratified the Convention on the Elimination of All Forms of Discrimination Against Women (CEAFDAW)[1] have entered significant reservations qualifying their adherence to various provisions.[2] The reservations entered by certain Muslim countries are notable because they amount to a rejection of central provisions of CEAFDAW, such as article 16, which requires the elimination of discrimination against women in all matters relating to marriage and family relations.[3] Muslim states have frequently invoked Islamic law as the reason for making these reservations. If individual Muslims objected to CEAFDAW as contrary to their religious beliefs, such objections could be properly termed religious. But, are CEAFDAW reservations entered by nation-states ever truly religious in character? Should the commitments to discriminatory policies that prompt such governmental reservations be regarded as exercises of religious freedom? I explain in this chapter why the answers to these questions should be negative.

II. THE POLITICAL NATURE OF "RELIGIOUS" RESERVATIONS

Governments do not have religious beliefs, but follow policies that reflect political calculations. Of course, governments may take religious factors and religious beliefs into account when they decide to uphold discriminatory features of Islamic law at the expense of CEAFDAW. They might be affected by factors such as: strategic alliances with groups or institutions that insist that Islam calls for subjugating women; worry that reforms expanding women's rights could fuel a fundamentalist backlash; a concern to maintain regime legitimacy by demonstrating fidelity to Islamic law; and the desire to win favor with rich donor nations, like Saudi Arabia, that sponsor a reactionary version of Islam. Or, governments might calculate that standing by traditional Islamic morality could serve as a useful prop for national identity. Such concerns are at best politico-religious.

Muslim countries' CEAFDAW reservations are the mutable outcomes of politics, whereas Muslims believe that their religion is universal and its values timeless. The versions of Islamic law that are in force in different Muslim countries vary dramatically in terms of their treatment of women, and are subject to revision and abrogation. The CEAFDAW reservations that Muslim countries enter in the name of upholding Islamic law are likewise diverse, and they, too, are subject to change. After entering CEAFDAW reservations insisting that Islamic law requires a certain treatment of women, countries may modify or discard these same reservations. Evolving political contingencies, not Islamic beliefs, turn out to be determinative factors.

CEAFDAW reservations invoking Islam need to be viewed as the products of skewed political processes that give men a monopoly of power and exclude input from precisely that segment of the population that will be most adversely affected by noncompliance with CEAFDAW. Only exceptionally do women enter the corridors of power in Muslim countries, and women as a whole have never attained the level of influence that would enable them to play a decisive role in defining national policies affecting women. Not surprisingly, governments of Muslim countries have discounted the views of feminists, who have decried their countries' CEAFDAW reservations and have expressed skepticism about the Islamic rationales that have been offered for these reservations.

Appeals to Islamic law to justify deviating from CEAFDAW have a political dimension in that they assume that citizens of Muslim countries are properly governed by Islamic law, an idea that Islamic fundamentalists promote with vigor but that is disputed by many Muslims. Outsiders may take away the impression that Muslim countries are permeated by a religious ethos, not appreciating that many members of these societies chafe under Islamic laws. Unlike secularists in more open societies, proponents of separation of religion and state in Muslim countries cannot denounce retrograde religious laws without imperiling their safety. Although secularist protests against application of Islamic law are infrequently voiced, secularists quickly take advantage of rare opportunities when they can speak out with relative impunity. Thus, as soon as the anti-fundamentalist battles of Algeria, Morocco, and Tunisia opened the door for the articulation of secularist perspectives, a group of North African feminists assertively proclaimed their distaste for religious law and called for adherence to CEAFDAW.[4]

To challenge the idea that laws discriminating against women rest on divine authority, feminists are deliberately emphasizing the bewildering diversity of national laws affecting women that claim to embody Islamic principles. Due to their utter irreconcilability, they cannot possibly all be valid statements of Islamic doctrine. Thus, a major women's advocacy group is named "Women Living Under Muslim Laws"; the name itself highlights that Muslim women are living under the conflicting positive *laws* enacted in various Muslim countries, rather than under *Islamic law* per se.[5]

Demonstrating how Islamic reservations to CEAFDAW are imbedded in the political strategies of individual regimes, Morocco made Islamic reservations[6] that were later explained as being an anti-fundamentalist prophylactic. In speaking to the CEAFDAW Committee in 1997, Morocco's representative struggled to defend Morocco's reservations, claiming that Islam represented "a total lifestyle and civilization, an integral part of Morocco's culture and traditions. It was also a rampart against fundamentalism and terrorism . . . a basic concern of his country was religious fundamentalism which would seek to impose intolerance."[7] Islam was thus envisaged as a part of Morocco's heritage that made for a stable identity that shielded the country against the inroads of fundamentalism and terrorism. Fear of the latter is natural, since the upsurge in fundamentalism in neighboring Algeria in the 1990s has culminated in devastating paroxysms of violence. If the Moroccan king's legitimacy as a traditional Islamic ruler were compromised by radical reforms, this might cause instability that ambitious fundamentalists could exploit for their own ends. Supporters of women's rights who accept this logic might agree that the regime's caution was warranted, fearing that women's rights might suffer badly if bold initiatives were undertaken that could provide fundamentalists with a means to mobilize support. Unimpressed by Morocco's defense, the Committee responded that religious fundamentalism was not restricted to Islamic countries; such attitudes existed in Christian countries as well.[8] As Morocco discovered, once a country dispensed with the protective cover of religious obfuscation, the logic of its reservations was open to critical scrutiny.

In contrast, the weaker Kuwaiti monarchy delayed confronting fundamentalists, whose influence increased after the Gulf War. Resistance to allowing women to vote had seemed to be ebbing until this recent surge in fundamentalism. An all-male parliamentary committee in March 1998 unanimously rejected a draft bill that would have crowned with success Kuwaiti women's long struggle to obtain the vote.[9] The rejection was reportedly based on a religious ruling by the *fatwa* department of the Islamic Affairs Ministry.[10] That is, after having entered a CEAFDAW reservation in 1994 indicating that Kuwait refused to enfranchise its women without claiming that Islam barred women from voting, Kuwait seemed poised to assert that Islamic law *did* require this bar. After ensuring that women would not be able to vote, Kuwaiti fundamentalists were planning to impose harsh restrictions on women's freedom, all in the name of Islam. To imagine that, once an Islamic label has been pasted on this regime of gender apartheid, principles of religious freedom should suffice to insulate it from criticism entails disregarding the obvious parallels with South African apartheid, where disenfranchised blacks were deprived of rights in a system approved by the Dutch Reformed Church.[11] When Kuwait's ruler, Sheikh Jabir al-Ahmad al-Sabah, decreed on May 16, 1999, that women had the right to vote, he provoked a storm of controversy. Some Islamic authorities supported this step, but fundamentalists denounced the decree as a violation of Islamic law, and it is unclear whether the decree will be upheld when the parliment reconvenes.

The example of Pakistan demonstrates how rank political expediency dictates how CEAFDAW reservations are characterized. Pakistan's energetic feminist leaders called for CEAFDAW ratification without reservation, but they encountered strong resistance from the Religious Affairs Ministry.[12] A government committee recommended CEAFDAW ratification with a temporary reservation to Article 2(f), which calls on states to take all appropriate measures to modify or abolish laws, regulations, customs, and practices that discriminate against women.[13] Women activists attacked this proposed reservation, saying it would negate the spirit of the convention.[14] After heated debates, Pakistan finally decided in March 1996 to ratify CEAFDAW with a sweeping reservation. The Prime Minister at the time, Benazir Bhutto, apparently had calculated that an unconditional ratification could provoke a fundamentalist challenge to her shaky government. Even though the reservation was designed to uphold what Pakistan routinely claims are Islamic requirements, it made no reference to Islamic law, offering the vague comment that Pakistan's accession was "subject to the provisions of the Constitution of the Islamic Republic of Pakistan."[15] The Pakistani Constitution contains many provisions supporting the supremacy of Islamic law, and thus this "constitutional" reservation would have the same impact as reservations making specific reference to Islamic law. Why, then, was the idea that Islamic law should override CEAFDAW only obliquely incorporated in this reservation? Pakistan was most likely eager to improve its image in the West and worried about the criticisms leveled at previous Islamic reservations. Therefore, the government of Pakistan was reluctant to tell the international community what Pakistani regimes routinely tell their domestic constituencies—that they are standing by policies of upholding Islamic law. Instead, it was attracted to a vague formula of "constitutional" reservations that had already been made respectable, at least in some eyes, by the United States, which has entered such reservations to human rights treaties.[16]

The case of Algeria provides another example of how political considerations dictate responses to CEAFDAW. In 1984, Algeria enacted a reactionary family law that embodies principles taken from medieval Islamic jurisprudence. The legislation passed despite women's protests over this and other discriminatory laws. Algeria finally ratified CEAFDAW in May 1996, reserving to central CEAFDAW provisions without any reference to Islam.[17] In formulating its CEAFDAW reservations, Algeria referred to its own family law as if it were nothing more than positive law.[18] Threatened by radical fundamentalism, Algeria's beleaguered government is attempting to retain Western support by positioning itself as a bulwark against fundamentalism. Therefore, where its international image is concerned, the government does not want to be associated with using Islamic law as a pretext for depriving women of human rights, even though it invokes Islam before domestic audiences to justify discriminatory features in its family law. Although other Muslim countries might seek to justify CEAFDAW reservations that are designed to shield similar state discriminatory laws by appeals to divine authority, it does not mean that their policies are any less the results of political choices.

As the Pakistani and Algerian cases prove, political considerations dictate whether governments decide to frame CEAFDAW reservations in Islamic terms—hardly the outcome one would expect if religious beliefs were behind these. Similar considerations appear to dictate the withdrawal of such reservations. During roughly the same period, two countries that had originally entered Islamic reservations to CEAFDAW decided to retract them in whole or in part: Bangladesh withdrew its reservation in July 1997 and Malaysia did so in part in February 1998.[19] These countries had not undergone sudden conversions from Islam to other faiths; like Pakistan and Algeria, the governments involved simply judged that it was inopportune to have on record an official statement saying that they upheld Islamic laws at the expense of CEAFDAW.

III. WESTERN MISCONCEPTIONS
ABOUT MUSLIM COUNTRIES' RESERVATIONS

Unfortunately, literature published in the United States has contributed to the misconception that religious beliefs lie behind Muslim countries' CEAFDAW reservations. Lessons seem to be mistakenly extrapolated from the U.S. system, where the state embraces no single religion and where it is bound to avoid interfering in the free exercise of religion. From the fact that the U.S. government is bound to respect the religious beliefs and practices of minority communities, authors glide to the unfounded conclusion that when Middle Eastern Muslim countries reserve to CEAFDAW, they aim to uphold the religious freedoms of their citizenry. Authors miss the following three crucial points: first, that in almost all Muslim countries in the region, Islam is the state religion (Turkey being the notable exception); second, that the official version of Islamic law is typically applied to individuals and groups regardless of their own religious convictions; and third, that dissent from the official version of Islam tends to be treated like political opposition and sometimes even like treason, often with lethal consequences. Further, authors seem to imagine that a secular CEAFDAW is clashing with Islamic beliefs, when in reality there is a clash of views within Muslim societies over whether there is any Islamic authority for discriminatory laws and policies affecting women and over whether Islamic law should in any case be the governing standard.

For example, in discussing Muslim countries' reservations to CEAFDAW, Theodor Meron has written as if they were mandated by a unitary Islam that stood above politics, with states merely acting as agents for Muslims' beliefs. According to Meron, "[g]iven the force of religion in many societies," states might resist CEAFDAW obligations that are incompatible with specific religious practices that may bar or impair the achievement of the equality of the sexes.[20] Imagining that women's equality clashes with this abstract "force of religion," he goes on to assert: "The attainment of the goal of equality of women may therefore require encroachment upon religious freedom."[21] That Muslims' beliefs might be offended by being forced to conform their lives to reactionary, state-imposed versions of Islamic law seems never to occur to Meron, who opines that "(t)he application of religious laws may itself constitute the observance and practice of religion."[22] In a bizarre transmogrification, coercive governmental imposition of discriminatory laws that will at best correspond to the religious views of one segment of the population becomes religious observance and practice implicating religious *freedom* of all—a freedom that would be menaced by CEAFDAW!

One should inquire: Whose religious practice is at stake? Whose religious freedom would be menaced—that of the nation-state imposing these laws or that of individuals? For clarification, consider Egypt's CEAFDAW reservations that appeal to "firm religious beliefs" as the basis for maintaining Egypt's discriminatory laws affecting women,[23] implying a correspondence between these laws and Egyptians' beliefs. In reality, no such shared understanding of how Islamic law applies to women underlies these Egyptian laws.[24] Egyptian personal status rules result from state policies of co-opting and manipulating Islam and delegitimizing feminists' protests.[25] They reflect the regime's hopes to buttress its Islamic credentials and its tottering legitimacy by forming strategic alliances with al-Azhar and other pillars of conservative Islam.[26] Much criticized by feminists, Egypt's laws also fail to win the approval of Islamic fundamentalists.[27] Thus, Egyptian laws affecting women flout the "firm religious beliefs" of Egyptians at both ends of the religious spectrum, and, of course, they ride roughshod over the beliefs of Egyptian secularists.

Meron may imagine that the kind of national Islam imposed by Egypt's government should be equated with religion. Although he refers often to the Declaration on the Elimination of All Forms of Intolerance and of Discrimination Based on Religion or Belief,[28] Meron seems to overlook that the protection afforded therein is not merely for "religion"—such as state religion—but for the *belief* of one's choice. He implicitly discounts the beliefs of individual dissidents and feminists, as if they did not rise to the level of "religion." He shows no concern that he has dismissed out of hand the beliefs of Muslims who support CEAFDAW principles and who may decry discriminatory laws in countries like Egypt as being based on patriarchal customs, not on Islam.

Donna Sullivan, in examining Islamic reservations to CEAFDAW, states that "[t]he most comprehensive challenges mounted by states to the international norms guaranteeing women's rights, and their application, have been couched as defenses of religious liberty."[29] Her own examples support neither this proposition nor her claim that "[s]tates that implement religious law, and believers themselves, have contended that many practices that violate women's human rights are manifestations of the freedom of religion or belief, and as such are entitled to protection under international law."[30]

In none of the CEAFDAW reservations entered by Muslim countries has the need to protect *freedom* of religion been cited to justify their noncompliance with the Convention. Indeed, it would be a tricky tactic for Middle Eastern countries to invoke this principle, since they do not in practice uphold freedom of religion and some have denounced this freedom in public forums. In 1990, all Muslim countries endorsed The Cairo Declaration on Human Rights in Islam,[31] which is noteworthy for failing to make any provision whatsoever for freedom of religion. Furthermore, even where Muslim countries do provide for religious freedom in their constitutions, they may disregard or nullify this freedom in practice.[32] Some of the countries most allergic to CEAFDAW, such as fundamentalist Afghanistan, Iran, and the Sudan, are among the most egregious violators of religious freedom in the world. For such countries, it verges on the grotesque to conceptualize the problem as one of governmental concern for religious freedom constituting an obstacle to the acceptance of CEAFDAW.

Meron and Sullivan proceed as if international law potentially provides a basis for saying that in the case of conflicts, concern for principles like religious freedom should override the liberty and equality rights of women. However, as Courtney Howland has rightly concluded, there is no warrant in international law for compromising women's human rights in this fashion.[33] After making the mistake of assuming that Muslim countries are restricting women's rights in the interest of protecting religious freedom, Meron and Sullivan seem to assume that applying a balancing test would limit the nefarious impact that privileging religion would have on women's rights and freedoms. They indicate that they would only accept religious reservations to CEAFDAW that are tied to authentic or significant aspects of religion. In connection with this balancing enterprise, Meron imagines that outsiders can speak of "genuine doctrinal features" of religion.[34] This is actually highly problematic. The international community has no basis for saying that the more isolated or unusual view is not as genuine a doctrinal feature as features that enjoy more powerful support and seem more strongly grounded in religious authority. After all, a "genuine" feature would be either one that is true or sincerely adhered to. A "doctrinal" feature would involve something to be taught and believed. What are the objective criteria for the international community to use in deciding which Islamic beliefs are true or sincerely adhered to, or for deciding what Muslims should be taught and should believe?

Sullivan seems to have relied on Meron in proffering similar categories. She contends that in evaluating religious reservations to CEAFDAW one can dismiss "spurious and fraudulent claims."[35] She seems to think that one should determine "the importance of the religious law or practice to the right of religious freedom," which is to be done by assessing "the significance accorded that practice by the religion or belief itself."[36] But, this assumes that there is a uniform, uncontested version of religion and a uniform, uncontested religious belief stipulating the relative significance of various laws and practices that is available to guide outsiders' assessments. This is a generally dubious proposition and one certainly inapplicable to Islam. Howland accurately observes that factoring in the relative importance of a religious law in determining the scope of women's rights "is impermissible under international law" and that it is "unworkable on a practical basis."[37]

Experience shows why a scheme of evaluating the importance or genuineness of religious reasons for deviating from CEAFDAW is impracticable. Muslim countries are prepared to claim that harmful practices and discriminatory laws are warranted by Islam even when such claims seem virtually impossible to substantiate. An Egyptian woman diplomat has recounted with palpable scorn the far-fetched assertions made in 1987 to defend practices violating CEAFDAW.[38] She notes how Islamic rationales were offered to the CEAFDAW committee by an Asian Muslim country for the practice of throwing acid in a woman's face as punishment and by an African Muslim country for the rule that, when a man died, his wife was to be treated as part of his movable property to be inherited by his brother.[39] However, once put on the spot, the delegates were at a loss to explain what the Islamic authority for these practices would be.[40] Apparently hoping to find a way to resolve such disputes by reference to Islamic law, the CEAFDAW Committee then requested that a study of the status of women under Islamic law be prepared.[41] That it should have proposed such a study suggests that even within the United Nations human rights system there is sympathy for the view that religious principles—as long as these can be shown to be important or "genuine doctrinal features"—may be considered in interpreting women's rights.

If religion were actually the issue, one would have expected Muslim countries to welcome a study of Islamic doctrines regarding women. Instead, Muslim countries strongly opposed this project.[42] The very countries urging the notion that there should be Islamic exceptions to CEAFDAW requirements do not want the international community to examine what the relevant Islamic doctrines are. With no way to devise a method to differentiate between genuine and spurious religious claims, ultimately, all appeals to Islam would have to be taken at face value. Obviously, if otherwise unacceptable deviations from CEAFDAW could automatically be justified by appeals to religion, there would be no limit to subsequent curbs on women's rights.

IV. CONCLUSION

The Islamic reservations that have been entered to CEAFDAW provide valuable material for examining what religious reservations to CEAFDAW mean. Critical appraisals should dissuade those advocating respect for religious difference and religious freedom from imagining that Islamic reservations to CEAFDAW warrant special accommodation. Religious reservations when offered by governments simply mean that states are refusing to comply with CEAFDAW and are hoping that invoking religious grounds for their noncompliance will win them special indulgence.

NOTES

1. Convention on the Elimination of All Forms of Discrimination Against Women, *adopted* Dec. 18, 1979, G.A. Res. 34/180, U.N. GAOR, 34th Sess., Supp. No. 46, at 193, U.N. Doc. A/34/46 (1979), 1249 U.N.T.S. 13 [hereinafter CEAFDAW].

2. A reservation is "a unilateral statement . . . made by a State, when signing, ratifying . . . a treaty, whereby it purports to exclude or to modify the legal effect of certain provisions of the treaty in their application to the State." Vienna Convention on the Law of Treaties, *adopted* May 23, 1969, art. 2 (d), 1155 U.N.T.S. 331, U.N. Doc. A/CONF. 39/27 (1969). Subject to conditions in particular treaties, states may enter reservations when ratifying treaties that restrict the effect of the treaty, subject to the condition that the reservation may not be incompatible with the object and purpose of the treaty. For a further discussion of reservations to CEAFDAW, see Ann Elizabeth Mayer, *Reflections on the Proposed United States Reservations to CEDAW: Should the Constitution be an Obstacle to Human Rights?,* 23 HASTINGS CONST. L.Q. 727, 731–41 (1996).

3. For examples of state reservations, see U.N. Doc. CEDAW/SP/1998/2, Feb. 6, 1998, at 20–21, 24, 28, MULTILATERAL TREATIES DEPOSITED WITH THE SECRETARY-GENERAL: STATUS AS OF 31 DECEMBER 1997, at 173, 174, 175, U.N. Doc. ST/LEG/SER.E/16, U.N. Sales No. E.98.V.2 (1998) (hereinafter MULTILATERAL TREATIES) (reservations of Egypt, Iraq, and Libya respectively). *See* ANN ELIZABETH MAYER, ISLAM AND HUMAN RIGHTS: TRADITION AND POLITICS 124–25 (Boulder, CO: Westview Press, 3d. ed., 1999).

4. Zakya Daoud, *En marge de la Conférence mondial des femmes de Pékin: la stratégie des féministes maghrébines,* MONDE ARABE MAGHREB MACHREK, Oct.-Dec. 1995, at 105–19.

5. *See* Seema Kazi, *Muslim Law and Women Living under Muslim Laws, in* MUSLIM WOMEN AND THE POLITICS OF PARTICIPATION: IMPLEMENTING THE BEIJING PLATFORM 141, 142–43 (Mahnaz Afkhami & Erika Friedl, eds.) (Syracuse: Syracuse University Press, 1997).

6. *See* MULTILATERAL TREATIES, *supra* note 3, at 176.

7. *See UN Committee on Elimination of Discrimination Against Women Concludes Consideration of Morocco's Report,* M2 PRESSWIRE, Jan. 22, 1997, *available in* LEXIS, World Library, ALLWLD File.

8. *Id.*

9. *See Kuwait Women's Efforts for Political Rights Thwarted,* XINHUA NEWS AGENCY, Mar. 2, 1998, *available in* LEXIS, World Library, ALLWLD File.

10. *Id.*

11. For a discussion of the parallels between gender apartheid and South African apartheid on the basis of religion, see Courtney W. Howland, *The Challenge of Religious Fundamentalism to the Liberty and Equality Rights of Women: An Analysis under the United Nations Charter,* 35 COLUM. J. TRANSNAT'L L. 271 (1997).

12. *See Pakistan—Women: Activists Pressure Government to Ratify CEDAW,* INTER PRESS SERVICE, June 21, 1995, *available in* LEXIS, World Library, ALLWLD File.

13. *See* CEAFDAW, *supra* note 1, art. 2(f), at 196, 1249 U.N.T.S. at 16.

14. *See Pakistan—Women: Activists Pressure Government to Ratify CEDAW, supra* note 12.

15. *See* MULTILATERAL TREATIES, *supra* note 3, at 177.

16. For example, see the United States reservation to the International Covenant on Civil and Political Rights, *adopted* Dec. 16, 1966, G.A. Res. 2200 (XXI), U.N. GAOR, 21st Sess., Supp. No. 16, at 52, U.N. Doc. A/6316, 999 U.N.T.S. 171, 6 I.L.M. 368 (1967), MULTILATERAL TREATIES, *supra* note 3, at 121, 131. For a discussion of U.S. reservations, see Mayer, *supra* note 2, at 754–67.

17. *See* MULTILATERAL TREATIES, *supra* note 3, at 171–72.

18. *Id.* at 171.

19. *See Multilateral Treaties Deposited with the Secretary-General, UN, New York ST/LEG/SER. E, Convention on the Elimination of All Forms of Discrimination against Women* (visited Apr. 13, 1999) <http://www.un.org/Depts /Treaty/final/ts2/newfiles/part_boo/iv_boo/iv_8.html>

20. THEODOR MERON, HUMAN RIGHTS LAW-MAKING IN THE UNITED NATIONS: A CRITIQUE OF INSTRUMENTS AND PROCESS 155 (Oxford: Clarendon Press, 1986).

21. *Id.*

22. *Id.* at 156.

23. *See* U.N. Doc. CEDAW/SP/1992/2, *supra* note 3, at 11–12; MULTILATERAL TREATIES, *supra* note 3, at 173.

24. *See* Azza M. Karam, *Women, Islamisms, and State: Dynamics of Power and Contemporary Feminisms in Egypt, in* MUSLIM WOMEN AND THE POLITICS OF PARTICIPATION, *supra* note 5, at 18, 26–28.

25. *Id.* at 24, 27.

26. *Id.* at 26.

27. *Id.* at 23.

28. Declaration on the Elimination of All Forms of Intolerance and of Discrimination Based on Religion or Belief, *adopted* Nov. 25, 1981, G.A. Res. 36/55, U.N. GAOR, 36th Sess., Supp. No. 51, at 171, U.N. Doc. A/36/51 (1981), 25 I.L.M. 205 (1982).

29. *See* Donna J. Sullivan, *Gender Equality and Religious Freedom: Toward a Framework for Conflict Resolution,* 24 N.Y.U. J. INT'L L. & POL. 795, 795 (1992).

30. *Id.*

31. *See* The Cairo Declaration on Human Rights in Islam, June 9, 1993, U.N. Doc. A/CONF.157/PC/62/Add. 18, at 2, The World Conference on Human Rights, Prep. Comm., 4th Sess., Provisional Agenda, Item 5, *reprinted in* MAYER, *supra* note 3, at 203.

32. For a general discussion of how Middle Eastern Muslim countries disregard freedom of religion, see MAYER, *supra* note 3, at 149–74; AMNESTY INTERNATIONAL, AFGHANISTAN: GRAVE ABUSES IN THE NAME OF RELIGION (New York, NY: Amnesty International, 1996); AMNESTY INTERNATIONAL, IRAN: VICTIMS OF HUMAN RIGHT'S VIOLATIONS 4–6 (New York, NY: Amnesty International, 1993); AMNESTY INTERNATIONAL, SAUDI ARABIA: RELIGIOUS INTOLERANCE: THE ARREST, DETENTION AND TORTURE OF CHRISTIAN WORSHIPPERS AND SHI'A MUSLIMS (New York, NY: Amnesty International USA, 1993).

33. *See* Howland, *supra* note 11, at 324–77.

34. *See* MERON, *supra* note 20, at 159–60.

35. *See* Sullivan, *supra* note 29, at 813.

36. *Id.* at 822.

37. *See* Howland, *supra* note 11, at 345, n.317.

38. *See* Mervat Tallawy, *International Organizations, National Machinery, Islam, and Foreign Policy, in* MUSLIM WOMEN AND THE POLITICS OF PARTICIPATION, *supra* note 5, at 128.

39. *See id.* at 135–36.

40. *See id.* at 136.

41. *See id.;* Report on the Seventh Session of the Committee on the Elimination of Discrimination Against Women, Sixth Session, U.N. GAOR, 42d Sess., Supp. No. 38, U.N. Doc. A/42/38, at 80.

42. *See* ANDREW BYRNES, REPORT ON THE SEVENTH SESSION OF THE COMMITTEE ON THE ELIMINATION OF DISCRIMINATION AGAINST WOMEN AND THE FOURTH MEETING OF STATES PARTIES TO THE CONVENTION ON THE ELIMINATION OF ALL FORMS OF DISCRIMINATION AGAINST WOMEN 6–7 (International Women's Rights Action Watch: 7th cedaw/iwraw report, 1988).

Chapter 11 🐊

Women's Equal Right to Freedom of Religion or Belief: An Important but Neglected Subject

Bahia G. Tahzib-Lie[1]

I. INTRODUCTION

Numerous international human rights provisions deal with the promotion and protection of the right to freedom of religion or belief.[2] The expression "freedom of religion or belief" is used inclusively and broadly, to connote freedom of theistic, nontheistic, and atheistic beliefs as well as freedom not to profess any of these beliefs.[3] Numerous international human rights provisions address women's equal entitlement to human rights, particularly in the fields of political participation, employment, health care, education, legal capacity, and family life.[4] It is a surprising fact, however, that no global human rights instrument has specifically articulated women's equal entitlement to the right to freedom of religion or belief. Only one fairly recent regional instrument explicitly acknowledges that women have this right.[5] These findings prompt this chapter's discussion on the meaning of women's equal right to freedom of religion or belief.

II. EQUAL ENTITLEMENT TO THE RIGHT TO FREEDOM OF RELIGION OR BELIEF

The right to freedom of religion or belief is enshrined in various human rights instruments adopted at both global and regional levels. It is clear from the relevant provisions in these instruments that the enjoyment of this right is not the exclusive preserve of a particular group of individuals. The relevant provisions refer to "everyone" having the right to freedom of religion or belief. Differences in matters such as race, language, gender, or religion may not provide grounds for discrimination.[6] Specific treaty provisions may also state that women and men are equally entitled to civil and political rights.[7] Such rights are understood to include the right to freedom of religion or belief. Yet women's equal right to freedom of religion or belief has not been specifically articulated in any global instrument on women's rights.[8] Even the Convention on the Elimination of All Forms of Discrimination Against Women does not explicitly provide for women's equal right to freedom of religion or belief.[9] However, it certainly reaffirms that women may not be discriminated against with respect to any of their human rights, and so it may be concluded that the fact that a woman is a woman must not be a reason to restrict her right to freedom of religion or belief.[10]

Despite the absence of a global provision on women's equal right to freedom of religion or belief, the number of pronouncements condemning religious intolerance and the discrimination against women has gradually increased in international fora in recent years. For instance, in 1993, the 171 states gathered at the Second World Conference on Human Rights not only recognized every individual's right to freedom of religion or belief but also called upon all governments to take all appropriate measures in compliance with their international obligations and with due regard to their respective legal systems to counter intolerance and related violence based on religion or belief, including practices of discrimination against women.[11] They also stressed "the eradication of any conflicts which may arise between the rights of women and the harmful effects of . . . religious extremism."[12]

Moreover, the United Nations (UN) Commission on Human Rights has urged states "[i]n conformity with international standards of human rights, to take all necessary action to combat hatred, intolerance and acts of violence, intimidation and coercion motivated by intolerance based on religion or belief, including practices which violate the human rights of women and discriminate against women."[13] The Commission has also stressed the need for its Special Rapporteur on religious intolerance "to apply a gender perspective, *inter alia* through the identification of gender-specific abuses, in the reporting process, including in information collection and in recommendations."[14]

The Special Rapporteur on religious intolerance initially named some countries where women were the principal victims of religious extremism and sent out communications to some countries on the question of women and religion.[15] Recently the Special Rapporteur has included women among his sensitive priority issues[16] and announced that special attention will be given to the status of women from the perspective of religion.[17] He specifically proposed initiating and developing closer cooperation with the Special Rapporteur on violence against women and the Committee on the Elimination of Discrimination against Women (CEDAW).[18] In addition, he recommended a joint study of discrimination against women attributable specifically to their status as women within churches and religions.[19] The relevance of such a study can be inferred from a recent global report: "[i]t is not an exaggeration to say that, as in so many aspects of life, women, half the human race, have been invisible within churches and religions which have been dominated by men. Women's modes of practice and organization may be, as with other minorities, invisible and ignored."[20]

In developing sensitivity to gender-specific violations of the right to freedom of religion or belief, it is instructive to know how this human right is defined under international law.

III. TWO-STRAND DEFINITION OF FREEDOM OF RELIGION OR BELIEF

International law provides a two-part definition of the right to freedom of religion or belief. Each part relates to a different domain, the first being the inner, private domain of the individual, referred to as the *forum internum,* and the second being the outer, public domain of the individual, the *forum externum.*[21]

A. The forum internum

Relevant human rights instruments provide varying definitions of the *forum internum* of freedom of religion or belief: "the right freely to profess a religious faith,"[22] "freedom to change his religion or belief,"[23] "freedom to maintain or to change one's religion or beliefs,"[24] "freedom to have or adopt a religion or belief of his choice."[25] The key verbs of the inner freedom are: to profess, to change, to maintain, to have, and to adopt. Their common denominator is that of individual choice in religion or belief.

The somewhat differing definitions are no coincidence. Within the UN, for instance, freedom to change has always been a bone of contention. Only the drafters of the Universal Declaration of Human Rights were able to expressly include this freedom in the text. Ever since then, a number of Islamic states have opposed the inclusion of the phrase "freedom to change" in international human rights instruments.[26] The reason for their continuing opposition is related to their considering the mere changing of one's mind and turning away from Islam as apostasy.[27] Even though this has resulted in a narrowing of the formulation of the *forum internum* freedom, it has been argued that this freedom should be interpreted as comprising all elements of the varying definitions.[28]

The *forum internum* freedom must be protected unconditionally.[29] No limitation is permitted in any circumstances, not even in a time of public emergency that threatens the life of the nation, such as public danger, war, civil strife, terrorism, or religious fundamentalism.[30] The rationale behind the absolute nature of the *forum internum* freedom is that it "falls primarily within the domain of the inner faith and conscience of an individual. Viewed from this angle, one would assume that any intervention from outside is not only illegitimate but impossible."[31]

Moreover, coercion that would impair the *forum internum* freedom is prohibited.[32] This no-coercion rule has been interpreted as including:

> the use or threat of physical force or penal sanctions to compel believers or non-believers to adhere to their religious beliefs and congregations, to recant their religion or belief or to convert. Policies or practices having the same intention or effect, such as, for example, those restricting access to education, medical care, employment or the rights guaranteed by article 25 and other provisions of the Covenant [International Covenant on Civil and Political Rights (hereinafter ICCPR)] are similarly inconsistent with article 18(2) [the no-coercion rule]. The same protection is enjoyed by holders of all beliefs of a non-religious nature.[33]

It is debatable whether more indirect forms of coercion including improper inducements are to be considered coercion.[34]

Understanding the scope of the *forum internum* freedom of religion is necessary for assessing situations in which women are not given much choice in their religion or belief. This is particularly true of women who disagree with the interpretation that religious leaders or society put on their religion, and of women who profess a religion or belief different from that of society at large ("dissenting women"). Reports of women, for instance, being abducted and forcibly converted to a particular religion[35] or forced to marry a man from a different religion and convert to his faith[36] chronicle clear violations of women's *forum internum* freedom of religion or belief. They exemplify situations in which dissenting women are specifically targeted. More attention ought to be given to gender-specific violations of the *forum internum* freedom and the kinds of society in which they take place.

B. *The forum externum*

Unlike the freedom belonging to the *forum internum,* international instruments have defined the *forum externum* of the right to freedom of religion or belief similarly: "freedom, either alone or in community with others and in public or private, to manifest his religion or belief in teaching, practice, worship and observance."[37] This outer freedom therefore applies to the manifestation of religious beliefs and has been interpreted as follows:

> The concept of *worship* extends to ritual and ceremonial acts giving direct expression to belief, as well as various practices integral to such acts, including the building of places of worship, the use of ritual formulas and objects, the display of symbols, and the observance of holidays and days of rest. The *observance and practice* of religion or belief may include not only ceremonial acts but also such customs as the observance of dietary regulations, the wearing of distinctive clothing or head coverings, participation in rituals associated with certain stages of life and the use of a particular language customarily spoken by a group. In addition, the *practice and teaching* of religion or belief includes acts integral to the conduct by religious groups of their basic affairs, such as, *inter alia,* the freedom to choose their religious leaders, priests and teachers, the freedom to establish seminaries or religious schools and the freedom to prepare and distribute religious texts or publications.[38]

Thus, the *forum externum* freedom encompasses a broad range of acts.[39] Unlike the *forum internum* freedom, the *forum externum* freedom is not absolute but contingent. The freedom to manifest one's religion or belief may be restricted because the "[m]anifestation of belief . . . impacts directly on society at large, so that limiting such manifestations may be a legitimate goal of overall social policy."[40]

States, however, may not limit the *forum externum* freedom in a manner that vitiates the right to freedom of religion or belief.[41] States may only apply limitations on the freedom to manifest one's religion or belief when three conditions are met. Limitations must be: (1) prescribed by law; (2) in pursuance of legitimate aims, specifically, public safety, order, health, or morals or the fundamental rights and freedoms of others; and (3) necessary to protect the specified, legitimate aim. Each of these three conditions leaves room for interpretation. States are considered to have a certain, but not unlimited, measure of latitude for interpretative purposes: a "margin of appreciation."[42]

The "prescribed by law" condition has been interpreted as follows: "The law must be accessible, unambiguous, drawn narrowly and with precision so as to enable individuals to foresee whether a particular action is lawful. . . . The law should provide for adequate safeguards against abuse, including prompt, full and effective judicial scrutiny of the validity of the restriction by an independent court or tribunal."[43]

The five specific grounds listed in the second condition constituting "legitimate" aims are open to such broad interpretation that they could easily serve as a pretext for "unwarranted forms of interference and discrimination 'based on religion or belief.'"[44] For this reason, the five grounds are "to be strictly interpreted: restrictions are not allowed on grounds not specified . . . in the Covenant [ICCPR], such as national security."[45]

The "public safety" ground has been defined to mean "protection against danger to the safety of persons, to their life or physical integrity or serious damage to their property."[46] The term "public order" has been elucidated "as the sum of rules which ensure the functioning of society. . . . Respect for human rights is part of public order (*ordre public*)."[47] Limitations on freedom to manifest one's religion or belief thus cannot be imposed merely to protect general notions of public order, such as national public policy, but only to protect public order narrowly construed.[48] The "public health" ground may be invoked "in order to allow a state to take measures dealing with a serious threat to the health of the population or individual members of the population. These measures must be specifically aimed at preventing disease or injury or providing care for the sick and injured."[49] It has been explained that the concept of morals "derives from many social, philosophical and religious traditions."[50] Therefore, limitations for the purpose of protecting morals must be based on principles not deriving exclusively from a single tradition or religion. In seeking to protect "the fundamental rights and freedom of others," "especial weight should be afforded to the rights from which no derogation may be made under the [ICCPR]."[51]

The meaning of "necessary" in the third condition is that limitations must "be applied only for those purposes for which they were prescribed and must be directly related and proportionate to the specific need on which they are predicated."[52] Thus, evaluating a limitation in accordance with this standard requires the assessment of the various factors in each particular situation. The principle of proportionality indicates that in imposing a limitation, the state must resort to the least restrictive way of achieving that aim.

In determining whether interference with the *forum externum* freedom is legitimate in a certain case, all three conditions must be satisfied. This is not often an easy test. For instance, in some countries all women are by law obliged to comply (in public) with a religious dress code.[53] Public order is often invoked as a ground for limitation. Is this interference with the *forum externum* freedom of women legitimate? The first two conditions may be fulfilled, but the question of whether the limitation meets the necessity condition is open to debate. For instance, the Special Rapporteur on religious intolerance has urged that "dress should not be the subject of political regulation and calls for flexible and tolerant attitudes in this regard, so as to allow the variety and richness of . . . garments to manifest themselves without constraint."[54]

Moreover, it could be argued that the interference is prohibited because restrictions may not be imposed for discriminatory purposes or applied in a discriminatory manner.[55] The Human Rights Committee (HRC) has recommended that "[i]nterpreting the scope of permissible limitation clauses, States parties should proceed from the need to protect the rights guaranteed under the Covenant [ICCPR], including the right to equality and non-discrimination on all grounds specified in articles 2, 3 and 26."[56] This recommendation makes it clear, inter alia, that gender-specific restrictions are not allowed. A study of restrictions on women's outer freedom of religion or belief would shed light on the nature and frequency of such restrictions.

IV. CONCLUSIONS AND RECOMMENDATIONS

As noted, except for one regional treaty, international human rights instruments have not ventured into specifically addressing women's equal right to freedom of religion or belief. Failure to do so has not detracted international human rights fora from stressing the importance of developing a gender-sensitive interpretation and application of the right to freedom of religion or belief, especially considering the harmful effects of religious intolerance and religious extremism. Nonetheless, further research into the enjoyment and protection of women's equal right to this freedom is required. Such research should, at a minimum, investigate women's experience in the following three subject areas: first, the discrimination against women attributable specifically to their status as women within religions and beliefs; second, the types of coercion that impair women's inner freedom of religion or belief (*forum internum*); and third, the types of restrictions existing on women's outer freedom of religion or belief (*forum externum*).

Studies of these topics should be conducted within and outside the context of the UN. Within the UN context, the Special Rapporteurs on religious intolerance and on violence against women, CEDAW, and HRC should be consulted and asked for input.

In addition, CEDAW and HRC might consider formulating a general recommendation or general comment on one or more of these topics. By way of interpretation and elaboration based on the experience gained through the supervisory activities of these treaty bodies, such statements would contribute to the development of the normative content of treaty provisions on freedom of religion or belief, the right to equality, and the prohibition of gender discrimination. Such statements would also promote more effective implementation of these treaty provisions.

Finally, it is recommended that any country-specific reports that scrutinize the right to freedom of religion or belief should include sections on the above topics.

NOTES

1. This paper is the sole responsibility of the author and does not necessarily reflect the opinions of the Netherlands Ministry of Foreign Affairs.

2. For a compilation of human rights provisions regarding freedom of religion or belief, see Appendix B of BAHIYYIH G. TAHZIB, FREEDOM OF RELIGION OR BELIEF: ENSURING EFFECTIVE INTERNATIONAL LEGAL PROTECTION 499–551 (The Hague: Martinus Nijhoff Publishers, 1996).

3. *See id.* at 1–3.

4. *See, e.g.,* Convention on the Elimination of All Forms of Discrimination Against Women, *adopted* Dec. 18, 1979, G.A. Res. 34/180, U.N. GAOR, 34th Sess., Supp. No. 46, at 193, U.N. Doc. A/34/46 (1979), 1249 U.N.T.S. 13 [hereinafter CEAFDAW]; Convention on the Political Rights of Women, *adopted* Mar. 31, 1953, 193 U.N.T.S. 135, 27 U.S.T. 1909 (1953).

5. *See* Inter-American Convention on the Prevention, Punishment and Eradication of Violence against Women, *adopted* June 9, 1994, art. 4(i), 33 I.L.M. 1534, 1536 (1994) ("Convention of Belém do Pará") (every woman has "[t]he right of freedom to profess her religion and beliefs within the law").

6. *See, e.g.,* U.N. CHARTER art. 55(c); International Covenant on Civil and Political Rights, *adopted* Dec. 16, 1966, art. 2(1), G.A. Res. 2200 (XXI), U.N. GAOR, 21st Sess., Supp. No. 16, at 52, U.N. Doc. A/6316, 999 U.N.T.S. 171, 6 I.L.M. 368 (1967) [hereinafter ICCPR].

7. *See* ICCPR, *supra* note 6, art. 3.

8. But article 4(1) of the Declaration on the Elimination of Violence against Women does, however, include a reference to religion. *See* Declaration on the Elimination of Violence Against Women, *adopted* Dec. 20, 1993, art. 4(1) G.A. Res. 48/104, U.N. GAOR, 48th Sess., 85th plen. mtg., Supp. No. 49, at 217, U.N. Doc. A/48/49 (1993), 33 I.L.M. 1049 (1994) ("States should condemn violence against women and should not invoke any . . . religious consideration to avoid their obligations with respect to its elimination").

9. *See* CEAFDAW, *supra* note 4.

10. *See* CEAFDAW, *supra* note 4, art. 1.

11. Vienna Declaration and Programme of Action: adopted by The World Conference on Human Rights, *adopted* June 25, 1993, part II, para. 22, U.N. Doc. A/CONF. 157/23, 32 I.L.M. 1661 (1993).

12. *Id.* at part II, para. 38.

13. Commission on Human Rights Resolution 1998/18, para. 4(c), 54th Sess., Agenda Item 18, UN Doc. E/CN.4/1988/L.34 (1998).

14. *Id.* at para. 7.

15. *See, e.g.,* U.N. GAOR, 52d Sess., Agenda Item 112(b), para. 31(a)(i), U.N. Doc. A/52/477 (1997) (Afghanistan); Commission on Human Rights, 53d Sess., Item 19 of the Provisional Agenda, para. 20(b)(i), U.N. Doc. E/CN.4/1997/91 (1996) (Afghanistan and Bangladesh).

16. *See* Commission on Human Rights, 54th Sess., Agenda Item 18, para. 110, UN Doc. E/CN.4/1998/6 (1998).

17. *See* U.N. GAOR, 52d Sess., Agenda Item 112(b), para. 89, UN Doc. A/52/477 (1997).

18. *See* Commission on Human Rights, 54th Sess., Agenda Item 18, para. 119, U.N. Doc. E/CN.4/1998/6 (proposal made pursuant to Commission on Human Rights Resolution 1997/43 of April 11, 1997, 53d Sess., 57th mtg., para. 4, U.N. Doc. E/CN.4/1997/50).

19. Commission on Human Rights, 54th Sess., Agenda Item 18, para. 119, U.N. Doc. E/CN.4/1998/6 (1998).

20. FREEDOM OF RELIGION AND BELIEF: A WORLD REPORT 13 (Kevin Boyle & Juliet Sheen, eds.) (London/New York: Routledge, 1997).

21. *See* TAHZIB, *supra* note 2, at 63–421.

22. American Declaration of the Rights and Duties of Man, art. III, Final Act of the Ninth International Conference of American States, Resolution XXX (Bogata, Mar. 30 - May 2, 1948), *reprinted in* THE INTERNATIONAL CONFERENCES OF AMERICAN STATES, SECOND SUPPLEMENT: 1942–1954, at 263, 264 (United States: Pan American Union, 1958).

23. Universal Declaration of Human Rights, *adopted* Dec. 10, 1948, art. 18, G.A. Res. 217A (III), U.N. GAOR, 3d Sess., pt. 1, 183d plen. mtg., at 71, U.N. Doc. A/810 (1948) [hereinafter Universal Declaration]; Convention for the Protection of Human Rights and Fundamental Freedoms, *opened for signature* Nov. 4, 1950, art. 9(1), 213 U.N.T.S. 222, 230 (1950) [hereinafter European Convention].

24. American Convention on Human Rights, *signed* Nov. 22, 1969, art. 12(1), 1144 U.N.T.S. 123, 128 (Spanish), 148 (English), 9 I.L.M. 673, 679 (1970) [hereinafter American Convention].

25. ICCPR, *supra* note 6, art 18(1); *see also* Declaration on the Elimination of All Forms of Intolerance and of Discrimination Based on Religion or Belief, *adopted* Nov. 25, 1981, art. 1(1), G.A. Res. 36/55, U.N. GAOR, 36th Sess., Supp. No. 51, at 171, U.N. Doc. A/36/51 (1981), 25 I.L.M. 205 (1982).

26. *See* ANN ELIZABETH MAYER, ISLAM AND HUMAN RIGHTS: TRADITION AND POLITICS 149–57 (Boulder, CO: Westview Press, 3d. ed., 1999).

27. *See id.*

28. *See, e.g.,* U.N. GAOR, 52d Sess., Agenda Item 112(b), paras. 66–76, UN Doc. A/52/477 (1997); Human Rights Committee, General Comments Adopted under Article 40, Paragraph 4, of the ICCPR: General Comment No. 22 (48) (art. 18), U.N. Doc. A/48/40 (Pt. I) 208, para. 5, at 208–209 (1993) [hereinafter General Comment on article 18 ICCPR]; TAHZIB, *supra* note 2, at 86–87, 167–68, 327.

29. General Comment on article 18 ICCPR, *supra* note 28, para. 3.

30. *See* ICCPR, *supra* note 6, art. 4(2); American Convention, *supra* note 24, art. 27(2).

31. ARCOT KRISHNASWAMI, STUDY OF DISCRIMINATION IN THE MATTER OF RELIGIOUS RIGHTS AND PRACTICES, at 16, U.N. Doc. E/CN.4/Sub.2/200/Rev.1, U.N. Sales No. 60.XIV.2 (1960).

32. *See* ICCPR, *supra* note 6, art. 18(2); TAHZIB, *supra* note 2, at 325–27.

33. General Comment on article 18 ICCPR, *supra* note 28, para. 5.

34. TAHZIB, *supra* note 2, at 326–27.

35. *See* U.N. GAOR, 51st Sess., Agenda Item 110(b), para. 105, U.N. Doc. A/51/542/Add.2, (1996) (Sudan); Commission on Human Rights, 52d Sess., Item 18 of Provisional Agenda, para. 66, U.N. Doc. E/CN.4/1996/95/Add.1 (1996) (Pakistan).

36. Commission on Human Rights, 54th Sess., Agenda Item 18, para. 62(e), U.N. Doc. E/CN.4/1998/6 (1998) (Iraq).

37. *See, e.g.,* Universal Declaration, *supra* note 23, art. 18; ICCPR, *supra* note 6, art. 18(1). For a similar definition, see, e.g., European Convention, *supra* note 23, art. 9(1). For less elaborate definitions, see, e.g., American Declaration of the Rights and Duties of Man, *supra* note 22, art. III; American Convention, *supra* note 24, art. 12(1); Organization of African Unity: Banjul Charter on Human and Peoples' Rights, *adopted* Jun. 27, 1981, art. 8, 21 I.L.M. 59, 60 (1982).

38. General Comment on article 18 ICCPR, *supra* note 28, para. 4 (emphasis supplied).

39. For a comprehensive list of examples, see Declaration on the Elimination of All Forms of Intolerance and of Discrimination Based on Religion or Belief, *supra* note 25, art. 6.

40. Roger S. Clark, *The United Nations and Religious Freedom,* 11 N.Y.U. J. INT'L L. & POL. 197, 215 (1978).

41. General Comment on Article 18 ICCPR, *supra* note 28, para. 8.

42. In developing the doctrine of the margin of appreciation, the European Court of Human Rights adopted the view that, in principle, the national or local authorities are in a better position to assess the situation and to determine the necessity of certain restrictions than an international court. *See* Angela Thompson, *International Protection of Women's Rights: An Analysis of Open Door Counselling Ltd. and Dublin Well Woman Centre v. Ireland,* 12 B.U. INT'L L.J. 371, 379–80, 396–400 (1994).

43. Principle 1.1 of the Johannesburg Principles on National Security, Freedom of Expression and Access to Information, adopted on 1 October 1995 by a group of experts in international law, national security, and human rights convened by Article 19, the International Centre Against Censorship, in collaboration with the Centre for Applied Legal Studies of the University of the Witwatersrand, Commission on Human Rights, 52d Sess., Item 8 of Provisional Agenda, Annex, UN Doc. E/CN.4/1996/39 (1996).

44. David Little, *Studying "Religious Human Rights": Methodological Foundations, in* RELIGIOUS HUMAN RIGHTS IN GLOBAL PERSPECTIVE: LEGAL PERSPECTIVES 45, 60 (Johan D. van der Vyver & John Witte, Jr., eds.) (The Hague: Martinus Nijhoff Publishers, 1996).

45. General Comment on Article 18 ICCPR, *supra* note 28, para. 8.

46. Principle 33 of the Siracusa Principles on the Limitation and Derogation Provisions in the International Covenant on Civil and Political Rights, Commission on Human Rights, 41st Sess., Annex, Item 18 of Provisional Agenda, at 5, UN Doc. E/CN.4/1985/4 (1984) [hereinafter Siracusa Principles].

47. *Id.* at 4, principle 22.

48. K.J. Partsch, *Freedom of Conscience and Expression, and Political Freedoms, in* THE INTERNATIONAL BILL OF RIGHTS: THE COVENANT ON CIVIL AND POLITICAL RIGHTS 209, 212–13 (Louis Henkin, ed.) (New York: Columbia University Press, 1981).

49. Siracusa Principles, *supra* note 46, at 4, principle 25.

50. General Comment on article 18 ICCPR, *supra* note 28, para. 8; *see also* Siracusa Principles, *supra* note 46, at 5, principles 27, 28.

51. Siracusa Principles, *supra* note 46, at 5, principle 36.

52. General Comment on article 18 ICCPR, *supra* note 28, para. 8.

53. *See, e.g.,* Commission on Human Rights, 54th Sess., Agenda Item 18, para. 60(a), U.N. Doc. E/CN.4/1998/6 (1998) (Afghanistan); Commission on Human Rights, 51st Sess., Item 22 of the Provisional Agenda, para. 27, at 10, U.N. Doc. E/CN.4/1995/91 (1994) (Algeria).

54. U.N. GAOR, 51st Sess., Agenda Item 110(b), para. 140, U.N. Doc. A/51/542/Add.2 (1996) (Sudan). *See also* Commission on Human Rights, 52d Sess., Item 18 of Provisional Agenda, para. 97, U.N. Doc. E/CN.4/1996/95/Add.2 (1996) (Islamic Republic of Iran).

55. General Comment on Article 18 ICCPR, *supra* note 28, para. 8.

56. *Id.*

Chapter 12

The Potential of International Law to Combat Discrimination against Girls in Education

Geraldine Van Bueren and Deirdre Fottrell[1]

I. INTRODUCTION

This chapter focuses particularly on a girl's right to education, because denial of, or interference with, this right facilitates the exclusion of girls from society, severely restricts their autonomy, and significantly contributes to the subordination of women later in life.

A girl's right to free quality primary education is so fundamental to the protection of her human rights that there is no provision for derogation from this right under the United Nations Convention on the Rights of the Child (Convention).[2] There are 191 state parties to the Convention, making it the most widely ratified human rights treaty.[3] Under the Convention, all children are entitled to free primary education, while secondary and higher education should be made accessible to all by the progressive introduction of free education.[4]

Despite these guarantees to free quality education, many children are denied education throughout the world as a result of the interplay between a range of socioeconomic and cultural factors, including religion. There is disagreement among scholars as to whether "religious"-based discrimination against girls (and women) is appropriately classified as "religion": some argue that it is rooted in theology;[5] some suggest that religion is often abused or used as a cover for cultural, economic, political, or other deeply rooted discrimination against girls;[6] and some believe that religion may be a source of empowerment and learning for women, and if appropriately understood, is not discriminatory;[7] and some hold more than one of these positions. This disagreement as to whether such discrimination is rooted in religion per se or is an abuse of religion, particularly in the context of what others in this volume have referred to as "fundamentalist," is not one that we need to answer in this context. However, these disagreements should be borne in mind through the rest of this chapter.

The potential exists in international law to advance the rights of girls to education and equality, even in the face of what might appear to be religious opposition as manifested in discriminatory domestic legislation or policies. A survey of existing norms supports the view that a state that fails to implement fully girls' right to education is failing to fulfill its obligations under international human rights law.[8] Every child's right to education is clearly provided for in unambiguous terms in the Convention. Moreover, international human rights law on the education of children is quite clear; it does not permit a state to rely on domestic religious law to excuse breaches of its international human rights obligations.[9]

In addition, these legal provisions ought to be implemented in concert with the changes called for by popular participation in accordance with international human rights law. Community and localized solutions are also necessary to advance girls' educational prospects. This is borne out by a number of United Nations Children's Fund (UNICEF) and state-sponsored schemes in South Asia and Africa put into effect following the World Conference on Education For All (EFA).[10]

II. HOW DOES INTERNATIONAL HUMAN RIGHTS LAW PROTECT A GIRL'S RIGHT TO EDUCATION?

Within the framework of international law, the right to education for children has focused on three issues: first, access to education, which at least in terms of primary education should be freely available to all children; second, the content and quality of education, which includes the obligation of states to respect the religious and philosophical convictions of parents; and third, the aims of education, which include the development of the child's personality.[11]

The right to education is found in article 26 of the Universal Declaration of Human Rights (Universal Declaration),[12] and this is elaborated upon by article 13 of the International Covenant on Economic, Social and Cultural Rights (ICESCR).[13] These provisions guarantee the child's right to quality education and establish that primary education should be free and compulsory. In addition, education must "be directed to the full development of the human personality and the sense of its dignity. . . ."[14] State parties to the ICESCR are obliged to undertake progressive implementation of these rights.

A. Convention on the Rights of the Child

The educational rights of children, however, were advanced considerably by the Convention, which "reconstruct[ed] the right of education as belonging to the child as well as to the parent."[15] The right to education is addressed in articles 28 and 29 of the Convention. Article 28 requires states to take a number of specific steps to guarantee the right to education, including: making primary education compulsory and free to all; developing different forms of secondary education (taking appropriate measures for, inter alia, financial assistance); and making higher education accessible to all on the basis of capacity.[16] In addition, state parties have an obligation to cooperate internationally toward the elimination of "ignorance and illiteracy," and particular account is to be taken of the needs of developing countries.[17]

Article 29 is more concerned with the content of the curriculum and stipulates that the aims of education should be, inter alia: the development of the child's personality, and his or her mental and physical abilities, to their fullest potential; the development of respect for human rights and the principles enshrined in the United Nations Charter; the development of respect for his or her parents and cultural identity; and preparation of the child for life in a free society, in the spirit of understanding, peace, tolerance, equality of sexes, and friendship among all peoples.[18]

These provisions are enhanced and given greater impact when they are placed in the context of the Convention as a whole. As Thomas Hammarberg notes, four central principles underpin the Convention and must be read into all provisions: first, "children's survival, protection, and development must be given priority"; second, "[t]he best interests of children should be a primary consideration whenever decisions are taken that affect them"; third, "their views should be heard and given due weight" in accordance with their evolving capacities; and, finally, "these principles apply to all children without discrimination of any kind."[19]

At different stages in their development these principles will assume greater importance for the child, but they provide a backdrop to all of the rights guaranteed in the Convention, and states are expected to reflect these values in their legislative and administrative polices.

B. Article 14 of the Convention

In addition, the Convention protects the child's right to freedom of thought, conscience, and religion in article 14.[20] This is significant in the context of this chapter, because this freedom of religion may be beneficial to girls in many ways. However, religion when distorted for political reasons is likely to have a negative impact on the girl child's education in two ways. First, there may be an outright denial or severe restriction of education; and second, an abuse of religions can influence the content of the curriculum to such a degree that the goals of education enshrined in the Convention are not met.[21]

Under Article 14(2), states are required to respect the rights of parents to "provide guidance and direction" to the child in their exercising of this right to freedom of religion. Several states—Roman Catholic and Islamic—have reserved to the Convention for a variety of reasons, and some to article 14 in particular. For example, a number of Islamic states have either entered reservations to specific articles including article 14, or have entered broad reservations to the Convention as a whole on the basis of Islamic law (which have the same effect as targeting article 14), and the Holy See and Poland have also entered a reservation to article 14.[22] These reservations reflect the desire to limit any possibility of the child having the freedom to adopt a religion of the child's choice, or to change religion.

The Convention prohibits reservations that are incompatible with the object and purpose of the Convention.[23] The Committee on the Rights of the Child (Committee), the interpretative body of the Convention, has taken issue with a number of states as to the reservations entered, but it remains to be seen whether those states will heed the Committee's comments.[24] It is arguable that the Committee ought to follow the lead of the Human Rights Committee, the interpretative body of the International Covenant on Civil and Political Rights (ICCPR), and take a firmer stand on reservations.[25] Under the ICCPR, children do have the right to change or adopt a religion.[26]

Parental wishes informed by religious considerations are protected under international human rights law, but they cannot be used to override the child's right of access to education. Article 26(3) of the Universal Declaration may be understood to provide parents with a right to choose the kind of education that is to be given to their children. This provision arguably reflected the common assumption that the interests of the child and those of the parents would always coincide. This provision, however, was not imported into the ICCPR or the Convention, as it would appear to run counter to the child's right to participate in all decisions that affect his or her future.

Article 18 (4) of the ICCPR obliges states to respect parental preferences in the matter of religious and moral education, but this obligation does not extend to other aspects of the curriculum.[27] The Human Rights Committee has confirmed that as long as a state is not indoctrinating children, but is providing information in a neutral and factual manner, the state will be in compliance with its international obligations.[28]

The primacy given to education under the Convention reflects the viewpoint that education is a precondition for the exercise of many other human rights and the deprivation of this right will have detrimental short- and long-term effects for both the child and the society. The most recent international instrument drafted by the Commonwealth, the draft Commonwealth Agenda for Action for Children, Asian chapter, also reflects this concern.[29]

C. Girls' Right to Education

For girls, discriminatory interference with education rights can limit their capacity, both as children and later, as adults, to enjoy and exercise other rights fully.[30] For example, the right to freedom of expression cannot be fully realized without literacy. For the society, a range of negative consequences can be traced to the lack of education for girls. Women who are educated and literate are less likely to marry young, their fertility rates are lower, their health and that of their children are better, and their children are more likely to be educated. Although education has long been central to the human rights agenda, it has recently been prioritized as a necessity by developmental economists, particularly as studies clearly demonstrate that a state's gross national product increases as resources and accessibility of education increase. The uneducated girl has been reconceptualized as a "largely untapped human resource."[31]

However, the recognition of the extent of the marginalization of, insensitivity to, and outright discrimination against girls as a phenomenon in education that has reached crisis levels across continents has only come about in the last decade.[32] Although the Convention does not make any reference to the particular importance of education for girls in its education-specific provisions, its approach to nondiscrimination and its holistic approach to children's rights has served as a catalyst for action to improve the rights of girls, including in education.[33] The Committee also recognized the threat posed to the rights of girls arising from their continued marginalization in education, and held a thematic discussion at its Seventh Session, which ultimately led to a contribution to the Fourth World Conference on Women, held in Beijing, in 1995.[34]

III. WHY ARE GIRLS DENIED THEIR RIGHT TO EDUCATION AND WHAT ROLE DO RELIGIOUS CONSIDERATIONS PLAY?

Although the causes of gender disparities in education are complex and sometimes regionally specific, Frank Dall has identified a number of common contributing factors and causes.[35] First, "persistent rural and urban poverty" is central to whether the girl has access to education. Often, the importance of the girl's labor to the survival of the household means that the cost of sending her to school is prohibitive. This factor was considered central at EFA, and suggested solutions included more appropriate curriculum content and new delivery systems.[36] Several states in conjunction with UNICEF have initiated programs that make education more gender-sensitive, more accessible, and more relevant to the girl's needs.[37] It is also possible that choosing to assign household tasks to the girl, rather than sending her to school, is based on religious and cultural factors.

Second, geographical factors are important. For example, the location of the school at a long distance from the home can discourage attendance because of parental concerns for the physical safety of the girl, and also because the length of time traveling to and from school will significantly interfere with the girl's household duties. The South East Asian participants drafting the Commonwealth Agenda for Action called for free transportation to and from school.[38]

A recent example is the Bangladesh Rural Advancement Committee (BRAC) program, which is a community-based effort aimed at dealing with both the poverty and geographical factors.[39] It involves parents, and the vast majority of its pupils are girls who have either dropped out of schooling or had no education at all.[40] Scholarships have also been provided in Bangladesh for the education of girls in rural areas, and offer a constructive approach in seeking to overcome the stereotyping of women.

Third, there is another range of factors that can make school a negative experience or affect parental decisions to send children to school. These include mixed-sex classes, exclusively male teachers, insensitivity, ignorance of girls' learning needs in the curriculum, and inflexible schedules that interfere with household duties.[41] Negative attitudes toward mixed-sex classes and male teachers, and attitudes concerning appropriate household duties for girls may well be informed by religious and cultural norms. Many of these factors can be mitigated or overcome through creativity and determination, particularly by promoting and exploring other types of informal education.[42]

Fourth, cultural constraints also clearly affect education. These are likely to have a religious dimension and may be rooted in a conceptualization of the role and function of a woman as residing solely in the private sphere. For example, extreme Islamists have set schools on fire, attacked teachers, and destroyed teaching materials because educational activities "alienate women from their 'proper' social roles and Islamic life-style."[43] Also, the girl is often regarded as an economic burden for the family,[44] and since her future is understood to be in the private sphere, there is a reluctance to educate her for the benefit of others, such as her future family. In 1995, the Committee, in a thematic discussion on the girl, noted that "the situation of the girl child was of particular concern in rural or remote areas under the strong influence of community and religious leaders and aggravated by the persistence of harmful traditions and beliefs."[45]

Where these practices are rooted in the law, they are incompatible with the provisions of the Convention. Where they reflect the parents' wishes, the states' obligations under the Convention are to promote the child as a rights holder, even if this challenges the traditional construction of girls in many communities. Governments may find that the observations of the Committee could serve as a useful tool for bolstering their attempts to change conservative culture at a local level.

IV. CONCLUSION

The education of the girl child cannot be divorced from the broader sociopolitical context. Where women are undervalued and discriminated against for whatever reason, the status of girls is correspondingly low. The Committee observed in 1996 that "[t]here was a need to ensure that a woman's life cycle would not become a vicious cycle, where the evolution from childhood to adulthood would be blighted by fatalism and a sense of inferiority. Only through the active involvement of girls, who are at the root of the life cycle, would it be possible to initiate a movement for change and betterment . . . of women."[46] One of the most pernicious consequences of denying girls their rights to education is the fact that, as women, they are thus hampered and limited in their participation in the debate about their status in society.

The recent joint call for action by nongovernmental organizations and governments in South East Asia on girls' education[47] and the appointment of a United Nations Special Rapporteur on Education should help focus states' attention on the practical measures necessary to implement equal access by girls to education. In addition, the potential of intergovernmental loan agreements needs to be urgently explored as a means of reducing the obstacles to girls' education. H. G. Wells may have been guilty of an overstatement when he wrote that, "[h]uman history becomes more and more a race between education and catastrophe,"[48] but if quality education is recognized as a provider of choices and an opportunity to climb out of poverty, then many girls have been left standing at the starting line.

NOTES

1. The authors would like to thank M. Siraj Sait for his help and assistance in researching this chapter.

2. *See* Convention on the Rights of the Child, *adopted* Nov. 20, 1989, G.A. Res. 44/25, U.N. GAOR, 44th Sess., Supp. No. 49, at 166, 170, arts. 28, 29 U.N. Doc. A/44/49 (1989), 28 I.L.M. 1448, 1467 (1989), *corrected at* 29 I.L.M. 1340 (1990)[hereinafter Convention]. The Convention makes no reference to derogations in circumstances of war or public emergency, and thus we would argue that the Convention allows for no derogations. On the Convention generally, see GERALDINE VAN BUEREN, THE INTERNATIONAL LAW ON THE RIGHTS OF THE CHILD (Dordrecht/Boston/London: Martinus Nijhoff, 1995).

3. *See* MULTILATERAL TREATIES DEPOSITED WITH THE SECRETARY-GENERAL AS OF 31 DECEMBER 1997, at 208, U.N. Doc. ST/LEG/SER.E/16, U.N. Sales No. E.98.V2 (1998) [hereinafter MULTILATERAL TREATIES].

4. *See* VAN BUEREN, *supra* note 2, at 232–62.

5. *See, e.g.,* Frances Kissling, *Roman Catholic Fundamentalism: What's Sex (and Power) Got To Do With It?,* in this volume.

6. *See, e.g.,* Marie-Aimée Hélie-Lucas, *What is Your Tribe?: Women's Struggles and the Construction of Muslimness,* in this volume (arguing that religious fundamentalisms are political movements, not religious movements).

7. *See, e.g.,* Section VII of this volume: Religious Challenges to Religious Fundamentalisms.

8. *See* VAN BUEREN, *supra* note 2, at 245–47.

9. *See also* Donna J. Sullivan, *Gender Equality and Religious Freedom: Toward a Framework for Conflict Resolution,* 24 N.Y.U. J. INT'L L. & POL. 795, 807 (1992).

10. The World Conference on Education For All (EFA) was organized by UNICEF and took place in Jomtien, Thailand, in 1990, and produced a Declaration and Framework for Action. *See* WORLD DECLARATION ON EDUCATION FOR ALL AND FRAMEWORK FOR ACTION TO MEET BASIC LEARNING NEEDS EDUCATION (New York, NY: The Inter-Agency Commission, 1990) [hereinafter EFA DECLARATION]; *see generally* MAGGIE BLACK, CHILDREN FIRST: THE STORY OF UNICEF, PAST AND PRESENT 215–44 (Oxford: Oxford University Press, 1996).

11. The right to education under international laws "extends to both adults and children, [however,] the principle of compulsory education is only applicable to children. It is a principle which implies that it is in the best interests of the child that children are not entitled to refuse education below a specific level. *See* VAN BUEREN, *supra* note 2, at 237.

12. *See* Universal Declaration of Human Rights, *adopted* Dec. 10, 1948, G.A. Res. 217A (III), U.N. GAOR, 3d Sess., pt. 1, 183d plen. mtg., at 76, art. 26, U.N. Doc. A/810 (1948) [hereinafter Universal Declaration].

13. *See* International Covenant on Economic, Social and Cultural Rights, *adopted* Dec. 16, 1966, G.A. Res. 2200 (XXI), U.N. GAOR, 21st Sess., Supp. No. 16, at 51, art. 13, U.N. Doc. A/6316, 993 U.N.T.S. 3, 8, 6 I.L.M. 360, 364 (1967) [hereinafter ICESCR].

14. ICESCR, *supra* note 13, at 51, art. 13(1), 6 I.L.M. at 364.

15. VAN BUEREN, *supra* note 2, at 256.

16. Convention, *supra* note 2, at 170, art. 28(1), 28 I.L.M. at 1467.

17. Convention, *supra* note 2, at 170, art. 28(3), 28 I.L.M. at 1467.

18. The provisions of the Convention have been supplemented and enhanced by the EFA DECLARATION, *see supra* note 10, and the education-related provisions of the World Declaration on the Survival, Protection and Development of Children [World Declaration] & Plan of Action for Implementing the World Declaration adopted at the 1990 World Summit for Children, *available in* INTERNATIONAL DOCUMENTS ON CHILDREN 410, 414 (Geraldine Van Bueren, ed.) (The Hague/Boston/London: Martinus Nijhoff Publishers, 2d ed., 1998).

19. *See* Thomas Hammarberg, *Foreword, in* IMPLEMENTING THE CONVENTION ON THE RIGHTS OF THE CHILD: RESOURCE MOBILIZATION IN LOW-INCOME COUNTRIES, at V (James R. Himes, ed.) (The Hague/London/Boston: Martinus Nijhoff Publishers, 1995) [hereinafter IMPLEMENTING THE CONVENTION].

20. *See* Convention, *supra* note 2, at 168, art. 14, 28 I.L.M. at 1462.

21. *See* VAN BUEREN, *supra* note 2, at 159–62.

22. *See* MULTILATERAL TREATIES, *supra* note 3, at 208–26. Algeria, Bangladesh, Brunei Darussalam, Indonesia, Iraq, Jordan, Malaysia, Maldives, Morocco, Syria, United Arab Emirates have entered specific reservations to article 14. Afghanistan, Egypt, Iran, Kuwait, Mauritania, Saudi Arabia have all entered general reservations based on Islamic law. Poland's reservation to article 14 is on the basis of "Polish customs and traditions." *See id.* at 217. *See generally* William A. Schabas, *Reservations to the Convention on the Rights of the Child,* 18 HUM. RTS. Q. 472 (1996); Lawrence J. LeBlanc, *Reservations to the Convention on the Rights of the Child: A Macroscopic View of State Practice,* 4 INT'L J. CHILDREN'S RTS. 357 (1996).

23. *See* Convention, *supra* note 2, art. 51(2).

24. *See, e.g.,* Concluding Comments on the Reports of Indonesia and Pakistan, U.N. GAOR, 51st Sess., Supp. No. 41, at 13, para. 19, 14, para. 32, U.N. Doc A/51/41 (1996).

25. *See* General Comment on issues relating to reservations made upon ratification or accession to the Covenant or the Optional Protocols therein, or in relation to declarations under article 41 of the Covenant, U.N. Doc. CCPR/C/21/Rev. 1/Add. 6 (1994); *see also* Vienna Declaration and Programme of Action: adopted by The World Conference on Human Rights, *adopted* June 25, 1993, U.N. Doc. A/CONF. 157/23, II., para. 5, at 14, II, para. 46, at 20, 32 I.L.M. 1661, 1674, 1680 (1993).

26. *See* International Covenant on Civil and Political Rights, *adopted* Dec. 16, 1966, G.A. Res. 2200 (XXI), U.N. GAOR, 21st Sess., Supp. No. 16, at 52, art. 18, U.N. Doc. A/6316, 999 U.N.T.S. 171, 6 I.L.M. 368 (1967) [hereinafter ICCPR]; VAN BUEREN, *supra* note 2, at 159.

27. VAN BUEREN, *supra* note 2, at 241.

28. *See* Hartikainen, et al. v. Finland, Communication No. 40/1978, *adopted* 9 April 1981 (12th Sess.), Annual Report of the Committee to the General Assembly through the Economic and Social Council, under Article 45 of Covenant and Article 6 of the Optional Protocol, Doc. A/36/40 (initially distributed as Official Records of General Assembly, 36th Sess., Supp. 40 (A/36/40)) 29 Sept. 1981, *in* II YEARBOOK OF THE HUMAN RIGHTS COMMITTEE, 1981–1982, at 313, 315 CCPR/3/Add. 1 (1989) (Annex XV); *see also* Kjeldsen, et al. v. Denmark, 1 Eur. Ct. H.R. 711, para. 53, at 731 (1976).

29. Commonwealth Agenda for Action for Children, drafted in Dhaka, Bangladesh, May 1998. Similarly, the marginalized position of the girl in South Asia led to the South Asian Area Regional Co-operation (SAARC) at the fifth regional summit in 1990 to declare a Decade of Action for the Girl Child from 1991–2000.

30. Despite widespread progress in access to education over the last three decades in developing states, gender gaps in education continue to be alarmingly high, particularly after the first three years of primary schooling, and most markedly in the regions of sub-Saharan Africa, South Asia, and the Middle East. *See* Frank P. Dall, *Children's Right to Education: Reaching the Universal, in* IMPLEMENTING THE CONVENTION, *supra* note 19, at 143, 155–58.

31. *Id.* at 147.

32. *See* U.N. Doc CRC/C/38, 8th Sess., para. 289, at 50 (Feb. 20, 1995).

33. For example, less than a year after the Convention was adopted, the EFA DECLARATION was made. *See* note 10 *supra*.

34. *See* U.N. Doc CRC/C/38, *supra* note 32, at 47, para. 275.

35. *See* Dall, *supra* note 30, at 157.

36. *See* EFA DECLARATION, *supra* note 10, at arts. 3(4), 5.

37. *See* LYDIA NYATI-RAMAHOBO, THE GIRL CHILD IN BOTSWANA: EDUCATIONAL CONSTRAINTS AND PROSPECTS (Gaborone, Botswana: UNICEF, 1992); THE COMMUNITY SCHOOLS PROJECT: MANUAL FOR TEACHERS AND SUPERVISORS (Egypt: UNICEF, 1992).

38. *See* Commonwealth Agenda for Action for Children, *supra* note 29.

39. *See* Dall, *supra* note 30, 163–65.

40. *See id.*

41. *See* EFA DECLARATION, *supra* note 10, at paras. 21 & 22.

42. *See* Dall, *supra* note 30, at 158.

43. *See* Amnesty International, *Bangladesh: Fundamental Rights of Women violated with virtual impunity,* ASA, Sept. 13, 1994, at 9–12.

44. *See* Nawal El Saadawi, *Women and Islam, in* THE NAWAL EL SAADAWI READER 73, 88 (London/New York: Zed Books, 1997).

45. *See* U.N. Doc. CRC/C/38, *supra* note 32, para. 287, at 49.

46. Report of the Committee on the Rights of the Child, U.N. GAOR, 51st Sess., Supp. No. 41, U.N. Doc. A/51/41, para. 1103, at 154 (1996).

47. *See* Commonwealth Agenda for Action for Children, *supra* note 29.

48. H.G. WELLS, THE OUTLINE OF HISTORY: BEING A PLAIN HISTORY OF LIFE AND MANKIND, Vol. 2, 594 (New York: The Macmillan Company, 1921).

IV

Religious Fundamentalism and National Laws

Chapter 13

The Two Faces of Secularism and Women's Rights in India

Ratna Kapur

I. INTRODUCTION

In this chapter[1] I examine several concepts that are important to understanding the impact that the rise of the Religious Right has had on women's human rights in contemporary India. In particular, I discuss the ways in which equality and secularism, the cornerstones of a liberal democratic state, have been deployed by the Hindu Right, and to some extent, validated by the Indian Supreme Court. I also address how the Hindu Right's agenda for women is related to its secular project.

The Hindu Right is a nationalist and right wing political movement devoted to creating a Hindu state. It includes: the Bharatiya Janata Party (BJP), the political arm of the Hindu Right, which is currently in power at the national level; the Rashtriya Swayam Sevak, the main ideological component of the Hindu Right; and the Vishwa Hindu Parishad, the expositors and promoters of the Hindu Right's religious doctrine. Other parties include the militant and virulently anti-Muslim *Shiv Sena*. These organizations collectively promote the ideology of Hindutva—an ideology that seeks to establish a Hindu state in India.

II. SECULARISM

Secularism has long been the site of political and constitutional struggle and controversy in India. The struggle to secure its place in the India polity has had many enemies. Increasingly, the enemies of secularism are waging their war not in opposition to secularism, but in and through it.

"[S]ecularism has become the subject of intensive political contestation in which right wing religious and fundamentalist forces endeavor to claim the secularist terrain as their own. In India, the Hindu Right . . . increasingly has staked out its own claim, arguing that it alone is committed to upholding secularism. Indeed, secularism has become a central and powerful weapon in the Hindu Right's quest for discursive and political power."[2]

By way of background, it is important to recognize that in India secularism has never been based on the idea of the separation of religion from the state.[3] Since gaining independence, almost all discussions of secularism have been based on the idea of *sarva dharma sambhava*—the equal respect of all religions. This approach to secularism "does not require a wall of separation between religion and politics, but rather, an equal respect of all religions within both the public and private spheres."[4] This concept was propounded by Mahatma Gandhi[5] and has been the governing model of secularism over the past 50 years.

The meaning to be given to this concept of secularism will depend in large part on the meaning given to equality. If equality is understood in a formal sense—treating likes alike—then secularism will insist on treating India's various religious communities alike. By contrast, if equality is understood in a more substantive sense—addressing disadvantage—then secularism will allow for an accommodation of difference between religious groups and the protection of the rights of religious minorities.

Indian secularism has, to a large extent, been based on a more substantive approach to the principle of equal respect and toleration of all religions, which has allowed for the protection of religious minority rights. The Hindu Right has increasingly been trying to cast itself as the true inheritors of India's secular tradition, that is, as promoters of positive or genuine secularism. But, contrary to the dominant understanding of secularism in India, the Hindu Right is committed to a vision of secularism based on a formal approach to equality. In its vision, secularism requires that all religious communities be treated the same. Any protection of the rights of religious minorities is cast as "appeasement," and a violation of the "true spirit" of secularism. Religious minorities are to be treated the *same* as the majority. Under this formal approach to equality, the majority becomes the norm against which all others are to be judged, and secularism ceases to be about the protection of the rights of religious minorities, but rather about the assimilation of minorities.

In the hands of the Hindu Right, secularism is twisted almost beyond recognition. For example, the principle of equal respect and toleration of all religions is used to establish the supremacy of Hinduism. According to the logic of the Hindu Right, since secularism is about toleration, and only Hinduism is tolerant (unlike Islam and Christianity, that proselytize), then only Hinduism is truly secular. The principle of protecting minorities virtually disappears. The various laws through which these minority rights have been protected are attacked as "special treatment" and as a violation of the constitutional mandate of equal treatment. Within this vision of the Hindu Right, secularism comes to be equated with a Hindu state, where religious minorities must be treated the same as the Hindu majority. Religious minorities are thus to be effectively assimilated into the Hindu majority. It is a vision in which there is no respect, no toleration, and no protection of religious minorities, and it is the antithesis of Indian secularism.

III. THE SUPREME COURT'S SEAL OF APPROVAL

Recent decisions of the Supreme Court involving the Hindu Right and the meaning of secularism in India reveal the inconsistent record of the Supreme Court and its recent failings in protecting against the erosion of India's secular foundation.

The 1994 *Bommai* decision involved a challenge to the declaration of Presidential rule in four states following the destruction of the Babri Masjid, a Muslim mosque, in Ayodhya by mobs of the Hindu Right.[6] The full constitutional bench of the Supreme Court upheld the validity of the declaration of Presidential rule. The "Court unanimously affirmed the importance of secularism to the Indian constitution, while emphasizing the distinctively Indian concept of secularism as the equal respect of all religions."[7] The decision not only contained statements about secularism— defining it as religious tolerance and equal treatment of all religious groups—but also a very strong condemnation of those political forces committed to undermining this constitutional ideal.

The *Bommai* decision recognized that the Hindu Right's strategy was an attack on the religious freedom of minorities and that it undermined secularism. *Bommai* represents a high-water mark in the Court's protection of secularism in recent years. It was a decision that came at a time when India was experiencing its most aggressive manifestation of communal politics. The mosque had been destroyed, communal riots had broken out around the country, and Presidential rule was declared in four states. The discourse of the Hindu Right was not sufficiently powerful to mask or to obscure the death and destruction that the forces of the Hindu Right had brought about.

But, a year later, in 1995, the Supreme Court delivered its opinion in the *Prabhoo* case, one of eleven cases that have come to be known as the *Hindutva* cases.[8] These cases represent a low-water mark in the Court's protection of secularism. In the *Hindutva* cases, "the election of Shiv Sena/BJP candidates in the December 1987 State elections in Maharastra was challenged on the grounds that the candidates had committed corrupt practices in violation of section 123 of the Representation of the People Act, 1951."[9] This section prohibits candidates from appealing to religion, race, caste, community, or language to further their chance of election, as well as prohibits candidates from promoting feelings of enmity between different classes of citizens on the grounds of religion, race, caste, community, or language.[10] Charges were brought against 12 members of the Hindu Right, including Bal Thackeray, the head of the militant *Shiv Sena,* and Manohar Joshi, Chief Minister of the State of Maharastra. Although the Court found several of the accused—most notably Thackeray—guilty of appealing to religion to gain votes, and promoting religious enmity and hatred, it also held that "Hindutva"—the ideological linchpin of the Hindu Right—simply represented "a way of life of people of the subcontinent."[11]

According to the Court in the *Prabhoo* case, Hindutva could not be equated with, or understood as, religious fundamentalism nor as a depiction of an attitude hostile to persons practicing other religions. Rather, Hindutva may be used "to promote secularism or to emphasize the way of life of the Indian people and the Indian culture or ethos or to criticize the policy of any political party as discriminatory or intolerant."[12] The Court held that Hindutva is neither an appeal to religion nor a promotion of religious hatred, and thus not a violation of the Act.

The Court's conclusion on the meaning of Hindutva is legally, historically, and politically insupportable. Even the most cursory glance at the historical and political context within which Hindutva has been given meaning would reveal that it is an appeal to religion and a promotion of religious enmity and hatred. The term had its modern-day genesis in the writings of the early leaders of the Hindu Right, who shaped its political and ideological agenda. The history of Hindutva demonstrates that the term has long been an appeal to religion. The writings of the ideological leaders described Hindutva as the mental state of the Hindu Race and the Hindu Nation—a race and a nation that were, at their very core, about religion.[13] It is the extent to which religion is the defining moment of the Hindu Race and Nation, which has made Hindutva, from its ideological inception, very much about the promotion of hatred and enmity toward religious minorities. Hindutva propagated the idea that the Christians' and Muslims' "holy land" lay elsewhere and that their presence in India made them a threat to the Indian Nation. This idea allowed the ideological leaders to construct Muslims and Christians as foreigners, aliens, and invaders.[14]

But, beyond this failure to recognize the highly communal nature of the contemporary deployment of "Hindutva" by the Hindu Right, the decision represents a further erosion of India's secular foundations. The Court held that the speeches in fact promoted secularism, stating that "[i]t cannot be doubted that a speech with a secular stance alleging discrimination against any particular religion and promising removal of the imbalance cannot be treated as an appeal on the ground of religion as its thrust is for promoting secularism."[15] In accepting, without any critical analysis, this discourse of secularism as secular, the Court has allowed a fundamentally nonsecular project (of Hindu supremacy and the assimilation of religious minorities) to be packaged, sold, and consumed as a secular one.[16]

Not surprisingly, the decision was immediately hailed as a victory by the Hindu Right. In its recent election manifesto, the BJP used the decision to continue to legitimize its model of secularism: "[e]very effort to characterize Hindutva as a sectarian or exclusive idea has failed as the people of India have repeatedly rejected such a view and the Supreme Court, too, finally endorsed the true meaning and content of Hindutva as being consistent with the true meaning and definition of secularism. In fact, Hindutva accepts as sacred all forms of belief and worship. . . . Hindutva means justice for all."[17]

IV. THE "NEW SECULARISM" AND WOMEN'S HUMAN RIGHTS

The Hindu Right has taken on board a broad range of women's rights issues, both within the majority community and the minority community.[18] "The Uniform Civil Code, violence against women, obscenity, women's education, and employment have all been taken up by women within the Hindu Right, and articulated as a part of the Hindutva agenda for women."[19] It is not always obvious how this women's rights agenda is related to its project of "new secularism." This obscuring is partly because the Hindu Right's official position on women is slathered over with the rhetoric of equality. One glance at their recent election manifesto substantiates this position. Their promises under their *nari shakti* (Empowerment of Women program) include: enactment of a Uniform Civil Code (UCC), based on progressive practices from all traditions, to ensure, inter alia, the right to adopt for women, the prohibition of polygamy, and the elimination of discriminatory divorce laws; enforcement of the principle of equal wages; enactment and enforcement of anti-sexual harassment codes; enactment of special laws against domestic violence against women; and prevention of the media's projection of women in any manner that demeans or hurts their dignity.[20] The BJP also seeks the immediate passage of a bill that would reserve for women 33 percent of the seats in all elected bodies, including the National Parliament, as well as to "[a]ctively promote the legal and economic rights of women which must be equal to those of men and not subject to the debilitating clauses of personal laws."[21]

But their election promises must be viewed in the context of their broader political program on cultural nationalism, the role of the family, and their targeting of the practices of the Muslim minority community. Indeed, the connection between women's rights and "new secularism" is most visible in relation to the rights of minority women. The Hindu Right has attempted to position itself as the guardians of the rights of women from minority religious communities as part of its more general project of undermining the very legitimacy of these communities. This strategy is seen no more clearly than in the controversies around the UCC and the reform of Muslim personal law. But, this is not the only area in which the Hindu Right's project of "new secularism" can be seen. The particular way in which it has taken issues, such as violence against women, on board is very much related to a Hindutva discourse that seeks to restore women to the position of respect they enjoyed as wives and mothers in the mythical, golden age of Hindu society.[22]

A. The Uniform Civil Code

The controversy over the UCC has exploded in the public arena since the mid-1980s. The storm erupted over the reform of Muslim personal law. The Hindu Right has time and again moved into these controversies as the true guardians of the rights of minority women. This move has been played out under the sinister shadow of Hindutva and the Hindu Rights' "new secularism" project. The Hindu Right constructs the Muslim community and its practices as discriminating against women, and hence barbaric and uncivilized. Part of the "civilizing" mission of the Hindu Right is to do away with these practices, and enact a UCC, based on the unstated, but very present practices of the Hindu majority community. The stench of majoritarianism is disguised in the sweet fragrance of secularism.

The Shah Bano controversy involved a divorced Muslim woman, seeking rights to maintenance from her lawyer husband under the Criminal Procedure Code, a secular code. She won her case in the Supreme Court, which held that the secular law would come into operation at the point where the personal law ceased to provide for the divorced woman.[23] However, the case triggered a storm of controversy and Muslim cries of their religion being in danger. The government subsequently enacted in 1986 the Muslim Women's (Protection of Rights on Divorce) Act (MWPRA),[24] which virtually robbed Shah Bano and the entire Muslim women's community of the limited rights to maintenance that they enjoyed under the secular law, and threw them back onto Muslim personal law.

It is within this context that the demand for a UCC reaches a crescendo. This demand means different things to different people. In the discourse of the Hindu Right, the demand for a UCC is all about secularism. The Hindu Right insists that *all* women must be treated the same, that is, that Muslim women must be treated the same as Hindu women. "Any recognition of difference is seen to constitute a violation of secularism. . . . [A]ny recognition of difference between women in different religious communities is seen to violate the constitutional guarantees of equality," which, the Hindu Right states, requires formal equal treatment.[25] The Hindu Right's approach is more about the discourse of secularism than the discourse of women's rights. The enactment of the MWPRA is regarded by the Hindu Right as just another example of pandering to minorities, and hence violating secularism. It is also seen as violating equality because Muslim women are being treated differently from Hindu women.

There have been several subsequent efforts to enact the Hindutva agenda on secularism and women's equality. In the case of *Sarla Mudgal,* the Supreme Court had to consider the legal implications when Hindu men, originally married under Hindu law, subsequently convert to Islam and enter into second marriages.[26] Specifically, the Court had to consider whether the second marriage could be solemnized, whether the first marriage still existed, and whether the husband would be guilty of the offense of bigamy. The Court held that the second marriage would not be valid without first dissolving the first marriage. One judge commented on the need to enact a UCC, stating that Hindus along with Sikhs, Buddhists, and Jains had forsaken their sentiments in the cause of national unity, but other communities had not.[27] This comment implies "that all other religious communities have been secularized, and that it is only the Muslims and Christians who are standing in the way of 'national unity and integration.'"[28]

The judge's language casts Muslims as the barbaric, uncivilized Other, a rhetoric that is disturbingly similar to that of the Hindu Right. The view expressed is that "all religious communities must be treated the same, and in this view, it is the dominant Hindu community which is to be the norm against which equality is judged."[29] Like the *Prabhoo* case, the *Mudgal* decision was claimed by the Hindu Right as a victory. The Hindu Right makes continuous references to these Supreme Court decisions to bolster their call for the enactment of a UCC. The UCC is a means for realizing the Hindu Right's vision of secularism—the formal equal treatment of all religious communities.[30] The Hindu Right's version of equality for women—treating all women the same, but treating them differently from men—would also be realized by the UCC.[31] While fighting for the enactment of a UCC, the Hindu Right casts itself as the defender of women's rights within minority communities. The UCC, of course, is not seen as a threat to Hindu norms and values because the Hindu Right's version of the UCC is based on existing Hindu norms and practices.[32] The Hindu Right's UCC takes advantage of the majoritarianism that is implicit in a formal model of equality.

B. Violence against Women

The issue of violence against women is one in which the connection between secularism and the Hindu Right's agenda for women is somewhat less obvious. Violence against women has long been a central issue to the secular women's movement in India. But, recently, it has also come to be central to the agenda of the Hindu Right, which routinely condemns atrocities against women, including rape, dowry, female infanticide, sex selection, and sexual harassment.[33] The appropriation of issues of violence against women by the Hindu Right is not a wholesale adoption of the concerns of feminists and women's groups. Rather, the Hindu Right's approach to violence against women is derived in part from its highly conservative approach to protecting and promoting the family, including redefining women's roles as wives and mothers, as well as from its revivalist Hindutva discourse, which seeks to restore women to the position of honor and respect that they enjoyed in a mythic golden age of Hinduism.[34]

The issue of violence against women in the public sphere is framed within the Hindu Right's discourse of communalism, and thus the Muslim man is cast as the perpetrator of sexual violence against women, playing into the stereotype of Muslim men as lustful and rapacious.[35] This stereotype, which characterizes the discourse of the Hindu Right, serves the dual function of "demonizing the Muslim community and deflecting attention away from the sexual violence caused by the Hindu male."[36] At no point is the patriarchal authority of the Hindu male challenged. To the contrary, the demand for harsh penalties—a demand to punish Muslim men who have dishonored Hindu women and by implication Hindu men and the Hindu community—is a reaffirmation of the patriarchal control of Hindu men over Hindu women. Rape in a communal discourse becomes a harm inflicted against a community, a violation of the community honor rather than a violation of an individual woman's right to bodily integrity.[37] The communalization of violence against women in the public sphere also provides women within the Hindu Right an "external" enemy to focus on that allows them to vent their personal and political anger about sexual violence without directing it toward their own community.[38]

Some newer issues that the BJP proposes to take up include: a vigorous campaign against child prostitution; amending the law to "make clients as culpable as commercial sex-workers"; increasing the number of women in the police force; and increasing the number of "Crimes Against Women Cells" (units dealing with crime against women).[39] The BJP's strategy appears to be closely related to the promotion of traditional family values and to its revivalist discourse in which women are to be restored to the position of respect and honor, as mothers and wives, that they ostensibly enjoyed in a by-gone era. These concerns constitute part of its simultaneous campaign to strengthen Hindu society and Hindu cultural values in keeping with its project of Hindutva.

V. COUNTERMANEUVERS

In recognizing that the discourse of secularism and equality are highly contested terrains, lawyers, women's groups, and human rights activists need to formulate strategies that will counter the meaning accorded to these terms by the Hindu Right. They need to learn from the lessons of recent history, in which the prioritizing of gender has resulted, in part, in a polarization of religious communities, a splintering of women's identity into unconnected meaningless fragments, and left the door ajar for a secular politics whose color is saffron. They need to think about a vision of secularism that is premised on a substantive notion of equality, that is, where one's gender and/or religious identity is not merely erased by brute majoritarianism, but is recognized and compensated if it has been the cause of historical disadvantage. There should be a recognition that this suturing of gender and religious identity is not a free-fall into the chasm of religious fanaticism or fundamentalism, but rather, a meaningful and important strategy for advancing the cause of secular politics in India.

NOTES

1. This chapter is based on: Brenda Cossman & Ratna Kapur, *Secularism's Last Sigh?: The Hindu Right, the Courts, and India's Struggle for Democracy,* 38 HARV. INT'L L.J. 113 (1997)[hereinafter Cossman & Kapur, *Secularism's Last Sigh?*]; Brenda Cossman & Ratna Kapur, *Secularism: Bench-Marked by Hindu Right,* 38 ECON. & POL. WKLY. 2613, 2620–25 (1996) [hereinafter Cossman & Kapur, *Secularism: Bench-Marked*]; and RATNA KAPUR AND BRENDA COSSMAN, SUBVERSIVE SITES: FEMINIST ENGAGEMENTS WITH LAW IN INDIA (New Dehli/Thousand Oaks/London: Sage Publications, 1996) [hereinafter KAPUR & COSSMAN, SUBVERSIVE SITES]. My thanks to Brenda Cossman in particular for allowing me to draw upon our collaborative work.

2. Cossman & Kapur, *Secularism's Last Sigh?, supra* note 1, at 113.

3. *See* Asgar Ali Engineer, *Secularism in India—Theory and Practice, in* SECU-
LARISM AND LIBERATION: PERSPECTIVES AND STRATEGIES FOR INDIA
TODAY 38, 39–41 (Rudolf C. Heredia & Edward Mathias, eds.) (New
Delhi: Indian Social Institute, 1995).

4. KAPUR & COSSMAN, SUBVERSIVE SITES, *supra* note 1, at 237.

5. *See* Engineer, *supra* note 3, at 43–44.

6. *See* Bommai v. Union of India, 3 S.C.C. 1 (1994).

7. Cossman & Kapur, *Secularism's Last Sigh?, supra* note 1, at 153; *see* Cossman
& Kapur, *Secularism: Bench-Marked, supra* note 1, at 2624.

8. Prabhoo v. Prabhakar Kasinath Kunte et al., 1995 S.C.A.L.E. 1, 24.

9. Cossman & Kapur, *Secularism's Last Sigh?, supra* note 1, at 119; *see* Cossman
& Kapur, *Secularism: Bench-Marked, supra* note 1, at 2613.

10. *See* Representation of the People Act, 1951, §123(3), (3A), INDIA A.I.R.
MANUAL.

11. Prabhoo, 1995 S.C.A.L.E. at 24; *see* Cossman & Kapur, *Secularism's Last
Sigh?, supra* note 1, at 114.

12. Prabhoo, 1995 S.C.A.L.E. at 24–25.

13. *See* VINAYAK DAMODAR SAVARKAR, HINDUTVA: WHO IS A HINDU? 115–16
(Savarkar Sadan, Bombay: Veer Savarkar Prakasha, 5th ed. 1969); M.S. GOL-
WALKAR, WE OR OUR NATIONHOOD DEFINED 26 (Mahal, Nagpur: M.N.
Kale, 3d ed. 1945).

14. *See* SAVARKAR, *supra* note 13, at 100–101, 113–15; GOLWALKAR, *supra* note
13, at 45–53.

15. Prabhoo, 1995 S.C.A.L.E. 11–12.

16. *See* Cossman & Kapur, *Secularism's Last Sigh?, supra* note 1, at 151.

17. BHARATIYA JANATA PARTY, ELECTION MANIFESTO—OUR VISION, OUR
WILL, OUR WAY 3 (1998) (chapter 2), *available in* (visited Oct. 9, 1998)
<http://bjp.org/manifes/chap.1.htm> [hereinafter BJP, MANIFESTO].

18. *See* BJP, MANIFESTO, *supra* note 17, at 12–13 (chapter 10); *see also* KAPUR
& COSSMAN, SUBVERSIVE SITES, *supra* note 1, at 247–273.

19. *See* KAPUR & COSSMAN, SUBVERSIVE SITES, *supra* note 1, at 247.

20. *See* BJP, MANIFESTO, *supra* note 17, at 12–13 (chapter 10).

21. *See* BJP, MANIFESTO, *supra* note 17, at 12 (chapter 10).

22. *See* KAPUR & COSSMAN, SUBVERSIVE SITES, *supra* note 1, at 233–34.

23. Mohammed Ahmed Khan v. Shah Bano Begum, 1985 A.I.R. (S.C.) 945,
950–51.

24. *See* VI INDIA CODE (Act No. 25 of 1986).

25. *See* KAPUR & COSSMAN, SUBVERSIVE SITES, *supra* note 1, at 256.

26. *See* Sarla Mugdal, President, Kalyani and Ors v. Union of India and Ors,
J.T. 1915 (4) (S.C.) 331.

27. *Id.* at 345–46.

28. *See* KAPUR & COSSMAN, SUBVERSIVE SITES, *supra* note 1, at 259.

29. *See id.* at 260.

30. *See id.*

31. *See id.*

32. *See id.* at 261.
33. *See id.* at 248–49.
34. *See id.* at 233–34.
35. *See id.* at 249.
36. *See id.* at 249.
37. *See id.* at 250.
38. *See* Tanika Sarkar, *The Women of the Hindutva Brigade,* 25 BULL. CON-CERNED ASIAN SCHOLARS 16, 19 (Dec. 1993).
39. *See* BJP, MANIFESTO, *supra* note 17, at 12–13 (chapter 10).

Chapter 14

Religion and Patriarchal Politics: The Israeli Experience

Frances Raday

I. INTRODUCTION

R eligion, subcultures, and the family share a common attribute in legal systems—they have all been regarded, at various times and in various contexts, as being outside the reach of political and legal regulation. These spheres of life are regarded, in constitutional democracies, as either private or autonomous. The members of these groups are given the right to determine their own ethical ideology and practice. This right to autonomy within a subgroup has gone variously under the rubrics of freedom of religion, multiculturalism, or the right to privacy. Religious freedom, cultural autonomy, and family privacy are usually treated as wholly separate topics. Yet there is a common thread that ties them all together from a feminist standpoint, and it is this commonality that I want to emphasize here. The patriarchal norms of family life are in no small part the result of patriarchal religious heritage and the object of ongoing religious politics. The customs of family life vary according to the patriarchal traditions of subcultures. Hence the sources of the patriarchal norms of all three institutions are inextricably interwoven.

Criticism of the sociolegal reticence in interfering with patriarchal rule within the family, often under the guise of protecting the privacy of the family, has begun to be articulated in feminist writing. There has, however, been far more ambivalence in critiquing the legitimacy of religious and cultural autonomy than in critiquing the negation of gender justice within the family. There are feminists who regard religious and subculture autonomy as legitimate and requiring "diverse feminism" or intersectionality.[1]

The argument, based on theories of multiculturalism, is that the Western model of feminist justice is ill-adapted to women of religion or women from other cultures.[2] This demand for cultural and religious subgroup autonomy is antithetical to the universality of the principle of equality between the sexes. Since so much of subgroup tradition is directed to bolstering the patriarchal family hierarchy, the multiculturalist approach results ultimately in foiling demands for intervention to ensure gender justice in the family.

The argument that women themselves demand religious or cultural subgroup autonomy is given as proof of the legitimacy of granting such autonomy. However, the notion that women have participated in the subgroup's consensus rests on shaky ground once their socialization to inequality is considered and the unbearably heavy price that they would have to pay for non-conformity in the subgroup is recognized. Under such conditions, women's sharing in the common understanding of a patriarchal tradition cannot be verified.[3]

II. THE ISRAELI EXPERIENCE

Because of Israel's special social, political, and legal situation with regard to the three monotheistic religions, an examination of the family through the prism of religion and subculture in the Israeli context encourages insights regarding the interconnection between these spheres that is often disguised or forgotten in modern Western constitutional democracies. From the Israeli perspective the connections seem clearer. The Israeli legal system provides an example of the way in which deference to religious and subculture norms operates to impose patriarchy on women. Deference to religious values—Jewish, Muslim and Christian—over the right of women to equality in the family has been formally institutionalized in the legal system.[4]

The Israeli model is striking because the imposition of patriarchal religious values on family life persists in the context of a strong democracy that has provided a high level of constitutional and legal protection for women's right to equality, affirmative action, and accommodation in other spheres of social and economic endeavor. Israel has radically progressive legal rules on: equal employment opportunity and equal pay, including comparable worth; parental rights in the workplace; sexual harassment in all contexts; the right to affirmative action appointments to high positions in the public service and to the boards of government company directorates; and conscription for army service and volunteer admission to combat units in the army such as the elite pilots' course. Even as regards the family, there are progressive legal rules in matters that are not ruled by religious norms concerning violence in the family, the division of matrimonial property between couples both married and cohabitant, and abortion. It is against these achievements of gender equality norms that the religious regulation of marriage and divorce has to be examined.

The centrality of religion in Israel's political and legal system is derived from a complex historical and political reality. The new state was created from the ashes of the Holocaust, and a prime motivating factor for its founders, as indeed for the United Nations, which gave it *de jure* recognition, was to save the vestiges of the Jewish people with its rich cultural heritage. That cultural heritage was expressed, in large part, through the religious authorities of Judaism—the Bible, the Talmud, and the Gemarra—that had served Jews as history, ethical philosophy, and law through the centuries. In addition, the Ottoman Millett system, which Israel inherited from the British Mandate, granted autonomy over matters of personal status to the three major communities living in Palestine—Jewish, Muslim, and Christian.[5] Israel still retains the Millett system at least in part because the religious political parties, who have consistently held the balance of power in Israel's coalition government system, would oppose any changes.[6] The religious autonomy for communities resulting from the Millet system is perceived, from the perspective of the communities, as a central element of their national-cultural identities and autonomy.[7]

By retaining the Millett system, the Knesset (Israeli parliament) effectively signed over the fate of women in each of the three communities to the religious institutions of that community. It must be noted that belonging to one of the communities is not a question of religious choice but of birth status. True, "only" the jurisdiction to determine personal status was vested in these institutions. However, the situation of women in the family is not a marginal matter. Women's status in the home plays an important role in determining the extent of their autonomy and of their equality of opportunity in socioeconomic terms, too. The delegation of powers to the religious institutions of the various communities amounts to the incorporation of patriarchy within the legal system on two levels. First, it excludes women from participation in policymaking or public office in those spheres of public life delegated to autonomous regulation by the institutions of the religious communities. Second, it subjects women to patriarchal norms in the spheres of social activity regulated by these institutions, particularly the family.

A. Women's Exclusion from Public Office or Ceremony

The patriarchal doctrine of all the recognized religions results in religious institutions being almost exclusively male; women are excluded from participation in policymaking, administration, and the judiciary. Because Israel delegates jurisdiction over matters of personal status to these religious institutions by statute,[8] women are barred *under the law* from appointment to the judiciary on matters of marriage and divorce.[9] In a way that is equally disempowering, women are excluded from all the various religious forums that authoritatively interpret the religious-legal norms that govern their existence.

The exclusion of women might be regarded as an accidental relic from a patriarchal past. However, as late as 1988, the rabbinical establishment pressured the Minister of Religion to prevent a woman, who had been elected to a religious council,[10] from sitting on the council, and pressured the Mayor of Tel Aviv to prevent the inclusion of women in the electoral board for municipal rabbi. Both instances led to petitions to the High Court of Justice, where the women won their cases.[11]

The impact of exclusion, and attempted exclusion, of women from the public arena in all areas of life that fall under religious influence is dramatically illustrated by the saga of the Women of the Wall (WOW). The Women of the Wall are Orthodox Jewish women who wish to pray by the Kotel, the Western Wall of the Temple in Jerusalem. The Kotel is a site of great religious, historical, national, and cultural symbolic significance to Jews everywhere. The WOW's manner of prayer is customary for men but not for women; the members pray in a group, aloud, from the Torah Scroll, and wear prayer shawls. The WOW's prayer in this manner has been greeted with violent opposition, including physical and verbal abuse, from other Orthodox worshippers, male and female.[12] WOW's numerous petitions to the Supreme Court have resulted in the Court's recognition of their freedom of worship in principle but, up to now, the denial of their right to exercise that freedom in practice.[13]

B. The Patriarchal Regulation of Women's Lives

The promotion of religion in the Israeli legal system has extended the impact of religious patriarchy beyond the practicing religious subgroups to all women born into the different communities, without regard to the women's consent or nonconsent. As noted at the beginning of this chapter, the notion that even religious women have consented in this context rests on very shaky ground.[14] Not only are actively religious women subjected to inegalitarian norms but so also are secular women whose consent is not merely suspect but totally nonexistent. The right to marry, to divorce, or to remarry in a way that will be officially recognized by the legal system is governed by religious precepts, Jewish, Muslim, and Christian, and *all* women in Israel are subject to these religious norms.

There are important areas of family law that are regulated by secular law and in these areas there is in principle a right to equality between the sexes. Thus, there is a right to equality for women in the family on issues of matrimonial property, with a presumption of shared ownership of all matrimonial property for the purposes of its division on divorce. There is the right to equality in matters of custody and guardianship. However, the subjection of women to the decisions of the religious courts for the divorce proceedings undermines their assertion of these other rights in the civil courts.[15] The interaction between the two concurrent jurisdictions results frequently in women's waiver of their formal rights under the secular law, since they find themselves ultimately at the mercy of the religious courts when it comes to determination of their marital status.

Moreover, ultra-Orthodox religious women do not apply to the civil courts because they would be considered traitors by their communities if they did so, and hence the jurisdiction of the religious courts is exclusive on all matters for them.[16] The religious courts systematically ignore the requirement of equality for women, which is imposed on them by law under the Women's Equal Rights Law with regard to matrimonial property and custody issues. The nature of the resultant legal regime governing women's family lives is clearly patriarchal.

1. Judaism

As regards the Jewish population, "the establishment of patriarchy is most clearly expressed in the ultimate power of the male not to release his wife from the bonds of marriage."[17] If the husband does not agree to give his wife a *get* (divorce writ), then there is no jurisdiction, religious or secular, that can free her from the marriage.[18] The rabbinical courts may recommend that the husband divorce his wife or may even order him to do so, but if he refuses to comply, she remains married to him.[19] The rabbinical courts have rarely ordered a husband to give a *get,* and, as a matter of current practice, they have refrained from such orders on the ground that a *get* that a husband gives against his free will is of doubtful validity.[20] A 1995 amendment to the law bestowed new powers on the rabbinical courts to cancel certain civil rights—for example, suspension of driving license or passport—of husbands who refuse to obey an order that does not compel but merely obliges him to give a divorce to his wife. This power seems to be used more liberally by the rabbinical courts than was the imprisonment power.

The inequality between men and women becomes even more apparent when the asymmetries between husbands and wives is further examined. Regardless of the remedies against recalcitrant husbands, the refusal of the husband to divorce his wife results in the wife's legal inability to remarry[21] and to set up any kind of new, informal family life as a practical matter. If she has a sexual relationship with another man, then she risks being considered a rebellious wife and, consequently, losing her rights to spousal maintenance payments or child custody.[22] Moreover, if at any future time her husband dies or releases her from the marriage, she will be prohibited from marrying her lover.[23] Any child that she has had by a lover while still married "will be considered a '*mamzer*' and will not be eligible to marry under Jewish law except if he/she marries another '*mamzer*' or a convert to Judaism."[24] Even secular women are generally reluctant to penalize their children in this manner, particularly since only religious marriage is recognized by the state.[25]

Although a wife's consent to a divorce from her husband is also required,[26] it does not have the same implications as the requirement of a husband's consent. If the wife refuses her consent, the husband may nonetheless be able to acquire a rabbinical license to remarry.[27] Moreover, if he sets up a new family without that license, he will not suffer the penalties that are imposed upon an undivorced wife. This asymmetry derives from the fact that originally, polygamy was allowed under Jewish law and hence multiple sexual associations of a married man were not considered as repugnant as those of a married woman.

Finally, women suffer an additional disadvantage. If a woman is widowed before the couple had children, the widow must obtain a *haliza* (a release) from her deceased husband's brother before she is free to remarry.[28] This situation has the potential for blackmail and humiliation of the widow by the deceased husband's family.

2. Islam

Muslim norms regarding the marital relations are also patriarchal. For example, Islamic law has been understood to allow polygamy; a man may take up to four wives.[29] Polygamy, however, is prohibited as a crime under Israeli law and this prohibition applies to all communities.[30] However, the existence of polygamy among certain Arab communities, particularly the Bedouin, has been well-documented.[31] Despite this evidence, there are no reports of prosecutions, evidencing the state's toleration of women's inequality under religious patriarchy.

Some writers claim that polygamy is not invariably adverse to women's interests.[32] However, such claims must be regarded as incapable of objective verification. In an equality analysis, whatever the subjective advantages claimed for polygamy, "[t]he practice must be regarded as inegalitarian so long as it is asymmetrical between the sexes."[33] The polygamy of Muslim law prohibits the marriage of one woman to a number of husbands and is therefore clearly patriarchal. Indeed, in judging the nature of polygamy, the context of the culture in which it is permitted should be analyzed as a whole and, in the case of Muslim culture as interpreted and practiced by significant sectors of the Arab community in Israel, that culture can leave little doubt as to its patriarchal nature.[34] Strong evidence of this is the phenomenon of family honor killings, that is, the killing of women who have betrayed the family honor by their sexual "misconduct"—this includes being the victim of rape where the rapist refuses to marry the victim—carried out by the woman's father and brothers.[35] Honor killings are obviously prohibited in Israel as murder under the criminal law. However, according to Manar Hassan, the police tend to ignore the practice on the premise that this is part of an autonomous cultural pattern.[36] It has been claimed that there are between 20 and 40 family honor killings each year that go uninvestigated and unpunished.[37] The result, she says, is that the state has, in essence, recognized "the right of patriarchal tradition to determine the punishment to be meted out to rebellious daughters."[38]

Muslim women suffer from the reverse problem from that of Jewish women as regards divorce. While Jewish women suffer from the difficulty of acquiring release from marriage, Muslim women suffer from the ease with which a marriage can be terminated. Under Muslim law, a man may unilaterally divorce his wife with full and immediate effect.[39] Although such unilateral divorces without a court order are prohibited by Israeli law,[40] the Muslim court that has jurisdiction of such cases applies Muslim law and thus is not foreclosed by the legal prohibition from legitimizing such divorces by court decree.[41]

Muslim women also suffer a disadvantage with respect to the right to custody of their children. When Muslim women who are widowed or divorced remarry, the custody of their children goes to the father or to his family members where he is deceased.[42] Such a holding by a *Ka'adi* (Muslim court) was challenged and the High Court of Justice held that although custody law could not be applied in a discriminatory fashion against women, the Muslim court could still take into account the norms of Muslim law.[43] This custody rule causes intolerable emotional hardship for women and many prefer not to remarry in order to avoid losing contact with their children.

3. Christianity

The situation of the much smaller minority of Christian women is less clear. There are 13 recognized denominations of Christianity, and Christian women are under the jurisdiction of their particular denomination.[44] These denominations include the Latin Patriarchate (Roman Catholic Church), the Eastern Orthodox Patriarchate, the Evangelist Episcopalian

Church, and various other denominations.[45] Thus, there are a number of versions of Christian canon law in effect in Israel. The norms of at least some of these churches, such as the Roman Catholic Church, the Orthodox Church, and Evangelical churches have been analyzed as being patriarchal in other contexts, particularly with regard to the wife having either an explicit or implicit duty to obey her husband.[46] There is no reason to suppose that these denominations are less patriarchal in Israel, where the state has delegated power to their courts.

4. Women's Control of Their Bodies: Differences among the Religious Communities

There are differences between the three religious communities on the issue of women's autonomy over their own bodies. On the issue of marital rape, Jewish law prohibits forced intercourse within marriage, and, in 1980, the Israeli Supreme Court, relying on Jewish law, unanimously held that imposition of sexual intercourse by a man on his wife without her consent was rape within the meaning of the Criminal Code.[47] Although the Supreme Court expressly indicated that a similar ruling would not be applicable to Muslims if Muslim law was different on this issue, Justice Ben Porat, the only woman justice sitting on the case, reserved her opinion on this point.[48]

As regards abortion, unlike some denominations of Christianity, Jewish law is not dogmatically opposed to abortion. The concept of Jewish law is that it is permissible to abort a fetus that is "threatening" the mother.[49] Thus, there has not been virulent religious opposition to abortion and the power of the religious parties has not been directed to securing full prohibition or prevention of abortion in Israel. Abortion is available on a wide range of grounds, but the ground of social hardship was repealed due to successful religious pressure in 1978.[50] In July 1998, the religious parties proposed administrative measures—demographic strategy—to persuade Jewish women who are pregnant not to have an abortion and to monitor women who have had abortions in order to persuade them not to have any further abortions. Feminist and secular organizations are organizing to oppose this pernicious proposition to invade women's privacy and limit their freedom of choice.

III. CONCLUSION: RELIGIOUS HAVENS OF INJUSTICE

It seems clear that religious and cultural subgroups are, like the family, organizations within the constitutional power of the state and there can be no meaningful gender equality in a society that leaves them as "havens" of injustice for women, inviolate from the police power of the state.

Where spheres of justice are defined in terms of subgroups, entrenching autonomy at the level of the subgroup will merely empower the dominating elite of that group and ignore the problems of inequality within the group. Where, within the subgroup, there is pervasive domination of a sub-subgroup, such as women, this policy will result in the suppression of the autonomy of that sub-subgroup's members. As we near a new century, it is clear that religion and subcultures, as well as the family, remain bastions of patriarchal culture that threaten women's hard-won equality in Western constitutional democracies.

NOTES

1. *See* Eva Brems, *Enemies or Allies? Feminism and Cultural Relativism as Dissident Voices in Human Rights Discourse,* 19 HUM. RTS. Q. 136 (1997) (discussing different feminist theories in international context).

2. For a general discussion of the issues of cultural relativism and the human rights of women, see Section II of this volume, Responses to Religious Fundamentalist Assertions of Cultural Relativism. For a discussion of this issue in the Israeli context, see Frances Raday, *Religion, Multiculturalism and Equality: The Israeli Case,* 25 ISRAELI YEARBOOK ON HUMAN RIGHTS 193 (1995) (hereinafter Raday, *Multiculturalism*).

3. *See* SUSAN MOLLER OKIN, JUSTICE, GENDER, AND THE FAMILY 66 (Basic Books, Inc., 1989).

4. *See* Women's Equal Rights Law, 1951, sec. 5, 5 L.S.I. 171, 172 (1950–51).

5. *See* King's Order in Privy Council, 1922–1947, arts. 47, 51; Law and Administration Ordinance, 1948, Sec. 11, 1 L.S.I. 9 (1948), 3 L.S.I. 73 (as amended) (1949); MENASHEH SHAVAH, 1 HA-DIN HA-ISHI BE-YISRA'EL [1 THE PERSONAL LAW IN ISRAEL] 69–76 (Hebrew) (Tel-Aviv: Masadah, 3d ed., 1991); Frances Raday, *Israel—The Incorporation of Religious Patriarchy in a Modern State, in* 4 INT'L REV. COMP. PUB. POL'Y 209, 210 (JAI Press Inc., 1992) (hereinafter Raday, *Religious Patriarchy*).

6. *See* Raday, *Multiculturalism, supra* note 2, at 195. At least one of the religious parties has been included in the coalition of every government, including when there was a national unity government and no coalition party was needed.

7. *See id.* at 194.

8. *See* King's Order in Privy Council, art. 47, 51, 52, 54; Rabbinical Courts Jurisdiction Act (Marriage and Divorce) Law, 1953, 7 L.S.I. 139 (1952–53); Druze Religious Courts Law, 1962, 17 L.S.I. 27 (1962–63).

9. *See* Raday, *Multiculturalism, supra* note 2, at 227.

10. Religious councils are statutory bodies that deal, on a local level, with the provision of religious services. Jewish Religious Services (Consolidated Version) Law, 1971, 25 L.S.I. 125 (1970–71).

11. *See* H.C. 153/87 Shakdiel v. Minister of Religious Affairs et al., 42(2) P.D. 221; H.C. 953/87 Poraz v. Mayor of Tel-Aviv et al., 42(2) P.D. 309.

12. *See* Haim Shapiro, *Women at the Wall,* Mar. 30, 1989, JERUSALEM POST.

13. *See* H.C. 257/89, 2410/90, Hoffman et al. v. The Commissioner of the Cotel et al., 48(2) P.D. 265; Raday, *Multiculturalism, supra* note 2, at 216–217.

14. *See* text accompanying note 3 *supra.*

15. Raday, *Multiculturalism, supra* note 2, at 233.

16. *Id.*

17. *Id.* at 230.

18. ARIEL ROSEN-ZVI, DINE HA-MISHPAÒAH BE-YISRAEL: BEN ÒKODESH LE-ÒHOL [ISRAELI FAMILY LAW: THE SACRED AND THE SECULAR] 138–9 (Hebrew) (Tel Aviv: Papyrus, Tel Aviv University, 1990); HAIM H. COHN, HUMAN RIGHTS IN JEWISH LAW 171–72 (London: The Institute of Jewish Affairs; New York: Ktav Publishing House, 1984).

19. ROSEN-ZVI, *supra* note 18, at 255–60; COHN, *supra* note 18, at 172–73.

20. *See* MOSHE CHIGIER, HUSBAND AND WIFE IN ISRAELI LAW 184, 264 n.28 (Jerusalem: Harry Fischel Institute for Research in Talmud and Jurisprudence, 1985); PINHAS SHIFMAN, 1 DINE HA-MISHPAHAH BE-YISRA'EL [1 FAMILY LAW IN ISRAEL] 297 (Hebrew) (Jerusalem: Mak 1984–1989); Eliav Schchatman, *Ma-amad Ha-ishah Be-dine Nisu-in Ve-gerushin [The Status of Women in Marriage and Divorce], in* MA-AMAD HA-ISHAH BA-HEVRAH UBA-MISHPAT [WOMEN'S STATUS IN ISRAELI LAW AND SOCIETY 380, 415–34 (Frances Raday et al., eds.) (Hebrew) (Tel Aviv: Schocken Publishing House Ltd., 1995) [hereinafter WOMEN'S STATUS].

21. Penal Law 1977, sec. 176, L.S.I.: Special Volume (1977) (imprisonment imposed on married woman who marries another man or on married man who marries another woman).

22. BENZION SCHERESCHEWSKY, DINE MISHPAHAH [FAMILY LAW IN ISRAEL] 200–13 (Jerusalem: Rubin Mass Ltd., 4th ed., 1992).

23. *Id.* at 195–213 ; COHN, *supra* note 18, at 173.

24. Raday, *Multiculturalism, supra* note 2, at 231; SCHERESCHEWSKY, *supra* note 22, at 353–55.

25. *See* Raday, *Multiculturalism, supra* note 2, at 231.

26. COHN, *supra* note 18, at 172–73. Such consent was not originally required under biblical law, but the *herem* of Rabbi Gershom in the tenth century C.E. changed this when it also disallowed polygamy.

27. SHIFMAN, *supra* note 20, at 178–79; COHN, *supra* note 18, at 172.

28. *See* Raday, *Multiculturalism, supra* note 2, at 231.

29. *See* JOHN L. ESPOSITO, WOMEN IN MUSLIM FAMILY LAW 20 (Syracuse, NY: Syracuse University Press, 1982).

30. Penal Law 1977, sec. 176, L.S.I.: Special Volume (1977).

31. Stephen Adler, *Ha-ishah Ha-beduit Ve-havtahat Hah-nassah Ba-Mishpahah Ha-poly-gamit [Bedouin Woman and Guaranteed Income in the Polygamous Family], in* WOMEN'S STATUS, *supra* note 20, at 133 (Hebrew).

32. *See, e.g.,* SAFIA IQBAL, WOMEN AND ISLAMIC LAW: REVISED EDITION 1991 165–75 (Shandar/Market/Chittli/Qabar/ Delhi: Adam Publishers & Distributors, 1991).

33. Raday, *Multiculturalism, supra* note 2, at 232 (footnote omitted).

34. *See* Manar Hassan, *Growing up Female and Palestinian in Israel, in* CALLING THE EQUALITY BLUFF: WOMEN IN ISRAEL 66, 66–72 (Sharon Ne'eman, trans.) (Barbara Swirski & Marilyn P. Safir, eds.) (New York: Pergamon Press, Inc., 1991).

35. *See id.* at 71.

36. *See id.* at 71–72.

37. *See id.* at 71.

38. *See id.* at 72.

39. *See* ESPOSITO, *supra* note 29, at 30–33.

40. *See* Women's Equal Rights Law, 1951, sec. 8(b), 5 L.S.I. 171, 172 (1950–51).

41. *See* Raday, *Multiculturalism, supra* note 2, at 232.

42. *See* H.C. 187/54, Briya v. Ka'adi of Shar'arite Muslim Court in Acco, et al., 9 P.D. 1193.

43. *Id.*

44. *See* King's Order in Privy Council, 1922–1947, art. 2 & Second App. (listing Eastern Orthodox; Latin [Catholic]; Gregorian Armenian; Armenian Catholic; Syrian Catholic; Chaldean Uniate; Greek Catholic Melkite, Maronite and Syrian Orthodox). Since then, the government has recognized the Evangelist Episcopalian Church in 1970 and the Bahá'í faith in 1971, as well as the Lutheran and Anglican denominations.

45. *Id.*

46. Raday, *Multiculturalism, supra* note 2, at 232–33; Courtney W. Howland, *The Challenge of Religious Fundamentalism to the Liberty and Equality Rights of Women: An Analysis under the United Nations Charter,* 35 COLUM. J. TRANSNAT'L L. 271, 289–96 (1997).

47. Cohen v. The State of Israel 35 (3) P.D. 281 (1980).

48. Cohen v. The State of Israel 35 (3) P.D. at 293–94.

49. *See* DAVID M. FELDMAN, BIRTH CONTROL IN JEWISH LAW 275, 284 (New York: New York University Press, 3d. ed., 1995).

50. *See* Raday, *Religious Patriarchy, supra* note 5, at 221.

Chapter 15

Family Disputes Involving Muslim Women in Contemporary Europe: Immigrant Women Caught between Islamic Family Law and Women's Rights

Marie-Claire S.F.G. Foblets

I. INTRODUCTION

This chapter discusses the question that arises when the judge in a family court in Europe is obliged to consider the degree of recognition to be given to family laws practiced and obeyed by immigrant communities that clash with the domestic legal culture. I will focus on the position of Muslim women in that debate.

In almost all European countries today, massive migration since the sixties and the seventies[1] from the former colonies of the Western powers have caused major changes in the area of international family law. As a result, European courts are facing a huge increase in the number of cases that require the court to decide which law, the law of the Muslim immigrant's country of origin or the law of the host country, to apply to a family dispute. Courts are being confronted with a plethora of foreign family law codes that, in spite of a near universal movement toward gender equality, still discriminate against wives and mothers in favor of husbands and fathers. These foreign laws do not meet the host country's standards of gender equality and nondiscrimination. For example, civil judges are petitioned repeatedly to recognize *talaq,* the Islamic law of unilateral repudiation by a Muslim man of his wife. However, courts usually do *not* grant divorces on more permissive grounds than those available in their own jurisdiction, but the arguments on which the judges base their decisions vary. Some courts insist on gender equality as a basic legal principle of forum law and therefore deny validity to unilateral divorces insofar as they systematically privilege one gender, the male, over the other.[2] Other courts, on the contrary, do not protect gender equality but argue against unilateral dissolution of the marriage for reasons pertaining to the proceedings, such as publicity, right of the wife to be properly defended before the divorce judge in the home country, and the like.[3]

As is apparent, the question of the appropriate choice-of-law model to use is becoming increasingly important and filled with conflict. There is also increased pressure from certain parts of the Muslim community to apply the country of origin's law to the Muslim immigrant.[4]

I recently had an occasion to deepen my reflection on this issue. I was offered, by the Belgian Minister of Justice, the opportunity to collect data on the legal problems actually encountered by Moroccan Muslim women in Belgium[5] with regard to their family life.[6] From January 1 to December 31, 1997, I collected, with a team of young researchers,[7] materials on family disputes involving Moroccan women domiciled in Belgium through three types of sources: inventories of the jurisprudence since 1980;[8] interviews (about 100) of law practitioners (magistrates, advocates, public officials, police officers, and so on); and, most important, interviews with about 80 Moroccan men and women.

In this chapter, I will review the current choice-of-law models used by courts, the problems with these models, and suggest a solution based on my research data involving Moroccan women.

II. THE DRAMATIC LACK OF ADAPTATION OF CENTURY-OLD LEGAL TECHNIQUES

The issue of the recognition to be given to non-Western legal cultures that claim legal protection in Europe touches on a highly sensitive, socially and politically, problem area. It has forced an open discussion of the degree of cultural tolerance to be shown by the courts in the host country and the role of judges when handling disputes involving immigrants from non-Western countries. Problems related to marital property law, inheritance, the mutual rights and obligations of spouses, adultery and cohabitation, inheritance and transfer of property, child custody, conflicts of nationalities within one family, and so on, sharply manifest how difficult it has become for family judges in Europe to achieve justice in conflicts involving disputants of non-Western origin, who, for the mere reason that they have kept their foreign nationality, continue to resort—at least partially—to the principles of their country of origin's legal system.

Cross-cultural conflicts of law leave the judge who has to deal with family disputes in an awkward position: he or she is compelled to act as a multistate decision maker in a way that will affect relationships among family members who, by definition, are not confined to the judge's culture. Cross-cultural family conflicts require the judge to consult unfamiliar foreign law which, he or she may find, is as unsatisfactory as European law (the *lex fori*) because both were framed in reference to local circumstances with scant regard for transnational realities. The techniques that are used by the courts to resolve international family disputes are generally called choice-of-law rules. There are currently four competing choice-of-law models that have developed: nationality, domicile, the choice of the "better law," and party autonomy.

A. Nationality

With respect to choice-of-law situations, European civil law since the middle of the nineteenth century looks to the national law of a person to resolve questions concerning her or his family relations and all matters linked—directly or indirectly—with that person's personal status.[9] Thus, the choice of law in these situations will depend upon a person's nationality (the nationality of their origin if nationality has been retained) even if the conduct in question did not take place in the person's state of origin but wholly within another state's jurisdiction. The usual reason given for this approach is that it corresponds to the expectations of individuals.

The repercussions of this position, when interpreted in present-day context, may be odd. Courts thus may find themselves compelled to recognize conduct as legal under foreign law that, in some cases, may be contrary to the basic principles of the forum's law (i.e., that of the host country), for the mere reason that the parties concerned—notwithstanding a life-long residence in the host country—have kept their nationality of origin. For example, polygamy and *talaq* are among the most controversial practices that have at times been legitimized by European judges in application of discriminatory matrimonial laws still in force in the parties' country of origin.[10]

B. Domicile

Another approach to the choice-of-law process is the solution traditionally applied in England, the United States, and Canada.[11] In these countries, the question of whether a legal system is applicable to a particular situation is dependent upon the parties' domicile (their permanent place of residence) rather than their nationalities. One of the main advantages of this type of solution is that it releases the courts from being required on principle to defer to the law of the nationality of origin in immigrant family disputes.

However, this approach also has its problems. For example, a Muslim man, according to the law of his nationality, may have a right to polygamy. If he becomes domiciled in England, thereby becoming subject to English matrimonial law, and while domiciled there marries, the marriage becomes a monogamous marriage and he cannot exercise his right to polygamy since the exercise of this right would be against English law. If the couple goes to his country of origin and become domiciled there, his English marriage—if it is still considered as a marriage at all—will be transformed into a Muslim marriage and not be regarded as an obstacle to the exercise of his polygamous privileges. This would occur regardless of the expectations the wife had when she entered a monogamous marriage in England.

C. Nationality and Domicile: The Choice of the "Better Law"

The problems arising from either nationality or domicile choice-of-law approaches have induced European courts and legislatures to search for other solutions. Some courts and legislatures have started to mitigate the sharp distinction between nationality and domicile by the notion that, over the years, a person might have lost a "true social connection" with his or her national law.[12] Some courts therefore have ventured to substitute domicile for nationality whenever the law of the domicile appears to be the "most closely connected" law.[13]

In this manipulative way of dealing with conflicts issues, also called the "better law" or "proper law" approach,[14] courts, in cross-boundary family disputes, may either stress the intent of the parties to stay in the country of residence or the objective links that connect the situation with the host state in order to justify their preference for the law of the domicile over the national law of the parties. Or, they may instead prefer to emphasize nationality over domicile in order to achieve results that appear to be more appropriate to the particular circumstances of the case.

The problems with this approach are that: first, it confers broad powers on the courts without providing guidance on how to use these powers correctly; and, second, it undermines predictability because the case decisions are so highly individualized that they have little precedential value.

D. Party Autonomy

For several years now some scholars have therefore advocated a greater role for party autonomy in conflicts issues involving immigrant disputants.[15]

Party autonomy, also called *optio iuris,* means that the parties themselves choose the law that is applicable to their legal relationships.

Party autonomy made its entrance into the area of international family law in the second half of the seventies.[16] Party autonomy was primarily seen as a remedy to unpredictability in the application of conflict-of-law rules: the power to designate the applicable law is a means by which parties can preclude any uncertainty with respect to the result of the conflict-of-law issues and at the same time know exactly with which legal norms they are expected to comply.

Although many courts still remain relatively reluctant to apply this solution to family relationships, the *optio iuris* model nonetheless has been emerging in different European countries over the last few years as a response to problems regarding the choice of surnames[17] and also in allowing spouses to protect themselves with regard to the status of their common property by making an ante-nuptial contract.[18] In practice, the parties' choice is generally confined to a choice from among a number of *relevantly* connected legal systems—either the common national or the common domiciliary law.[19] However, with respect to matrimonial property, the spouses may, prior or during the marriage, choose the law of either party's present nationality or domicile, as well as the *lex rei sitae* (the local law where the property is located) with respect to real estate.[20] Prior to the wedding, fiancés may also choose the law of either party's domicile.[21] Parties are not allowed to choose any other law. Party autonomy is also subject to the restriction that the choice does not prejudice the weaker party.[22]

III: THE CASE OF MOROCCAN WOMEN CLAIMING PROTECTION UNDER BELGIAN (SECULAR) LAW

A. Muslim Women's Choices: Religious Laws and Social Reality

As a consequence of immigration, Islam has, since the late 1980s, become the most important religious group in Belgium after Catholicism.[23] The Muslim community is steadily growing, showing a clear will to manifest itself as a religious group and claiming protection of the fundamental rights and liberties to express and freely manifest its convictions in both the private and the public area.[24] The numeric importance of Muslims in Continental Europe, combined with the problematic, but until today still valid, principle that courts are to favor preservation of cultural distinctiveness of foreigners and newcomers and therefore give preference to the law of the nationality of origin, results in a situation that touches the core of the issue being deliberated by this book: religious laws clashing with the basic principles of protection of women's fundamental rights.

The problem is even more intricate since: first, Muslims originating from countries that officially adhere to Islam do not lose their nationality of origin, not even after having acquired the (new) nationality of the country of residence;[25] and, second, most Muslims who are actually living in Europe demonstrably keep in touch with their countries of origin, including investing their savings there, spending long yearly holidays with family that have remained there, choosing fiancés there, and so on.

Multiple citizenship, on the one hand, and on the other, the increased risk of "limping" situations—situations (such as recognition of marriage, divorce, paternity) where the same cases are resolved differently in different countries[26]—create an urgency to find appropriate alternative solutions that both solidly protect the constitutional and human rights prevailing in the host country and allow Muslims (and other minorities) to conform to their religion, if that is their wish.

My research study for the Belgian Minister of Justice gives an important insight into what this wish may be. Our findings indicate that the vast majority of the Muslim women interviewed are unequivocally claiming protection under Belgian law. The data examines three sociological generations of Moroccan women, each of them experiencing in its own way the dilemma of religious law versus women's rights.[27]

A first generation of women, aged 60 to 70, struggle with the consequences of polygamy; their husbands most often have taken a second wife in the country of origin. These women have the feeling of being solely the property of their husband. They refuse to consent to *talaq*—their repudiation at the initiative of the husband—as they are afraid that the husband will then make a claim in Belgium for family reunification with his second wife (who is in the country of origin) as soon as the first marriage is dissolved.

The second generation comprises women aged 20 to 40. Most of them have at a very young age been given away into an arranged marriage by their parents to a relative in the country of origin. A cultural clash results between the two spouses because of their differing expectations; a European, Muslim woman has completed her school education and does not fit neatly into a marriage where the husband, who has grown up in a Muslim country, expects his wife to submit to his authority. Ninety percent of these marriages collapse.

The third or intermediary generation is made up of women of all ages who have been entitled to immigrate on the basis of family reunification: they have been married to a husband who has immigrated to Belgium many years ago and who has selected a fiancé in the country of origin with the sole purpose to keep control over her and the marriage as, at the time of her marriage, she neither knows Belgium nor has adopted a Western lifestyle. Most women of this intermediary generation feel extremely lonely in Belgium. They have no family or relatives of their own in Belgium. They are treated badly by their husband, who dominates them in all aspects of life. Yet, returning to their country of origin is not a real possibility. This third category of women tends to maintain high expectations by way of the protection offered under Belgian law. They find it very unfair to be repudiated by their husband because the dissolution of the marriage endangers their right to permanent residence in Belgium.

Thus, all three groups of women resist a choice-of-law rule that in principle connects them with the law of the nationality of origin.

B. The Proposed Solution: The Domiciliary Principle Enhanced by Party Autonomy

The proposal arising from this research is *not* to maintain the still valid principle of the law of the nationality. Rather the law of the domicile, *in casu* Belgian law, should be applied in Belgium, except for those couples who, at the time of their marriage, have explicitly expressed the wish to remain governed by the law of their nationality of origin (Moroccan law) for all aspects of their marital relationship. With respect to those couples who chose party autonomy, *both* spouses, husband and wife, must have fully and freely consented to that choice.

Party autonomy may act as a valuable substitute for the automatic application of Belgian law. It is premised on the understanding that parties know better than anybody else, and *a fortiori* better than the judge, which substantive law is most effectively to govern their relationship, and thus the reliance on the parties' choice yields results that are superior to heteronomous adjudication by a conflicts judge. As such, party autonomy in the choice-of-law process reflects the same values and objectives as those embodied in contracts law: the parties' choices are the core of their legal relationship. Inasmuch as the courts are respectful of the parties' decisions, the court establishes the facts and subjects them to the rule of law provided by the parties involved. The certainty of the outcome has been increased.

It is important to understand that party autonomy should not result in structurally enforcing the weakness of wives within marriage. This result will be avoided because courts still have control over the parties' choice, and are enjoined to scrutinize party agreements to determine if they properly meet various legal standards. There are at least four limitations in law on party autonomy that courts must use in their evaluation of the legality of the party agreements.

First, courts must determine that the parties' consent was freely given. This determination includes a finding that the Muslim wife who has chosen to retain the laws of her personal status of origin (Moroccan law) has been well-informed concerning the consequences of that choice.

Second, the parties' choice may require the court to weigh the various interests involved. In the search for a just solution to the choice-of-law problem, all the relevant interests—and not just the interests of the parties, but also the interests of the surrounding host society (public order arguments)—must be taken into consideration by the court. For instance, the court will necessarily exclude choices of laws that structurally prejudice the interests of the weaker party, most often the wife.

Third, the parties' choice must necessarily implement the legal principles prevailing at the time of the marriage[28] unless these principles have been changed at the time of the enforcement of the agreement. They must also reflect the legal convictions held by the general public in the host society.[29] A choice of law by the parties should be overridden when the consequences of the choice are not justifiable under the current legal norms of the host society. For example, under no circumstances may party autonomy allow the parties' agreement to rely upon Moroccan rules of maintenance and child custody that are preferential for the husband, because the agreement would thereby be evading the legal principle of nondiscrimination that protects the wife under the domestic law of the host country.

Fourth, the parties' choice of the applicable law may not result in the recognition of privileges that they would not otherwise enjoy under the objectively applicable law as proposed—the law of domicile.[30] Neither can the choice place them—or one of them—in a better position than other citizens in the same situation. Thus, a Moroccan husband could not gain the advantages of unilateral divorce and polygamy since these would not otherwise be available. For example, Moroccan spouses who, after 20 years of continuous residence in Europe, have lost any true social connection with Moroccan law may not prejudice the protection that the wife would enjoy under domestic matrimonial law of the host country by a previously executed agreement that Moroccan law controlled their marriage. Thus, the choice to submit the case to Moroccan law will most probably be denied any validity in the country of residence in Europe because the discrimination of the wife in relation to her husband under Moroccan law negatively affects the wife's position to the sole benefit of the husband. The spouse's choice for Moroccan matrimonial law will most probably be considered fraudulent and therefore null and void.[31]

In sum, party autonomy does not entail the recognition of an unlimited freedom to choose, without restriction, the applicable law in international cases. In fact, party autonomy in conflict-of-law situations does no more than reflect a similar evolution in substantive law; ultimately, it is the protective rationale and the social function of the law that keep control over the choice-of-law process. The development of the concept of party autonomy in private international law may be viewed in connection with the popularization (as well as the individualization) under domestic law of the freedom of ordering granted to contracting parties for a growing number of issues.

C. The Limits of the Proposal

If party autonomy is to become a key legal concept in contemporary society with respect to family relationships, then is it to be offered not just to Muslims originating from foreign countries but also to converted Europeans? Our proposal so far restricts the *optio iuris* model to categories of people of foreign origin who have kept their nationality of origin. The principle of *optio iuris* should not be extended beyond this group, for that would mean a return to religious pluralism in a way that denies the secular foundation of state law and the protections resulting from the separation of state and religion in our countries since the late eighteenth century.

III. CONCLUSION

Whether immigrant women will effectively make use of party autonomy and the way they will do it is very much a matter of their view on Muslim identity in the diaspora. It is also unclear whether Muslim women will be able to resist the pressures within their tradition to opt for Islamic Moroccan law that privileges the husband. This resistance or choice is the responsibility of the women themselves.[32] The hope is that the formula of *optio iuris* may offer for them a solid platform for identity building in a plural context.

For the time being, we continue to collect reactions to our suggestions. The Belgian Minister of Justice has so far been extremely satisfied with the study, mainly because it responds to the needs of law practitioners through its emphasis on application of Belgian law in as many cases as possible. However, we expect critical comments from the Moroccan representatives in Belgium, since their jurisdiction over Moroccan nationals in Belgium is considerably reduced by our proposal.

NOTES

1. *See* L'EUROPE ET LES RÉFUGIÉS: UN DÉFI? [EUROPE AND REFUGEES: A CHALLENGE?] (Jean Yves Carlier & Dirk Vanheule, eds.) (The Hague/London/Boston: Kluwer Law International, 1997); ELSPETH

GUILD, THE DEVELOPING IMMIGRATION AND ASYLUM POLICIES OF THE EUROPEAN UNION: ADOPTED CONVENTIONS, RESOLUTIONS, RECOMMENDATIONS, DECISIONS AND CONCLUSIONS (The Hague/London/Boston: Kluwer Law International, 1996).

2. *See* Bruxelles, Chambre 3e civ., June 30, 1981, Journal des Tribunaux, 656, comment M. Taverne; Revue trimestrielle de droit familial, June 30, 1982.

3. *See* Cassation [Supreme Court], Dec. 11, 1995, Revue trimestrielle de droit familial, 1996, 165, comment J. Y. Carlier; Revue du droit des étrangers, 1996, 185, comment M.-C. Foblets; Rechtskundig Weekblad, 1995–1996, 1339, comment J. Erauw.

4. On the emerging claims of Muslim communities in matters of family law in Europe, see, for example, JØRGEN S. NIELSEN, MUSLIMS IN WESTERN EUROPE 100–17 (Edinburgh: Edingburgh University Press, 2d ed., 1995); Jørgen S. Nielsen, *Introduction: Muslims, Christians and Loyalties in the Nation-State, in* RELIGION AND CITIZENSHIP IN EUROPE AND THE ARAB WORLD 1, 3–6 (Jørgen S. Nielsen, ed.) (London: Grey Seal Books, 1992); Sebastian Poulter, *Cultural Pluralism and Its Limits: A Legal Perspective, in* BRITAIN: A PLURAL SOCIETY 3, 5–13 (London: Commission for Racial Equality, 1990).

5. Moroccan immigrants constitute the largest group of Muslims in Belgium. Moroccan women, therefore, are the most representative group of Muslim women in the country.

6. For an extensive review of the study, its methodologies, its interviews, and its full report, see MARIE-CLAIRE FOBLETS (DIR.), FEMMES MAROCAINES ET CONFLITS FAMILIAUX EN IMMIGRATION: QUELLES SOLUTIONS JURIDIQUES APPROPRIÉES? [IMMIGRANT WOMEN FROM MOROCCO INVOLVED IN FAMILY DISPUTES: WHAT ARE APPROPRIATE LEGAL SOLUTIONS?] (Marie-Claire Foblets, ed.) (Antwerp/Apeldoorn: Maklu-Uitgevers nv, 1998).

7. The researchers on the project were: Nouhza Bensalah, a sociologist and Arabist; Jinske Verhellen, a lawyer and anthropologist; Annabel Belamri, a lawyer; and, Goedele Franssens, a lawyer.

8. We collected over 200 published court decisions.

9. FRIEDRICH K. JUENGER, CHOICE OF LAW AND MULTISTATE JUSTICE 63–64 (Dordrecht/Boston/London: Martinus Nijhoff Publishers, 1993).

10. *See* Paul Lagarde, *La théorie de l'ordre public international face à la polygamie et à la répudiation. L'expérience française [The theory of public policy in private international law with respect to polygamy and repudiation: the French experience], in* NOUVEAUX ITINÉRAIRES EN DROIT. HOMMAGE À FRANÇOIS RIGAUX [NEW DIRECTIONS IN LAW: A TRIBUTE TO FRANÇOIS RIGAUX] 263–82 (Brussels: Bruylant, 1993) [hereinafter NOUVEAUX ITINÉRAIRES]; Bertrand Ancel, *Le statut de la femme du polygame [The status of the wife of a polygamous husband], in* LE DROIT DE LA FAMILLE À L'ÉPREUVE DES MIGRATIONS TRANSNATIONALES 105–24 (Paris: Librairie Géneral de Droit et Jurisprudence, 1993).

11. JUENGER, *supra* note 9, at 61–63.

12. Some legislatures have displaced nationality as the primary connecting factor in cases where either of the spouses no longer has a "true social connection" with his or her country of citizenship. *See, e.g.*, arts. 1(2), 1(1b), Wet van 25 maart 1981 houdende regeling van het conflictenrecht inzake de ontbinding van het huwelijk en scheiding van tafel en bed en de erkenning daarvan ('Wet Conflictenrecht Echtscheiding'), Staatsblad, 1981, at 166 (Dutch).

13. *See* HR, Feb. 9, 1979, NJ 546, at 1824–32 [Netherlands' highest court].

14. For the first suggestion of this approach, see J. H. C. Morris, *Torts in the Conflicts of Laws,* 12 MOD. L. REV. 248 (1949) which was then further elaborated on, see J. H. C. Morris, *The Proper Law of a Tort,* 64 HARV. L. REV. 881 (1951).

15. For a full discussion of *optio iuris,* see JEAN-YVES CARLIER, AUTONOMIE DE LA VOLONTÉ ET STATUT PERSONNEL. ETUDE PROSPECTIVE DE DROIT INTERNATIONAL PRIVÉ [AUTONOMY OF CHOICE AND PERSONAL STATUS: A SURVEY OF INTERNATIONAL PRIVATE LAW] 254–80 (Brussels: Bruylant, 1992).

16. *See* Alfred E. von Overbeck, *L'irrésistible extension de l'autonomie en droit international privè [The Inexorable Growth of the Principle of Party Autonomy in Private International Law], in* NOUVEAUX ITINÉRAIRES, *supra* note 10, at 619–36; Raymond Vander Elst, *Liberté, respect et protection de la volonté en droit international privé [Freedom of, Respect for, and the Protection of party choice in private international law], in* NOUVEAUX ITINÉRAIRES, *supra* note 10, at 507–16.

17. *See* W. E. Elzinga & G.-R. De Groot, *Naar een liberaler naamrecht [Towards a more liberal law on names],* HARTMANS TIJDSCHRIFT VOOR STUDENTEN OPENBAAR BESTUUR 108–126 (1984).

18. Such agreement may be made either before or during the marriage and may subsequently be amended.

19. This is true, for example, of article 3 of the proposed Hague Convention of 1978 on the Law Applicable to Matrimonial Regimes, see Willis M. Reese, *The Thirteenth Session of the Hague Conference,* 25 AM. J. COMP. L. 393 (1977); *see also* Kurt G. Siehr, *Domestic Relations in Europe: European Equivalents to American Evolutions,* 30 AM. J. COMP. L. 37, 51 (1982).

20. *See* CARLIER, *supra* note 15, at 233–383; MARIE-CLAIRE FOBLETS, LES FAMILLES MAGHRÉBINES ET LA JUSTICE EN BELGIQUE. ANTHROPOLOGIE JURIDIQUE ET IMMIGRATION 347–87 (Paris: Karthala, 1994).

21. *See* CARLIER, *supra* note 15, at 233–383.

22. *Id.*

23. *See* NIELSEN, *supra* note 4, at 70.

24. *See generally* FELICE DASSETTO, LA CONSTRUCTION DE L'ISLAM EUROPÉEN. APPROCHE SOCIO-ANTHROPOLOGIQUE [THE CONSTRUCTION OF EUROPEAN ISLAM. A SOCIO-ANTHROPOLOGICAL STUDY] (Paris: L'Harmattan, 1996).

25. *See* A. KESSMAT ELGEDDAWY, RELATIONS ENTRE SYSTÈMES CONFESSIONNEL ET LAÏQUE EN DROIT INTERNATIONAL PRIVÉ 35 (Bibliothèque de droit international privé, vol. X) (Paris: Librairie Dalloz, 1971).

26. "Limping situations" include disagreement among states about, among other things, (1) whether to recognize the existence of a marriage, of a divorce, of paternity, and so on; (2) how to decide when a rule is discriminatory; (3) how to promote coexistence among separate normative systems; and so on. As a result, a woman may well be considered divorced (for example, via *talaq*) in her country of origin, whereas she will be considered still married in the host country.

27. For a full review of the interviews with the women and the data that is discussed in text, see FOBLETS, *supra* note 6, at 59–104.

28. *See* Dal Basco v. Bern, Decision of June 3, 1971, 97 BGE I 389, 409.

29. *See* Cardo v. Cardo, Decision of July 11, 1968, 94 BGE II 65, 71.

30. JUENGER, *supra* note 9, at 229.

31. There could also be situations in which the court would determine that the chosen legal system benefits in a fraudulent way, not just the stronger party in the relationship, but all parties involved where, for example, a speedy divorce suits the interests of both spouses. The court would then be indifferent as to the choice of law made by the parties and will employ its own choice-of-law rules.

32. On this responsibility, see MUSLIM WOMEN'S CHOICES: RELIGIOUS BELIEF AND SOCIAL REALITY (Camillia Fawzi El-Sohl & Judy Mabro, eds.) (Providence/Oxford: Berg, 1994).

V

The War over Women's Bodies:
Sexuality and Reproduction

Chapter 16

Finding Our Feet, Standing Our Ground: Reproductive Health Activism in an Era of Rising Fundamentalism and Economic Globalization

Lynn P. Freedman

I. INTRODUCTION

Women's bodies—their reproductive capacities and sexualities—are both the symbolic currency and the physical, tangible tools used by virtually all fundamentalist movements in their drive to re-order the world according to their own phantasms. It thus becomes relatively easy to catalogue the direct and immediate consequences of fundamentalist power plays on women's reproductive health and sexuality. In the United States, for example, we see the direct results of Christian fundamentalist strategies in the bombing of abortion clinics and in highly orchestrated campaigns to take over local school boards—the ideal perch from which to censor sex education and impose theologically driven, fear-based "abstinence only" curricula for all adolescents.[1] In Afghanistan we see the dramatic consequences for women's health when Taliban decrees ordering total gender segregation in health-care facilities are imposed in a war-decimated environment: the principle of gender segregation is deemed to outweigh the principle of life, as women are literally turned away from hospital doors even in emergency situations when the sure and certain result is death.[2]

One could go on and on: the list is distressingly varied and long. These confrontations with fundamentalism must be fought strategically in each place, taking careful gauge of the context and consequences. But it is also important for us to step past the specifics of particular engagements and to give serious attention to some of the broader dynamics that shape the impact of fundamentalism. Specifically, we need to understand how different fundamentalisms collude with each other, and how they interact with other socially conservative forces even while they co-opt the language and concepts of progressive movements.

We need to understand how these dynamics relate to our own strategies and space as reproductive health and rights movements. Five years after the high-water mark of the 1994 United Nations International Conference on Population and Development (ICPD), held in Cairo, international reproductive health activism is now entering a crucial phase. As the pressure builds to abandon the ICPD agenda as unrealistic and too expensive, and as the alignments that women's movements built in Cairo begin to tremble, we will need to get a better, deeper, and stronger grip on the basic principles that make transnational reproductive health activism both possible and desirable. In short, we need to find our feet and stand our ground.

II. COLLUSION AND CO-OPTION

One of the most enduring characteristics of fundamentalists is their incredible certainty that they own the truth. Whatever else this means, it is a quality that enables them to employ different modes of public presentation and strategic action as circumstances warrant, always keeping their primary end goal clearly and confidently before them. Particularly at the international level, maneuvering on the world stage, two aspects of this chameleon-like quality should draw our attention.

First, despite their ideological rigidity, fundamentalist groups make strategic alliances for particular purposes as suits their ultimate goals. Sometimes alliances are struck across different fundamentalist movements such as when the Vatican-led Christian fundamentalists joined with right-wing Muslim groups in opposition to the Cairo conference.[3] More often, alliances are struck between fundamentalists and other socially conservative forces who may not themselves be identified as fundamentalist. This regularly happens, for example, when a conservative government or political party needs the support of the Religious Right to maintain or legitimate its power, as is the case with the Republican party and the Christian right in the United States, or the Likud government and the religious parties in Israel, or Nawaz Sharif's recent efforts to woo the Religious Right in Pakistan. As a result, the whole edifice of government moves to the right, tinged with the ideological agenda of religious extremists.

Second, the concepts, language, and discourses normally associated with progressive movements are co-opted, distorted, and then re-deployed by fundamentalists in service of their own ends. Such is the case, for example, with concepts such as "multiculturalism,"[4] "rule of law"[5] and "secularism."[6]

Played out in the international arena, this dynamic of collusion and co-option has two main effects. First, alliances with mainstream organizations lend legitimacy to fundamentalist political projects, effectively shielding their ultimate goals—often anti-democratic in the extreme—from serious scrutiny. Second, by co-opting their critics' language and discourse, fundamentalists effectively silence their natural opponents. The result is that progressive movements lose their footing and stumble. Forced into reactive and defensive stances, derailed from their primary focus into side skirmishes, such movements are increasingly sapped of their transformative potential.

In describing this dynamic, I do not mean to ignore the fact that fundamentalist groups do themselves change and develop; they diversify, splinter, and sometimes even self-destruct in internecine warfare. Nor do I mean to imply that there is a fundamentalist hiding under every rock. Indeed, I want to be careful not to attribute to fundamentalist movements some kind of mystical power to infiltrate all quarters with flawless coordination. Nevertheless, I think we have been dangerously inattentive to the ability of fundamentalists to dress in sheep's clothing: to make strategic alliances and to co-opt the language and concepts of progressive movements. The near total lack of attention to these issues, particularly at the international level, among those in the health field seeking to promote the ICPD agenda and implement the reproductive health paradigm, is a case in point.

III. THE REPRODUCTIVE HEALTH PARADIGM AND THE IMPLEMENTATION OF THE ICPD AGENDA

I use the term "reproductive health paradigm" to refer to a view of reproductive and sexual health and rights that found its fullest—even if still imperfect[7]—official, public expression in the declarations and programmes that emerged from the ICPD[8] and the Fourth World Conference on Women held in Beijing in 1995.[9] The ICPD Programme, in particular, can be seen as the culmination of more than a decade of work by women's movements throughout the world, coming from different perspectives and situations, and building on many years of local activism on women's health and rights issues.[10] The broad coalition of women's advocates who participated in the Cairo process made effective use of the research data and theoretical developments that had been generated from within the population/family planning and maternal-child health fields, as well as the human rights and "women-in-development" fields—and so was able to build alliances with academics, program professionals, and policymakers in those arenas as well.

The result at the international level was an effective challenge to the dominant paradigm for thinking about, researching, and acting on women's reproductive health and sexuality. That challenge included the following four critiques: a critique of biomedical approaches that view women's health as a technical problem centered on women's bodies as isolated mechanical systems to be "fixed" through application of expert knowledge; a critique of population control measures that posit women's fertility as the primary threat to development and use women's wombs as the primary tools of target-driven state social engineering policies; a critique of patriarchal social structures that rob women of the ability to control their reproduction, protect their health, enjoy their sexuality, and participate fully in the lives of their societies; and a critique of economic development policies (especially structural adjustment programs) that decimate already rickety health and social welfare systems, while throwing onto women a disproportionate burden for ensuring the survival of families and communities within the brave new world such policies are creating.

The reproductive health paradigm is not only a critique of dominant modes of thinking. It is also a positive vision about women's health, and this positive vision was articulated in the ICPD Programme of Action and endorsed by 184 countries.[11] There are four key elements of that vision: first, health must be viewed holistically with reproductive issues planted firmly within the wider context of a woman's overall physical and emotional health and well-being over the course of the life span; second, reproductive health is premised on a woman's right to make decisions about childbearing and to have the means to implement such decisions, and to express and enjoy her sexuality, free from coercion, violence, and discrimination; third, women's reproductive health and reproductive rights are grounded in the enjoyment of a wider set of human rights, including economic, social, and cultural rights, which are also key to their societies' broader health and social development; and, finally, because the purpose of health programs is to facilitate the fulfillment of this vision of reproductive health and rights, such policies and programs need to be dramatically reoriented to incorporate women and women's perspectives in the planning and implementation.

A. Rising Fundamentalism and Economic Globalization

Certainly reproductive health and rights activists in each country and community face specific obstacles to implementation of the principles of this new paradigm in their local settings. But surveying the situation at an international level, we can see that the reproductive health movement is caught between two forces: rising fundamentalism and economic globalization. At first blush, these two phenomena might seem to pull in opposite directions with fundamentalists re-bordering the world through identity politics while transnational capital seeks to span all borders of identity, geography, and culture in the drive to create global markets. The challenge is to understand how they actually reinforce each other and, together, threaten to sap the power of reproductive health activism to work toward true social change.

Take the concept of "choice" as an example. Perhaps the most basic and important principle in the evolving reproductive health paradigm is its nuanced understanding of the relationship between an individual and the broader community or, translated into rights language, the connection between liberty and equality. Within the reproductive health paradigm, there is a developing understanding of the ways in which health is linked to the ability of an individual woman to be an agent in her own life, to be able to make and implement decisions. But this is not a neoliberal vision of autonomous selves; rather it is a vision that sees women's lives as deeply embedded in the wider social structures of family, community, and state. Thus, for reproductive health advocates, "choice" is a complex notion that seeks to capture both the concept of individual dignity and its connection to structural issues of social justice.

But what happens to the concept of "choice" in the hands of today's free marketeers, as globalization decimates public health and social welfare systems and transforms the state into an agent for privatization? The fundamental principle of the reproductive health paradigm—a woman's right to control over her body—is delinked from questions of equality and community. "Choice" gets co-opted and distorted into a discourse of personal responsibility for health, and a battery of self-help measures come to define the health marketplace. Increasingly, the solution to poor health is believed to lie in individual lifestyle choices assumed to be within our control: eat right, exercise regularly, stop smoking, use condoms, and so on.[12] For the affluent, the result is crass consumerism.[13] For the poor, it means personal responsibility and blame for ill health because of the "willful" failure to follow the prescriptions of the new lifestyle doctors.[14]

This perversion of "choice" operates in a broader assault on women's movements. Emptied of political content and stripped from its social and economic context, "choice" gets marketed as a kind of cartoon feminism, or what Zillah Eisenstein has called "western feminism for export": "[g]litzy advertising and romanticized displays [that] fantasize the freedom of the 'west'" are exported around the world.[15] What started as a complex vision of social transformation is then further re-deployed by social conservatives who characterize it as selfish, crass, and immoral—and the essence of cultural imperialism. Any assertion by women of "liberty" or "choice"—an essential response in the face of fundamentalist measures—is identified with a creeping decadence destroying families and communities and also, in the South, with the encroachment of the "West" and an assault on "authentic" indigenous culture. Such re-deployment of "choice" is used effectively to silence women—both women in the North afraid of being labeled racist and/or imperialist, and women in the South, afraid of being labeled traitors to their collectivities or stooges for Western interests.

Moreover, the perversion of "choice" is given an added boost from some parts of the population establishment (important allies for women's advocates at the ICPD) who shy from any direct efforts to address the power imbalances and structural inequalities that are acknowledged to affect both health and fertility. Instead, they claim to be implementing the ICPD agenda by incorporating only a narrow, diminished—almost rhetorical—concept of "choice" into long-standing family planning programs still intended, above all else, to lower total fertility rates.

The result is that the language of women's reproductive health activism has been assimilated by all players and is used to draw new lines in the sand; the logic of women's reproductive health activism has been quietly shelved as women's movements are forced into defensive postures on multiple opposing fronts. This is, in essence, what Rosalind Petchesky has called the "fault line" in the ICPD Programme: "between the politics of the body, sexuality and reproduction on the one hand and the politics of social development and global economic transformation on the other"—a place which she rightly deems "highly dangerous" for feminists.[16] Fundamentalists help create this fault line; they then exploit it through a process of collusion and co-option. Their negative use of "choice" forces feminists into a politics of the body, sexuality, and reproduction that, in the fundamentalist framework, is made to seem antithetical to a politics of social justice.[17]

I want to suggest that a similar story may now be unfolding with another central concept of reproductive health activism: the critique of biomedicine and the advocacy of holistic approaches to women's health. In this case, however, fundamentalists are poised to use the feminist concept "affirmatively" to support their own destructive politics of identity.

The privatization of health care has created new space and incentives for the promotion of a broader set of health strategies beyond allopathic medicine. There is growing emphasis not just on self-help measures designed to enable the individual to take control over her health, but also on alternative therapies and, particularly, holistic treatments. This is certainly true in the United States, where businesses offering organic foods, natural medicines, and holistic therapies have suddenly appeared virtually everywhere, from shopping malls to mainstream magazines and even in the promotional literature of managed care companies.[18] But it is also true in Southern countries, where indigenous medicine and practitioners, who may have been providing the bulk of health care all along, are gaining new recognition by government health officials and international donors alike. There is much to celebrate in this development, as the women's health movement's long-standing critique of biomedicine implies. But there is also cause for concern.

This is not the first moment in history when supporters of holistic approaches to health—approaches that reject mechanistic views of biology in favor of the "whole body"—have contended with high-tech biomedicine for dominance of the health professions. A recent article by historian Anne Harrington revisits what is perhaps the most horrifying episode of modern medicine, the story of the Nazi doctors.[19] Since the revelations of the Nuremberg war crimes trials in 1949, the prevailing view of Nazi medicine has been what Harrington calls "Nazi medicine as objectivity run amok," in which "the most pernicious energy driving the engine of Nazi medical science had not been its racism, anti-Semitism, political agendas, and so on; it had been its perverse fidelity to an obscene objectivity that ultimately found it possible to see all activities through the lens of expediency, scientific 'interest,' and efficiency."[20] In this view, such objectivity "masked" the suffering of the individual human beings who were the victims of the Nazi death machine, and enabled doctors to perform the most gruesome acts seemingly without feeling or remorse.

In contrast to this widely accepted account, Harrington goes back to the origins of Nazi medicine in the interwar years, a time of economic desperation for Germany, and traces a different strand of Nazi medicine, only recently attracting scholarly attention—what she calls "Nazi holism."[21] Nazi holism gained adherents precisely because of its challenge to the objectification of the body, its assault on the very idea of the body as machine and on medicine as neutral, detached, and technical. Harrington tells the deeply unsettling story of how the holistic critique of Western biomedicine originating in the 1920s in Germany—with its "'wholeness'/'mechanism' battle imagery"—would, in the course of the following decades, begin to "fold into the goals and politics" of Nazism:

"Jewishness as a racial condition—the Jewish way of thinking and being—was perceived as a disorganizing and sterilizing force to be contained and conquered by the answering racial power of German-Aryan 'wholeness.'"[22]

In this discourse the physical body is no longer a shared fact of the human condition. Different bodies need different health care. Thus, difference is constructed through biology, and biology—*addressed through specific approaches to health and health care*—is mobilized around identity. Holistic medicine, building on folk therapies and natural, indigenous materials becomes a key resource in this process. The Dachau concentration camp, for example, had a massive plantation, worked by some 800 to 1200 prisoners, for experimentation with traditional German herbal remedies.[23]

The echoes of Nazi holism are sometimes heard quite clearly today in the discourses of fundamentalist movements. Perhaps the most blatant example is the Rashtriya Swayamsevak Sangh (RSS) in India, which organizes as a grassroots movement through, among other things, a rigorous program of exercise and physical body-building activities.[24] The emphasis on health, exercise, and physical prowess in on-the-ground mobilizing strategies feeds the broader discourse about Hindu racial purity in which the strength of the Hindu nation is threatened by the corrupt and polluted bodies of the Muslim "other."[25]

It is, of course, important for health activists to be attentive to such echoes. But Harrington challenges us, as progressive movements, at a deeper level by showing that the "spin" given to the story of the Nazi doctors in the years following the revelations of the Nuremberg trials is as much about "us" as it is about Nazism. Harrington does not deny the element of truth captured by the explanation of Nazi medicine as "objectivity run amok." But she questions why, at the same time that we embrace this explanation, we have closed our eyes to the competing "holistic" strand of Nazi medicine. Perhaps, she hints, the story of Nazi holism is too de-stabilizing to our own efforts to address what we now perceive as the faults and failures of modernity: "[P]art of the task of confronting human suffering is to recognize that products of our own moral imagination—especially those that shine for us the most brightly—can, if we let them, become seductions, myths of goodness that we can be tempted to serve, even at the expense of the human beings in whose name they were allegedly first constructed."[26]

B. Reproductive Health Activism

The fault line that creates a cleavage between a politics of the body and a politics of social justice becomes an even more dangerous place for reproductive health activists when the products of our own imagination—the principles of the reproductive health paradigm—are emptied of political content and hijacked through a disarming process of collusion and co-option. Within reproductive health and rights movements there is, certainly, an appreciation of the politics of the body on the one hand and the politics of social justice on the other, but there is dangerously little understanding of why it is the linkage between the two that gives the reproductive health paradigm its transformative power. Without a firm understanding of and commitment to the linkage itself, the reproductive health movement can be derailed by both its allies who pull it and its opponents who push it onto one side or the other of the fault line. For a movement that teeters in this precarious spot, the risk of seduction is real indeed. That is why it is crucial for reproductive health activists to stay engaged in the different levels of implementation of the ICPD agenda with a deepened commitment to the linkage.

First, we will need to have a much better grasp of how the fault line is created and exploited by various international forces. The kind of collusion and co-option described here is only a tiny part of the puzzle. The actual causal connections between economic globalization and rising fundamentalism need much greater elaboration.[27] This will require, among other things, a much better understanding of how local realities are, in fact, inextricably linked to transnational forces.

Second, we will need to move beyond our own rhetorical flourishes to recognize that there is nothing inherent in the critique of biomedicine, the promotion of holistic approaches to health, or even the advocacy of an abstracted right to choose, that prevents these concepts from being turned against us. Unless such concepts are grounded in a political vision of health that *insists* on linking individual health and human dignity to public health and social justice, we will find ourselves perpetually stranded at the fault line.

The factual basis for such a vision of health is beginning to emerge through academic work in epidemiology[28] and demography.[29] It is further developed through activist work of the kind undertaken in comparative research-action projects such as that of the International Reproductive Rights Research Action Group[30] or the Women and Law in the Muslim World Programme of Women Living Under Muslim Laws,[31] both of which seek to document the diverse ways in which women themselves understand, articulate, and act on their own entitlements, grounded in the wider conditions of their lives.

A political vision of health requires not only a strong factual basis, but also a conceptual framework that can convert scientific insights into political claims of entitlement.[32] Most critically, such a framework must be able to address *simultaneously* both the challenges to social justice posed by economic globalization and the challenges to individual liberty posed by rising fundamentalism. At the international level, human rights law and discourse provide perhaps the most effective tools for doing this. But as human rights law and discourse evolves it will need to retain the flexibility and sensitivity to move back and forth between the local and the international if it is to give effective voice to women's true concerns and to the real multilayered conditions that shape their lives. In an era of economic globalization and rising fundamentalism, only a vision that can work both transnationally and in dramatically different local settings has any hope of mounting a serious defense against such forces.

IV. CONCLUSION

The Cairo conference was a hugely important moment in the development of a political vision of health as scientific insights, political discourse, and mobilizing strategies came together to gain, in the ICPD Programme of Action, the first level of global commitment to a new paradigm. Now, as the hard work of implementation grinds on and the risks of co-option and division intensify, it becomes increasingly urgent to deepen our understanding of and strengthen our commitment to the fundamental values in which the paradigm must be grounded. In short, we need to find our feet, or we will never be able to stand our ground.

NOTES

1. *See* Susan D. Rose, *Christian Fundamentalism: Patriarchy, Sexuality, and Human Rights,* in this volume; Patricia Donovan, *School-Based Sexuality Education: The Issues and Challenges,* 30 FAM. PLAN. PERSP. 188 (1998).
2. PHYSICIANS FOR HUMAN RIGHTS, THE TALIBAN'S WAR ON WOMEN: A HEALTH AND HUMAN RIGHTS CRISIS 64–73 (U.S.A.: Physicians for Human Rights, 1998).
3. *See* Mark Nicholson, *Fears of Violence Stalk Cairo Conference,* FIN. TIMES, Sept. 1, 1994, at 4.
4. *See* Kenan Malik, *The Perils of Pluralism,* Index on Censorship, No. 3/97, May 1997, *reprinted in* WOMEN LIVING UNDER MUSLIM LAWS, DOSSIER 20, at 138, 141 (Marie-Aimée Hélie-Lucas & Harsh Kapoor, eds.) (Grabels, France: Women Living Under Muslims Laws, 1997).
5. *See* Mahnaz Afkhami, *Gender Apartheid and the Discourse of Relativity of Rights in Muslim Societies,* in this volume, at text accompanying footnote 13.
6. *See* Ratna Kapur, *The Two Faces of Secularism and Women's Rights in India,* in this volume; Brenda Cossman & Ratna Kapur, *Secularism: Bench-Marked by Hindu Right,* 38 ECON. & POL. WKLY. 2613, 2620–25 (1996); Brenda Coss-

man & Ratna Kapur, *Secularism's Last Sigh?: The Hindu Right, the Courts, and India's Struggle for Democracy,* 38 HARV. INT'L LAW J. 113, 139–170 (1997).

7. *See* Rosalind Pollack Petchesky, *From Population Control to Reproductive Rights: Feminist Fault Lines,* 6 REPROD. HEALTH MATTERS 152, 152 (1995); Rhonda Copelon & Rosalind Petschesky, *Toward an Interdependent Approach to Reproductive and Sexual Rights as Human Rights: Reflections on the ICPD and Beyond, in* FROM BASIC NEEDS TO BASIC RIGHTS: WOMEN'S CLAIM TO HUMAN RIGHTS 343, 353–56 (Margaret A. Schuler, ed.) (Washington, DC: Institute for Women, Law and Development, 1995).

8. *See* Programme of Action of the International Conference on Population and Development, *adopted* Sept. 13, 1994, U.N. Doc. A/CONF. 171/13 (preliminary version) (1994) [hereinafter Cairo Programme].

9. *See* Beijing Declaration and Platform for Action adopted by Fourth World Conference on Women, *adopted* Sept. 15, 1995, U.N. Doc. A/CONF. 177/20 (preliminary version), 35 I.L.M. 401 (1996).

10. *See* T. K. Sundari Ravindran, *Women's Health Policies: Organising for Change,* 6 REPROD. HEALTH MATTERS 7, 7–8 (1995).

11. *See* Cairo Programme, *supra* note 8.

12. *See* ALAN PETERSEN & DEBORAH LUPTON, THE NEW PUBLIC HEALTH: HEALTH AND SELF IN THE AGE OF RISK 64–72 (Australia: Allen & Unwin Pty. Ltd., 1996).

13. *See id.* at 67.

14. Lynn P. Freedman, *Human Rights and the Politics of Risk and Blame: Lessons from the International Reproductive Health Movement,* 52 J. AM. MED. WOMEN'S ASS'N 165, 165–66 (1997).

15. ZILLAH EISENSTEIN, HATREDS: RACIALIZED AND SEXUALIZED CONFLICTS IN THE 21ST CENTURY 109 (New York/London: Routledge, 1996).

16. Petchesky, *supra* note 7, at 159.

17. Lynn P. Freedman, *The Challenge of Fundamentalisms,* 8 REPROD. HEALTH MATTERS 55, 56, 64 (1996); Lynn P. Freedman, *Reflections on Emerging Frameworks of Health and Human Rights,* 1 HEALTH AND HUM. RTS. 315, 332 (1994) (citing, e.g., Vatican statements that Cairo conference was "'basically about a type of libertine, individualistic lifestyle' being imposed by the United States under the sway of 'a pervasive feminist influence' that amounted to 'cultural imperialism'").

18. *See* David M. Eisenberg, et al., *Trends in Alternative Medicine Use in the United States, 1990–1997,* 280 JAMA 1569 (1998).

19. Anne Harrington, *Unmasking Suffering's Mask: Reflections on Old and New Memories of Nazi Medicine,* 125 DAEDALUS 181 (1996).

20. *Id.* at 184.

21. *Id.* at 185–95.

22. *Id.* at 188–89.

23. *Id.* at 194.

24. *See* Harsh Kapoor, *Culture, médias, vie social: les fronts du national hindouisme,* 343 ECONOMIE ET HUMANISME 12, 12 (1997); Joseph S. Alter, *Somatic Na-*

tionalism: Indian Wrestling and Militant Hinduism, 28 MOD. ASIAN STUD. 557, 564–70 (1994).

25. PETER VAN DER VEER, RELIGIOUS NATIONALISM: HINDUS AND MUSLIMS IN INDIA 10, 72–73 (Berkeley/Los Angeles/London: University of California Press, 1994); Alter, *supra* note 24, at 568–70.

26. Harrington, *supra* note 19, at 200.

27. *See* Shelley Feldman, *(Re)presenting Islam: Manipulating Gender, Shifting State Practices, and Class Frustrations in Bangladesh, in* APPROPRIATING GENDER: WOMEN'S ACTIVISM AND POLITICIZED RELIGION IN SOUTH ASIA 33 (Patricia Jeffery & Amrita Basu, eds.) (New York/London: Routledge, 1998).

28. *See* Bruce G. Link & Jo Phelan, *Social Conditions as Fundamental Causes of Disease,* J. HEALTH & SOC. BEHAV., Extra Issue 1995, at 80.

29. *See* ROGER JEFFERY & PATRICIA JEFFERY, POPULATION, GENDER AND POLITICS: DEMOGRAPHIC CHANGE IN RURAL NORTH INDIA (Cambridge: Cambridge University Press, 1997).

30. For an example of the International Reproductive Rights Research Action Group's collaborative research and analysis, see NEGOTIATING REPRODUCTIVE RIGHTS: WOMEN'S PERSPECTIVES ACROSS COUNTRIES AND CULTURES (Rosalind P. Petchesky & Karen Judd, eds.) (London/New York: Zed Books Ltd, 1998).

31. *See* Farida Shaheed, *Linking Dreams: The Network of Women Living Under Muslim Laws, in* FROM BASIC NEEDS TO BASIC RIGHTS: WOMEN'S CLAIM TO HUMAN RIGHTS, *supra* note 7, at 305, 320.

32. *See* Freedman, *supra* note 14, at 165.

Chapter 17

Roman Catholic Fundamentalism: What's Sex (and Power) Got to Do with It?

Frances Kissling

I. INTRODUCTION

I would like to start this chapter with a reflection and some observations on the process followed by all of us who attended the May 1998 conference on Religious Fundamentalisms and the Human Rights of Women (from which this book developed). I was absolutely fascinated by the fear that speakers—many of whom are among the most courageous women active in politics today—showed when confronted with time limits. Each of us was allotted a brief amount of time to speak, a time we felt was far too short to make our cases. In traditional fashion, we bemoaned our fate, and moderators, with greater and lesser success, slipped little yellow pieces of paper to each person as their time elapsed.

To some extent this small example of ritual reminded me of the profoundly different ways in which the secular world and the religious world approach the power of ritual. So when my time to speak arrived, I brought some props with me: a bell and some flowers. This is what some of us in the religious world refer to as "smells and bells." No little torn-off strips of yellow legal pads for religionists; that lacks subtlety. Instead, raw power needs to be combined with symbols of gentleness; as one's time expires, a bell is sounded. When one's time has completely expired one is presented with a flower, the symbol of peace used visibly to invoke obedience—the time to be silent.

We have much to learn from these smells and bells. Whether we choose to use them or not, we need to better understand how religions gain obedience and engage the hearts as well as the minds of people. In the context of smells and bells, I'd like to offer some reflections on Roman Catholic perspectives on reproductive health and human rights. The official positions and approach of the Roman Catholic Church (Church) meet commonly accepted definitions of fundamentalism and serve as an obstacle to women's well-being and autonomy. In order to understand the vehement public opposition of the Vatican to the international policy consensus to legalize and make available under public auspices contraceptives, sterilization, abortion, and even fertility treatments, one needs to understand the Church's perspective on sexuality and the modern secular state. With the rise of religious fundamentalism in many religious institutions, we also see links between the Roman Catholic approach to church-state relations and that of fundamentalist Jewish, Christian, and Islamic projects. I will also discuss some aspects of conservative efforts to cast religious believers and institutions as victims, thus seeking even greater special privileges.

II. ROMAN CATHOLIC FUNDAMENTALISM

The discourse on modern religious fundamentalism includes the idea that such fundamentalism is not religious. Because most fundamentalists who claim to possess absolute truth regarding the structure of family, sexual relationships, and reproduction seek laws that would enshrine their views in state and international policy, religiously based fundamentalist projects are seen through a political lens. Moreover, many of the scholars and advocates studying and reacting to religious fundamentalism are trained in disciplines such as the law and political science or have a long history of activism on the political left or in feminist movements, and thus may fail to recognize the religious aspect. Women active within religious traditions, as well as scholars of religion and theologians, have not been particularly active in studying or challenging religious fundamentalist policies. To the extent that we all have an obligation to review and approve or oppose policy initiatives on the basis of the effect that they would have on the common good, a secular understanding of religious fundamentalism and a secular challenge to it are critical.

An effective challenge, however, requires a deeper understanding of the religious basis of the positions and actions undertaken by fundamentalists. The experience and knowledge of those working within religious structures, as well as of progressive theologians and religious scholars, has led them to conclude that the public policy projects of religious fundamentalists are profoundly religious. For example, official Roman Catholic efforts to prevent the legalization of abortion, to limit public funding for contraception and sterilization, to limit if not outlaw divorce and remarriage, and to deny gay rights legislation if it can be construed to accept the "homosexual lifestyle" are based on a long-standing assumption regarding the rights of the church relative to the state. This assumption is not merely fueled by a desire to control, but is rooted in a theological understanding of the relationship of God to people from which one may extract an understanding of the relationship of society and the state to God.

Catholicism contains a long-standing and deep-seated hostility to the concept of the plural and secular state. A plural, secular state challenges patriarchal notions of the proper relationship between men and women and between people and God. While the Church's hostile view was modified somewhat by the Second Vatican Council (1962–65), it is on the rise again within the conservative or fundamentalist Vatican government now in power. It should be noted that Roman Catholicism cannot be viewed as wholly conservative or wholly liberal. For example, the Church is ruled by a pope whose views on human rights in the world include support for the forgiveness of Third World debt side by side with blindness to the need for human rights within the church.[1] The former position leads many to view this Pope as a great intellectual within the Church. The latter position has confirmed that he is most likely the greatest intellect of the fifth century and is ruling the Church as we move into the twenty-first century.

The belief that the church and state are one was set in stone in the early centuries of the Church. The Church and right wing Catholics' hostility to the concept of an independent state is a profoundly religious stance. It is based on religious teachings and religious ideas about the world that started when Constantine converted to Catholicism. At that moment, Catholicism shifted from being a marginal, counter-cultural movement within Judaism to a dominant state religion. The history of Roman Catholicism from Constantine forward is indeed of an institution that sees itself—and its religious role—as the entity that anoints and appoints state leaders. This role of the Church is clear in much of European history where the Church crowned Europe's kings and queens.

The Church bolsters its position with respect to the state by relying on Thomistic theology that, in turn, developed theories of natural law. These theories asserted that religious positions taken by the Church—from the existence of God and the divinity of Jesus to theories about sexuality and reproduction—are based on immutable laws of nature, accessible to all humans regardless of faith and binding on them. Under this approach, states are regarded as having no right to enact laws that contradict natural law, but rather have a duty to enact these "natural" laws as part of secular law. It was not until the Second Vatican Council that the Church acknowledged the separation of church and state as a legitimate religious and political concept. In its Declaration on Religious Liberty, the Church accepted a limited role for itself in the state policy process and greater freedom for the modern state.[2]

Yet, the 35 years since the Second Vatican Council is a mere moment in time for the 2000-year-old Church, and its new 35-year-old approach to the separation of church and state is looking increasingly fragile. In the current fundamentalist climate within the Church, a school of thought has emerged that seeks to apply Catholic natural law conclusions to U.S. law. This movement is lead by well-known legal scholars such as Robert Bork and Robert George.[3] These scholars have gone so far as to claim that the current Supreme Court's decisions on privacy so violate natural law that they can rightfully and legitimately be resisted.[4]

These views are "in favor" in the Vatican and among Catholic fundamentalists, and are manifested in various Church initiatives in the secular world that fail to acknowledge any separation between the Church and state. For example, in Poland, the Church argued that the Polish Constitution should start with the statement that Poland is a Catholic country.[5] In 1995, the Vatican delegation to the United Nations requested that Catholics for a Free Choice's (CFFC) credentials as a nongovernmental organization to the Fourth World Conference on Women, held in Beijing, be withdrawn because CFFC was not "Catholic."[6] There are two particularly extraordinary aspects about the Vatican's request, both based on its concept of the relationship between church and state and the related concept of its authority in this relationship. The Vatican assumed that, first, UN criteria for recognition meant that the UN could decide which groups were "really" Catholic and which were not (an extrapolation of power from the mere position of authority of the UN); and, second, that the UN would do this based upon the Vatican's legitimization or approval of that group, as if the Vatican were a state.

The strongest sign of the fact that the Church sees itself as both a religion and a secular government is its recognized status at the UN as a permanent observer nonmember state[7]—a status that it shares with Switzerland. From the way the Vatican conducts itself at the UN, it would appear that it sees little difference between itself, the Vatican State, and the United States. However, the Vatican is unique among UN members in that it believes itself to be infallible on some matters under consideration by the UN. In the UN, a body that strives so diligently for consensus and compromise, an "infallibility" perspective is surely problematic.

The Vatican presents quite an image as a state. It points with pride to the 160 plus countries that recognize it as a state and exchange ambassadors with it.[8] There are no women ambassadors from the Vatican, and it is only in recent years that any country appointed a woman as its ambassador to the Vatican.[9] At present, there are fewer than a half-dozen women representing countries at the Vatican. The Vatican has about 1000 male citizens and an electoral body comprised of men appointed by the Pope. Given the lack of democratic procedures, it could certainly be regarded as an anomalous, if not rogue, state. The Vatican State's small geographic area consists primarily of tourist attractions, museums, a post office, and a radio station.[10] Under the criteria used by the UN to admit the Vatican, EuroDisney should similarly be able to seek statehood.[11]

III. WOMEN, SEXUALITY, AND POWER

Against this background of the Vatican State's position on state and church relations and the growth of fundamentalism in other religions aimed at claiming state power, one looks with concern on the current lobbying and legislative efforts of conservative Christian groups. Conservative Protestants and Catholics have been active in claiming that Christians in the United States are discriminated against and derided by a secular elite and that Christians (and others, but the emphasis is on Christians) in many countries are subject to profound discrimination including denial of the right to practice their faith.[12] In the United States, these groups have successfully sought legislation that requires the U.S. government to monitor religious persecution and to implement sanctions against countries who are found to persecute groups and individuals on the basis of religious belief.[13] This approach, in effect, elevates state persecution based on religious belief or membership to a high degree of human rights scrutiny—over and above other human rights violations.

While there are serious instances of state persecution on the basis of religious belief, and these surely should be addressed with the same vigor as are other human rights violations, there is some concern that this effort is designed more to enhance the status of conservative Christianity. It is certainly as reasonable to assert that religious institutions are guilty of oppressing their members (and others) as it is to assert that a state is guilty of persecuting believers. For example, women especially have had a hard time achieving equality within most faith groups.[14]

There is thus a suspicion that this new effort to cast religions as oppressed institutions follows very quickly upon the increased public understanding of the ways in which religion violates or is used to violate the human rights of women. For example, the Church has been especially active in seeking exemptions from new laws that require nondiscrimination in employment. In the United States, teachers have been fired because they were divorced and remarried or because they have become pregnant out of wedlock.[15] Should the state be protecting the religious tenets of certain members or leaders of a religion, or protecting all women, including those whose reproductive behavior is considered sinful by certain religious leaders? There has also been an increasing number of claims of exemption by Church officials for their hospitals from providing reproductive health care including contraception.[16] For those committed to sexual and reproductive health and rights, the question of religious exemptions that favor faith groups rather than consumers is extremely troubling.

The move for exemptions is not only within the United States. Roman Catholic bishops in Great Britain and other countries are challenging proposed European Union provisions that prevent discrimination against homosexuals, claiming that their religious beliefs prevent them from hiring homosexuals in schools as well as in other Church institutions.[17] Where should state protection lie? Should it protect religious tenets as described by Church leaders, or individuals whose sexual identity is unpopular with some religious leaders?

To some extent, the ease with which government officials seek to accommodate religious institutions indicates the extent to which our understanding of religion can best be characterized as pre-Enlightenment. Perhaps there was a time when distinct religious denominations enjoyed near absolute concurrence with positions by their members. But, it is clear that that is no longer the case. Indeed, in the case of Catholicism, large majorities of Catholics disagree with certain policy and moral positions taken by Church leaders. This is especially true on matters related to women's rights, sexuality, and reproduction. Not only are many Catholics supportive of allowing women to make reproductive decisions on the basis of a personal, informed conscience, but they also reject Church explanations for the basis of Roman Catholic teaching in opposition to abortion.[18]

There is a growing understanding among Catholics that the Church's opposition to legal abortion may be rooted more in a vehement hostility and fear of women and sexuality than in the hostility to the secular state as discussed above. While Church leaders have claimed that their opposition to abortion is based on Church teaching that requires that human life be absolutely protected from conception to natural death, a review of Church documents and core teachings regarding conscience show this to be a less than candid or full exposition of Church teaching. Like most religions, the Church has taken no position on when the fetus becomes a person or at what moment the fetus is given a soul by God. A 1974 Church document on this matter, the Declaration on Procured Abortion issued by the Vatican Congregation on the Faith, states that it "[e]xpressly leaves aside the question of the moment when the spiritual soul is infused. There is not a unanimous tradition on this point and authors are as yet in disagreement."[19] This view meshes well with that expressed in the U.S.

Supreme Court decision in *Roe v. Wade,* which notes that neither law nor medicine are able to answer the question of when life begins.[20] A more recent Church document, the Encyclical Evangelium Vitae, which condemns abortion in all circumstances as a crime against life, did not take the definitive step of declaring the Church's opposition to abortion infallible.[21] This is significant because "the word 'infallibly' had been considered for the formulas in earlier drafts."[22] Given the Pope's unrelenting campaigning against abortion, there is no doubt that Church leaders would have taken this step if they could have.

The Church's claim that opposition to abortion is based on an absolute commitment to life has also been undercut by the unwillingness of Church officials to unequivocally condemn all killing in war, self-defense, or capital punishment. Taking life is sometimes permitted in Church law and the fact that the Church does not grant women some leeway in making reproductive decisions reflects a persistent culture of sexism, not respect for life.

Liberation theologians have noted that the Church itself needs to be subjected to political analysis. It is a social organization with a government that acts in its own interest as well as seeking to serve the common good. The governing structure of the Church is designed to reinforce male rule. In order to rule in the Church, there are two simple qualifications. First, you need to be a man—not necessarily a good one or a smart one. Second, you need to pledge that you will not have sex, but you do not necessarily need to keep that vow. The purpose of those two qualifications is to rule out women, who are regarded as historically suspect in any event. They also serve to rule out the vast majority of Catholics who, like most people, regard sexuality as an integral component of human life.

Women and sexuality are the historic and modern bane of fundamentalists, including Roman Catholic fundamentalists. Ever since Eve, women have been seen as the source of evil, and sex has been one of the greatest sins. It is no accident that those religions that are most welcoming of women into the ordained ministry, and accept married clergy, have the most positive positions on abortion and family planning. While none laud abortion as a positive moral good, all see it as a moral option, minimally a necessary but tragic choice. Can there be any doubt that official Catholic attitudes toward sexuality and women are determinant in the oppositional, indeed, fundamentalist position taken by the Church?

Precisely what is the Church's position on sexuality and women? Through the eighteenth century, Church leaders debated whether any sexual activity, even in marriage, could be free of sin. A general rule of thumb was that the greater the pleasure in sex, the more sinful it was. Even now, for Church leaders, steeped in natural law and in personally celibate lifestyles, sex is understood in terms of "nature," and is to be directed toward procreation. Thus, the Church's mandate is that every sex act must be open to procreation. The use of contraception or sterilization is a clear sign that one has rejected Church teachings on sexuality. Abortion, of course, is the most obvious sign that one does not accept the Church's position.

In the mid-1950s, the Church allowed that there could be another legitimate goal of sexuality between a married heterosexual couple other than procreation: the unitive function. In addition to procreation, the Church regarded sex as serving to unite the couple in love and draw them closer together in fulfilling their task of raising a family. While Church documents did not speak directly of pleasure, the unitive function was popularly understood to support pleasure in sex. The Church, however, has now moved into a fundamentalist mode with a fundamentalist pope, and pleasure is no longer a popular idea. Women, whom early Church leaders saw as temptresses leading men astray and whose sexual persona distracted men from their task of worshipping God, have again become problematic in the eyes of the Church. Both the taboo on sex for pleasure and the insistence that sex occur only in marriage and be directed primarily toward procreation have reemerged with a vengeance.

While posturing as a friend and supporter of women's rights, the current Church administration actually sees women primarily through the lens of motherhood, and advocates for women on this basis. Under this view, even motherhood must be desexualized. The little girl in grammar school learns this message very early on. Indeed, she learns she will never reach a state of being in which the Church respects her, because the model she is given for her life is the Virgin Mother. This is a model no woman can meet. Women cannot be both virgins and mothers.

Instructions to women from the earliest days of the Church focused on controlling women's sexuality. St. Jerome, an early misogynist Church leader, was steeped in Greek philosophical dualism. The body was bad, especially women's bodies, and the spirit was good, especially men's spirits. St. Jerome advised women not to dress up, but rather to wear the ugliest clothes possible, to walk close to walls, and never lift their eyes to men. Indeed, women were to make themselves as physically unattractive as possible in order to avoid their bodies distracting men's souls and spirits. According to this world view, men have no responsibility for their sexual feelings. If there is sexual misconduct, women are to blame.

I will close this chapter with a story that illustrates the difficulty that Roman Catholicism has had in developing an ethic based on a positive view of sexuality. Roman Catholicism, like much of patriarchal society, tends to view sex as something to be limited, not something to be welcomed. An early attempt by the Church to put forward a positive vision of sexuality is illustrative of this tendency. During the Renaissance, the Church decided to address the question of when married couples could have sex. The Church brought together a group of experts on sexuality— monks—and sent them to the mountains to develop a code on sexual relations. Their conclusion was that there should be no sex when a woman is menstruating, pregnant, or lactating; no sex during the 40 days of Lent; no sex during the 25 days of Advent; no sex on holy days or ember days; no sex on Fridays and no sex on Sundays. While these rules no longer apply and we are reassured by Church leaders that sex within a lifelong heterosexual marriage is regarded as a positive good, the taboo on a sexual life directed primarily to the expression of love nonetheless remains central to the fundamentalist project within Roman Catholicism.

The fundamentalist project aims to control women and preserve male power. What those in the Church who challenge this project seek is a major social transformation of how women are viewed and how their sexuality is enhanced, appreciated, and honored. To liberate women from motherhood, to see them as persons in their own right, is to challenge directly male control of the family and to establish the blueprint for a social structure—and perhaps a Church structure—in which power and decision making are equally shared between men and women.

NOTES

1. *See God's Politician,* IRISH TIMES, Oct. 19, 1998, at 52.
2. DECLARATION ON RELIGIOUS LIBERTY, Vatican II, *Dignitatis Humanae,* 7 December 1965, *reprinted in* VATICAN COUNCIL II: THE COUNCILIAR AND POST COUNCILIAR DOCUMENTS 799, 804–05 (Austin Flannery, O.P., ed.) (Northport, NY: Costello Publishing Co., 1992).
3. *See* ROBERT H. BORK, SLOUCHING TOWARDS GOMORRAH: MODERN LIBERALISM AND AMERICAN DECLINE 272–95 (New York, Regan Books, 1996); ROBERT P. GEORGE, MAKING MEN MORAL: CIVIL LIBERTIES AND PUBLIC MORALITY (Oxford: Clarendon Press, 1993).
4. *See* BORK, *supra* note 3, at 96–119; GEORGE, *supra* note 3, at 93–97, 210–17.
5. *See* Anthony Barker, *Solidarity Chief Demands Godly Polish Constitution,* REUTERS WORLD SERVICE, Feb. 25, 1997, *available in* LEXIS, News Library, Non-US File.
6. *See* Julia Preston, *U.N. Summit on Women Bars Groups; China, Vatican Block Opponents' Admission,* WASH. POST, Mar. 17, 1995, at A36.
7. *See* Yvette Delph & Kathy Toner, *First Among Equals,* 18 CONSCIENCE 2 (1997).
8. *See God's Politician,* IRISH TIMES, Oct. 10, 1998, at 52.
9. *See* Ruth Gledhill, *Britain Sends First Woman Ambassador to Vatican,* TIMES, Mar. 11, 1995, *available in* LEXIS, News Library, Non-US File.

10. *See* Delph & Toner, *supra* note 7, at 4.

11. Frances Kissling, *The Challenge of Christianity,* 44 AM. U. L. REV. 1345, 1345 (1995).

12. *See* Christian Coalition Press Releases 1997, *Fighting Religious Persecution Worldwide a Christian Coalition Top Priority* (visited Nov. 20, 1998) <http://www.cc.org/publications/ccnews/ccnews97.html>.

13. *See* International Religious Freedom Act of 1998, Pub. L. No. 105–292, 112 Stat. 2787, Oct. 27, 1998.

14. *See* Section VII of this volume, Religious Challenges to Religious Fundamentalism.

15. *See* Geary v. Visitation of the Blessed Virgin Mary Parish School, 7 F.3d 324 (3d Cir. 1993); Boyd v. Harding Academy of Memphis Inc., 88 F.3d 410 (6th Cir. 1996); *see also* Jendi B. Reiter, *Sex and the Single Teacher,* LEGAL TIMES, May 18, 1998, at S46.

16. *See* Karen Brandon, *Religion, Medicine Collide on Birth Care; Catholic Affiliations Cut Women's Options,* CHI. TRIB., July 7, 1998, at 1; Victor Cohn, *Catholic Hospitals: Balancing Medical Advances and Papal Valued,* WASH. POST, June 9, 1987, at Z12.

17. *See* Martin Pendergast, *Rights, Privileges, and "Public Authorities,"* 19 CONSCIENCE 25, 25–27 (1998).

18. *See* Kathy Toner, *Is Anyone Listening?,* 17 CONSCIENCE 3 (1996).

19. Sacred Congregation for the Doctrine of Faith, Declaration on Procured Abortion 26 n.19 (Boston, MA: Daughters of St. Paul, n.d.).

20. *See* Roe v. Wade, 410 U.S. 113, 159–62 (1973).

21. *See* POPE JOHN PAUL II, ENCYCLICAL EVANGELIUM VITAE, *reprinted in* 24 ORIGINS 689, 709–11 (1995); Laurie Goodstein, *Nations Conspire 'Against Life,' Pope Declares: Abortion, Contraception Decried,* WASH. POST, Mar. 31, 1995, at A1, A38.

22. *Pope stepped back from making encyclical statements infallible,* NAT'L CATHOLIC REP., Apr. 7, 1995.

Chapter 18

Reconciling the Opposites: Equal but Subordinate

Asma M. Abdel Halim

> I decided to take a look at the Paradise I am promised after life if I behave
> well. I advise you to do the same if you are a Parsi, a Catholic, a Protestant,
> a Jew, or . . . you're in for a big surprise! Parsi, Catholic, Protestant, Jewish
> and Moslem paradises are not designed to make women happy! So what are
> they designed for? Between you and me, we had better organize ourselves
> to sort this out before we die. Who wants to be faced with problems just
> when you decide to have a long, peaceful sleep?
>
> —Fatima Mernissi[1]

I. INTRODUCTION

The concept of patriarchy in the Muslim world has been the focus
of reformers who are trying to improve the status of women,
and the focus of traditionalists and fundamentalists who are trying to legitimize the concept. Muslim scholars are thus hard at work
trying to prove or disprove the equality of the sexes. So far, the best that
they have been able to do is to declare that women and men are equal
in human "dignity."[2] Although a number of scholars have advocated the
equality of women and men in Islam, they have ended their advocacy
by surrendering to the shari'ah.[3] Polishing the old ideas to look new
does not help women, because the polishing rarely goes to the root
cause of the discrimination—discrimination based on sexual roles. Reformists have kept the old concepts while trying to change the consequences of those concepts. This strategy inevitably fails because sooner

or later the reformist will come face to face with the original concept that keeps women subordinate to men.

The status of Muslim women thus far has been articulated along the lines of traditional interpretations of the shari'ah (the body of Islamic law derived primarily from the Qur'an and secondarily from the Sunnah—the sayings and exemplary customs and habits of the Prophet Muhammad). These interpretations have focused on sex and sexuality as the determining factor for rights and duties. The concept of "gender"—that differential social roles for women and men are socially constructed rather than dependent on "natural" sexual differences—is an anathema to Muslim fundamentalists for the very reason that it delinks the status of women from their sexuality. This chapter discusses various examples of how women's sexuality has been interpreted by Muslim scholars to be the most important factor for determining women's rights and duties in Islam, and suggests alternative approaches.

II. DEFINING WOMEN'S STATUS ACCORDING TO SEXUAL BEHAVIOR

Women's sexuality is dealt with in relation to its effect on men, who are regarded as the center of social life in Islamic societies. The traditional interpretative approach to the Qur'an regards women as lustful creatures whose sexuality is obstructive to the performance of men's duties and carries the seeds of destruction of the world.[4] While men's pursuit of women is widely accepted as a natural instinct, women's sexual responses are seen as temptations to be repressed and avoided. *Hejab* (as interpreted by traditionalists and fundamentalists) thus requires segregation of women and men and dictates that if women go outside their homes, they should be fully covered, often including veiling the face, in order not to attract men's attention.[5] Some religious commentary has gone so far as to find that "[t]he whole of a woman's body is a pudendum except her face and hands."[6] The "veil" that covers a woman's body from head to toe is intended to operate as a curtain of protection between the woman and the man. Yet, the "veil" in practice further eroticizes women's bodies by its very focus on the illicit quality of women's bodies. The veiled erotic body becomes central to men's lives and the benefits of that body are negotiated according to men's terms. Men are thus presented with the dilemma of learning to want to avoid and being required to avoid that which is central in their lives. The responsibility for resolving that dilemma is delegated to women; women must fully cover their tempting bodies in order to protect men.

Some women have tried to argue that *hejab* is beneficial for women because it gives them their own domain and guarantees them freedom of movement.[7] This very argument shows how women have become convinced that they can only be free if they are isolated and that men are not capable of, and should not have responsibility for, controlling their sexual urges.

An examination of the interpretations of two Qur'anic verses that are understood to be dealing with *zina* (fornication) demonstrates how the desire to retain the view of women as sexual temptresses and the source of evil has affected these interpretations, and have dictated the result that women's status is determined by their sexual behavior. The Qur'anic verse 4:15 may be translated as:

> Regarding your women who are guilty of fornication, call to witness four of you against them. And if they testify (to the truth of the allegation) then confine the women to the houses for the rest of their lives or (until) Allah provides them with a way out (of this punishment).[8]

A number of scholars regard this verse as being abrogated by a later verse in the Qur'an[9] (the Qur'an was not all revealed to Muhammad at the same time, but was revealed in a piecemeal fashion over time) that punishes both men and women who commit *zina* by flogging of 100 lashes.[10] These interpreters regard the latter verse as dealing only with a change in the punishment for *zina*. Such interpretations insist on retaining a view of women as the source for sexual misconduct. But, in fact, the later verse could be viewed as representing a paradigm shift in the Qur'an. This shift was away from the view that women's erotic bodies were responsible for sexual misconduct and should be shut away from the outside world. Instead, under the latter verse, women are regarded as equal to men: women and men are equally responsible for fornication; women and men must bear the same punishment; and women and men are both restricted in the same way with respect to who they marry—they may marry only fornicators or unbelievers. Hence, this verse is a move toward gender equality.

A second example regarding *zina* also demonstrates how interpreters insist on focusing on women's sexual behavior as determining their status in a way that they do not on men's. Verses six, seven, eight, and nine of Surat al-Nour of the Qur'an legislate a procedure that allows a man to prove his wife's *zina* without the usual obligation to produce four witnesses to give evidence. Essentially, the husband's evidence suffices if he swears four times in the name of Allah that he is telling the truth, and a fifth time that Allah's curse will be upon him if he is lying. The wife may avert the punishment of adultery if she swears four times in the name of Allah that her husband is lying, and a fifth time that the wrath of Allah will be upon her if her husband has told the truth.[11] After these oaths, the marriage is dissolved immediately.

There is no equivalent verse that is understood to provide the same procedure for a wife to use against her husband if he has committed *zina* that has only been witnessed by the wife. Rather, it is understood that a woman must have four witnesses to charge her husband with *zina*.

However, there is nothing in these verses that prevents interpreting them as to allow both men and women to use this procedure in the same way. For example, it would not be unreasonable to argue that a principle of equality between both male and female fornicators applies with respect to the restrictions as to who they might marry, and must therefore apply to the procedure that actually determines the issue of fornication. In addition, because of the cardinal rule that a fornicator should only be married to a woman who is also a fornicator, there are good grounds for using the same rule to enable women to obtain a divorce from a man whose marriage is illegal on this basis. An advantage of my interpretation is that it would stop men who are fornicators from abusing the power that they have by virtue of interpreting this procedure as unavailable to women in a context where a woman's right to divorce is otherwise limited to very narrow grounds.[12] For example, a wife who desires a dissolution of her marriage because of her husband's fornication is unable to use the above procedure, and instead, may be vulnerable to paying property to her husband in order to obtain his consent to dissolution of marriage through *khul'*—which allows women to offer property to get a divorce for reasons that are not grounds for a divorce. In a world of AIDS, when the right to a safe sexual relationship has become a matter of life and death, women are, in essence, compelled to stay married to promiscuous men because they do not have four witnesses to prove *zina*.

A. Female Circumcision: Is it an Islamic Tradition?

Islam inherited from Arab tribal societies an obsession with women's sexuality.[13] Prior to Islam, sexual play and the eroticizing of women's bodies were *de rigeur* in the poetry of the Arabian peninsula, the main literature of that time. The poetical descriptions of love affairs and women's bodies reveal a time when women were considered as nothing more than erotic sexual objects.

In their quest to maintain control over women's sexuality, Muslim societies found no difficulty in adopting female circumcision (FC), a local tradition that predated Islam.[14] Obviously, FC is a very direct way to control a woman's sexuality, and fits well into Islamic interpretations that a woman's sexuality is dangerous, needs to be controlled, and should not be

enjoyed by the woman herself. Yet, there is no apparent religious foundation in Islam for assuming that FC is mandated by Islam.

Despite there being no foundation in Islam, a number of Muslim religious leaders have stated that FC is mandatory in Islam. For example, in
Egypt in 1996, the Minister of Health provoked debate by prohibiting FC
being performed by doctors and other healthcare workers because it
caused serious health problems for women. Realizing that FC serves as a
means of control of women, fundamentalists quickly imported Islam into
the debate to silence the voices against FC. Sheikh Gad al Haq, the former
head of Al-Azhar university, the first Islamic university and a source for Islamic *fatwas* (religious opinions) for hundreds of years, issued a long *fatwa*
that addressed both male and female circumcision and stressed that FC was
mandatory in Islam.[15] Despite conservative and fundamentalist Muslim
zealots' condemnation of Egypt as un-Islamic and sinful, they nonetheless
wasted no time in availing themselves of state court where they invoked
their version of Islam against the Minister of Health.[16] The lower court
used every technicality it could find to strike down the decision of the
Minister of Health's ruling. Finally, the highest appellate court upheld the
Minister's decision to ban FC in medical facilities.[17] Yet, Egypt is still without a law—rather than an executive ruling by a minister—that prohibits
FC in general or protects women who resist the practice.

Although the current head of al-Azhar, Mohammed Sayyed Tantawi, has
now issued a *fatwa* that FC is not mandatory in Islam,[18] it is still possible to
see in the Egyptian example the same, tired theme of fundamentalist men interpreting Islam in a manner to enhance the patriarchal control of women's
sexuality. Yet the Qur'an itself expressly denounces the deliberate infliction of
harm and deplores any changes to God's creations.[19] In fact, bodily integrity
is part of the three objectives of Islamic jurisprudence, and it is being sacrificed for purposes of enhancing patriarchal control over women's sexuality.

B. The Status of Women in Marriage

In many states with Muslim majorities, the personal or family law is governed by Islamic law, and particularly the shari'ah. For example, in
Sudan, under Islamization, the Personal Law for Muslims Act (Personal
Law) was enacted in 1991, and with respect to women's rights, it does
not deviate much from the shari'ah.[20] Under Sudan's Personal Law, an
unmarried woman must have a *wali* (a male guardian). Women may not
contract their own marriage, nor serve as the guardian for another
woman. A *wali* has the responsibility to negotiate and conclude the marriage contract, and the exclusive right to judge the suitability of the

woman's future husband.[21] Although a woman must consent to the marriage, her ability to prevent the marriage is limited to challenging the *wali* in court—which may not be successful. The law does not treat her as a human being who may make choices concerning crucial aspects of her life. Her role in life is to provide sexual services for her husband and to bring social prestige to her family by being married to a socially and financially acceptable man chosen by her *wali*. She is defined in terms of what she can do for others.

Under the marriage contract and the law, "the wife is required to obey the husband and care for him by protecting herself and his property."[22] The wife's duty to obey has been justified by some traditionalists and fundamentalists as an exchange for the husband's duty of "protection" in the form of an obligation to provide basic financial support during marriage.[23] Yet this exchange is by no means equal; the woman is under control of her husband and vulnerable to him. In addition to the wife's duty to obey, a woman cannot leave her home without her husband's approval. The husband is regarded as having a right to confine his wife to the home, and so he may withhold his approval. The rationale behind the rule is that the woman's duty under the marriage contract is to be at her husband's disposal at all times so that the husband may fulfill his sexual needs whenever he desires.

Again, with respect to sexual relations in marriage, male interpreters have viewed the Qur'an through a patriarchal lens. Interpretations assert a man's role as the initiator and controller of sexual relations in a marriage and as the controller of women's sexuality. Qur'anic verse 2: 223 is often cited as support for male control over sexual relations. The verse is understood to affirm the legality of sexual relations in a marriage at all times, and that in this marital context sex is nothing to be ashamed of.[24] The legalizing of sexual relations in this verse occurred in a context where beliefs at the time allowed sodomization of women.[25] The verse also tells the man that his wife is a tilth for him to cultivate, and that he may approach her as he likes (subject to Qur'anic verse 2:222's prohibition of intercourse during menstruation). Much of the debate of male interpreters concerning this verse focused on whether the verse meant that husbands could sodomize their wives.[26] The verse was interpreted to give men the exclusive right to control the sexual relationship. Any sense that the woman may have a role in sexual relations, or was the initiator in asking the Prophet about this issue,[27] has been ignored.

It is important to note in this context that in the early days of Islam, women challenged men's willingness to give up sexual relations so as to spend their nights worshipping God.[28] Characterizing this behavior as a threat to her sexual rights, a woman came to the Prophet and asked whether his message involved enticing a man to leave his matrimonial bed in order to spend the night worshipping Allah and thereby eliminating a woman's right to sexual pleasure. The answer to that challenge was clear: celibacy is not part of Islam and women have a right to a satisfying sexual life in the marriage.[29] This answer is not always followed in interpretations and seems to have been forgotten in the interpretation of Qur'anic verse 2:223.

C. Marital Rape

The above-mentioned exclusive right of access to the woman's sexual organs has led to the belief and interpretations that disobedience of the wife or refusal of the wife to engage in sexual intercourse may justify her subjection to a forcible sexual relationship, or what is known as marital rape.[30] This is premised on the belief that a wife may not refuse sex to her husband and so her not consenting to sex is impossible.[31] The legal justification that is used to support marital rape is again that the marriage contract is one of exchange. The argument is that the wife received consideration for the marriage contract in the form of dowry and receives maintenance (food, clothing, and a home) during the marriage in return for her obedience and sexual accessibility. By concluding the marriage contract, the woman has consented to unlimited sexual accessibility by the husband. Therefore, a woman who disobeys is in breach of the marriage contract, and the husband can enforce his right to accessibility by forceful means. Yet, there is no basis in the Qur'an for this legitimation of forced sexual access.

Even if Qur'anic verse 4:34 is taken to its extreme, it is understood to stipulate the following actions to be taken in the case of disobedience of the wife: first, she is to be admonished; second, the husband is to desert her in bed; and, third, he is to beat her lightly.[32] When all of the above fails, two arbitrators, one from the wife's family and one from the husband's family, are to be appointed to decide whether the marriage should continue.[33] Under no circumstances does this verse sanction forcible sexual relations. Marital rape is simply illegal in Islam. Even the beating is supposed to bring about a consent, not to serve as an excuse to rape. The question, of course, that remains unanswered is: should a consent obtained by a beating be valid? Perhaps the social circumstances at the time of this Sura would lead to an affirmative answer. But the question that we should be concerned with is: Under current social circumstances, should a husband be empowered by the law to obtain such a consent? The answer must be "no." There are definite limits even under traditional interpretations of Qur'an; an excessive beating of a wife may allow her to obtain a divorce.

Moreover, the rule that applies in cases of resistance by men to marital duties is Qur'anic verse 4:128, which states that if a woman fears ill-treatment or desertion on the part of her husband, they (the couple) should seek a reconciliation between them.[34] Thus, under this verse, as under the others noted, there are no circumstances in which sexual relations may occur in the marriage without consent. Again, some interpreters have insisted on understanding these verses in a way designed to ensure male control over sexual relations and over women's sexuality.

D. The Pleasures of Paradise

Does a woman's role as a passive object serving both as sexual temptation for men and as a receptacle for men's pleasure change in the role assigned to women after death? As Fatima Mernissi notes in the quote at the beginning of this article, paradise in the next world has not been designed for women. According to certain interpretations, sexual pleasures are heaped on men alone in the next world. In interpreting the Qur'anic verse that promises believers *houris* (extra-terrestrial, wide-eyed, beautiful females), Muslim scholars have virtually competed as to who can award the highest number of *houris* to each male believer.

In the twentieth century, particularly in Iran and Sudan, the promise of *houris* wives in the hereafter helped recruit young men as fighters and shaped their political views. These young fighters were promised *houris* if they became martyrs in a *jihad* (religious struggle) or wars that assumed a divine status. In contrast to how the Qur'an has been interpreted to make sure that women's sexuality is under control and repressed, men are encouraged to focus and obsess on sexual pleasures—not as a vice that women should be protected from, but as something legitimate to indulge in.

III. CONCLUSION

Muslim women's claim to their human rights is destined to be treated by fundamentalists as a move by lustful women seeking to Westernize the life in Muslim societies. The demand by women in Saudi Arabia to have driver's licenses caused a tempest, and Abd al-Aziz ibn Abdallah ibn Baz, the leading Muslim scholar in the country, called on the ruling monarchy to beware the lust of women that could destroy the society.[35]

Muslims have to face the fact that women's demand of their human rights has nothing to do with "Western" ideas. Women have challenged the rules since the early days of Islam. Women's challenges to patriarchal interpretations of the Qur'an, the Sunnah, and the shari'ah have been, and are, based on the awareness of their humanity—a humanity that is, and should be, confirmed in Islam. Muslim women challenging patriarchal rules are not seeking to convert to other religions or to denounce their religion. Instead, they are seeking to invoke the best that there is in Islam and that supports them as full human beings.

NOTES

1. Fatima Mernissi, Women in Moslem Paradise (New Dehli: Kali for Women, 1986) (no page numbering).
2. The Cairo Declaration on Human Rights in Islam, June 9, 1993, U.N. Doc. A/CONF.157/PC/62/Add. 18, at 2, The World Conference on Human Rights, Prep. Comm., 4th Sess., Provisional Agenda, Item 5, article 6(a) (1990), *reprinted in* Ann Elizabeth Mayer, Islam and Human Rights: Tradition and Politics 203–08 (Appendix B) (Boulder, CO: Westview Press, 1999).
3. *See* Abdelwahab El-Affendi, Turabi's Revolution: Islam and Power in Sudan 173–75 (London: Grey Seal, 1991).
4. *See* Abul A 'La Maududi, Purdah and the Status of Woman in Islam 2, 121–23 (Al-Ash 'ari trans. ed., 1972) (1939) [hereinafter Maududi, Purdah).
5. *See* Maududi, Purdah, *supra* note 4, at 163–216; Safia Iqbal, Woman and Islamic Law 52–59 (Delhi: Adam Publishers & Distributors, rev. ed. 1991).
6. *See* Andrea B. Rugh, *Reshaping Personal Relations in Egypt, in* 2 The Fundamentalism Project: Fundamentalisms and Society 151, 172 (Martin E. Marty & R. Scott Appleby, eds.) (Chicago/London: The University of Chicago Press, 1993).
7. *See* Iqbal, *supra* note 5, at 50–60.
8. Author's translation.
9. *E.g.,* S. Abul A'la Maududi, The Meaning of the Qur'an (Vol. II) 307, 309 n.26 (Delhi: The Board of Islamic Publications, 1971).
10. Qur'an 24:2–3 (Surat al-Nour), *in* Abdullah Yusuf Ali, The Holy Qur'an: Text, Translation and Commentary 896 (Beirut/Lebanon: Dar al-Arabia, n.d.) [hereinafter Ali, The Holy Qur'an].
11. Qur'an 24:6–9 (Surat al-Nour), *in* Ali, The Holy Qur'an, *supra* note 10, at 897–98.
12. *See* John L. Esposito, Women in Muslim Family Law 29–30 (Syracuse: Syracuse University Press, 1982); Jamil J. Nasir, The Status of Women Under Islamic Law and Under Modern Islamic Legislation 92–101 (London/Dordrecht/Boston: Graham & Trotman, 2d. ed., 1994).
13. *See* Fatima Mernissi, The Veil and the Male Elite: A Feminist Interpretation of Women's Rights in Islam 182 (Mary Jo Lakeland, trans.) (Reading, MA/Menlo Park, CA/New York/Ontario/Wokingham, UK/Amsterdam/Bonn/Sydney/Singapore/Tokyo/Madrid/San

Juan/Paris/Seoul/Milan/Mexico City/Taipei: Addison-Wesley Publishing Company, 1991) (Editions Albin Michel S.A., 1987).

14. There are three main types of FC: clitoridectomy; excision—the removal of all or part of the labia minor; and, infibulation—the removal of the whole labia minora and majora and the stitching together of the two sides of the vulva leaving a small orifice for flow of urine and entry for intercourse. *See* NAHID TOUBIA, FEMALE GENITAL MUTILATION: A CALL FOR ACTION (NY: Women Ink., 1993); Nahid Toubia, *Female Circumcision as a Public Health Issue,* 331 NEW ENG. J. MED. 712, 712–16 (1994).

15. GAD AL HAQ ALI GAD AL HAQ, AL-KHITAN, AL-AZHAR (Jumada al Awola, Cairo: 1415 hijri).

16. *See Lawsuits Filed against Health Ministers over Ban on Female Circumcisions,* AGENCE FRANCE PRESSE, Oct. 2, 1996, *available in* LEXIS, News Library, Non-US File.

17. *See Egyptian Court Supports Ban on Female Circumcision,* DEUTSCHE PRESSE-AGENTUR, Dec. 28, 1997, *available in* LEXIS, News Library, Non-US File; *FGM in Court and in Culture: An Advocacy Lesson from Egyptian Women,* 11 International Women's Rights Action Watch: The Women's Watch, Dec. 1997, at 1.

18. *See Egypt's Top Administrative Court Recommends Banning Female Circumcision,* AGENCE FRANCE PRESSE, Nov. 3, 1997, *available in* LEXIS, News Library, Non-US File.

19. *See* Qur'an 95:4 (Surat al-Teen), *in* ALI, THE HOLY QUR'AN, *supra* note 10, at 1759 & n.6199.

20. *See* Asma Mohamed Abdel Halim, *Challenges to the Application of International Women's Human Rights in the Sudan, in* HUMAN RIGHTS OF WOMEN: NATIONAL AND INTERNATIONAL PERSPECTIVES 397, 400–05 (Rebecca J. Cook, ed.) (Philadelphia: University of Pennsylvania Press, 1994).

21. *See* Sudan Personal Law for Muslims Act of 1991, sec. 22; Halim, *supra* note 20, at 400–05

22. Halim, *supra* note 20, at 402.

23. *See* Courtney W. Howland, *The Challenge of Religious Fundamentalism to the Liberty and Equality Rights of Women: An Analysis Under the United Nations Charter,* 35 COLUM. J. TRANSNAT'L L. 271, 282–85, 307–13 (1997).

24. *See* Qur'an 2:223 (Surat al-Baqara), *in* ALI, THE HOLY QUR'AN, *supra* note 10, at 88.

25. *See* MOHAMED ALI AL SABOUNI, MUKHTASAR TAFSEER IBN KATHEER, vol. 1, 195 (Beirut: Dar al Jeel, 1995).

26. *See* MERNISSI, *supra* note 13, at 145–47.

27. *Id.*

28. *See* 7 THE TRANSLATIONS OF THE MEANINGS OF SAHIH AL-BUKHARI: ARABIC-ENGLISH, Book 62, no. 1 (Dr. Muhammad Mushin Khan, trans.) (New Delhi: Kitab Bhavan, 5th ed., 1984).

29. *Id.*

30. MERNISSI, *supra* note 13, at 154–60.

31. *See* Rugh, *supra* note 6, at 171; HUDA KHATTAB, THE MUSLIM WOMAN'S HANDBOOK 40 (London: TA-HA Publishers, 1993).

32. *See* Qur'an 4:34 (Surat al-Nisa), *in* ALI, THE HOLY QUR'AN, *supra* note 10, at 190.

33. *See* Qur'an 4:35 (Surat al-Nisa), *in* ALI, THE HOLY QUR'AN, *supra* note 10, at 220–21.

34. *See* Qur'an 4:128 (Surat al-Nisa), *in* ALI, THE HOLY QUR'AN, *supra* note 10, at 191.

35. *See* JAN GOODWIN, PRICE OF HONOR: MUSLIM WOMEN LIFT THE VEIL OF SILENCE ON THE ISLAMIC WORLD 211–13 (Boston/New York/Toronto/London: Little, Brown and Company, 1994).

Chapter 19 ★

Buddhism and Human Rights in the Thai Sex Trade

Lucinda Joy Peach

"My name is Nuj and I am 18 years old. I grew up in a village in Mae Sai district, a town on the northern border between Thailand and Burma. . . . Since I was small I remember seeing women . . . wearing thick make-up and beautiful dresses, and walking in and out of the brothels that were mushrooming in the village. . . . Mae Sai revolved so much around the sex business; daughters are sold to local agents as well as agents from Bangkok. The women who work in the sex trade in Bangkok can send home a lot of money to build big houses and to buy cars. When you see people getting these things, the whole business appears quite attractive. . . . Champa is a local sex worker who has made a fortune working in Bangkok. She always came up to Mae Sai to recruit women to go south. When she asked me to work as her housekeeper in Bangkok, I decided to go with her. . . . I lived with Champa and her husband, Yonguth, who beat me and forced me to work as a prostitute. . . . Throughout the three years I worked in that massage parlour, I never received any money for my body. . . . After work, Champa would bring me back to the flat, and she locked me in the room where I could watch TV. . . . [F]inally I decided to escape. . . ."[1]

I. INTRODUCTION

The trafficking in women and children for prostitution and sex tourism in Thailand involves the most blatant violations of women's human rights. Yet because this phenomenon is undergirded by cultural and religious attitudes, beliefs, and practices, especially regarding gender roles and relationships, that legitimate its continuation, it has largely evaded the efforts of international human rights law to curb its proliferation.[2]

Scholars and activists have only begun in recent years to attend to the tremendous influence of religion on the recognition and enforcement of human rights, especially women's rights. Most recent scholarly attention given to the religious oppression of women's rights has focused on Islam, Hinduism, and Christianity, religions typically deemed to have "fundamentalist" elements. It has also tended to emphasize ways that fundamentalist religions overtly violate women's human rights, and has overlooked more subtle forms of repression, such as the religious dissemination of negative images and stereotypes of women.[3] As I will illustrate in this chapter, even though Buddhism is not, in general terms, a "fundamentalist religion" (even though aspects of Theravāda Buddhism can be characterized as fundamentalist),[4] aspects of Buddhist culture in Thailand present serious obstacles to the recognition and enforcement of women's human rights, especially with respect to the trafficking of women for prostitution. As Thanh-Dam Truong observes, "[t]he trade in women in Thailand arose from social conditions which were external to Buddhism as a body of thought, but has been consolidated by the biases inherent in Buddhism."[5]

II. TRAFFICKING IN WOMEN FOR PROSTITUTION AND SEX TOURISM

Although it has roots in the colonial period, the sex trade in Thailand began to take its modern form with the stationing of U.S. troops in Asia during the Korean and Vietnam Wars.[6] It has continued to thrive and grow since that era, fueled by an influx of foreign "tourists," many of whom come to Thailand for the sex industry alone.[7] Since 1982, Thailand has earned more foreign currency from tourism than any other economic activity, and a significant percentage of this has been earned through sex tourism.[8] It is "conservatively estimated" that ten percent of Thai women aged 18 to 24 are engaged in prostitution.[9]

Human Rights Watch and other commentators have detailed the conditions under which many women from Thailand and Burma, some still teenagers, are encouraged, coerced, or even sold by their families into the burgeoning sex trade in Thailand. These women are often forced into a system of debt bondage that makes their debt incredibly difficult to "pay off."[10] They are often virtually imprisoned, made to work in impoverished conditions, physically abused, underpaid, and deprived of basic rights to liberty and to receive needed medical treatment. They are frequently arrested for violating laws against prostitution (a double standard since the "clients" and pimps are not arrested), especially upon trying to escape.

They are often returned to the brothels by law enforcement personnel (or, in the case of Burmese women, returned to the Myanmar government to risk prosecution for leaving the country without permission), or subjected to prolonged detention (frequently sexually and otherwise physically abused while in detention), or both.[11]

In addition to these violations of their liberty, many of these women are even deprived of the conditions necessary to protect themselves from HIV, which has resulted in an AIDS epidemic rapidly spreading throughout Thailand and more slowly within Burma. The risk of HIV transmission has only encouraged sex-trade procurers to seek younger and younger women, especially from the hill tribe regions, to insure their "cleanliness" from the deadly disease.[12]

Trafficking and the sex trade are maintained by a number of interdependent factors, many of which are completely separate from religion. These include the inadequacies of international human rights laws relating to the trafficking of women (especially regarding enforcement),[13] the Thai government's unwillingness and/or inability to adhere to its international obligations or to enforce its domestic laws,[14] and the dismal economic opportunities in Thailand that provide few alternative means for women to earn as much money as they can through prostitution and sex work. Lack of other employment opportunities encourage many Thai families to sell their daughters into debt bondage in order to help maintain the rest of the family.

In turn, the trafficking and sex tourism industries in Thailand "are a reflection of the sad reality of an international society which aims at economic growth and maximizing profit by exploiting powerless groups in poor countries."[15] These are all certainly significant contributors to the perpetuation of trafficking and the sex trade. Religion is not a necessary element of trafficking, as this problem also exists in societies that do not have a strong religious dimension, such as those of the former Soviet Union. Nonetheless, a number of aspects of the Buddhist culture of Thailand provide an atmosphere in which trafficking is allowed to flourish, and enhance the difficulties of using international human rights law to protect the human rights of women and children who are victims of the sex trade.

III. BUDDHISM AND TRAFFICKING IN WOMEN

The influence of Buddhist culture on the sex trade is evident in several, very different but interrelated ways. The center of Thai culture, Theravāda Buddhism—the earliest and most orthodox of the three great traditions of Buddhism that developed in India after the death of the Buddha in 544 B.C.E.—has been the central norm shaping the nation's social institutions and legal order.[16] There is no formal separation of church and state in Thailand. Instead, there is a close, mutually supportive and interdependent relationship between government and Buddhist institutions, especially the Thai Theravāda Sangha (Sangha), the male monastic establishment.[17] According to Thanh-Dam Truong, "[a]s a social and political institution, the Buddhist religion was a foundation of feudal law, and it still provides the people with a world-view, shapes their consciousness, and acts as a subjective form of power which provides legitimacy to social relations."[18] Thus, Buddhism influences the public sphere as well as the private one.

First, Buddhist teachings help to shape gender identity, especially through cultural valuations of women as both inferior to men and as the embodiments of sexuality. Buddhist scriptures emphasize that women are attached to the material world of the senses and emotions, in contrast to men, who are able more easily to transcend their embodied and worldly existence for spiritual goals. Women's identity is depicted as embodied and social, embedded in relationships with others, and dependent on things of this "world."[19]

Women are also identified with sex, especially as sexual temptresses who present obstacles for monks attempting to maintain their vows of celibacy.[20] Scholars have suggested that such images of women, which appear in many early Buddhist texts, indicate that monks consider women's sexuality as a threat to their pursuit of the spiritual path and to the stability of the monastic order as a whole.[21] The use of the female body as a symbol of attachment to the world of sensuality is a common theme throughout the Buddhist world, beginning with the story of the Buddha's renunciation from lay life. The Buddha's struggle under the Bodhi tree for Enlightenment years later involves rejecting the sensual enticements of Mara's "daughters," who have been sent to seduce him away from his spiritual goal.[22]

Second, in Buddhist understandings, to be born a woman is considered to be the result of previous bad karma.[23] In fact, many Buddhist scriptures state, among a number of derogatory and misogynistic comments about women, that a woman can only achieve Enlightenment after having been reborn as a male. Women's stated desire to be reborn as males illustrates how significant the doctrines of female inferiority and karma are in shaping women's valuation of their own gender identity in Buddhist culture.[24] The denigration of women in Buddhist teachings facilitates women's involvement in the sex trade by conveying attitudes that through prostitution women fulfill their role expectations as sexual and inferior beings.[25]

Third, although prostitution is believed to accumulate negative karma by reinforcing craving and attachment to the sensual world of desire (which perpetuates bondage to this world of *samsara* or suffering), it is not considered to be a "sin" in Buddhism as it is in Christianity, Islam, or other religions.[26] Prostitutes are not necessarily viewed negatively in Buddhist teachings. The *Vinaya* (part of the Buddhist canon that sets forth the moral precepts for monks) can be interpreted as sanctioning prostitution by listing ten kinds of wives, including "those to be enjoyed or used occasionally" and "those who were temporary or momentary wives."[27] The earliest Buddhist scriptures include narratives involving prostitutes, sometimes as friends of the Buddha, whose generosity helps to sustain the Sangha.[28] Thus, Buddhist teachings do not condemn prostitution as some other religious teachings do.

Buddhist doctrines of karma and merit-making are connected to the gender-biased monastic establishment in ways that also enable trafficking and prostitution to flourish. One method of "correcting" or reversing previous bad karma is to create "merit" through good works, basically understood as acts of generosity.[29] Merit can be "made," not only for the actor, but also for others, through "dedicating" it for their benefit. Traditional Thai Buddhist values of respect and honor for parents motivates children to make merit in order to satisfy their indebtedness to their parents.

Males can favorably improve their karma and make merit for their parents through entering the Sangha, even temporarily.[30] Indeed, most young men become monastics on a temporary, "novice," or "apprentice" basis, usually for only a few months. This form of merit-making is unavailable to girls and women, since the order of nuns died out centuries ago in Theravāda Buddhist countries and has not been reintroduced, in part because of the opposition of the orthodox male monastic establishment (even though male orders have been reintroduced in several other Buddhist countries after having disappeared). Some women do become "renunciants," known as "ten precept women" because of the vows they take to adhere to fundamental principles of Buddhist practice, but they are not given the social respect or financial support accorded to the male Sangha.[31]

The exclusion of women from the official monastic institution itself contributes to the denigration of the status of women in Buddhist cultures by providing "evidence" of their spiritual inferiority.[32] As Thomas Kirsch explains, "[t]he monk's role is the most esteemed role in Thai society and . . . women are categorically denied admission to this role. Thus, men and women stand in qualitatively different relations to Buddhist values and norms."[33] Besides raising a son who will enter the order, women's "merit making" activities are limited to practicing generosity by giving *dana* (donations—usually money, food, and other provisions) to temples and individual monks, who act as "fields of merit" for donors.

After having fulfilled his filial obligation by temporarily ordaining as a monk, the son is "thereafter formally freed from his familial and other primordial attachments."[34] In contrast, the daughters, especially the youngest in a family, feel an ongoing responsibility to take care of their parents, which they can satisfy by earning money to provide for them. Prostitutes have told researchers with pride how they can please their parents and their communities by sending money home.[35] Family members may willfully neglect to inquire how the money that their daughters send home was earned, especially as it can be used to make merit by giving lavish donations to the local temple.[36]

Thus, women's inferior status serves to legitimate or even excuse their involvement in "immoral" or karmically negative activities like prostitution.[37] At the same time, lacking other options for merit-making, women's work in the sex industry, if temporary, can be justified and remedied based on understandings of karma.[38] Buddhist teachings indicating that prostitutes can later overcome the negative karma they have accumulated as prostitutes by renouncing sex work and abiding by the precepts thus indirectly serves to encourage women's continued participation in prostitution.[39] At the same time, because participation in the Sangha is socially highly respected, whereas participation in sex-work is not, the connections between trafficking and merit-making serve to perpetuate the male domination of society.

Although the all-male Sangha does not condone the sexual exploitation of women through trafficking and coerced prostitution, it has not formally opposed the practice either. According to Buddhist teachings, prostitution violates the prohibition of sexual misconduct, one of the basic five precepts taken by lay Buddhists as well as monks (along with not killing, stealing, lying, or drinking alcohol). Even though "Buddhist monks should in principle be opposed to prostitution[,] . . . there has been little evidence of their involvement in activities to change the attitudes of the people."[40] In fact, the Abbot of Rim Mon monastery told researchers: "We must be reasonable. . . . Besides, what is wrong if the employers of the girls make merit at the local temple or visit the village?"[41] This attitude should not be all that surprising, given that the trafficking in women results in supporting the male monastic establishment by enabling women to earn money, part of which is given to support the Sangha.

More generally, Thai Buddhist attitudes toward wealth contribute to the affirmation of capitalist expansion, which indirectly supports trafficking and sex tourism. Given the benefits that the Sangha receives from trafficking and the sex trade industry as part of Thai capitalist expansion, it has little incentive to object to these practices.[42]

Because of the direct influence of religion on government in Thailand, Buddhist views of women also have shaped their legal status in ways that hinder the enforcement of both international human rights law and domestic laws prohibiting trafficking and the sex trade. Thai law historically formalized discrimination against women, legitimating male dominance over women in marriage, divorce, and allocation of marital property.[43] Although the law has been changing toward formal equality, changes "have been made without adequate provision for implementation, creating a substantial rift between law and practice."[44]

All of these influences undermine the ability of international human rights law to protect women who are victims of trafficking and the sex trade. International human rights law is premised on a conception of humans as independent, autonomous individuals. Yet this conception of the human conflicts with Buddhist cultural constructions of female identity. The Buddhist religion does not itself recognize a concept of human rights, even though several scholars have argued that the resources within Buddhism exist for such recognition.[45] Recognition of women's human rights is made especially difficult in Thailand because Buddhist culture views women as socially embedded in family, kin, and community rather than as self-determining, independent individuals.[46] Thai women are socialized to be relational and family oriented rather than autonomous individuals. Since human rights cannot be asserted without "an awareness to a legitimate claim to reasonable control and determination of one's own life,"[47] it is questionable that international human rights law can be of much use to Thai women who lack such an awareness.

The absence of support in the Buddhist religion for women to develop as individuals entitled to protection of their human rights is reinforced by the lack of a developed legal tradition based on individual rights in Thailand.[48] Consistent with Buddhist principles promoting peace, harmony, and equanimity, larger forces in Thai society and culture value harmony of social relationships, avoiding confrontations, and resolving disputes by informal means such as tolerance, community or moral pressure, or informal systems of dispute resolution rather than individual rights and rule-oriented systems involving bureaucratic institutions like courts. Given their socialization, it is unreasonable to expect that Thai women will even be aware they have "human rights," never mind take action to enforce them on their own behalf. Thus, women's religious understandings of their gendered identity also serves to inhibit the effectiveness of international human rights law in addressing trafficking.

IV. RECOMMENDATIONS AND CONCLUSIONS

Given the several obstacles to the recognition and enforcement of international human rights law to protect and empower women who are victims of trafficking and the sex trade in Thailand, alternative approaches need to be considered. Undoubtedly, prostitution would be less attractive for many women if they were able to earn comparable incomes in less exploitative ways. Of course, the ultimate solution to this problem requires shifting the balance of power between nations that currently functions to exploit the labor of workers in developing countries, especially women workers. This will require reconfiguring the gendered power relations not only within Thailand, but also in the nations that support the Thai sex trade, and among the nations that govern the global economy.

The appeal of prostitution would also be lessened if the bonds of indebtedness that women feel toward their parents (and that parents feel toward the Sangha) could be satisfied in ways other than showering them with money. If women's ordination were established in Thailand, women would also have an opportunity to "make merit" for their families by ordaining in the Sangha, as their brothers are now able to do.[49] Such developments would require enormous changes in Thai culture and social institutions, however, and there seems little reason for optimism that they will be realized in the near future, especially in view of the recent financial crisis in Thailand.

In the meanwhile, a more modest but perhaps more easily achievable goal is to empower women to view themselves as entitled to the protection of their human rights. Thai philosopher Suwanna Satha-Anand has proposed reinterpretation of sacred Buddhist texts as a way to achieve this goal in the context of trafficking and prostitution victims.[50] Since Thailand does not have a well-developed tradition of human rights, especially women's rights, Satha-Anand claims that "cultural empowering of women is crucial to creating more awareness of this problem as a rights issue in a society where economic, legal, historical, and cultural conditioning are working *against* the recognition of women's human rights."[51] Certainly, the positive resources exist within Buddhist teachings—the affirmation of women's capacity for Enlightenment, for example, along with principles of respect and compassion for others—to contribute to such empowerment and reversal of the cultural images of women's inferiority.

Since religion is a significant, if not core, aspect of identity for many women around the world, conflicts between religion and women's international human rights cannot be resolved simply by restricting the former in favor of the latter. Given the pervasive influence of Buddhism in shaping personal and community identity in Thailand, Satha-Anand's reinterpretation strategy has the virtue of not forcing women to choose between their religiously shaped identity and the independent, individualistic identity that is assumed by international human rights laws. Scriptural reinterpretation more effectively addresses what Satha-Anand describes as "women's self-formation process,"[52] which international women's human rights law neglects. Scriptural reinterpretation is also less likely to alienate or motivate opposition from fellow citizens or government officials than international human rights strategies, which may be perceived as inappropriate meddling by Western outsiders into the integrity of local culture and tradition.

This approach is not without its own difficulties, however, as evidenced by the limited success that feminists in other religious traditions have had with this strategy. Nonetheless, scriptural reinterpretation currently presents a more feasible strategy for empowering women victimized by trafficking and the sex trade in Thailand than international human rights law. In addition, practical strategies such as those proposed by the Women in Development movement to enable women to attain economic independence—such as providing education, literacy training, micro-credit, and communal land ownership—also may be effective—either instead of or in addition to international human rights law—for addressing the problem of trafficking in Thailand.

In conclusion, among the many limitations and criticisms of international human rights discourse, one of the most significant is its failure to recognize and address the role of culture, especially religion, in shaping personal identity and subjectivity. This brief analysis of the role of Buddhist cultural values in the trafficking of women for prostitution and sex tourism in Thailand reveals the limitations of legal rights strategy for empowering women who lack "rights consciousness" and suggests the need to first attempt more local strategies, such as scriptural reinterpretation, that enable women to recognize themselves as deserving of their human rights.

NOTES

1. SIRIPORN SKROBANEK ET AL., THE TRAFFIC IN WOMEN: HUMAN REALITIES OF THE INTERNATIONAL SEX TRADE 1–2 (London/New York: Zed Books Ltd., 1997).
2. *See* Stephanie Farrior, *The International Law on Trafficking in Women and Children for Prostitution: Making it Live Up to its Potential,* 10 HARV. HUM. RTS. J. 213, 214 (1997); Report of the Special Rapporteur on Violence Against Women: Its Causes and Consequences, Feb. 12, 1997, U.N. Commission on Human Rights, 53d Sess., Item 9a, at 3–5, 21, U.N. Doc. E/CN.4/1997/47 (1997) [hereinafter Special Rapporteur].
3. *See* Sara Hossain, *Equality in the Home: Women's Rights and Personal Laws in South Asia, in* HUMAN RIGHTS OF WOMEN: NATIONAL AND INTERNATIONAL PERSPECTIVES 465, 473–74 (Rebecca Cook, ed.) (Philadelphia: University of Pennsylvania Press, 1994); Special Rapporteur, *supra* note 2, at 34–37.
4. *See* Donald K. Swearer, *Fundamentalistic Movements in Theravada Buddhism, in* 1 THE FUNDAMENTALISM PROJECT, FUNDAMENTALISMS OBSERVED 628, 628

(Martin E. Marty & R. Scott Appleby, eds.) (Chicago/London: University of Chicago Press, 1991); Charles F. Keyes, *Buddhist Economics and Buddhist Fundamentalism in Burma and Thailand, in* 3 THE FUNDAMENTALISM PROJECT, FUNDAMENTALISMS AND THE STATE 367, 368 (Martin E. Marty & R. Scott Appleby, eds.) (Chicago/London: University of Chicago Press, 1993).

5. THANH-DAM TRUONG, SEX, MONEY AND MORALITY: PROSTITUTION AND TOURISM IN SOUTHEAST ASIA 131 (London/New Jersey: Zed Books Ltd., 1990).

6. *See* Catherine Hill, *Planning for Prostitution: An Analysis of Thailand's Sex Industry, in* WOMEN'S LIVES AND PUBLIC POLICY: THE INTERNATIONAL EXPERIENCE 133, 134–35 (Meredeth Turshen & Briavel Holcomb, eds.) (Westport, CT: Greenwood Press, 1993).

7. *See id.* at 137–38.

8. *See* RITA NAKASHIMA BROCK & SUSAN BROOKS THISTLETHWAITE, CASTING STONES: PROSTITUTION AND LIBERATION IN ASIA AND THE UNITED STATES 10, 116–17 (Minneapolis: Fortress Press, 1996); Hill, *supra* note 6, at 136–37.

9. Swearer, *supra* note 4, at 655.

10. *See* Special Rapporteur, *supra* note 2, at 23.

11. *See* HUMAN RIGHTS WATCH WOMEN'S RIGHTS PROJECT, HUMAN RIGHTS WATCH GLOBAL REPORT ON WOMEN'S HUMAN RIGHTS 207–08, 216–17, 220–22 (New York: Human Rights Watch, 1995); Special Rapporteur, *supra* note 2, at 23–24.

12. *See* HUMAN RIGHTS WATCH WOMEN'S RIGHTS PROJECT, *supra* note 11, at 225.

13. *See* Farrior, *supra* note 2, at 213–14.

14. *See* HUMAN RIGHTS WATCH WOMEN'S RIGHTS PROJECT, *supra* note 11, at 225–30; Siriporn Skrobanek, *Exotic, Subservient and Trapped: Confronting Prostitution and Traffic in Women in Southeast Asia, in* FREEDOM FROM VIOLENCE: WOMEN'S STRATEGIES FROM AROUND THE WORLD 121, 124 (Margaret Schuler, ed.) (New York: UNIFEM, 1992).

15. Skrobanek, *supra* note 14, at 129.

16. *See* Swearer, *supra* note 4, at 629–31, 655–56; Thomas A. Kirsch, *Text and Context: Buddhist Sex Roles/Culture of Gender Revisited,* 12 AM. ETHNOLOGIST 302, 315 (1985); Frank Reynolds, *Dhamma in Dispute: The Interactions of Religion and Law in Thailand,* 28 L. & SOC'Y. REV. 433, 436 (1994).

17. *See* Swearer, *supra* note 4, at 655; Keyes, *supra* note 4, at 386–87.

18. TRUONG, *supra* note 5, at 131.

19. *See* Kirsch, *supra* note 16, at 303–04.

20. *See* TRUONG, *supra* note 5, at 134; SUSAN MURCOTT, THE FIRST BUDDHIST WOMEN: TRANSLATIONS AND COMMENTARIES ON THE THERIGATHA 119–27 (Berkeley, CA: Parallax Press, 1991).

21. *See* Alan Sponberg, *Attitudes toward Women and the Feminine in Early Buddhism, in* BUDDHISM, SEXUALITY, AND GENDER 3, 19–20 (José Ignacio Cabezón, ed.) (Albany, NY: State University of New York Press, 1992);

Karen Christina Lang, *Lord Death's Snare: Gender-Related Imagery in the Theragatha and the Therigatha,* 2 J. FEMINIST STUD. RELIGION 63, 64 (1986); DIANA Y. PAUL, WOMEN IN BUDDHISM: IMAGES OF THE FEMININE IN MAHAYANA TRADITION 3–10 (Berkeley, CA: University of California Press, 2d ed., 1985); Nancy Falk, *An Image of Women in Old Buddhist Literature: The Daughters of Mara, in* WOMEN AND RELIGION 105, 108 (Judith Plaskow & Joan Arnold, eds.) (Missoula, MT: Scholars' Press, 1974).

22. *See* PAUL, *supra* note 21, at 6–7; Falk, *supra* note 21, at 110; MURCOTT, *supra* note 20, at 122.

23. *See* CHATSUMARN KABILSINGH, THAI WOMEN IN BUDDHISM 31 (Berkeley, CA: Parallax Press, 1991); Suwanna Satha-Anand, *Looking to Buddhism To Turn Back Prostitution in Thailand, in* THE EAST ASIAN CHALLENGE FOR HUMAN RIGHTS 193, 197–98 (Joanne R. Bauer & Daniel A. Bell, eds.) (New York: Cambridge University Press, forthcoming, 1999).

24. *See* TRUONG, *supra* note 5, at 135.

25. *See* KHIN THITSA, PROVIDENCE AND PROSTITUTION: IMAGE AND REALITY FOR WOMEN IN BUDDHIST THAILAND 23 (London: CHANGE International Reports: Women and Society, 1980).

26. *See* BROCK & THISTLETHWAITE, *supra* note 8, at 62–63; Charles F. Keyes, *Mother or Mistress But Never a Monk: Buddhist Notions of Female Gender in Rural Thailand,* 11 AM. ETHNOLOGIST 223, 236 (1984).

27. TRUONG, *supra* note 5, at 136.

28. *See* MURCOTT, *supra* note 20, at 119–138.

29. *See* KABILSINGH, *supra* note 23, at 31.

30. *See* Kirsch, *supra* note 16, at 308.

31. *See generally* KABILSINGH, *supra* note 23.

32. *See* Nancy Eberhardt, *Siren Song: Negotiating Gender Images in a Rural Shan Village, in* GENDER, POWER, AND THE CONSTRUCTION OF THE MORAL ORDER: STUDIES FROM THE THAI PERIPHERY 73, 78 (Nancy Eberhardt, ed.) (Madison, WI: Center for Southeast Asian Studies, 1988).

33. Kirsch, *supra* note 16, at 304.

34. *Id.* at 308.

35. *See* Juree Vichit-Vadakan, *Women and the Family in Thailand in the Midst of Social Change,* 28 L. & SOC'Y REV. 515, 518 (1994).

36. SKROBANEK ET AL., *supra* note 1, at 72–74.

37. *See* Eberhardt, *supra* note 32, at 78.

38. *See* BROCK & THISTLETHWAITE, *supra* note 8, at 196–97.

39. *See* Keyes, *supra* note 26, at 236.

40. SKROBANEK ET AL., *supra* note 1, at 77–78.

41. *Id.* at 78.

42. *See* Keyes, *supra* note 4, at 389.

43. *See* THITSA, *supra* note 25, at 5–7.

44. *Id.* at 5.

45. For example, the Journal of Buddhist Ethics recently held a Conference on Human Rights where most scholars who attended took this position. For

a compilation of these scholars' papers, see Journal of Buddhist Ethics, *Journal of Buddhist Ethics Conference on Human Rights* (visited Sept. 2, 1998) <http://www.frontiernet.net/~ahimsa/.jbe/jbe_home.html>. *See* Padmasiri De Silva, *Human Rights in Buddhist Perspective, in* HUMAN RIGHTS AND RELIGIOUS VALUES: AN UNEASY RELATIONSHIP? 133 (Abdullahi A. An-Na'im et al., eds.) (Grand Rapids, MI: William B. Eerdmans Publishing Co., 1995).

46. *See* Vichit-Vadakan, *supra* note 35, at 516; *see also* BROCK & THISTLETHWAITE, *supra* note 8, at 193–94.

47. Satha-Anand, *supra* note 23, at 211.

48. Ted. L. McDorman, *The Teaching of the Law of Thailand,* 11 DALHOUSIE L. J. 915, 927 (1988); De Silva, *supra* note 45, at 142.

49. For a full discussion of the issue of women's ordination in Buddhism, see Suwanna Satha-Anand, *Truth Over Convention: Feminist Interpretations of Buddhism,* in this volume.

50. Satha-Anand, *supra* note 23, at 204–11.

51. Satha-Anand, *supra* note 23, at 194.

52. Satha-Anand, *supra* note 23, at 206.

VI

Nonlegal Remedies, Resistance, and Exit

Chapter 20

Women Educating Women in the Afghan Diaspora: Why and How

Sakena Yacoobi

I. INTRODUCTION

Much has been written about the current situation in Afghanistan.[1] Rather than review that situation, I will focus on how Afghan women—despite the current turmoil—are educating Afghan girls and women. In response to the rapidly diminishing presence of foreign assistance to both Afghan citizens and Afghan refugees in Pakistan that began in 1995, several colleagues and I formed the Afghan Institute of Learning (AIL). The immediate purpose for this organization was to continue support for schools that had been started for Afghan refugee children in Pakistan during the war between Afghanistan and the Soviet Union. The majority of these children live in refugee camps that are not of the temporary type existing in Africa but that are as permanent as the villages once inhabited by these refugees in their own country. There are, however, many significant differences—all of which impact on the type, style, and urgent need for education.

AIL is a program encompassing over 3,000 Afghan students in 24 pre-schools and 33 schools. Six hundred of these students are girls being educated in 20 temporary one-room home schools within Afghanistan. Of the first and second grade students, some 5 to 10 percent are boys. The AIL program has 250 teachers, 10 master-teachers, 10 health educators, 5 administrative staff, 2 supervisors for the Afghan schools, and 6 logistical support personnel. The 2 Afghan school supervisors are men (because it is necessary for them to travel into Afghanistan alone and women are not permitted to travel alone in Afghanistan) as are the 6 support personnel, consisting of 2 male drivers and 4 male "chowki-dars."[2] All other students and personnel including teachers, trainers, and the like are women, and all of us are Afghan. Many of us—if not most of us—are doing jobs that we probably would not have been doing if the war and dislocation of our people had not occurred. But interestingly enough, our teachers are so gifted and/or well-trained that the results we get far exceed those in schools being run according to the more traditional style of education common to Afghanistan.

We are proud of what we have accomplished, what we are doing on a daily basis, and of the total impact that we are having on the lives of our students, their families, and even their communities. We have a strong sense of purpose and long-range goals. We see what we are doing as being vital and even *crucial* to the survival of some semblance of an educated Afghan population to participate in the future redevelopment of our country. The war and disruption of life in Afghanistan has resulted in a current illiteracy rate of over 99 percent. But, in addition, in the 20 years since 1978, we have actually lost 3 generations of educated Afghans. One generation of elders escaped the country and now resides in exile in Europe, the United States, or Australia. Yet, many of these people are now reaching the end of their natural lives. The second lost generation was killed during the 20 years of war with the Soviets and during the continuing civil war. The third lost generation are their children, who have had no educational training, but for training in fighting, guns, weapons, and bombs.

The children we teach will need to make up for those three generations of lost leaders, teachers, physicians, and the like. Our charge, therefore, is a big responsibility. Any success we have encourages us to the next step. As women, we can see how important a role we do in fact play.

The AIL has another important impact on Afghan refugees that we are only just beginning to appreciate ourselves. Almost every one of the 283 people on our staff supports with her salary—meager as it may be—at least 4 to 5 other people. This means that our program is helping to keep alive about 1,500 people.

II. OBJECTIVE OF AIL

Those of us who are involved with the AIL firmly believe that the education of girls is the best investment in the future growth and development of our nation. We are aware of international statistics showing that a developing nation that emphasizes education for women reaps improved health for all of its citizens, better standards of living, increased family incomes, and general improvement in all indices measuring development. A bright future for Afghanistan does not seem much of a possibility without the educated participation of the female half of our population. In addition, within the context of our society, girls and young women between the ages of 3 and 20 are among the most disadvantaged and therefore deserve our attention for this reason as well.

In "educating" our young women, we have several objectives beyond the obvious ones of literacy, skill in mathematics, science, language, and social studies. We also see that increasing the knowledge base of our children will give them a necessary self-confidence. These children need empowerment, both as individuals and as Afghan citizens, in order to confront and conquer the challenges that they will most certainly face throughout life. Much of the integrity of life and lifestyle known by their parents and grandparents when living in villages in Afghanistan has been destroyed during 20 years of exile and life in a refugee camp. Identity itself is confused. Culture, traditions, and economic and social status are disrupted, in transition, or even lost. All of these are important elements to support and reinforce during the educational process. Even though our students live in what could be described as large but primitive villages in discombobulated communities within a foreign country, they must emerge from their education with a sense of self, a sense of purpose, and a commitment to the future of their families, their communities, and their country.

III. TRAINING TEACHERS TO PROVIDE QUALITY EDUCATION

AIL's emphasis is on training teachers that we regard as the key to a successful school. Much of our teacher training includes elements that would seem obvious from a Western perspective. These skills and orientation, however, are very new approaches to education for the people of Afghanistan.

AIL has several different training levels and programs. Master-teacher trainers undergo an intensive four month training program with both classroom and in-class training. Regular teachers receive a twenty-four-day version of the same program. They then practice what they have learned in their own classrooms and are monitored and evaluated by the teacher trainers. Occasionally, AIL also runs three-hour workshops for nearby refugee camp schools and three-day workshops for faraway refugee camp schools. Successful completion of the full programs requires no more than three absent days and an 80 percent score on the final examination. Certificates are given.

The emphasis in all of these training activities is on student success. Teachers are shown how to interact with students in a friendly way, to be respectful of them, to refrain from using physical punishments, and to inquire about their absences from school in order to learn if there are problems or illnesses at home that might affect the student's performance and psychological health. Teachers are taught how to design lesson plans on a daily basis (a strict requirement in AIL schools) that are realistic and have an objective transparent to the student. We teach the importance of creativity in approach, particularly in activating cooperation and participation of both students and teachers in designing classroom teaching materials. In an environment lacking financial resources, the ability to put to use ordinary things from home and the bazaar becomes invaluable. For example, gravel and beans may be used for counting exercises and used office paper for drawing and coloring. We encourage teachers to involve parents in their children's school lives. In this respect, teachers are also trained to explore the ethnic, religious, cultural, social, economic, and other circumstances of the children's lives for two reasons: first, they may need to be sensitive about these in the educational materials they design; and, second, the children themselves need to learn about their heritage so that they can be more effective as adults working within their communities.

We also train our teachers in certain management skills that permit them to participate in administration and office work required to run a school. In some cases, they will ultimately become school principals or other types of school administrators. We have a training module in leadership that encourages teachers to value each other, to think in terms of a "team," and to help and assist one another. Finally, we impart techniques for involving parents and the larger community in coming up with "in kind" contributions to the school. For example, we welcome soap from a shopkeeper father or beans for an afternoon snack. Many of our schools actually exist because parents wanted them so badly that they did everything they could to bring them into being. They are equally eager to find ways, no matter how meager, to continue supporting their children's education.

IV. EMPHASIS ON PRE-SCHOOL EDUCATION

Upon completion of the basic 24-day teacher trainer module, the very best of our teachers are assigned to our pre-school education program. The reason for this is simple: we have learned as have others around the world that sound early preparation is the most valuable thing we can give our children. In fact, our pre-school-educated children consistently rank at the top of their first and second grade programs. In our case, there are other reasons why strong intervention and teaching at this level are of major importance. Many of our kids need special psychological and social help at this age. These children do not know how to play; often their "play" consists of throwing dirt at each other. They do not laugh and they have insufficient language and physical skills. Many have been traumatized by war, fighting, bombs, and fear. Their living conditions are not good; two or three families often share one or two rooms. All of these problems are addressed in a special 20-day pre-school education training module for those teachers assigned at this level. The curriculum for pre-school includes language preparation (phonetic alphabet and reading, and vocabulary development) in four languages—Farsi, Pushtu, Arabic, and English—as well as an understanding of numbers and exercise/play in art work, such as drawing. The level of accomplishment of these little children is quite extraordinary.

V. HEALTH EDUCATION

Over time we have learned that health education is an important and totally necessary adjunct to our basic education program. We have developed therefore a training course for educators in this topic. Candidates for health education must have completed the twelfth grade or be university graduates. The three month course focuses on physiology, pathology, microbiology, and preventive health techniques. Many of these trainees will end up in clinics and must have familiarity with the human body and its functions. In addition, personal hygiene and cleanliness are taught. In the nutritional segment, we emphasize that a very healthy diet of beans and rice with occasional supplements of fruits and vegetables will go a long way toward furthering good health. Reducing meat and oil intake is both healthier and less expensive. The course dwells on disease prevention through control of environment and nutrition. The health educators and then the women and children learn to avoid and prevent standing water from occurring, because it serves as a breeding home for flies and mosquitoes. An exciting initiative is our child-to-child health program. Children, who are taught about hygiene and environmental management at school, go home and share the health issues that they have learned with other children who are not in the school. It has proven to be the most cost-effective way that we have found of spreading the word. Within the schools, every grade level has a total of five minutes health education every day and every week a special health topic presentation is given.

VI. HOME SCHOOLS INSIDE AFGHANISTAN

We consider one-room schools in Afghanistan to be a temporary if necessary solution to the current problem. For true education to take place, we believe a larger group of students to be invaluable. Interaction between and among many teachers and many students ferments the kind of learning process we espouse. Nevertheless, AIL supports 20 one-room schools for girls in Herat and Kabul. These schools are reaching people who due to the civil war were suddenly considered unreachable. These schools are like the one-room schoolhouses of the prairies in early America, consisting of one teacher, students from grades one to six, a minimum of fifteen and a maximum of thirty in the room, and minimal, if any, resources. AIL supervisors go in and out of Afghanistan to assist and monitor these rudimentary educational places. Given the uncomfortable circumstances within which these schools must operate, cultural, religious, and ethnic sensitivity on the part of the teachers has become one of the most important things. They must learn who their students are and what background they come from, and then reinforce the behavior considered appropriate by their context in order that their students be supported by the families and communities in question. AIL has prepared a teacher's guide for those running the Afghan home schools to aid them in being aware of the various outside factors affecting the students.

VII. SCHOOL SUPPORT SYSTEM

To the degree that funds are available to AIL, we support our systems of schools as much as possible. In some cases, we provide the teachers. In other cases, we pay teacher salaries. In some schools, we contribute all or some of the rent. In a few, we provide a salaried administrator or supervisor. We consistently do teacher evaluations in an effort to keep the high quality of teaching to which we are so dedicated. And we are always ready to support in every way we can think of the confidence and self-esteem of the students. In the back of our minds is the constant fear of what a country would be like with total illiteracy, no support, and no foreign assistance in a context where the rest of the world is concerned about connecting the students to the internet. Afghanistan will soon be 100 years behind the rest of the world. We are only barely treading water just to retain a small proportion of our people being able to read and write their own names.

VIII. THE FINAL WORD

We are doing a lot. We want to do more. We would like to expand our program to include 5,000 students. For this, we need much help. Our women want an education. Their families want them to be educated. Their communities are even contributing to that educational process. Many of our teachers are married women with families of their own. This means that in order to do their teaching jobs, their husbands, children, and other relatives are supporting them in having these jobs.

Political systems and problems come and go. Leaders come and go. Through it all, ordinary people thirst for what has become a basic in our world: the right to an education and what it brings to all of us—understanding, tolerance, and friendship among racial and religious groups and communities, and ultimately understanding within an entire nation.

NOTES

1. For a discussion of some of the issues raised by the civil war in Afghanistan, see Mahnaz Afkhami, *Gender Apartheid and the Discourse of Relativity of Rights in Muslim Societies;* Christine M. Chinkin, *Cultural Relativism and International Law;* and Lynn Freedman, *Finding Our Feet, Standing Our Ground: Reproductive Health Activism in an Era of Rising Fundamentalism and Economic Globalization* in this volume.
2. A chowki-dar sits at the gate and regulates traffic into the school. Only males are chowki-dars.

Chapter 21

Challenging Christian Fundamentalism: Organizing an Alternative to the Religious Right in Your State*

Cecile Richards

I. INTRODUCTION

The Religious Right movement has had a significant impact on public policy and political dialogue in the United States. The backlash against women's rights and the political efforts to undermine the progress that women have made in the United States are rooted in the Religious Right movement and its political manifestation of fundamentalism.

I speak to a lot of women's groups these days, and I have been struck by how often a woman will come up to me after a speech and say, "now you know, I'm not a feminist, but. . . ." Then you can fill in the blank: "I really think women should get equal pay; I support reproductive freedom; I am worried about the Promise Keepers;" and the like. How did we get into this predicament that intelligent, educated women think that feminism means something other than a belief in the political, economic, and social equality for women? I imagine there are socioeconomic reasons why feminism is misunderstood. But I'd like to give at least partial credit to our friends on the Religious Right.

It was three years ago that I got to know someone who more than anyone else influenced me to get involved in this work: the Reverend Pat Robertson, founder of the Christian Coalition. Let me share what the Reverend Robertson has to say about feminism: "The feminist agenda is not about equal rights for women. It is about a socialist, anti-family political movement that encourages women to leave their husbands, kill their children, practice witchcraft, destroy capitalism, and become lesbians."[1]

That's a pretty tall order for most feminists. Unfortunately, we usually dismiss these types of statements because they are so extreme. However, in the absence of a response to the Religious Right, people reading this rhetoric or watching it on television—the 700 Club show—may begin to wonder that maybe everyone else agrees with Robertson. We are long overdue for religious and community leaders to speak up and counter the misinformation and rhetoric of the Religious Right.

Just as the Religious Right has redefined what women's equality is about, they have seized the opportunity to be the defining spiritual voice on morality and family values,[2] at a time when progressive leadership has not. Unfortunately, we have too often been unable or unwilling to speak out on social issues that truly concern people: the breakup of families, the rise in single parenting, and the decline in social morals. By default, the Religious Right is seen as the movement that cares about these issues. As the world has become a more complicated place, Christian fundamentalists are only too willing to simplify the problems for mainstream Americans. They have created easy scapegoats for societal ills, blaming gays, immigrants, working women, or poor people.[3]

The Religious Right movement also threatens our very democracy through attacking everything public: our public schools; public libraries; public television; public arts; and the like.[4] The movement represents a serious challenge to values that we share, such as the free expression of ideas and thought, the celebration of our ethnic and cultural diversity, and the belief in equality of all people regardless of gender, ethnicity, race, religion, or sexual orientation. That sums up the bad news about the Religious Right.

The good news is what we have learned over the last three years of working in Texas at our not-for-profit organization, the Texas Freedom Network. We've discovered that despite the formidable grassroots organization that the Religious Right has developed in this country, their movement and agenda are still only supported by a small minority of voters. The question is whether we will be able to mobilize the overwhelming majority of people who agree with us on most issues.

In this chapter, I discuss the nature of the Religious Right political movement, its future, and the threat that it poses to women's rights. I will also share in more detail what we've learned in Texas so that you too can fight the Religious Right.

II. THE RELIGIOUS RIGHT

I would like to start with my definition of the Religious Right: *a far right political movement that misuses religion in order to promote a political agenda.* Although many followers of the Religious Right may be motivated by their religious beliefs, their agenda is to achieve political power. The Christian Coalition is not working on getting more folks to go to Sunday school.

The Religious Right movement has changed dramatically in the past 15 years. In the past, the Religious Right was largely a televangelistic phenomenon, led by charismatic preachers whose fortunes rose or fell depending upon the personalities involved.[5] Early leaders included the Reverend Jerry Falwell, Jim and Tammy Faye Baker, and so on. They focused on hot button social issues such as abortion, women's liberation, pornography,[6] and sex education in the schools.[7]

But the movement has changed, and in several important ways. First, the organizations on the Religious Right are no longer dependent upon personalities. For example, the departure of Ralph Reed from the Christian Coalition has not caused the organization to shut down.[8] In fact, his leaving allowed new leaders such as James Dobson and Gary Bauer to replace Reed as national Religious Right spokespeople.

Second, there are several more organizations than in the past, including significant national groups, each one of which is financially stable, has a multimillion dollar budget, and a diversified fundraising base.[9] They are not going out of business anytime soon.

Third, the Religious Right organizations today are politically sophisticated, using polling, focus groups, direct mail, television, and the internet. They are also usually more successful at these methods of organizing than their progressive counterparts.[10]

Fourth, despite their nonprofit status, Religious Right groups are almost exclusively focused on electoral politics. The Christian Coalition, for example, is organized like a political party, precinct by precinct.[11] They print and distribute millions of voters' guides to influence elections, conduct candidate training, and, in Texas, they even hold their annual conference at the Republican party convention.[12]

Fifth, their political agenda has diversified beyond the social agenda of years past. According to the Christian Right, there is an official "Christian" position on every issue from the right to carry a concealed handgun to eliminating legal services for the poor.

Finally, the most important difference from the past is how the Religious Right has developed allied grassroots organizations.[13] They are able to mobilize incredibly rapidly. Hundreds or thousands of calls and faxes can be made, and are made, overnight on any given issue. Because of this extensive political network, the Religious Right is one of the most effective lobbying forces. And, they can lobby effectively at all levels, from the local school board to the U.S. Congress.[14]

In terms of the future and how the Religious Right will impact on women's issues, there are two important considerations. First, their focus will remain on electoral politics. The Religious Right and their organizations control the Republican parties in many states, and are a formidable group to deal with.[15] Because of their ability to mobilize 10 to 15 percent of the voters in any election, they will continue to have disproportionate political influence.

Moreover, their grassroots organization in the Republican party will allow them to train the party activists, leaders, and candidates of tomorrow. It will become increasingly important to reach out to moderate women and men in the Republican party in order to support them in preventing the Religious Right from determining the party's position on key women's issues.

Second, national Religious Right groups will begin to move back to primarily a moral and social political agenda. In line with this, they will continue to lead the efforts to turn back economic and political gains made by women. Their attitude toward women was clearly demonstrated by the Congressional leaders they elected in 1994. In the debate over the deficit and welfare reform, leadership beholden to the Religious Right was eager to blame women for all of society's ills. They condemned poor women who stayed at home to care for their children, saying that they were the cause of the national deficit, and they condemned middle-class women who left home in order to work, blaming them for the destruction of the American family. Women simply can not win!

Although in recent years the Christian Coalition, under the leadership of Ralph Reed, had attempted to move into more mainstream economic issues, the tide seems to be moving back to the social issues that brought the Religious Right into prominence and energized its troops in the beginning: banning contraception and sex education for teens, eliminating gay rights, restricting abortion, and the like.

Nowhere is the regressive approach to women's role in society more apparent than with the newest, largest, and fastest growing movement of male Christian fundamentalism: the Promise Keepers. This movement is significant because of its size, appeal, and link to other Religious Right organizations such as Focus on the Family and Gary Bauer's Family Research Council.[16] The founder of the Promise Keepers, Bill McCartney, was a supporter of the militant anti-abortion group Operation Rescue, as well as the Coalition for Family Values that opposed antidiscrimination legislation for gays and lesbians in Colorado.[17]

Coach McCartney has said, "[t]he strongest voice in America is the Christian male."[18] It seems that leaves out a large number of us "Other" Americans. One of the Promise Keepers' more popular speakers, Tony Evans, has written that "the primary cause of this national crisis [the decline of family structure] is the feminization of men."[19]

The Promise Keepers justify putting women back in their place in exchange for husbands becoming more responsible to their families. This movement is particularly significant because of the support it has had from many wives.[20] I fear we will see the backlash against women's rights in this country manifest itself in a kinder, gentler form of patriarchy, where women themselves are the primary collaborators.

We are already seeing the impact of the Promise Keepers' message. In May 1998, the nearly sixteen-million member Southern Baptist convention announced a proposal to change their core document to call upon "husbands to 'protect and lead their family,' and wives 'to submit graciously to the servant leadership of her husband'"[21] This is scary stuff.

It is particularly alarming that so many are unwilling to speak out about the danger of the Promise Keepers because it is a "religious" organization and therefore not political. Imagine if there were a religious organization preaching in stadiums to hundreds of thousands of people that any other group in this country were inferior or subordinate—they would be blasted by every political leader and news organization in the country. But somehow, as long as the religious organization is "just" talking about women, it's okay for them to do so.

III. THE TEXAS EXPERIENCE: ORGANIZING AN ALTERNATIVE TO THE RELIGIOUS RIGHT

My frustration at people unwilling to speak out against the Religious Right caused me three years ago to quit my job and form the Texas Freedom Network (TFN), a non-partisan, grassroots organization of religious and community leaders. We work to provide an alternative to the Religious Right in Texas. We do a wide range of activities, including: monitoring the activities of the Religious Right in Texas; training leadership around the state and across the country in how to stand up to this movement; educating the media and providing a balance of coverage on issues such as public education and religious and individual liberties; and advocating for rational public policy at the state and local level, particularly to counterbalance the political activities of the Religious Right.

We've learned through our grassroots organizing that the political agenda and rhetoric of the Religious Right is supported by a very small percentage of people. Voters, regardless of political party, generally do not want people with extreme political views to represent them, either on the local school board or in the U.S. Congress. But unless we are doing our part to educate voters, inform the public and mobilize our supporters, the Religious Right will continue to be successful on many issues that we care about.

With respect to advocacy and organizing, there are several ways that you can make a difference. First, get to know the opposition. Get on their mailing lists, attend their meetings, and read their literature. Identify national organizations with whom they are affiliated and use this knowledge. If you do not know who is active in your state, there are several national groups that have this information, primarily People for the American Way in Washington, DC. Learn where the Religious Right stands on issues that you care about, and how they are impacting women's issues in your area.

Second, educate the media. We must constantly educate the press on who the Religious Right is and what they are doing. The press also needs to know that you can provide another point of view on a given issue on which the Religious Right is involved. We learned over and over again that alerting the media to public policy positions of the Religious Right can be very effective. For example, in 1996, the Religious Right opposed the social studies textbooks that were to be adopted by our state board of education.[22] They wanted to remove material on the poet Langston Hughes because he was a communist, and they complained that the books had an overly negative portrayal of slavery in the south.[23] You can imagine the media's reaction when we informed them. For the first time, three television stations covered the textbook hearings. As a result, the books were adopted without the requested changes.

Third, work with clergy. Because of the use and misuse of faith in the political arena, it became clear that we needed to have clergy who could offer an alternative religious voice to the Religious Right. As a result, in 1996 we organized the Texas Faith Network, an interdenominational group of religious leaders and laity whose faith supports a politic of compassion not reflected in the message of the Religious Right. They are active on issues across the state, and are often asked to speak to state and local organizations. By mobilizing clergy, you undercut both the religious base of the Religious Right and neutralize the issue of religion.

Fourth, learn from the other side. In the Religious Right's campaigns to prohibit sex education, to censor books on reading lists, to pass restrictions on reproductive freedoms, and so on, they use many effective tools that we too can adopt. For example, it is important to: develop a database of supporters; make sure the press knows to call you; organize a public forum to educate others on your issues; and meet your legislators and city council members. The point is that most of what the Religious Right does is nothing more than hard work—which we can do too.

Fifth, remember that the Religious Right is a growth industry. Their finances, grassroots organization, political sophistication, and determination are not to be underestimated. Sometimes, because we believe their ideas are extreme, we want to dismiss the Religious Right as marginal. This is a real mistake.

Also, you should think twice before negotiating with the Religious Right on an important issue. Our experience is that you can never buy peace and that there is no advantage to reaching a compromise with them. For most of us, we see politics and public policy as reaching for the middle ground, bringing together competing views and interests. The Religious Right does not see it that way. Fundamentalists often believe that their position on issues such as abortion, women's equality, or prayer in school is directly connected to their own salvation, and compromise is not an option for them. Moreover, many of the Religious Right regard themselves as being a persecuted minority for which a compromise is not possible or not to be honored.

IV. CONCLUSION

Margaret Sanger said "[n]o woman can call herself free who does not own and control her body."[24] For if we can control decisions about childbearing, we can also control decisions about our work, our career, and our relationships. It is this freedom for women that the Religious Right ultimately cannot tolerate.

The Religious Right anti-abortion movement describes itself as pro-life, and nothing could be further from the truth. They believe that the right to life begins at conception and ends at birth! The same national, right wing groups that fight against reproductive rights have worked to eliminate every social program that benefits the very children that they claim to care about. They have fought against Headstart, pre-kindergarten programs, reduced-price breakfast and lunch in schools, school nurses, Aid to Families with Dependent Children, child health care coverage, and access to day care.[25] The most incredible of all is that they fight at the state and national level against *every effort to educate young people about contraception and family planning* that could reduce the number of unintended pregnancies.[26]

It is also hard to understand how a national movement that claims to be based upon Christianity could be the foremost opponent of public education, and of opportunities for women and people of color, and the least accepting of those from different religious backgrounds.

We can shake our heads in disbelief, or we can wake up and get busy. We will either be in the courthouses, in the statehouses, and in the streets fighting for our future, or we will have no one but ourselves to blame.

I believe in our democracy, and I support the right of Pat Robertson and the entire Christian Coalition to be politically active. It's just high time that we were as active as they are. It's time to quit complaining about assaults on women's rights and time to get organized. I will not sit back and let the Religious Right determine the future for my children, my community, or my country. I hope you won't either. Thank you and God bless.

NOTES

* This chapter is an edited version of the speech given at the Conference on Religious Fundamentalisms and the Human Rights of Women at the George Washington University Law School on May 19, 1998. Footnotes have been added.

1. Letter from Pat Robertson to contributors of the Christian Coalition to gain support to defeat an Equal Rights Initiative in Iowa, *quoted in* Maralee Schwartz & Kenneth J. Cooper, *Equal Rights Initiative in Iowa Attacked,* WASH. POST, Aug. 23, 1992, at A15.

2. *See* Matthew C. Moen, *From Revolution to Evolution: The Changing Nature of the Christian Right,* SOC. OF RELIGION, Fall 1994, at 345, 349.

3. *E.g.* Robert H. Knight, *Nobody Has to Be Gay,* Speech given at Harvard University Third Annual National Coming Out of Homosexuality Day (Oct. 10, 1997) (transcript available in <http://www.frc.org/podium/pd9711hs.html>); Family Research Council, *Immigration and the American Family* (visited Nov. 20, 1998) <http://www.frc.org/infocus/if95b3cu.html>; Gary L. Bauer, Written Testimony to the United States House of Representatives Ways and Means Subcommittee on Human Resources (Mar. 12, 1996), *reprinted in* AT THE PODIUM, <http://www.frc.org/podium/pd96dlwl.html> (discussing impact of welfare on illegitimacy rates).

4. *E.g.,* Family Research Council, *Keeping Libraries User and Family Friendly* (visited Nov. 20, 1998) <http://www.frc.org/fampol/fp98epn.html>; Robert H. Knight, *The Failures of Reform: Why CPB, NEA and NEH Must Be Zeroed Out* (visited Nov. 20, 1998) <http:// www.frc.org/insight/is95f2cu.html>; Molly Ivins, *Right-Wingers Target NEA Grants,* ARIZ. REPUBLIC, Feb. 1, 1995, at B5; *see* PEOPLE FOR THE AMERICAN WAY, A RIGHT WING AND A PRAYER: THE RELIGIOUS RIGHT AND YOUR PUBLIC SCHOOLS (Washington, DC: People for the American Way, 1997).

5. *See* JEFFREY K. HADDEN & ANSON SHUPE, TELEVANGELISM: POWER AND POLITICS OF GOD'S FRONTIER 4–19 (New York: Henry Holt and Company, 1988).

6. *See id.* at 216–28.

7. *See* Susan D. Rose, *Christian Fundamentalism: Patriarchy, Sexuality, and Human Rights* in this volume.

8. *See* Ralph Reed, Jr., *Statement by Ralph Reed, Jr. Concerning His Resignation from the Christian Coalition,* (visited Nov. 20, 1998) <http://www.cc.org/publications/ccnews/ccnews97.html>; Peter Baker & Laurie Goodstein, *Christian Coalition Rearranges Top Posts,* WASH. POST, June 12, 1997, at A15.

9. Such groups include the Christian Coalition, the Eagle Forum, Focus on the Family, the Family Research Council, and the Promise Keepers.

10. *See* JUSTIN WATSON, THE CHRISTIAN COALITION: DREAMS OF RESTORATION, DEMANDS FOR RECOGNITION 54–60 (New York: St. Martin's Press, 1997).

11. *See id.* at 58.

12. *See id.* at 56–60.

13. *See id.* at 62–65.

14. *See* PEOPLE FOR THE AMERICAN WAY, BUYING A MOVEMENT: RIGHT-WING FOUNDATIONS AND AMERICAN POLITICS (Washington, DC: People for the American Way, 1996).

15. *See* Moen, *supra* note 2, at 353.

16. *See* Nancy Novosad, *Promise Keepers Seek Power as Well as God,* NEWSDAY, Sept. 19, 1996, at A53.

17. *See* Joe Conason et al., *The Promise Keepers are Coming: The Third Wave of the Religious Right,* NATION, Oct. 7, 1996, at 11, 14.

18. *See Colorado Coach Draws Fire Again,* CHI. TRIB., Jul. 29, 1992, at 3.

19. Thomas B. Edsall, *Movement Seeks to Revive Traditional Role for Men,* WASH. POST, Aug. 1, 1994, at 6.

20. *See* Julia Duin, *Women Join Promise Keepers to Express Their Own Gratitude,* WASH. TIMES, Oct. 5, 1997.

21. *See* Jeffrey Weiss, *Baptist Proposal Asks Wives to be Submissive; Core Document Addition Also Says Couple Equal Before God,* DALLAS MORNING NEWS, May 12, 1998, at 15A.

22. *See* Steve Ray, *Textbook debates heat up: Critics object to minority depiction,* CORPUS CHRISTI CALLER TIMES, Oct. 25, 1996, at A10, A16; *see, e.g.,* Mel & Norma Gabler, *Texas Watchdogs Target History Textbooks: You Can Make a Difference,* 3 TEXAS EAGLE FORUM: TORCH 7 (Summer 1996).

23. *See* Ray, *supra* note 22, at A10, A16.

24. MARGARET SANGER, WOMAN AND THE NEW RACE 94 (New York: Maxwell Reprint Company, 1969) (1920).

25. *See, e.g.,* Robin DeJarnette, *Universal Child Day Care: The Latest Threat to the Family* (visited Nov. 20, 1998) <http://www.frc.org/insight/is97hlcc.html>.

26. *See* Rose, *supra* note 7; PEOPLE FOR THE AMERICAN WAY, TEACHING FEAR: THE RELIGIOUS RIGHT'S CAMPAIGN AGAINST SEXUALITY EDUCATION (Washington, DC: People for the American Way, 1994).

Chapter 22

Gender-Based Asylum in the United States: A View from the Trenches

Paul Nejelski

I. INTRODUCTION

Having been an United States Immigration Judge for eight and a half years, I am no stranger to violence against women. I vividly remember a day in August of 1989 spent observing as part of my training as a new judge. The scene was the Immigration Court in the detention facility at 201 Varrick Street in New York City.

At 8:30 A.M., the first case involved a 30-year-old man convicted of raping his mother, who sat terrified next to her son. He was finishing his 2-year prison sentence and wanted to stay with his mother, but the judge ruled that he be deported to his native Poland and to his wife and children who waited for him there. The second case involved a 26-year-old man who had beat his wife senseless, thereby violating a protective court order to stay away from her. The judge ordered that the man be deported back to the Dominican Republic. In the next case, a 51-year-old man, who was finishing his 7-year prison term for stabbing his wife 14 times, was ordered deported to Nigeria.

But the most troubling incident occurred at lunch when a colleague casually mentioned a case that had previously come before the court. A 40-year-old man was ordered deported to Syria after a conviction for raping his sister-in-law. During the attack, she jumped from a window and was killed. The woman's husband (that is, the brother of the alien on trial) came to court to testify to the good character of the attacker: "A brother is forever, but a woman is . . . ," and he blew some imaginary dust from his outstretched palm to show his contempt for his wife, for women, and for the honorable court.

For me, in the last eight and a half years, thousands of cases followed. Many involved violence against women. But certainly the most poignant were those where the violence was condoned or even encouraged in the name of religion. I wondered then, and I wonder now, at the institutionalized hatred for women found in parts of the major religions. Where religion should liberate and comfort, too often it is misused to enslave and torment women throughout the world. Consequently, an appropriate question for this book is: "to what extent can women fleeing the hardships of religious fundamentalism find refuge in the United States?"

II. IMMIGRATION LAW IN THE UNITED STATES

An applicant may be eligible for political asylum in the United States upon the showing that she meets the statutory definition of a "refugee."[1] "Refugee" is defined consistently with the 1967 Protocol Relating to the Status of Refugees, thereby conforming U.S. national law to its international obligations.[2] A refugee is a person who neither can return to her home country nor can avail herself of the protection of her home country because of "persecution or a well-founded fear of persecution on account of race, religion, nationality, membership in a particular social group, or political opinion."[3] An immigration judge is given the power under section 208 of the Immigration and Naturalization Act (INA) to grant asylum to applicants who have established by a preponderance of the evidence that they: (1) were persecuted or reasonable persons in their circumstances would have a well-founded fear of persecution; (2) the persecution was or will be inflicted on account of their race, religion, nationality, membership in a particular social group, or political opinion; and (3) the harm was or is reasonably feared to be inflicted by a state actor or someone that the state is unable or unwilling to control.[4]

In assessing whether the level of treatment received amounts to "persecution,"[5] the Immigration and Naturalization Service (INS) and the courts, in recent years, have recognized that women may suffer harm that is specific to women,[6] such as sexual abuse, rape, infanticide, genital mutilation, forced marriage, domestic abuse, and forced abortion.[7] However, gender is not expressly mentioned in the statutory language. Thus, in order to prevail on an asylum claim, the applicant must show that the gender-based persecution is "on account of" one of the five statutory grounds:

race, religion, nationality, membership in a particular social group, or political opinion.[8]

Female asylum applicants have primarily relied on two of these categories in asserting their gender-based claims: political opinion and membership in a particular social group. The Third Circuit Court of Appeals stated that it had "[l]ittle doubt that feminism qualifies as a political opinion within the meaning of the relevant statutes."[9] A woman, therefore, who has received or fears severe harm due to her beliefs on how women should be treated or what status they should hold within their country, culture, religious or ethnic group could be deemed to have been persecuted because of her political opinions.[10]

The Board of Immigration Appeals has interpreted the phrase "particular social group" to be a "group of persons all of whom share a common, immutable characteristic. The shared characteristic might be an innate one such as sex, color, or kinship ties."[11] The Third Circuit, using this language, concluded that as a legal matter either gender alone or gender in combination with other factors could provide the basis for a particular social group.[12] However, no court has found that as a factual matter, an applicant has shown that she has been persecuted solely on account of her gender.[13]

Once she has established that she has suffered or has a well-founded fear of suffering persecution on account of one of the five statutory categories, the applicant must also establish that the persecution was either by a state actor, or by someone from whom the government is either unwilling or unable to protect her.[14] Violations of serious human rights by a nonstate actor, therefore, qualify as statutory persecution where it can be shown that the state has failed to provide the applicant meaningful protection and enforcement of the laws.[15]

For the purposes of this chapter, I will limit myself to discussing issues that arise in satisfying these requirements prescribed for the granting of political asylum and will omit discussion of closely related issues, including restriction on removal,[16] the application of the United Nations Convention Against Torture and Other Cruel, Inhumane or Degrading Treatment or Punishment,[17] and the new summary procedures for arriving aliens claiming asylum.[18] It should be noted, however, that besides asylum and restriction on removal, an eligible applicant may qualify for legal temporary or permanent residence in the United States through a variety of forms of relief such as Temporary Protective Status,[19] cancellation of removal,[20] or adjustment of status.[21] Consequently, any lawyer representing an alien or a judge in Immigration Court should consider, in addition to asylum, a variety of forms of relief.

III. CASES

During my tenure as an immigration judge, I have granted asylum on numerous occasions to women fleeing the hardships of fundamentalist religious persecution occurring in countries such as Sudan, Pakistan, Iran, Afghanistan, and areas of Latin America. In writing my decisions, I referred to various sources, including academic writing, INS guidelines, and appellate decisions. However, I primarily relied on basic asylum law developed in the United States based on international principles. Many cases will be contingent upon whether the applicant has satisfied the statutory grounds themselves, such as "political opinion" or "membership in a particular social group." The general asylum case law developed by the Board of Immigration Appeals[22] is helpful in supplementing the nuances that surround the requirements for each category.

Courtney Howland has already described in her 1997 article the two major decisions that I decided involving women's rights in conflict with religious fundamentalism:[23] *In re A and Z* and *In re M.K.*[24]

In *In re A and Z,* the respondents were a mother and child. The mother was a 51-year-old native of Syria who was married at 18 to the son of a prominent family in Jordan. For the next 32 years, her husband beat her with his fists, a belt, and even a tennis racquet. He threatened her with a knife; and, on one occasion, when he was in a drunken rage, fired a pistol into a room where she was hiding.

In granting this woman asylum, I stated:

> The respondent has been targeted for abuse because she is a woman who seeks to have her own identity, who believes in the "dangerous" Western values of integrity and worth of the individual. She is not content to be a slave. She wants to get an education, to read books, to have a career of her own, to have some control over her life. . . . The emancipation of women is one of the most important world-wide political and social movements of this century. Precisely because of its importance, the freedom and equality of women is dangerous and threatening politics to her husband, his society, and his government. The respondent's husband has beaten and abused the respondent for three decades, but the respondent and her twelve-year-old son remain unbowed. They now seek protection in this country for their political belief in the importance of individual freedom. Not just freedom for adult males, but freedom for women and children too. They shall have the protection they seek under the asylum and withholding of deportation laws of the United States.[25]

In approaching the more novel asylum claims presented by women, including spousal abuse, genital mutilation, or retaliation for reporting a rape for criminal prosecution, I did *not* say: "let's create special treatment for women." Rather, the question I always asked was: "Would I be justified in granting asylum if the applicant was a man?" In *In re A and Z*, my question was: "Would a man be entitled to asylum if he could show three decades of mental and physical abuse, denial of employment, house arrest, and so forth all *on account of* his "political opinion"? A denial of the man's asylum application based on such facts alone would be hard to imagine. Why should the result be any different in *In re A and Z* because the victim is a woman? If anything, the plight of the woman in *In re A and Z* was much more desperate because her spouse—instead of offering assistance— was in fact the primary agent of state and cultural repression.

In *In re M.K.* I granted asylum to a 29-year-old Sierra Leone woman based on three factors: (1) persecution relating to her forcibly-imposed female genital mutilation; (2) persecution due to her spousal abuse; and (3) persecution relating to her political party activism.[26] In my decision I emphasized that, in granting asylum in that case, the United States is not creating a standard of behavior that we are forcing on other societies.[27] Rather, I stated:

> [w]e are creating the standard by which this country will serve as a refuge for women who are being persecuted because of their gender. This standard is pursuant to United States domestic law and reflects our traditional commitments to justice, equality, individual autonomy, freedom of belief and expression, and democratic government. This standard is also consistent with international law and our commitments relating to the protection of human rights and refugees.[28]

I was able to grant asylum to a woman from El Salvador based on the events and treatment that she received after she had been abducted and repeatedly raped by a stranger.[29] After she escaped, the victim reported the offense to the police, who then arrested the attacker. The attacker's family in turn threatened the victim and beat members of her family in retaliation. The victim fled the country realizing that she could not obtain protection from the state. I granted the woman asylum because, in the context of that *macho* culture, she was being persecuted "on account of" her political opinion and her participation in a particular social group.[30] The social group was determined to consist of "women in El Salvador who have been sexually abused and are being punished for having reported this abuse to the authorities."[31]

Just before I retired from the bench in February 1998, I granted asylum to a woman and her two daughters from Afghanistan because of the clear threat posed to these three Westernized women by the ruling Taliban regime.[32] It was such a strong case that—based on the very thorough evidence presented by the alien's attorney—the INS trial attorney recommended a grant of asylum and waived any appeal from my decision.

IV. A VIEW FROM THE TRENCHES

In recent years, the unity and clarity of asylum law has been eroded by Congress. Various interest groups have convinced Congress to create favorable treatment for individual countries (Poland),[33] religion (Jews from the former Soviet Union),[34] or practices (coerced family planning).[35] As a humanitarian, I was delighted to grant relief whenever I could and, consequently, applied these special treatment provisions of the law in specific cases where appropriate.

But as a believer in the rule of law, I favor the universal application of section 208 itself. The proper question it seems to me is whether an individual meets the same standard for asylum relief as applied equally to all applicants. The alternative is to turn our asylum law into a large television quiz show in which the audience applauds each contestant based on the ability of special interest groups to fill the auditorium. A claimant from Nicaragua regardless of the merits of the case? Congress says "Lots of Nicaraguans vote in Florida, let's grant permanent residence." A claimant from Sudan or Bangladesh? "No votes, no special interest groups—case denied." Is this rule by law or rule by mob?

The Immigration Court is unique to the extent that the litigants either win all or lose all. The alien is either allowed to stay in the United States or ordered deported. In other civil litigation, the amount of money in controversy is negotiable or may be divided by the court. In criminal law, charges may be raised or lowered, sentence suspended, a variety of dispositions possible. But, generally speaking, in the Immigration Court, it is the "Winner Takes All."

This is significant because the stakes in Immigration Court are high. The judge's robe that I wore had on the back collar a small string noose as a reminder that our decisions could involve life or death for the litigant appearing before us.

Despite these high stakes, the evidence presented in my court by both sides—the alien *and* the government, was often painfully inadequate. In all the years I sat as a judge, the INS never presented an expert witness on country conditions in an asylum case.

With the adversarial system used by our courts, the judges must rely on the parties to present the written and oral evidence on which we can base our decision. The need for relevant written and oral evidence is high. Telling the story of repression by religious fundamentalism—over and over again if necessary—is essential in our case-by-case adjudication. I could only render strong, positive decisions in cases such as *In re A and Z* or *In re M.K.* because I had excellent expert witnesses and documents from the aliens' representatives to make my conclusions supportable. In *In re A and Z,* for example, a clinical psychologist who had personally evaluated the family testified, along with a disinterested woman from Jordan who described the repressive laws and customs.[36] In *In re M.K.* I relied heavily on the testimony of a medical doctor who was the director of Maternal-Fetal Medicine at Georgetown University, and who had personally examined the alien.[37] Crucial testimony was also received from a public health expert with extensive experience and travel in Africa.[38]

Cases involving rape present particularly difficult credibility problems. The claim of rape is frequently made in war-torn countries such as Somalia, El Salvador, or Afghanistan. I have worked with attorneys and expert witnesses such as psychologists or rape crisis counselors to develop evidence necessary to prove a case.

Feminist activists have occasionally argued that in cases involving women's issues only women should participate as interpreters, counsel, or judges.[39] Their reasoning is that female applicants might be intimidated or inhibited from discussing sexual violations. My own experience is that neither gender has a monopoly on ignorance or insensitivity. For example, I have seen women attorneys for the government be extremely harsh and unsympathetic in cases involving allegations of violence to women.

Where little evidence is presented to provide credible corroboration, I have had to deny asylum claims. A strong claim for asylum may also be denied because of overriding policies. Congress has drastically withdrawn asylum where the applicant has been convicted of a crime. A sentence of one year or more imprisonment for one of the crimes listed in the INA makes an alien an "aggravated felon" and thereby ineligible to apply for asylum.[40] "Negative factors" such as firm resettlement or having left a safe haven may also result in a denial of asylum.

Because of the attractions of living in the United States, thousands of weak or frivolous claims are filed each year. Precisely because the stakes are high in immigration proceedings, fraud is a great temptation for applicants in hopes that it will help them achieve their goal. The alien generally does not suffer any additional penalty if caught committing perjury. Numerous immigration lawyers, however, have been convicted and disbarred for fraud, but those cases generally involved fraudulent marriages or business-related visas.[41]

The INS Forensic Laboratory has been extremely useful in identifying fraudulent documents. False or altered passports are their specialty, but the

Forensic Lab has been increasingly helpful in finding fraudulent photos, marriage or death certificates, political party membership cards, and a host of other documents.

V. CONCLUSION

In conclusion, there is good news. Individual asylum claims based on violence from religious fundamentalists have been granted. There is also bad, or at least sobering, news. Credibility and fraud are always at issue. Cases cry out for, but rarely receive, the necessary expert testimony and relevant corroborating evidence. The view from the trenches is that the logistics of cases—evidence, expert testimony, and issues of fraud—are extremely important because immigration law is not self-enforcing.

NOTES

1. Refugee Act of 1980, Pub. L. No. 96–212, 94 Stat. 102 (1980) (codified at 8 U.S.C. 1101 et. seq.).
2. *See* The 1967 Protocol Relating to the Status of Refugees, Jan. 31, 1967, 19 U.S.T. 6223, 606 U.N.T.S. 267.
3. Immigration and Naturalization Act [hereinafter INA] §101(a)(42)(A), 8 U.S.C. §1101(a)(42)(A) (Supp. II 1996).
4. *See* INA §208(a), 8 U.S.C. §1158(a)(Supp. II 1996); *see* I.N.S. v. Cardoza-Fonseca, 480 U.S. 421 (1987).
5. Although the INA does not define "persecution," the Board of Immigration Appeals (BIA) has defined it as harm or suffering inflicted upon a person to punish that individual for possessing a belief or characteristic that the persecutor seeks to overcome. *See* Matter of Acosta: In Deportation Proceedings, 19 I & N Dec. 211, 222–23 (BIA 1985).
6. *See* U.S. DEPARTMENT OF JUSTICE: IMMIGRATION AND NATURALIZATION SERVICE INTERNATIONAL DIVISION, MEMORANDUM: CONSIDERATIONS FOR ASYLUM OFFICERS ADJUDICATING ASYLUM CLAIMS FROM WOMEN (May 26, 1995) [hereinafter INS GUIDELINES]; Fatin v. I.N.S., 12 F.3d 1233, 1240 (3d Cir. 1993); *see also* Nancy Kelly, et al., *Guidelines for Women's Asylum Claims,* 71 Interpreter Releases 813 (June 1994).
7. *See* INS GUIDELINES, *supra* note 6, at 9; Deborah Anker, et al., *The BIA's New Asylum Jurisprudence and Its relevance for Women's Claims,* 73 Interpreter Releases 1173 (Sept. 1996); Kelly, *supra* note 6.
8. INA §208(b), 8 U.S.C. §1158(b) (Supp. II 1996); *see* Matter of Acosta: In Deportation Proceedings, 19 I & N Dec. 211, 226 (BIA 1985).
9. Fatin v. I.N.S., 12 F.3d 1233, 1242 (3d Cir. 1993).
10. *See* INS GUIDELINES, *supra* note 6, at 11.
11. Matter of Acosta: In Deportation Proceedings, 19 I & N Dec. 211, 233 (BIA 1985).

12. Fatin v. I.N.S., 12 F.3d 1233, 1240–41 (3d Cir. 1993); *but see* Gomez v. I.N.S., 947 F.2d 660, 664 (2d Cir. 1991) ("possession of broadly-based characteristics as youth and gender will not by itself endow individuals with membership in a particular group.")

13. *See* INS GUIDELINES, *supra* note 6, at 13.

14. *See id.* at 16–17.

15. *See* Matter of Kasinga, Interim Dec. No. 3278 (BIA 1996) (upholding gender-based asylum claim in which agent of persecution was applicant's community and tribe and government did not provide protection against female genital mutilation).

16. *See* INA §241(b)(3), 8 U.S.C. §1231(b)(3) (Supp. II 1996); INA §208, 8 U.S.C. 1158 (Supp. II 1996).

17. *See* U.N. Convention Against Torture and Other Cruel, Inhumane or Degrading Treatment or Punishment, *opened for signature* Feb. 4, 1985, G.A. Res. 39/46, 39 U.N. GAOR, Supp. No. 51, at 197, U.N. Doc. A/RES/39/708 (1984), 23 I.L.M. 1027 (1984), *modified in* 24 I.L.M. 535 (1985). For an analysis of how the Torture Convention can be used as an alternative for refugees who are otherwise ineligible for asylum or withholding of removal, see Kristen B. Rosati, *The United Nations Convention Against Torture: A Detailed Examination of the Convention as an Alternative for Asylum Seekers,* IMMIGRATION BRIEFINGS, Dec. 1997, at 1.

18. *See* INA §235(b), 8 U.S.C. §1225(b) (Supp. II 1996).

19. *See* INA §244, 8 U.S.C. §1254 (1994).

20. *See* INA §240A, 8 U.S.C. §1229(b) (Supp. II 1996).

21. *See* INA §245, 8 U.S.C. §1255 (1994).

22. The Board of Immigration Appeals has national application, unlike the regional circuit court decisions.

23. *See* Courtney W. Howland, *The Challenge of Religious Fundamentalism to the Liberty and Equality Rights of Women: An Analysis under the United Nations Charter,* 35 COLUM. J. TRANSNAT'L L. 271, 354–56 & nn.353, 355, 357 (1997).

24. *See In re* A and Z: In Deportation Proceedings (A 72–190–893, A 72–793–219) (Exec. Office for Immigration Review, Arlington, Va.) (Dec. 20,1994) (unpublished opinion), *reported in* 72 Interpreter Releases 521 (Apr. 17, 1995) (on file with editor); *In re* M.K.: In Deportation Proceedings (A 72–374–558) (Exec. Office for Immigration Review, Arlington, Va.) (Aug. 9,1995) (unpublished opinion) (on file with editor).

25. *In re* A and Z: In Deportation Proceedings (A 72–190–893, A 72–793–219), *supra* note 24, at 14.

26. *See In re* M.K.: In Deportation Proceedings (A 72–374–558), *supra* note 24, at 22–23.

27. *See id.* at 21.

28. *Id.*

29. *See In re* Maria Ana Andrades: In Deportation Proceedings (A 70–671–603) (Exec. Office for Immigration Review, Arlington, Va.) (Feb. 26, 1997) (unpublished opinion) (on file with editor).

30. *See id.* at 6–8.

31. *Id.* at 6; *see also* Matter of Sharmin (A73–556–833) (Exec. Office for Immigration Review, New York, NY) (Sept. 27, 1996), *reported in, IJ Grants Asylum to Battered Bangladeshi Woman,* 74 Interpreter Releases 174 (Jan. 27, 1997).

32. *See In re* Ahmad Qasemi, Zakia Qasemi, Muzhda Qasemi, Saleha Qasemi: In Exclusion Proceedings (A 29–104–445; A 29–104–442; A 29–104–443; A 29–104–444) (Exec. Office for Immigration Review, Arlinton, Va.) (Jan. 5, 1998) (unpublished opinion) (on file with editor).

33. *See* Act of Dec. 22, 1987, Pub. L. No. 100–204, sec. 902, 101 Stat. 1331 (1987) (codified at 8 U.S.C. sec. 1255a (1994)); 8 C.F.R. sec. 245a.4 (1997); 64 Interpreter Releases 1391, 1392 (1987); *see also* 67 Interpreter Releases 72 (1990).

34. *See* Lautenberg Amendment, Pub. L. No. 101–167, Title V, §599D, 103 Stat. 1261(1989) (codified at 8 U.S.C. §157 (1994); *In re* Igor Fiodosy Zabelin: In Deportation Proceedings (A71–960–487) (Exec. Office for Immigration Review, Arlington, Va.) (Dec. 15, 1995) (unpublished opinion) (on file with editor). For a detailed opinion considering the applicability of the Lautenberg Amendment to section 208 asylum requests, see *In re* Saamova-Soyfer: In Deportation Proceedings (A29–757–816) (Exec. Office for Immigration Review, Philadelphia, Pa.) (May 9, 1995) (unpublished opinion) (on file with editor).

35. *See* INA §101(a)(42)(B), 8 U.S.C. §1101(a)(42)(B) (Supp. II 1996).

36. *In re* A and Z: In Deportation Proceedings (A 72–190–893, A 72–793–219), *supra* note 24, at 6, 11–13.

37. *In re* M.K.: In Deportation Proceedings (A 72–374–558), *supra* note 24, at 3–6.

38. *See id.* at 3–7.

39. *See* Deborah E. Anker, *Women Refugees: Forgotten No Longer?,* 32 SAN. DIEGO L. REV. 771, 776 n.13 (1995); Nancy Kelly, *Gender-Related Persecution: Assessing the Asylum Claims of Women,* 26 CORNELL INT'L L.J. 625, 630 & n.21 (1993).

40. *See* INA §101(a)(43), 8 U.S.C. §1101(a)(43) (1994); INA §208(b)(2)(B)(i), 8 U.S.C. §1158(b)(2)(B)(i) (Supp. II 1996).

41. *See, e.g.,* United States v. Zalman, 870 F.2d 1047 (6th Cir.); *see also* 8 C.F.R. §292.3(a)(3) (1997).

Chapter 23

Tales of Subversion: Women Challenging Fundamentalism in the Islamic Republic of Iran

Azar Nafisi

I. THE PAST

I will begin with a tale. Its plot centers on a woman and poet known as Tahereh. Tahereh was not her real name; it was the title bestowed on her by Bab, a religious leader and the precursor of the Baha'i faith in Iran. It means "the pure." Tahereh was born in Qazvin, Iran, in 1814, to a well-known and influential clerical family.[1]

She lived at a time in Iran when clerics and despots shared power and the "law" was religious law. Perhaps the best way to judge that time is by its rules regarding women. Women were veiled from head to toe, and when talking to men who were not members of their immediate family or their husbands, they had to hide behind a curtain. Polygamy was an accepted practice, women's age of consent for marriage was nine, the punishment for adultery was death by stoning, and women's public education was banned.

Because of her father's enlightened views, Tahereh and her sister were allowed to continue their studies under his and his brothers' tutelage. Tahereh's exceptional talent and zeal for knowledge matched her extraordinary beauty. Despite the high degree of her scholarship and attainments,[2] she was given in marriage to her cousin at the age of 14.[3] Marriage to a husband from an orthodox and highly religious family, and the birth of two sons, did not deter Tahereh from her studies.

As a result of those studies, she became attached to the teachings of the most controversial religious leaders of her time, the Babis. At a time when women were not allowed to leave their house without their husband's permission, Tahereh left her husband and family and became one of the Babi movement's most effective and outspoken leaders.[4] She urged radical changes in religious doctrines that she insisted must change and be renewed with time. She was so effective an orator that wherever she went she gathered large followings, especially among women.

The followers of Bab and later of Bahaullah posed a dangerous threat to Iran's powerful Islamic clergy, and Tahereh became a particular threat. In the year 1848, at a gathering of Babi followers in the hamlet of Badasht, Tahereh appeared unveiled, and abrogating the laws of Islam, proclaimed the advent of a new faith. "Consternation immediately seized the entire gathering. . . . To behold her face unveiled was to them inconceivable."[5] Many men escaped in horror, and one slashed his throat at such an act of sacrilege by a woman.[6] It was then that the Babis announced their independence from Islam, and proclaimed their faith as a new faith.[7]

Tahereh's unveiling became synonymous with the abrogation of Islamic law. To the followers of her abandoned faith she was worse than a heathen; she was a heretic, the evil "Other" who had betrayed her own. To her followers she was an enigma, a puzzle to be worshipped without being understood.

Not surprisingly, Tahereh was soon put under house arrest.[8] The tale ends with her death. The government, too apprehensive about executing her publicly, secretly planned her death and had her strangled.[9]

This chapter is not about Tahereh's Babi movement. Rather it is about Tahereh's great granddaughters and great great granddaughters living in a country now called the Islamic Republic of Iran (Islamic Republic). Tahereh's legend is the context that will make these women's lives understandable.

The image of Tahereh in Badasht now haunts the Islamic Republic. As an Iranian woman living in the Islamic Republic until 1997, I often felt that a time warp had occurred and I was back to living in Tahereh's times. Understanding women's lives in the Islamic Republic and their resistance to fundamentalism starts with understanding the past, and in finding answers to the questions raised by Tahereh's tale: Why did Tahereh have to be taken away and killed secretly? What danger did a single woman present to those powerful men? Why did a man kill himself because she lived the way she did?

II. THE CHALLENGE OF THE PAST

The first challenge to the Islamic Republic is the challenge of the past. The Islamic regime took power in the Islamic Revolution in 1979 in the name of the past, putting forward the story that modern Iran was an aberration, a fabrication imposed on the country by the Imperialists and their domestic agents. It claimed that there never had been any genuine move to change the society and to bring it into the modern world. The new rulers attacked the West's "cultural invasion," which they alleged had led to the destruction of traditional Islamic culture. They branded all moves to create new spaces for women from the time of Tahereh to the present as part of foreign plots to dominate and subjugate Iran. The Babis' and Bahais' persecution and destruction was, and is, justified because they were declared to be not only heretics but also spies and agents of imperial powers. Yet there are other accounts that belie and contradict this version of history.

Unlike many intellectuals who created the idea and ideal of a modern Iran, Tahereh had no contact with the West, and was not influenced by Western thought. She was a religious woman, not an ardent feminist.[10] She is important because she articulated an urge centered in the very religion that she negated. She questioned the religious fundamentalism of her times that blended so well with despotic rule. To question that fundamentalism meant questioning the fundaments of the society.

If it were only Tahereh who challenged the existing system, we would mainly remember her as an exceptional and colorful legend. But in the decades following her death, many more Iranians questioned the basic tenets that ruled the country. Most of these Iranians felt instinctively that central to change in society was the fate of its women. Their adversaries also felt this. From the very start, the concept of change and the idea of modernization was bound to the demand for more spaces, more rights, for women and minorities. In this way, women became gauges with which we have been measuring where Iranian society is going and where it has been.

Iran's modern history abounds in images of women who fought for their freedom of choice. They were not as dramatic or messianic as Tahereh. Yet many were the women who participated in the long struggle for Iran's modernization culminating in the 1906 Constitutional Revolution. In the years before and after the Constitutional Revolution, women from different strata of society took part in almost all the major events that helped change the course of Iranian society.[11]

The Constitutional Revolution heralded the dawn of a new Iran, but it did not grant rights to the women who had so ardently fought for it. It did, however, provide spaces within which women could fight and achieve some rights. And fight they did—with the support of some progressive men. They created health clinics and public schools for women, organized the first women's organizations, and published the first women's publications. Long before Reza Shah made the removal of the veil mandatory, many women under the pain of infamy, banishment, and at times exile, refused to wear the veil. In 1906, some women marched in the streets of Tehran, taking off their veils and demanding the full recognition of their rights, and aroused such public outrage as to force even the constitutionalists to call the march a "plot" by the reactionaries who had hired these "prostitutes" to discredit the Revolution.[12] By February 1907, 150 women had created an organization to fight "ancient traditions that are harmful and contrary to progress."[13]

The struggle against foreign domination and the resulting Constitutional Revolution did not prevent Iranian men and women from desiring to become part of the modern world. They saw themselves as part of an international community and were not shy of acknowledging their kinship to Western ideas and ideals. Iranian women were also aware of women's movements in other parts of the world.[14] Nor were progressive Westerners afraid of acknowledging their solidarity with the modernizing efforts by the women of the East. As an American, Morgan Shuster, remarked, "[t]he Persian women since 1907 had become almost at a bound the most progressive, not to say radical, in the world. That this statement upsets the ideas of centuries makes no difference. It is the fact."[15]

It was not surprising that the reactionaries both in the conservative clerical and royal ranks who had opposed the struggle for Iran's modernization should manifest this opposition most virulently in relation to women's struggle for their rights. Certain conservative clerics felt that the most poisonous aspects of the West were cultural, especially in relation to the rights of women and minorities. The most outspoken of the clerics issued a *fatwa* (religious edict) against women's education.[16] The clerics' attacks on progressive women, and on girls' public schools, further encouraged the opponents of women's rights who attacked young female students and their teachers on the streets, spat on them, and called their behavior "unchaste" and "immoral."[17]

From those earlier times right through to the present, women had to fight for their space in Iranian society. Despite contemporary fundamentalists' claims to the contrary, this was true during the Pahlavi era as well. Every right seemingly granted to women during the Pahlavi era was the result of efforts and struggles of women who fought for these changes against fundamentalist factions and patriarchal attitudes.[18] For example, in 1963, when women finally won the right to enfranchisement, Ayatollah Khomeini (little known then) opposed women's enfranchisement and organized riots in various cities.[19] He later opposed the passage of the Family Protection Law (which gave women the right to divorce and generally strengthened women's rights in child custody, marriage, and divorce)[20] and the appointment of women as judges. He warned that in granting these rights to women the government was obeying foreigners and not Islamic laws.[21]

When in 1979 the fundamentalists tried to regain the power they had lost at the beginning of the century, they revived the old slogans and resurrected the images of their old enemies. Their pretense that they were, and are, returning to the past—a past unencumbered by imperialism or struggle for women's rights—is an obvious lie since it is clear that Iranian women have been struggling for their rights for over a century and a half, not as domestic agents of imperialists, but for themselves and for their country. Women's rights as the site of struggle in Iran since the advent of the Islamic revolution is the *continuation*—not a repetition—of a struggle that goes back over a century and a half. The very "past" that fundamentalists rely on for their legitimacy challenges the truth of their claim.

III. THE PRESENT

The man who slashed his throat because of Tahereh's unveiling, along with the men who silenced and strangled Tahereh, are back: they are the fundamentalists attempting to lead the Islamic Republic of Iran. The main targets of these new rulers are minorities, intellectuals, and, of course, women. From the very start, the Islamic regime, under the guise of attacking the West's "cultural invasion," focused on cultural issues. They found that the most obvious manifestations of "decadent Western culture" were women—the way they looked and the public spaces they occupied.

When the Islamic revolution triumphed, women had been involved in all aspects of Iranian life. During the first half of the seventies "the number of girls attending elementary school rose from 80,020 to 1,508,387; the number of girls attending vocational training schools rose tenfold; the number of women candidates for the universities rose seven times. By 1978, 33 percent of all university students were women and they had begun to choose fields other than traditionally female occupations."[22]

In employment, before the Islamic Revolution, priority had been given to training women for semiskilled and skilled work. "All laws and regulations were revised to eliminate sex discrimination, and equal pay for equal work was incorporated into the body of all government rules. All regulations regarding housing, loans, and other job benefits were adjusted to eliminate discrimination."[23] Women were active in all walks of life; they worked in universities, the police force, and as judges, pilots, and engineers—in every field except religious activities. In 1978, 333 of 1660 candidates to local councils were women. "Twenty-two were elected to Parliament, two served in the Senate. There were one cabinet minister, three sub-cabinet under secretaries (including the second highest position in the Ministries of Labor and Mines and Industries), one governor, an ambassador and five mayors."[24]

These figures are important not only to judge women's losses and gains after the Islamic Revolution, but to understand why women took such an active part in the Revolution. They saw themselves as part of the society, as a force with a voice, and a choice. They, like the majority of those who supported the Revolution, were asking for more rights, more political participation, and greater freedom of expression because they had reached a state of maturity where these rights and freedoms seemed to be inalienable. So, women "marched and shouted their will. That it was in support of a destructive force came from political naiveté which only time and experience can correct."[25]

Although reactionary clergy during the Constitutional Revolution tried to force Iranian women to leave the scene, it was impossible to do so because women were so much part of Iranian society. The same was true in the Islamic Revolution. This explains why the new rulers in the Islamic Republic picked women as their main target. They annulled progressive laws, including the Family Protection Law,[26] and brought back the old laws that had dominated society in Tahereh's times: polygamy; the age of consent for girls was lowered from 18 to 9; women were barred from many public offices, from 140 academic disciplines, and from many jobs in engineering, medicine, and fields deemed to be masculine territory;[27] and women were expelled from many secretarial jobs because their presence was regarded as a temptation to their bosses. One by one women's rights were taken away from them. Universities, schools, and even buses became segregated, and women had to obtain their husbands' permission to work. In passing these laws, the new rulers not only made a statement against women, but against a century-long struggle for modernity.

The most obvious symbol of the new regime was the "veil," defined as a black, body-length garment that covered women's hair and head down to her toes. The regime claimed that the unveiling of Iranian women had been solely the work of Imperialists and their domestic agents. In 1979, Ayatollah Khomeini ordered the reveiling of women. Unlike what has been claimed by some in the West, the imposition of the veil *was* met with protest. *One hundred thousand* women poured into the streets protesting Khomeini's edict.[28] The regime had to back down temporarily. Its vigilantes, however, continued attacking and harassing unveiled women in public. In 1980, the regime made the veil mandatory in government buildings and public places. Many women resisted and protested this act, and were, as in former times, attacked and beaten by vigilantes supported by the government and denounced by the "progressive" forces. After all it was not only a "backward" Ayatollah who had claimed that women's hair had to be covered, but the Islamic Republic's French-educated, first president, Bani Sadr.[29] It was Leftist intellectuals who condemned women who protested against veiling as "a handful of fashion models and painted dolls" who "are turning this insignificant issue (of veiling) into a major affair as if it is as important as democracy and the country's independence."[30]

Three years later the veil became mandatory for all women regardless of their religion, creed, or nationality. It took four years and use of coercion and force to impose the veil on women. The punishment for deviating from the dress code was jail, monetary fines, and a flogging of up to 76 lashes. In order to implement the "law," the regime created vice squads, special courts, and jails for "moral offenses." These courts and their guards had permission to raid public places or private homes, in search of alcoholic drinks, "decadent" music, video films, playing cards, sexually mixed parties, or unveiled women. Bazaars and shopping malls were surrounded and raided. Young girls were arrested for not wearing the proper clothing and/or for walking together with boys in the streets. Lipsticks, nail polish, and Reebok shoes were treated as lethal weapons. Young girls were subjected to virginity tests, to flogging, and jail sentences.

The fact that the Islamic Republic had to use so much energy and violence to insist on segregation and veiling to such an extent demonstrates that the issue of veiling belied its claim that it was merely acting in accordance with time-honored traditions of the society. Could the Islamic regime literally turn the clock back? Could it regain the ground that was lost at the turn of the century? This was a test both for the regime and for the forces that believed in a modern Iran.

IV. THE CHALLENGE TO THE PRESENT

In the first year after the Islamic Revolution's victory there were many sit-ins, demonstrations, and protests against the reactionary measures taken by the regime against women. As a result, the new regime learned to impose its laws gradually as it consolidated its power and repressed the democratic forces in the country. The Revolutionary Guards and "Islamic" vigilantes aided repression by attacking women in the streets, beating them up, and throwing acid in their faces if they were not veiled or dressed according to the "Islamic" dress code.

Despite Ayatollah Khomeini's earlier opposition to women's enfranchisement, he decided that women's voting power was politically necessary—even if religiously unacceptable. Rather than denying women the right to vote, he made the passage of new restrictive laws possible by creating new rifts or exploiting old ones among the ranks of women.

Women were divided into the good and the bad; the good were "women of Islam" and the bad were "agents of Satan." It was in the interest of the good to destroy the bad. This created a rift between women who were characterized as either agents of the West or emissaries of the regime. This rift was further encouraged by Leftist organizations that, in the name of fighting Western decadence, resisted women's attempts to defend their freedoms. An authoritarian attitude became the norm not only for the more reactionary elements of the regime, but for "progressive" groups as well. The main struggle now, as in the past, was not against an outside enemy, but against the enemy within.

The regime's approach was to replace modern women with "Islamic" ones. Many of the "good" women were placed in high positions not because of their merit but because they were related to the men in power. As such they became mouthpieces for their fathers, husbands, or male relatives. Some of these women used their position to attack the rights of women, and to advocate what the religious leaders prescribed.

But gradually some women in public office became more sensitized to the plight of women in general, and they began working for change. Secular women had the most important role in creating this change in the political and social climate. The majority of secular women could not be easily dispensed with because they had information and skills that were needed in various fields.[31] This situation in itself put women from different camps side by side. As time went by, both sides realized that they had more in common with each other than they had differences. Many of the women who were in power gradually took on the same role as those whom they had previously criticized as Westernized.

One area that solidified the bond between women was that of the law. The Islamic Republic had changed the laws, claiming that they were unjust and products of alien rule and exploitation. Once the "alien rulers" were gone and the new laws were implemented, the truth or falsity of these claims were tested in actuality. The Islamic laws inevitably led to women making a critical reappraisal of the basic tenets that had created them. For example, the imposition of the veil raised discussions concerning the right to freedom of choice. Some Islamic women considered that they had the right to practice their religion according to their own interpretations. If some chose to wear the veil, that was their right and privilege, but if others chose not to, that was also their privilege. In imposing the veil, the Iranian government not only infringed the rights of Muslim women, but of secular women, and of women from other religions and denominations. With this realization, it became clear to many that the law did not protect women, but violated their basic right of freedom of choice and expression. Iranian women from all walks of life discovered that the hardest obstacle to their lives was the rule of law itself.

And women's protest continues. Of course, once the veil was made mandatory, conventional forms of protest became impossible. Yet, Iranian women, especially young girls, have turned the veil into an instrument of protest: they wear it in attractive and provoking ways; they leave part of their hair showing from under their scarves; they allow their colorful clothing to show from underneath their uniforms; and they walk in a provoking manner. Their defiant way of wearing the veil is a constant reminder to the ruling elite that this is one battle that will never be won.[32]

It is not surprising therefore that, in 1997, after the victory of the Iranian football team in Australia, millions of Iranians—against the government's repeated warnings—poured into the streets celebrating with dancing and loud music. This was called the "Football Revolution." The most striking feature of this "revolution" was the thousands of women who, by breaking the police barricades, entered the football stadium banned to women by the government. Some celebrated by taking their veils off.

The Iranian regime's efforts at "Islamization" has taken a heavy toll on society, especially on women, who were its main targets. But it did not leave the regime unscathed. The government has claimed that only a handful of "Westernized" women have opposed its laws, but now years after the Revolution its most outspoken and daring opponents are the youth, the children of Revolution. In July 1993, vice squads detained 802 men and women in Tehran for violating the dress code. The officials reported that 80 percent of the detainees were under the age of 20.[33]

Those who were, and are, not part of Iranian society should not be deceived by its portrayal of Iranian women as docile and satisfied with the regime. The fact of the matter is that for the past 20 years both the public and private arena has been the scene of a protracted struggle about women's rights and freedoms.

As in Tahereh's times, women in today's Iran have become an essential part of the larger movement for the creation of democracy and civil society. The women's movement continues its century-and-a-half struggle for rights and freedoms with the aid of secular women, Muslim women, and women from other religions, and a large portion of society who have now come to question the very laws they had taken for granted for so long. It is in this way that Tahereh has come back. Her murderers were the ones to resurrect her and give her a special place in the hearts and minds of her great granddaughters, and their daughters' daughters. Those men have come back, but again they will have to slash their own throats.

NOTES

1. *See* ABBAS AMANAT, RESURRECTION AND RENEWAL: THE MAKING OF THE BABI MOVEMENT IN IRAN, 1844–1850, 295 (Ithaca/London: Cornell University Press, 1989).

2. *See* 'ABDU'L-BAHA, MEMORIALS OF THE FAITHFUL 190–91 (Marzieh Gail, trans. & annon.) (Wilmette, IL: Bahá'í Publishing Trust, 1971).

3. *See* AMANAT, *supra* note 1, at 297.

4. *See generally* FARZANEH MILANI, VEILS AND WORDS: THE EMERGING VOICES OF IRANIAN WOMEN WRITERS 77–99 (Syracuse: Syracuse University Press, 1992).

5. THE DAWN-BREAKERS: NABÍL'S NARRATIVE OF THE EARLY DAYS OF THE BAHÁ'Í REVELATION 294–5 (Shoghi Effendi, trans.) (Wilmette, IL: Bahá'í Publishing Trust, 1962).

6. *See id.* at 295; MILANI, *supra* note 4, at 86 & 254 n.23 (quoting SHOGHI EFFENDI, GOD PASSES BY 32 (Wilmette, IL.: Bahá'í Publishing Committee, 1944)).

7. *See* MILANI, *supra* note 4, at 86.

8. *See* AMANAT, *supra* note 1, at 329; 'ABDU'L-BAHA, *supra* note 2, at 202.

9. *See* 'ABDU'L-BAHA, *supra* note 2, at 203.

10. *See* AMANAT, *supra* note 1, at 330.

11. *See* JANET AFARY, THE IRANIAN CONSTITUTIONAL REVOLUTION 1906–1911, 178–9 (New York: Columbia University Press, 1996).

12. HAIDEH MOGHISSI, POPULISM AND FEMINISM IN IRAN: WOMEN'S STRUGGLE IN A MALE-DEFINED REVOLUTIONARY MOVEMENT 30 (New York: St. Martin's Press, 1996).

13. *See* AFARY, *supra* note 11, at 184 & 372 n.40 (quoting *Notes et Nouvelles,* 2 REVUE DU MONDE MUSULMAN 213 (1907)).

14. *See id.* at 205.

15. *See id.* at 177 (quoting MORGAN SHUSTER, THE STRANGLING OF PERSIA (1912)).

16. *See id.* at 190.

17. *See id.*

18. For a discussion of these various struggles, see Mahnaz Afkhami, *Iran: A Future in the Past—The "Prerevolutionary Women's Movement," in* SISTERHOOD IS GLOBAL: THE INTERNATIONAL WOMEN'S MOVEMENT ANTHOLOGY 330, 331–35 (Robin Morgan, ed.) (New York: Doubleday, 1984). Mahnaz Afkahami herself is one of the pioneers in this struggle.

19. *See id.* at 331; *see also* HALEH ESFANDIARI, RECONSTRUCTED LIVES: WOMEN & IRAN'S ISLAMIC REVOLUTION 27 (Washington, DC: Woodrow Wilson Center Press; Baltimore/London: The Johns Hopkins University Press, 1997).

20. *See* Afkhami, *supra* note 18, at 333; ESFANDIARI, *supra* note 19, at 30–31.

21. MOGHISSI, *supra* note 12, at 46.

22. Afkhami, *supra* note 18, at 335.

23. *Id.* (footnote omitted).

24. *Id.* (footnote omitted).
25. *Id.* at 335 & 336 n.3
26. *Id.* at 336.
27. *See* Mahnaz Afkhami, *Women Post-Revolutionary Iran: a feminist perspective, in* IN THE EYE OF THE STORM: WOMEN IN POST-REVOLUTIONARY IRAN 5, 12 (Mahnaz Afkhami & Erika Friedl, eds.) (Syracuse: Syracuse University Press, 1994).
28. *See* AFARY, *supra* note 11, at 177.
29. *See* ESFANDIARI, *supra* note 19, at 146 & n*.
30. MOGHISSI, *supra* note 12, at 102–103.
31. *See* ESFANDIARI, *supra* note 19, at 43–45.
32. MOGHISSI, *supra* note 12, at 184.
33. *Id.*

VII

Religious Challenges to Religious Fundamentalism

Chapter 24

A Feminist Perspective on Jewish Fundamentalism

Paula E. Hyman

I. INTRODUCTION

This chapter provides an example of feminist strategies in response to patriarchy in general and fundamentalism in particular in one religious tradition—Judaism. It demonstrates how feminism can provide an alternative understanding of the past and an alternative vision of the future, as it creates an alternative social and cultural reality. For almost 30 years Jewish feminists have worked in the Jewish community, particularly in the United States but also in Israel and elsewhere, to assert the equality of women and to introduce egalitarianism as a fundamental communal value. Comprising a loosely structured movement with many different branches, Jewish feminists recognize the patriarchal nature of traditional Judaism but, with the exception of a small group of Orthodox feminists, also accept the legitimacy and authenticity of non-Orthodox forms of modern Judaism.[1] They do not presume that patriarchy and the consequent subordination of women are essential features of Judaism, as the feminist theologian Mary Daly has asserted vis-à-vis Catholicism.[2] Instead, they have taken on the task of creating a feminist Judaism because, in the words of the Jewish feminist theologian Judith Plaskow, they "refus[e] the split between a Jewish and a feminist self" and "find value and meaning in Judaism and in [their] own Jewish identity. . . ."[3] They are unwilling to leave the definition of Judaism to either traditionalists or fundamentalists. Jewish feminists have introduced manifestations of women's equality into contemporary Jewish life and have challenged the disabilities that women continue to suffer, particularly in divorce, under Jewish law.

Feminist successes have depended on the strength of secular civil society. In America the separation of church and state has enabled diverse forms of Judaism to flourish and has marginalized the voices of fundamentalists, who represent a tiny proportion of American Jewry. Fundamentalists comprise a radical subset of Orthodox Judaism, and Orthodox Jews in America, many of whom dissent from the fierce anti-modernism of the fundamentalists, account for no more than 10 percent of the Jewish population. In Israel the establishment of an official, Orthodox rabbinate, with authority (where Jews are concerned) over such personal status issues as marriage, divorce, and burial, has diminished the scope of secular civil society. Moreover, the structure of Israeli coalition politics has magnified the significance of the 20 percent of the Jewish population that identifies itself as Orthodox. Those two factors have compelled feminists to make use of the civil court system, under attack by some Orthodox Jews and their political parties, to struggle for the equality of women. The acceptance by a broad spectrum of the Jewish population of Israel of the establishment of the Orthodox rabbinate, which dates back to the time of the founding of the state and has its roots in the Ottoman Empire's millet system, has limited feminist gains. The impact of Jewish fundamentalism on women is therefore more significant in Israel than in the United States.

II. JEWISH FUNDAMENTALISTS

Much of the scholarly literature discusses Jewish fundamentalism in terms of *haredim* (ultra-Orthodox) and the messianic religious activism of Gush Emunim in Israel.[4] Scholars have identified two types of fundamentalists, the quiescent and the active (or the conservative and the innovative), and two fundamentalist strategies, withdrawal from the dominant secular society and conquest of that society by imposing the fundamentalists' vision of truth upon it.[5] Conservative and quiescent fundamentalists arouse little opposition; activists and innovative religious radicals do. The growing strength of the activists, particularly in Israel, and their triumphalist desire to control the public and private behavior of their fellow Jews have provided the greatest challenge to Jewish women.

The anti-modernist sentiment of fundamentalist movements characterizes much of contemporary Orthodox Judaism, though the system of textual interpretation of the Bible and Talmud does not allow for the literalism that characterizes American Protestant fundamentalism.[6] Orthodox Judaism, as distinct from traditional Judaism, emerged in the nineteenth century as a reaction to the Enlightenment, the civic emancipation of the Jews, and the emergence of various forms of Judaism that accepted Enlightenment values. As the historian Jacob Katz has pointed out, "[t]he claim of the Orthodox to be no more than the guardians of the pure Judaism of old is a fiction. In fact, Orthodoxy was a method of confronting deviant trends. . . ."[7] The form of Orthodoxy that prevails in both Israel and the United States derives from eastern Europe, where the influence of Enlightenment (and post-Enlightenment) concepts of rationalism, individualism, and social equality was muted until the twentieth century and where the civic emancipation of the Jews came late. Orthodox Judaism was more rigid in its approach to changing social conditions than was premodern traditional Judaism. Most important, it saw the distinction in gender roles that characterized *halakhah* (Jewish law), as one of the pillars of Jewish tradition.[8] Because Orthodox Jews in general share so many basic values with fundamentalists in their ranks—despite fundamentalists' rejection of the official religious establishment because it is not stringent enough—feminists confront a more formidable opponent than the numbers of Jewish fundamentalists alone would indicate.

As is generally acknowledged, women's subordinate status within Judaism is based on a male monopoly of the sources of learning, and hence authority, and a fear of uncontrolled female sexuality.[9] Women's subordinate status was manifest particularly in laws of divorce and property and inheritance rights, in their limited role in the public space of the community, and in their lack of access to Torah learning.[10] Despite the promulgation of the ideal of women's relegation to the domestic sphere, throughout history Jewish women have been actively involved in the public economic sphere.[11] Indeed, contemporary Jewish fundamentalist movements depend on married women to support their families by working outside the home while their husbands devote themselves to the study of Torah. In this way, Jewish fundamentalism differs from that of other religious traditions. The learning of Torah—by which is meant primarily the vast corpus of rabbinic literature found in the 70 tractates of the Talmud as well as the Hebrew Bible and rabbinic commentaries upon it—is a divine commandment for men within traditional, Orthodox, and fundamentalist Judaism. Men who achieved mastery of rabbinic texts were, and are, accorded high status within the community; with the acquisition of the title "rabbi," to which their mastery entitled them, they had the right to interpret *halakhah* and to adjudicate according to its rules. Women were exempt from Torah study; a minority of rabbis went so far as to forbid teaching Torah to them. In practice, until the modern period, and particularly the twentieth century, the distinction between exemption and exclusion was virtually irrelevant. The vast majority of women received little formal education in the Jewish texts whose study was an ideal to which all male Jews aspired. Most important, no women wielded authority as rabbis; the power of interpreting Jewish law lay entirely in male hands.

III. JEWISH FEMINISTS

Through scholarly writing, which has recuperated or reinterpreted classical Jewish texts, political activity, and the creation of egalitarian communities, Jewish feminists have subverted the markers of female subordination within Judaism. Highly educated and predominantly middle class, by the 1970s American Jewry, and its non-Orthodox rabbinate, were attuned to the basic claims of feminism.[12] Asserting that the failure of traditional Judaism to accept women as potential leaders and sources of authority and to consider them as appropriate as men to perform all religious rituals was historically contingent, and deprived the Jewish community of half of its potential human resources, feminists have succeeded in transforming women's roles in non-Orthodox forms of Judaism.[13] There are now more than 400 women rabbis in the Reform, Reconstructionist, and Conservative movements in the United States and a handful in Israel (unrecognized by the state, as are their male colleagues in non-Orthodox synagogues), and about 200 female cantors in American synagogues.[14] Women have equal status in the American non-Orthodox synagogue; they count in the *minyan* (the quorum necessary for prayer), serve as *shlihot zibbur* (prayer leaders), and are called to the Torah. The adolescent girl's entry into symbolic religious adulthood—her *bat-mitzvah*—is marked with the same importance and display of ritual skills as is the adolescent boy's *bar-mitzvah*.[15] Feminists have also created naming ceremonies for baby girls that have won widespread acceptance in the American Jewish community, leading the Orthodox to revive a Sephardic ceremony of welcome to a baby girl, the *seder zeved habat*.[16] Most important, with the popularity of the *bat-mitzvah,* the non-Orthodox denominations in North America are beginning to close the gender gap in Jewish education.[17]

Even Orthodox communities, which often segregate girls and boys in their Jewish learning, have responded to the perceived threat of feminism by providing significant Jewish education for females.[18] Indeed, within American Orthodoxy there has emerged a feminist movement that seeks to expand possibilities for women within the framework of *halakhah* and has focused on intensive Talmud education for women as a vehicle for the improvement of women's status. Orthodox feminists have raised the issue of women's status publicly—most recently in a conference held in New York that drew 2,000 participants—and have created a network of women's prayer groups that continue to function despite considerable rabbinic invective against them.[19]

Because of the pluralism of American Jewish religious life and the freedom of non-Orthodox Jews from ecclesiastical as well as state control, feminists have also succeeded in instituting changes in the language of prayer, which affirms and legitimates a particular view of the world. In non-Orthodox synagogues men no longer thank God for not having created them female; instead men and women alike bless God, in the language of the first creation story in Genesis, for having made them in God's image. Feminists have also spearheaded the adoption of gender-neutral language in the prayer books of the Reform and Reconstructionist movements and the beginnings of gender sensitivity in the Conservative movement's prayer book.[20] Jewish feminist theologians have infused traditional Jewish categories such as God, Torah, and Israel with feminist content and have proposed a radical transformation of the Jewish wedding ceremony.[21] Feminists have not denied the misogyny in classic Jewish texts and practice; indeed, feminist scholars, male and female, have explored the subject of gender within Judaism and Jewish history and have demonstrated its importance for understanding the changing consciousness of Jews in different cultural and political contexts.[22] As activists within the American Jewish community, feminists have established gender equality as an ideal and have transformed the experience of Jewish women and girls in the non-Orthodox synagogue and, to some extent, in communal institutions.[23] Feminists have been less successful, however, in persuading communal umbrella organizations that seek to bring diverse groups of Jews together in demonstrations of Jewish solidarity that the commitment to the equality of women is non-negotiable. When Orthodox needs—to suppress the voices of women, for example—are articulated as divine commandments, the rest of the community is expected to compromise its values, which are seen as voluntary, as socially constructed rather than God-given.

Jewish women in America experience themselves as unequal to men in religious terms only insofar as *halakhah* and its interpretation matter to them. When they seek a Jewish religious divorce, a *get,* which is required for remarriage under Conservative as well as Orthodox auspices, women discover their vulnerability. According to Jewish law, men alone may give a *get;* the woman accepts the document.[24] The ceremony, which is arranged by rabbis who constitute a court, is therefore structurally unequal, though many rabbis conduct the ritual so that divorcing husband and wife are not compelled to be in the room at the same time. Should a man refuse to grant his wife a *get,* she remains an *agunah* (a chained wife), unable to remarry in an Orthodox or Conservative ceremony.[25] He suffers no such penalty because *halakhah* allowed men more than one wife, although there has been a general ban on polygamy among Ashkenazi Jews (those of central and east European origin) for a thousand years. Should the woman remarry (in a civil or Reform ceremony) without having acquired a *get,* the children of her second union would be *mamzerim,* forbidden by Jewish law to marry any but other *mamzerim.*[26] Feminists have supported the Conservative practice of inserting a clause in the *ketubah* (the marriage contract that the bride and groom sign) that declares that the bride and groom agree "that should there be any contemplation of the dissolution of this marriage, or in the event of its dissolution in the civil courts, they will respond to the summons each may make to the other to appear before the *Beit Din* [Court] of the Rabbinical Assembly and of the Jewish Theological Seminary of America. . . . [and that] they are committed to abide by its rulings and instructions, so that both may live according to the law and teachings of our sacred Torah."[27] Feminists within the Orthodox community, which has not adopted a conditional clause inserted in the *ketubah,* also gained support for a New York statute that requires that if a marriage is solemnized by a religious leader, then an individual must take all steps to remove barriers to remarriage, and that effective barriers to remarriage must be taken into account in equitable distribution of property and maintenance.[28] The problem of *agunot,* however, remains significant, not only for the women unable to remake their lives but also as a symbolic reminder for all Jewish women of their lack of power in the *halakhic* system.

Feminists in Israel lack the communal support for feminism that has prevailed among American Jewry. They confront a political system that enhances the power of fundamentalists, who seek to impose their vision of truth within Israeli society through Orthodox political parties, which have proven necessary to virtually every government coalition. Despite their precarious position, feminists have organized, particularly through the Israel Women's Network, to challenge religious as well as secular disabilities that Israeli Jewish women suffer. They have used three strategies: creating publicity that highlights the diminishment of women's humanity; appealing to the secular Supreme Court; and increasing women's power within religious institutions. Feminists have brought to public attention the absence of women in high positions in the civil service and in politics, irrational closure of many army jobs to women, the sexual exploitation of women in advertisements, and the issues of rape and violence against women. Thus, they have initiated public debate on these matters. Feminists used the secular court system, in a precedent-setting case, to win a seat for Leah Shakdiel, a modern Orthodox feminist, on a local religious council, which allocates funds for religious institutions.[29] The Orthodox establishment had banned women from serving on the grounds that they could not exercise authority in religious matters. The Supreme Court, however, moves slowly and is itself increasingly embattled as fundamentalists seek to reduce its power and achieve a legal system governed exclusively according to Jewish law. Focusing on the plight of *agunot,* feminists supported legislation that imposes sanctions, such as the loss of a driver's license, on men who exploit their superior position in *halakhah* to control spouses seeking release from a marriage.[30] At the same time, they are training women in Jewish law so that they might, as *toanot* (arguers), plead women's cases in religious courts. Until the Orthodox monopoly over personal status issues is modified or eliminated, Israeli feminists must rely on such a triple-pronged approach.

In the realm of religious symbolism, some Israeli feminists, many of them of American origin, with the support of American Jewish feminists, have asserted their right to pray publicly at the Western Wall in Jerusalem.[31] At the beginning of each month they hold their early morning service in a special, unobtrusive spot set aside for them in the vicinity of the wall. Declared a synagogue, the area of the wall is under the authority of the official rabbinate, which bans women from praying with a Torah scroll. In order to demonstrate their fidelity to the legal process, they have refrained from violations of Orthodox regulations regarding women's prayer and have adhered to each legal decision as their case makes its way slowly through the secular court system. In persisting in their public prayer and challenging the right of the religious establishment to deny women the possibility of religious self-expression at a site that has national as well as religious significance, "Women of the Wall" provide a different model of Jewish female piety than what has dominated in Israeli society.

Jewish feminists struggle on different fronts in Israel and in the United States (and other countries of the Diaspora) to achieve their goal of equality for women. In the United States they have combined strategies of exit (from the ranks of Orthodoxy) and voice (protest and lobbying) to achieve change. In Israel, only the strategy of voice is available to them. Ultimately, the national political structure and prevailing social values have determined the success of the feminist project within various Jewish communities.

NOTES

1. On American Jewish feminism, see THE JEWISH WOMAN: NEW PERSPECTIVES (Elizabeth Koltun, ed.) (New York: Schocken Books, 1976); Ellen M. Umansky, *Feminism and American Reform Judaism, in* THE AMERICANIZATION OF THE JEWS 267 (Robert M. Seltzer & Norman J. Cohen, eds.) (New York/London: New York University Press, 1995); Paula E. Hyman, *Ezrat Nashim and the Emergence of a New Jewish Feminism, in* THE AMERICANIZATION OF THE JEWS, *supra,* at 284; Judith Hauptman, *Conservative Judaism: The Ethical Challenge of Feminist Change, in* THE AMERICANIZATION OF THE JEWS, *supra,* at 296; SYLVIA BARACK FISHMAN, A BREATH OF LIFE: FEMINISM IN THE AMERICAN JEWISH COMMUNITY (New York: The Free Press, 1993).

2. On Mary Daly's position, see MARY DALY, BEYOND GOD THE FATHER: TO-WARD A PHILOSOPHY OF WOMEN'S LIBERATION 3–4, 13–14 (Boston: Beacon Press, 1973).

3. JUDITH PLASKOW, STANDING AGAIN AT SINAI: JUDAISM FROM A FEMINIST PERSPECTIVE ix, xi (San Francisco: Harper & Row Publishers, 1990).

4. *See, e.g.,* Samuel C. Heilman, *Quiescent and Active Fundamentalism: The Jewish Cases, in* 4 THE FUNDAMENTALISM PROJECT: ACCOUNTING FOR FUNDAMENTALISMS 173 (Martin E. Marty & R. Scott Appleby, eds.) (Chicago/London: University of Chicago Press, 1994); Menachem Friedman, *Jewish Zealots: Conservative Versus Innovative, in* JEWISH FUNDAMENTALISM IN COMPARATIVE PERSPECTIVE: RELIGION, IDEOLOGY, AND THE CRISIS OF MODERNITY 148 (Laurence J. Silberstein, ed.) (New York: New York University Press, 1993) [hereinafter JEWISH FUNDAMENTALISM].

5. *See* Heilman, *supra* note 4, at 175, 184; Gerald Cromer, *Withdrawal and Conquest: Two Aspects of the Haredi Response to Modernity, in* JEWISH FUNDAMENTALISM, *supra* note 4, at 164.

6. In this I share the view of Jay Harris. Unlike Harris, however, I find the term "fundamentalist" a useful category to sum up certain anti-modern trends, and particularly the hierarchical world view in which the subordination of women is a central tenet. *See* Jay M. Harris, *"Fundamentalism": Objections from a Modern Jewish Historian, in* FUNDAMENTALISM AND GENDER 137 (John Stratton Hawley, ed.) (New York/ Oxford: Oxford University Press, 1994).

7. Jacob Katz, *Orthodoxy in Historical Perspective,* 2 STUD. CONTEMP. JEWRY 3, 4–5 (1986).

8. On the strict gender segregation advocated by fundamentalists, see Hava Lazarus-Yafeh, *Contemporary Fundamentalism: Judaism, Christianity, Islam, in* JEWISH FUNDAMENTALISM, *supra* note 4, at 42, 51–52. *See also* Helen Hardacre, *The Impact of Fundamentalisms on Women, the Family, and Interpersonal Relations, in* 2 THE FUNDAMENTALISM PROJECT: FUNDAMENTALISMS AND SOCIETY 129 (Martin E. Marty & R. Scott Appleby, eds.) (Chicago/London: The University of Chicago Press, 1993) (discussing Buddhist, Christian, and Muslim fundamentalisms).

9. *See* JUDITH ROMNEY WEGNER, CHATTEL OR PERSON?: THE STATUS OF WOMEN IN THE MISHNAH 19 (New York/Oxford: Oxford University Press, 1988); Judith Baskin, *The Separation of Women in Rabbinic Judaism, in* WOMEN, RELIGION, AND SOCIAL CHANGE 3, 8–14 (Yvonne Yazbeck Haddad & Ellison Banks Findly, eds.) (Albany, NY: State University of New York Press, 1985); JUDITH HAUPTMAN, REREADING THE RABBIS: A WOMAN'S VOICE 30–31 (Boulder, CO: Westview Press, 1998); DANIEL BOYARIN, CARNAL ISRAEL: READING SEX IN TALMUDIC CULTURE 167–96 (Berkeley/Los Angeles/Oxford: University of California Press, 1993).

10. *See* HAUPTMAN, *supra* note 9, at 10.

11. *See id.* at 11–12.

12. *See* JACK WERTHEIMER, A PEOPLE DIVIDED: JUDAISM IN CONTEMPORARY AMERICA 21–22 (New York: Basic Books, 1993).

13. *Id.* at 72–75.

14. *See* PAMELA S. NADELL, WOMEN WHO WOULD BE RABBIS: A HISTORY OF WOMEN'S ORDINATION 1889–1985 220 n.23 (Boston: Beacon Press, 1998). In 1996, the Conservative Cantors' Assembly informed me that it has 39 female members and the American Conference of Cantors informed me that 40 percent of its 350 members were women.

15. *See* FISHMAN, *supra* note 1, at 130–35.

16. *See id.* at 124–26.

17. *See id.* at 192, 196.

18. *See id.* at 192–96.

19. *See* BLU GREENBERG, ON WOMEN & JUDAISM: A VIEW FROM TRADITION 30–37, 92–97 (Philadelphia: The Jewish Publication Society, 1981); Rivka Haut, *Women's Prayer Groups and the Orthodox Synagogue, in* DAUGHTERS OF THE KING: WOMEN AND THE SYNAGOGUE 135 (Susan Grossman & Rivka Haut, eds.) (Philadelphia: The Jewish Publication Society, 1992).

20. *See, e.g.,* GATES OF PRAYER: THE NEW UNION PRAYERBOOK (New York: Central Conference of American Rabbis, 1975); GATES OF PRAYER FOR SHABBAT (Chaim Stern, ed.) (New York: Central Conference of American Rabbis, 1992); KOL HANESHAMAH: SHABBAT EVE (Rabbi David A. Teutsch, ed.) (The Reconstructionist Press, 2d. ed., 1993); SIDDUR SIM SHALOM: A PRAYERBOOK FOR SHABBAT, FESTIVALS, AND WEEKDAYS (Rabbi Jules Harlow, ed.) (New York: The Rabbinical Assembly and The United Synagogue of America, 1985).

21. *See* PLASKOW, *supra* note 3, at 25–169.

22. *See, e.g.,* PAULA E. HYMAN, GENDER AND ASSIMILATION IN MODERN JEWISH HISTORY: THE ROLES AND REPRESENTATION OF WOMEN (Seattle: University of Washington Press, 1995); JEWISH WOMEN IN HISTORICAL PERSPECTIVE (Judith R. Baskin, ed.) (Detroit: Wayne State University Press, 1991); DANIEL BOYARIN, UNHEROIC CONDUCT: THE RISE OF HETEROSEXUALITY AND THE INVENTION OF THE JEWISH MAN (Berkeley/Los Angeles: University of California Press, 1997); BOYARIN, *supra* note 9.

23. The record in communal institutions has been mixed. The Council of Jewish Federations reported that the percentage of female board members of federations had risen from 17 percent about 20 years ago to 32 percent in the early 1990s. *See* COUNCIL OF JEWISH FEDERATIONS, THE STATUS OF WOMEN IN THE LAY AND PROFESSIONAL LEADERSHIP POSITIONS OF FEDERATIONS 1 (New York: The CJF Research Department, 1994). However, in the largest Jewish communities, it was extremely difficult for women to enter into the top leadership of communal institutions. *Id.* at 2. Moreover, a very recent report of Ma'yan: The Jewish Women's Project finds that only 25 percent of board members of national Jewish organizations in 1994 were women. *See* POWER & PARITY: WOMEN ON THE BOARDS OF MAJOR AMERICAN JEWISH ORGANIZATIONS 3 (New York: Ma'yan: The Jewish

Women's Project, 1998). For a comprehensive analysis of gender equality in education, labor force participation, and occupational achievement in the American Jewish community, see MOSHE HARTMAN AND HARRIET HARTMAN, GENDER EQUALITY AND AMERICAN JEWS (Albany: State University of New York Press, 1996).

24. *See* RACHEL BIALE, WOMEN AND JEWISH LAW: AN EXPLORATION OF WOMEN'S ISSUES IN HALAKHIC SOURCES 79–80, 83–97 (New York: Schocken Books, 1984).

25. *See id.* at 102.

26. *See id.* at 103; FISHMAN, *supra* note 1, at 65–72.

27. Ketubah (English) (New York/The Rabbinical Assembly, 1990). This clause also appears in the two Aramaic versions of the Ketubah of the Conservative Movement (1982 and 1990), and all three are currently in use. Although the development of such a clause began in the 1950s, it is only in the past two decades, with the widespread impact of feminism, that its use has become common in Conservative synagogues. Interview with Rabbi Jon-Jay Tilsen, in New Haven, CT (May 14, 1998).

28. *See* N.Y. Dom. Rel. Law §253 (McKinney 1986); N.Y. Dom. Rel. Law §236B (5)(h), (6)(d) (McKinney Supp. 1998).

29. H.C. 153/87, Shakdiel v. Minister of Religious Affairs et al., 42(2) P.D. 221.

30. *See Israel cracks down on die-hard husbands,* AGENCE FRANCE PRESSE, Feb. 22, 1995; Sasha Sadan, *New Bill Would Penalize Men Who Refuse to Divorce,* JERUSALEM POST, Nov. 12, 1992. For a discussion of the legal issues of marriage and divorce in Israel, see Frances Raday, *Religion and Patriarchal Politics: The Israeli Experience,* in this volume.

31. *See* Haim Shapiro, *Women at the Wall—Not an Issue,* Dec. 3, 1989, JERUSALEM POST; Haim Shapiro, *Women at the Wall,* Mar. 30, 1989, JERUSALEM POST. For a discussion of the legal petitions of the Women of the Wall, see Raday, *supra* note 30.

Chapter 25 ▰

Truth over Convention: Feminist Interpretations of Buddhism

Suwanna Satha-Anand

I. INTRODUCTION

For better or for worse, Buddhism accepts two categories of truth, one ultimate and the other conventional. Buddhism denies that the expression of ultimate truth is related to a Supreme Being and, instead, points to a dynamic flow of interdependent conditions, radically nonanthropocentric, as reality. The expression of this reality might be called the "truth of nature," the ultimate truth, as opposed to what could be termed the "truth of convention." When a farmer plants rice in his field, a good or bad harvest is decided by "truth of nature"; whereas the price of the rice is decided by "truth of convention."

The ideal of Buddhism is for the individual to leave the everyday world of desire—the household life that is understood to keep the person bound to the world of *samsara* (suffering; the cycles of rebirth)—and to strive for ultimate truth rather than truth of convention. Buddhism's emphasis on ultimate truth and the leaving of the world of convention has led it to being characterized, and even criticized, as otherworldly and thus lacking in messages for social reform. However, as will be demonstrated, this dismissal of Buddhism is premature.

The issue of women's equality in Buddhist societies, such as Thailand, has been inextricably tied to the issue of how women are regarded in Buddhism with respect to the sanghas (the orders of monks and nuns). There are two main issues concerning the sanghas: first, whether the *bhikkhuni sangha* (nuns' orders)[1] should be established; and, second, if so, the nature of the institutional relationship between the male and female orders. In various countries, such as Thailand, where a *bhikkhuni sangha* was never established, the Thai Theravāda Sangha (Sangha) establishment (the monks' order only) have refused to establish a *bhikkhuni sangha* in contemporary times. This reluctance has been perceived as serving as legitimation for treating women unequally and for regarding them as being inferior to men in the general society.

Although there are a variety of issues of feminist concern in Thai Theravāda Buddhism, I have chosen the issue of female ordination for focused consideration because it is of central concern to both women's equality and to Buddhism itself. It involves major philosophical and institutional implications for Buddhism.

In this chapter, I demonstrate that the Buddha's initial reluctance and his final decision to establish the *bhikkhuni sangha,* together with the fact that he seemed to subordinate the nun order under the monk order, should not be regarded as a mere compromise that he made with his already existing monk order, but rather should be understood as a confirmation of the universality of Buddhist truth over truth of convention, as convention would have disallowed the nuns' order. This confirmation of universal Buddhist truth indicates that when truth of convention comes into conflict with Buddhist truth, the latter is to overrule the former. As the Buddha finally decided to allow female ordination, he was, in fact, respecting the rights of women to religious practice. Convention was thus overruled in favor of women's rights. This principle of truth over convention, in and of itself, can serve as a philosophical basis for women's rights in Buddhism.

II. THE RELUCTANCE OF THE BUDDHA

In order to analyze the significance of the Buddha's reluctance to allow female ordination, it is necessary to take a close look at the Buddhist canonical text, namely, *The Tripitaka* or the Buddhist Bible (which appears in both Pali and Sanskrit versions), of the ordination of the first nun. The story from the Pali text is divided into six passages, and the key events are as follows:

Scene 1. . . . [I]n Kapilavatthu, the Buddha is approached by his aunt Pajāpatī, who raised him as a child after his mother's death. She suggests that it would be good if women were allowed to become nuns, taking up the homeless life as full-time disciples rather than as lay followers. The Buddha tells her not to entertain this idea. . . . Pajāpatī repeats her request three times, without avail. . . .

Scene 2. . . . Having shaved their heads and put on monastic robes, Pajāpatī and a large group of Sakyan women follow the Buddha to Vesālī, where Pajāpatī waits outside the Buddha's door with "her feet swollen . . . sobbing and in tears." . . . [T]he Buddha's personal attendant Āanda inquires about her distress and offers to take up their cause. . . .

Scene 3. . . . Āanda[, m]aking the same request [to the Buddha], gets the same answer. Āanda tries a different approach, asking, "Lord, are women, having gone forth from home into homelessness . . . able to realize the fruits of . . . arhatship [Enlightenment]? The Buddha replies that indeed they are. Thereupon, Āanda points out that the women should then be allowed to become nuns, both because the Buddha acknowledges that they are capable of arhatship and because he owes a great debt to Pajāpatī, "foster-mother," nurse, giver of milk, who suckled him as a child.

Scene 4. . . . Conceding Āanda's point, the Buddha agrees to Pajāpatī's ordination if she will accept eight rules (in addition to the normal monastic rules): (1) Nuns, no matter how senior, must always defer to monks, no matter how junior. (2) Nuns must not spend the rainy season retreat in a residence where there is no monk. (3) Nuns must observe the fortnightly monastic observances under the direction of monks. (4) After the rainy season retreat nuns must formally report to a convocation of monks as well as to the other nuns. (5) A nun who has broken a monastic rule must be disciplined by both the order of monks and by that of the nuns. (6) Both monks and nuns are necessary for the ordination of new nuns. (7) Monks must never be abused or reviled in any way by a nun. (8) Nuns may be formally admonished by monks, but not monks by nuns.

Scene 5. . . . Āanda . . . reports the Buddha's decision . . . [to Pajāpatī]. Honored, Pajāpatī accepts the eight conditions . . . vowing she will never transgress them.

Scene 6. . . . On hearing Pajāpatī's reply, the Buddha then declares the prophecy that this compromise will result in the Dharma enduring for only 500 years rather than 1000, adding several . . . analogies of robbers attacking households, mildew attacking rice, and rust attacking sugar cane. Finally he says that establishing the eight rules is like building a dam so that water will not overflow a reservoir.[2]

Buddhist scholars have been challenged to offer consistent explanations for these recorded events leading to the ordination of women in Buddhism. Alan Sponberg argues that these passages reflect a position of the "multivocality" of Buddhism in regards to women and the feminine.[3] He finds that, on the one hand, Buddhism confirms the potential of women to achieve Enlightenment, and on the other hand, Buddhism allows "institutional androcentrism."[4]

Rita Gross argues that Buddhism allows gender hierarchy to exist between the orders of monks and nuns, as explicitly expressed in the rules for nuns, because the rules do not inherently hinder spiritual progress for women.[5] This is because "social reform was not the arena for [Buddhist spiritual] liberation anyway, and since prevailing codes for gender relationships were not thought to be spiritually harmful. . . . Buddhists had little incentive to bring their vision and their practice regarding gender into alignment with each other."[6]

Kajiyama Yuichi explains that:

> Gautama [the Buddha] hesitated to permit admission of women in the Order, not because women could not attain Enlightenment, but because he had to deliberate on problems which might arise between the Order of monks and that of nuns, and between the Buddhist Order and the lay society. . . . We should not interpret this event as showing discrimination against women by Gautama because he never even as much hinted that a woman had not the same chance as a man to become an arhat, or that she was in any way unfit by her nature to attain nirvāna.[7]

It seems that all of these explanations are based on making a distinction between the issue of women's spiritual potential and the reality of the monastic institution that relies on lay support for its existence. In other words, the argument is that Buddhism accepts the equality of the *natural* potential for Enlightenment of the two sexes, while recognizing the institutional necessity of one sex controlling the other. Rather than seeing these two issues as distinct, I analyze the issue of ordination by relating the two issues to each other and argue that the Buddha had no choice but to allow female ordination in order to remain philosophically consistent.

III. THE PRINCIPLE OF TRUTH OVER CONVENTION

For the purpose of argument, it would be fascinating to follow the logical implications of the situation if the Buddha were to have said "no" to female ordination. Would it really have led to longer life for his religion as indicated in his prophecy? There is already contrary evidence: the Buddhist religion has survived more than one thousand years, much longer than was prophesied of how long it would last without a nuns' order.

If the Buddha had denied female ordination, then such a denial would imply that his truth was not universal, for his truth would have been irrelevant to half of humanity. This position would obviously conflict with the affirmation in Buddhism that Buddhist truth is universal.

Or, if it were the case that women do not need ordination to become enlightened, then it would mean that the prerequisite for attaining ultimate truth, namely leaving a household life, is not universally applicable.

But again, this position would contradict previous affirmations that leaving the household life is a prerequisite for attaining ultimate truth.

A third alternative would be to say that women by nature cannot attain Enlightenment. This alternative implies that there are at least two natures, one male and the other female, or one superior and the other inferior. But this two-natures hypothesis would require a double version of Buddhist truths, one for each sex. It is obvious that the Buddha did not even consider this to be a logical possibility. On the contrary, it is recorded that there is one version of Buddhist truth for both sexes:

> And be it woman, be it man for whom
> Such chariot doth wait, by that same car
> Into Nirvana's presence shall they come.[8]

Moreover, there is no sexual distinction in The Four Noble Truths of suffering, of the source of suffering, of the cessation of suffering, and of the path to the cessation of suffering.[9] The prescriptions for liberation, the Eightfold Noble Paths, are meant to be universally applicable.[10] It would be ridiculous to say that the first four paths (right view, right intention, right speech, right action) are for men and the last four (right livelihood, right effort, right mindfulness, right concentration) are for women. Thus, it is clear that in order for the Buddha to remain logically consistent, he *had* to allow female ordination.

When the Buddha confirms women's potential to become fully enlightened, he is at the same time confirming the fact that obstacles hindering women toward Enlightenment are not inherent in women's nature, but rather essentially exist in human convention. Truth of convention is the source of his reluctance. But the Buddhist truth is universal, as all beings, whether male or female, necessarily go through the process of birth, old age, sickness, and death. It is clear that when convention came into conflict with Buddhist truth, the Buddha chose to uphold Buddhist truth. This principle of truth over convention explains the decision of the Buddha to allow ordination for women.

The universality of Buddhist truth also required the Buddha to make the decision to support the human rights of women, at least with regards to religious practice. The highest ideal, Enlightenment, had previously been linked with the necessity of the existence of the monk's sangha (an institutional setting regarded as one of the Three Jewels in which Buddhists seek liberation from *samsara*). Once the Buddha decided that women *did* have the potential to become enlightened, then logic required the establishment of an institution for women to practice their religion.

The permission of the Buddha to allow female ordination is a fine illustration of respecting women's rights. If the Buddha's initial reluctance indicates the force of convention, then his final decision to allow female ordination indicates his choice to respect women's rights over the force of that convention.

From this principle of truth over convention, it is possible to deduce what was envisioned as the function of a religious institution. If the Buddha's reasons for the establishment of *bhikkhuni sangha* are accepted and respected, it would mean that the role of that institution, and, of the monk sangha by extension, is to help women overcome obstacles imposed by convention in pursuing their path to Enlightenment. In other words, the role of the religious institution is to help *reduce* any prejudices against women, as spiritual agents, directly practicing their religion themselves rather than to legitimize or increase such prejudices. The Buddha's placing of the nun order under the auspices of the monk order implies that the monk order is now bestowed with an obligation to provide a congenial environment for women to practice religion. As the monk's sangha is an institution that stands for universal truth rather than conventional truth, then should it not be the role of the monks' sangha to remedy the shortcomings of the world of convention with regard to women's rights to spiritual liberation, as it has done for its male members?

IV. THE EIGHT SPECIAL RULES FOR NUNS:
WHY INSTITUTIONAL SUBORDINATION?

It is clear that the requirements of the *Gurudhammas* (the eight special rules for nuns) are irrelevant to women's spiritual practice as such. They do not effect any of the Four Noble Truths or the Eightfold Noble Paths to Enlightenment. Rather the rules appear to be aimed at regulating the relationship between the two sanghas, and to protect the nuns from the possible danger of living homeless in the forests. These rules nonetheless could be regarded as indicating the patriarchal nature of the Buddha, who, after all, did not instigate gender reform for the lay social order and did adopt some of the male-centeredness of the lay world into his religious order. But I would reject this characterization and argue instead that the institutional subordination of the nun order under the monk order should be understood primarily as a precautionary measure taken by the Buddha to secure the acceptance and the respect of the lay society for the nun order, and to maintain the lay world's respect for the male order, which was crucial for the survival of the religion at that time.

For example, when, at a later time after ordination, Pajāpatī requested a change of the first special rule so that monks and nuns would deal with each other solely on the basis of seniority,[11] the Buddha refused her request, stating that "even in other sects [non-Buddhist], which were subject to poor leadership, men did not rise or salute women under any circumstances."[12] In addition, "he declared it an offense if any monk should so behave toward a woman."[13] This incident reflects the social conditions of the time and the Buddha's understanding that it was necessary for religious organizations not to stray too far from what was deemed appropriate between the two sexes in order to win social acceptance for the organizations and to maintain their legitimacy in the lay world.

Moreover, if the Buddha had allowed female ordination without laying down proper regulations between the two sanghas, the two orders might have created an image of a "family" to the lay eyes. Since the ideal of Buddhism is to leave the household life and encourage a life of homelessness, this semblance of a "family" within the life of the renunciates would be counterproductive. It was therefore important for the Buddha to lay down those special rules, which among other things signify the absolute seriousness of the renunciates, as well as give both orders an "institutional" existence.

Besides, the Buddha was well aware of the difficulties for men of giving up sexual attachment to women, which is one of the requirements on the path to Enlightenment. As a former young, married prince, the Buddha was sexually experienced and recognized the power of human sexual attachment:

> Monks, I see no other single form so enticing, so desirable,
> so intoxicating, so binding, so distracting, such a hindrance
> to winning the unsurpassed peace from effort . . . as a woman's
> form. Monks, whosoever clings to a woman's form—infatuated,
> greedy, fettered, enslaved, enthralled—for many a long day
> shall grieve, snared by the charms of a woman's form. . . . [14]

He was aware that even without women living in the immediate vicinity of the monks' order, the monks had great difficulty overcoming their sexual attachment to women. His decision to make the nuns' order separate from but under the auspices of the monks' order had a practical element— the desire to maintain an environment for monks that would provide support for their renunciation of the world and also maintain their legitimacy with the lay world as renunciates.

Viewed in this way, it is perhaps best to understand this institutional subordination of nuns as arising out of the Buddha's practical considerations, rather than his patriarchalism. Despite the necessity of lay support and a congenial environment for his monks for the survival and prosperity of his religion, the Buddha decided to allow female ordination. It was also clear

that despite the *Gurudhammas,* the Buddha respected that women were ordained in order to follow the path for Enlightenment. For example, even in
his own lifetime, the Buddha prohibited monks to ask nuns to do housework for them;[15] women entered ordination for spiritual progress, not to
offer domestic services for monks. The Buddha clearly prohibited such acts
on the part of the monks, who might have brought with them into their
life of renunciation some assumptions about the role of women based upon
their previous household experience. Doing such housework would have
interfered with women's spiritual practice because their very role as renunciates required them to leave the world of households behind. Thus, such
housework would have undermined women's spiritual path in a way that
the *Gurudhammas* do not. In this example, there is again the Buddha's affirmation of the seriousness of women's ordination and of universal truth over
convention. The Buddha's practical considerations for lay support went as
far as necessary at the time, but never so far as to interfere with the actual
spiritual path of ordained women. Thus, to the extent that the Buddha's
practical considerations could be regarded as deference to the force of convention, the force of convention was nonetheless not permitted to control
the issue of whether women could be ordained and thus achieve their ultimate spiritual fulfillment.

There is also another point to be discerned from the Buddha's actions.
The Buddha was often very accommodating to lay society and desirous
of its support; this was necessary for the survival of the religion. Judging
from this accommodation, it is reasonable to argue that when the conditions of lay society change, the Buddha would desire the sangha to
change as necessary. Thus, the nature of the institutional subordination
of the nuns' order is not set in stone, but may change in accordance with
the Buddha's recognition of the necessity of accommodation to the
broader lay society in those matters that do not actually interfere with
the spiritual path.

V. THE IMPORTANCE OF FEMINISM
IN THAI BUDDHISM: APPLYING THE
PRINCIPLE OF TRUTH OVER CONVENTION

As noted at the beginning of this chapter, due to historical accident, the
bhikkhuni sangha was never established in Thailand. Without the possibility
of ordination, women have been relegated in Thai Theravāda Buddhism to
being the major lay supporters of the monk order throughout Thai history.
The result of this exclusion of women from ordination has been manifold.

It is important to understand that Buddhism holds great symbolic and
political significance for Thai society. According to the Constitution, the

King, the only person who does not enjoy religious freedom in the country, has to be a Buddhist. With regards to political authority, a noted Thai political scientist observes that, "[the] Thai state is sometimes characterized as a political manifestation of all Buddhist values and ideals based upon Buddhist cosmology."[16] The influence of Buddhism is also manifested through a close alliance between the Buddhist establishment and the Thai state. For example, the National Sangha Act of 1962 promulgated a highly centralized Sangha (the monks' order) as an arm of the state.[17]

Within a society where Buddhism plays such a central role in its religio-cultural and political life, denying women the possibility of ordination indicates severe limitations for women as agents of highest spiritual achievement. Such a denial helps legitimate notions that women are inferior, spiritually and in other ways; women are only fit for being lay supporters for monks' spiritual path rather than seeking the ideal path of Buddhism of leaving the household life themselves.

On a practical level, there are also repercussions resulting from the lack of a *bhikkhuni sangha*. Strict monastic rules in traditional Thai society prohibit women from getting too close to monks. As a result, girls had been excluded from educational opportunities because education was, as a practical matter, often under the control of monks and courtesans. As a result, it has been argued that the reestablishment of the *bhikkhuni sangha* would help reduce the number of Thai girls becoming prostitutes because the educational opportunities for girls would increase, especially in poor villages in rural areas. It has also been argued that the existence of the *bhikkhuni sangha* would reduce the number of women becoming prostitutes because they would have the opportunity to "make merit" for their family (and reduce the family's obligation to the Sangha) by joining the *bhikkhuni sangha* as men are able to do by joining the Sangha.[18]

In this context it becomes clear that the analysis of the reluctant decision of the Buddha in relation to female ordination is crucial to advancing the Buddhist feminist movement in Thailand and to improving the position of Thai women. As far as the Sangha establishment is concerned, this chapter's analysis of the Buddha's reluctant decision could be used as a basis for the consideration of the reestablishment of the *bhikkhuni sangha* in Thailand. As indicated, the institutional position so far has been an unconditional "no," with the major arguments against ordination being the lack of historical precedent and technical impossibility.[19] There are several responses to this unconditional "no."

First, if the historical precedent argument is taken seriously, then it leads to an untenable conclusion for Buddhism: historical accidents, namely the dying out of the nun order in Sri Lanka in the eleventh century and the nonexportation of the nun order to Southeast Asia, hold more weight than the Buddha's decision allowing for ordination. If this historical accident argument is not considered *a priori,* then the argument of technical impossibility is weakened as well, and does not serve as an absolute bar to ordination.

Second, according to my analysis of the Buddha's decision, the monk order has an obligation to provide a congenial environment for women to practice their religion. This obligation should be taken seriously by the Sangha.

Lastly, present-day lay society is much more open to women's concerns, needs, and rights. This change in attitude allows for the Buddha's approach of accommodation to the lay world, and thus the eight special rules of institutional subordination could change accordingly. Such accommodation is important in order to maintain lay support. It would also appear that ordination is a particularly healthy arena to be more accommodating to the lay world; it confirms the Buddha's choice of allowing women to be ordained and in that process reaffirms the principle of truth over convention. In this sense, modern-day convention in the lay world has become closer to the universal truth of Buddhism.

The principle of truth over convention should serve as a basis for future feminist interpretations and renegotiations of the Buddhist scriptures. It should also serve as a basis for institutional decisions of the Sangha in relation to the women's issues. What is at stake is not only the human rights of women, but also the philosophical universality and institutional integrity of Buddhism itself.

NOTES

1. The term "nun" in this chapter is used as equivalent of "*bhikkhuni*" or fully ordained almswoman.

2. For the purposes of brevity, I have shortened the translated version of the events leading to the establishment of the *bhikkhuni* order as given by Alan Sponberg in his well-presented article, Alan Sponberg, *Attitudes toward Women and the Feminine in Early Buddhism,* in BUDDHISM, SEXUALITY, AND GENDER 3, 14–15 (José Ignacio Cabezón, ed.) (Albany: State University of New York Press, 1992). The original version is in the Anguttara-nikaya IV; VIII.VI:51–52, Anguttara-nikaya, Kotami vagga, Kotami sutta, 23 PHRA TRAIPIDOK PHASATHAI [THE SIAMESE TRIPITAKA] 312–18 (Bangkok: Kromkan Sasana, Krasuang Suksathikan [Department of Religious Affairs, Ministry of Education, B.E.2530 [AD 1987]).

3. *See* Sponberg, *supra* note 2, at 3–4.

4. *Id.* at 13–18.

5. RITA M. GROSS, BUDDHISM AFTER PATRIARCHY: A FEMINIST HISTORY, ANALYSIS, AND RECONSTRUCTION OF BUDDHISM 214–15 (New York: State University of New York Press, 1993).

6. *Id.* at 214–15.
7. Kajiyama Yuichi, *Women in Buddhism,* 25 E. BUDDHIST 53, 60 (1982).
8. Majjhima-nikaya I:169, *quoted in* Yuichi, *supra* note 7, at 59.
9. For a background to Buddhism and a discussion of The Four Holy Truths, see RICHARD H. ROBINSON & WILLARD L. JOHNSON, THE BUDDHIST RELIGION 26 (Belmont, CA: Wadsworth, Inc., 3d ed., 1982)
10. *See id.*
11. Cullavagga, X:2.3, *quoted in* GROSS, *supra* note 5, at 37.
12. GROSS, *supra* note 5, at 37 (paraphrasing Cullavagga, X:2.3).
13. *Id.* (paraphrasing Cullavagga, X:2.3).
14. Anguttara-nikaya III:67–68, *quoted in* Sponberg, *supra* note 2, at 20.
15. *See* GROSS, *supra* note 5, at 37.
16. Chaiwat Satha-Anand, *Hijab and Moments of Legitimation: Islamic Resurgence in Thailand, in* ASIANS VISIONS OF AUTHORITY 279, 295 (Charles F. Keyes, et. al, eds.) (1994).
17. *See* Donald K. Swearer, *Fundamentalistic Movements in Theravāda Buddhism, in* 1 THE FUNDAMENTALISM PROJECT: FUNDAMENTALISMS OBSERVED 628, 655 (Martin E. Marty & R. Scott Appleby, eds.) (Chicago/London: The University of Chicago Press, 1991).
18. *See* Lucinda Joy Peach, *Buddhism and Human Rights in the Thai Sex Trade, in* this volume.
19. As *Garudhamma* rule 6 indicates, in order to ordain a new nun, one needs the presence of both orders of monks and nuns. As there is no existing nun order in the Theravāda tradition, the new ordination of nuns is therefore technically impossible.

Chapter 26

Religion and Women's Rights: The Fundamentalist Face of Catholicism in Brazil

Maria José F. Rosado Nunes

I. INTRODUCTION

This chapter reflects my personal experience as a feminist and a Catholic woman of the Brazilian Church. In this chapter, I analyze the difficulty that Roman Catholicism (Catholicism) has in accepting the modern notion of individual autonomy—which underlies the concept of human rights—particularly with respect to women. This difficulty is at the foundation of the conflict between human rights for women as conceived in liberal theory and Catholicism. I also explore how Latin American women have reformulated human rights for women so that they are integrated into the context of collective rights, and include, inter alia, social rights and reproductive rights. These visions of women's rights conflict with Catholicism, a conflict that has been particularly evident in Brazil. This chapter ends with examples of the Brazilian Church engaging in Catholic fundamentalist political action that has been aimed at making Brazil's laws correspond to traditional Catholic doctrine concerning sexuality.

II. HUMAN RIGHTS, CATHOLICISM, AND WOMEN'S RIGHTS

Emile Poulat, in his provocative text on the paradoxes and limitations of theories on "the rights of man," reminds us that this concept of rights should be understood in the context of modernity's ambition to forge, for the first time in the world's history, a universal consensus.[1] This ideology of rights is founded on an Enlightenment concept of mankind and was formed "by breaking away from Catholic principles."[2] Under a liberal conception of society, mankind, and the world, "the rights of man" are based on three suppositions: "an extensive, abstract concept of "humanity"; a concept of rights for which "humanity" is the only necessary condition; and the realization of the individual as a social unit resulting from these rights."[3] According to Poulat, these suppositions underlying the liberal theory of rights explains "the unending and perhaps insurmountable conflict between Catholicism and Liberalism, which never ceases to repeat itself. It is possible to consider this conflict in light of the new problems brought about by bioethics: contraception, abortion, euthanasia, and, in broader terms, sexuality. . . ."[4] The same can be said concerning international problems of economic and social importance.

We can see this conflict between Catholicism and Liberalism and the Catholic allergy to liberalism in the way law has developed and how the concept of nature has changed. Natural law, the common denominator of Christianity and modernity, has transformed itself in a radical way. "With modern science, like science itself, modern law repudiates the Christian conception of nature created by scholastic thought, according to Aristotle."[5] If the basis for Christian ideas is to be found in the affirmation of God as the primary cause and ultimate foundation, scientific thought and modern law are supported by the social contract and by reasoning—which discards appeals to divinity. "In this effort of scientific and legal construction emerges a new man: the *individual* and his *conscience,* master of himself, his judgments and his decisions."[6] The "man" born out of the Protestant Reformation is obliged to obey his conscience alone.

According to Christianity, all liberty is a gift from God; it is not inherent in the individual and is not a source of rights. "To the contrary, all efforts of the modern spirit will tend to abolish this arbitrariness and set it free, offering human nature something which until then depended on a higher order."[7] Such a transformation, in the legal realm, meant the invention of the individual as a "social unit and its corollary: one man equals one man."[8] This principle of individuality not only opposed the Catholic social order, but also the religious order. As such, a conflict of rights developed: "the right of the individual to freedom of conscience, opinion and religion; the right of Catholicism, held as a State religion, to represent the absolute truth and extract the social consequences which seemed to result. . . . Liberal individualism secreted social atheism: a lay society no longer needed God to govern its steps and kept Him in the sphere of private life, and in the intimacy of conscience and family."[9]

Poulat's discussion may help to shed light on the ways in which Catholic fundamentalism manifests itself by violating the fundamental rights of women. The analysis of this "unending and insurmountable" conflict between liberal ideas and Christian conceptions may help in understanding the reasons why Catholicism rises up against women's struggles for autonomy.

Feminism sets out to affirm rights and individual liberties by proclaiming that women, as social subjects, are citizens (with the right to vote) and that they, as individuals, are capable of generating life itself (with the right to control their own sexuality and reproductive capability). In the field of reproductive rights, "the issue of individual autonomy—so deeply valued by contemporary feminism—as a fundamental point of the exercise of liberty is the basic inspiration for the growth and adaptation of this field of law."[10] However, Catholicism propagates a traditional conception of women and identifies their essence in maternity. The roles reserved by Catholic doctrine for women are as wives and mothers. As such, the affirmation of individual rights for women becomes incompatible with the staunch affirmations of the Catholic religion. Patrick Snyder, while analyzing the position of the present pope, says that "[a]s an absolute, for Pope John Paul II maternity defines in one fell swoop the nature, dignity, vocation, and the temporal and spiritual essence of women."[11] This pope considers one of the errors of feminism to be exactly the fact that it aims to "'liberate' women . . . from that which is their specific vocation of mother and wife."[12]

In this way, the Catholic allergy to liberalism reaches modern conceptions of autonomy and the claims of women to their self-determination. These claims are also found within Catholicism itself. As Monique Dumais, a Catholic theologian, states, "One of the main claims of women is to control their own bodies. How can one feel like a person when that which is closest to one, one's own body, escapes one and is made dependent on others and under the authority of others?"[13]

III. HUMAN RIGHTS, FEMINISM, AND WOMEN'S RIGHTS IN THE LATIN AMERICAN CONTEXT

Within the liberal field of supporting individual rights, the notion of human rights has been, and continues to be, incorporated and restated by women. On the one hand, human rights theory deals with the incorporation of reproductive rights under the notion of women's rights. "Reproductive rights are a recent concept arising out of women's own reflection and includes individual, collective and social rights, in addition to other rights related to maternity, conception and contraception, family planning, among others which integrate fundamental rights."[14]

On the other hand, the critical vision of liberalism "as a political and economic doctrine in which the market is perceived as the driving force of the possibilities of choice, and accumulation and competition are the basic values sustaining it,"[15] leads to the suggestion of a Latin American perspective on human rights. The document prepared by the Ad Hoc Co-ordinating Committee of Non-Profit Organizations at the Regional Human Rights Conference held in Costa Rica in 1992 states, "[t]he application of neo-liberal policies and structural adjustment programs deny economic, social, cultural, civil, and political rights to our peoples since these measures have increased poverty and discrimination by polarizing our societies and leading discriminated groups to subsistence levels; women, Latin Americans of African and Native (South) American heritage, those living with HIV/AIDS, the disabled, those forced to relocate [desplazados], and migrant workers have all experienced a decline in their already anguishing situations."[16]

According to Irene León, the reformulation of human rights proposed by Latin American women includes economic, social, cultural, civil, and political rights, covering the area of individual rights as collective rights.[17] Calling for the inclusion of social rights and reproductive rights into the scope of human rights, women contribute to the development of the concept of citizenship and democracy, by "projecting a new model of society which demands social reform and a change in mental attitudes."[18]

Such a widening of rights allows for the possibility that a woman can control her sexuality and reproductive capability as part of the realization of feminine citizenship. That it is presently impossible for all women to experience safe, freely chosen maternity, to ensure the new being of a dignified life, and to gain access to contraception and abortion, relegates women to a position of submission and prevents them from exercising the right to control their own bodies and their own lives.

IV. THE FUNDAMENTALIST FACE OF CATHOLICISM IN BRAZIL AND WOMEN'S RIGHTS

Unlike what occurs in other countries, Brazilian feminists' relationship with the Catholic Church has not always been one of mutual opposition. In the 1970s, the Catholic Church in Brazil offered an important space for protest against the military dictatorship that existed from the 1960s through the 1980s. During this period, there were feminist and Left Wing party alliances with the Catholic Church.[19] The firm opposition to the military regime by key members of the Catholic hierarchy and the Church's privileged position in negotiations with the state greatly boosted the institution's credibility in the eyes of the Left Wing groups with which feminists were allied or to which they belonged. The women's movement was therefore able to find allies in the Catholic Church who supported campaigns for daycare centers, lowering the cost of living, freeing political prisoners, and the like.

Due to the Church's social penetration and its power to influence society, feminist struggles were thus amplified by this alliance. Through the action of the Ecclesiastic Base Communities (CEBs) in the 1970s, many poor Catholic women from outer urban communities and rural areas took on social and political struggles. According to their testimony in various surveys, it was the Catholic Church that motivated them to "leave their homes and take to the streets."[20] In this process, many of them met with feminists and assimilated their ideas, sharpening their critical awareness in relation to their own situations "as women" not only in society, but also in the Church itself.[21]

However, the alliance between the Catholic Church and the women's movement at times placed constraints on women's demands and limited the issues debated by the movement. As the military began liberalizing the regime in the 1980s and feminists explicitly extended their demands to include the right of women to freely decide sexual matters, including the right to interrupt unwanted pregnancy, the Church reacted adversely, and conflict entered into the relationship. This ambiguity in the Brazilian Catholic Church toward social issues is maintained by at once engaging in social discourse with respect to some issues while at the same time siding with conservative—or fundamentalist—positions of the Vatican on matters of sexual mores.

A few recent examples may help to illustrate the matter. The first example demonstrates the devotion of certain sectors of the Church to issues of social justice. In 1998, the worst drought in over 15 years afflicted the North of Brazil. Neither the government nor the media, and not even the president himself, addressed the problem, much less were prepared to do anything about it. Men, women, and children were dying. Finally, the Catholic bishops of Brazil broke the silence and dramatically announced to the starving that they had the right to loot the supermarkets for the food that they needed to live. In fact, the people had already begun this type of action, but the bishops gave their blessing in support. Television, radio, and newspapers then began reporting on the drought and the looting of food. Finally, the president spoke publicly for the first time about the problem. After having announced measures to help the needy population, he called on the courts to legally prosecute "those" who were encouraging the looting, in a clear reference to the bishops' action. But, it was in fact the Church's outspoken stance that finally provoked a response by the government to the crucial problem of the drought. Many judges and lawyers publicly supported the bishops by stating that stealing food in order to avoid starvation was not a crime and could be justified.

A second example concerns individual rights and social responsibility with respect to human reproduction in the cases of rape and pregnancy. In a rural part of the State of Rio de Janeiro, an 11-year-old girl was raped and became pregnant. She, with the support of her parents, decided to perform an abortion, which in this case is permitted by Brazilian law. Meanwhile, Catholic religious groups, supported by the local priest, pressured the girl and her family into changing their minds. Thus, the resource of religious argumentation was used to compel the maternity of a child who had become pregnant by the violence of rape.

Another recent episode is also revealing. Under Brazilian law, women may legally have an abortion in two cases: rape and whenever a woman's life is endangered.[22] But public hospitals do not provide this assistance, so poor women are not protected by this law, and many die. Provoked by continuous political action by the women's movement, legislators proposed a law forcing public hospitals to perform legal abortions. Congress held a special session to discuss the issue. Catholic feminists attended, including myself. A Catholic priest and his supporters also attended. He brought a young girl with him, making a ridiculous spectacle by presenting her to the entire session and saying, "[t]his child would not be alive if abortion were legal."

The cases mentioned above illustrate the two-sided nature of Brazilian Catholicism, and allow us to evaluate the difficulty faced by Catholic women in continuing to subscribe to this religious creed, and, at the same time, defend their feminist ideas. Their support of the Church's action in the struggle for social justice does not prevent them from criticizing Catholic positions with respect to sexual and reproductive rights.

Courtney Howland, in discussing a possible definition of religious fundamentalism, argues that "the experience of many religious women who have suffered under fundamentalism and fought to resist it" must be considered.[23] She states that "[f]undamentalism is real and has meaning for numbers of religious woman from different religions and countries who experience it as a very real threat to their freedom and often their lives. These women perceive themselves to be religious despite their resistance to fundamentalist trends within their religion, and may perceive themselves to be feminists despite the intensity of their religious belief."[24]

In reality, this is the experience of many Catholic women and feminists in Brazil. They sway between affirming their religious faith and the need to defend the more elementary rights of women in search of their autonomy. This is the context in which the fundamentalist face of Brazilian Catholicism should be analyzed. Returning to Howland's text, we find a conceptualization of religious fundamentalism that includes, on the one hand, principles of doctrine and, on the other hand, political action aimed at bringing national legislation in line with religious norms.[25] The doctrine of the Brazilian Catholic Church has always faithfully followed the sexual morals of Rome. The Roman Catholic position on sexuality and reproduction is well known, and has the effect of submitting women to their biological capabilities that allow them to generate new human beings. Women's demands for recognition of their moral capability to make decisions that are acceptable from ethical and religious standpoints, for recognition of their right to decide matters affecting their own lives and bodies, and for recognition of their experiences as appropriate for Christian reflection in the sphere of sexual morals, all produce situations of conflict within the Catholic Church. As Howland and many others bring to light, any change in the patriarchal organization of the family or attempt to enhance women's autonomy in the sphere of sexuality and reproduction threatens the basis of Catholic belief and tradition.[26]

Catholic doctrine pervades Brazilian culture. As has been noted:

> [T]he Catholic patriarchal order is so deeply rooted in our culture that it does not require justification; it imposes itself as self-evident and is considered "natural." Bourdieu points out the great difficulty in analyzing this cultural logic due to the fact that the institution, for more than a millennium, has been woven into social structures and mental thought processes and attitudes, such that analysts run the risk of using certain categories of perception and thought as instruments of knowledge which should rather be dealt with as objects of study.[27]

In the area of political action, the Catholic Church has a history of constant interference in issues relating to sexuality and reproduction. By making use of the considerable social power that it still enjoys in Brazil, this religious institution acts as a major pressure group by lobbying the government and Congress and by influencing the mass media. In maintaining its traditional principle of the inseparability of sexuality and procreation, its aim is to:

> influence or even define the content of social policy and legislation. The result of this is that dialogue with the representatives of the executive and legislative branches is, in general, continually under the censuring influence of a transcendental and theological order. This situation has resulted in the obstruction of, and delays in, the implementation of social programs, as in the case of the PAISM [Program of Total Assistance for Women's Health], which had its inauguration as an official program delayed because of the Church attempting to remove the IUD (intra-uterine contraceptive device) from

the list of contraceptive methods to be offered by the state social services. The controversy finally ended with the inclusion of this method, but meanwhile this had given the religious wing an opportunity to promulgate so-called "natural" methods. In addition, the Church has succeeded in delaying, or even in some cases entirely preventing, the distribution of informative materials produced by feminist groups at the request of the Ministry of Health.[28]

There are many other examples, as well. The case of abortion in Brazil is the clearest example of Catholic intervention in the most basic of women's rights: the right to control our own bodies; the right to live our sexuality in a free and responsible way; and the right to decide our own reproductive capacity. In the past few years, the Catholic Church, allied with other religious groups and backward forces of society, has been active in the Brazilian Congress in preventing women's access to the voluntary interruption of pregnancy. It has both tried to eliminate the laws that allow for abortion in some circumstances and to prevent further liberalization of the abortion laws. As demonstrated above, the Church also seeks to place obstacles in the way of allowing public health services to provide abortions in situations where the abortion would be legal, thereby effectively preventing poor women to exercise their rights under the law.

In conclusion, the Roman Catholic Church in Brazil, both due to its doctrine in dealing with sexual mores and reproduction and as a result of its political action in these areas, is one of the most powerful adversaries of the development and affirmation of women's reproductive health and rights. Its opposition to the expansion of the scope of autonomy of thought and action for women is what we characterize as the fundamentalist face of Brazilian Catholicism.

NOTES

1. EMILE POULAT, LE DISCOURS SUR LES DROITS DE L'HOMME. SES PARADOXES ET SES CONTRAINTES, EXTRAIT: ACTES DE LA IIIÈME RENCONTRE ISLAMO-CHRÉTIENE DROIT DE L'HOMME [A DISCOURSE ON THE RIGHTS OF MAN: ITS PARADOXES AND LIMITS (EXTRACTED FROM THE PROCEEDINGS OF THE THIRD ISLAMIC-CHRISTIAN CONFERENCE ON THE RIGHTS OF MAN)] 27 (Tunis: Centre D'études et Recherches Economiques et Sociales, 1986) (author's translation).
2. *Id.* (author's translation).
3. *Id.* at 28 (author's translation).
4. *Id.* (author's translation).
5. *Id.* at 29 (author's translation).
6. *Id.* (author's translation).

7. *Id.* at 32 (author's translation).

8. *Id.* (author's translation).

9. *Id.* at 33–34 (author's translation).

10. Maria Betânia Ávila, *Modernidade e Cidadania Reprodutiva*, 1 ESTUDOS FEMINISTAS, 382, 391 (1993) (author's translation).

11. Patrick Snyder, Le Féminisme selon Jean-Paul II: Une Négation du Déterminisme Corporel de la Femme [Feminism According to [Pope] Jean-Paul II: A Negations of Bodily Determinism of Women], at 5 (n.d.) (author's translation) (manuscript on file with author and editor).

12. *See* Snyder, *supra* note 11, at 3 (quoting Pope John Paul II, *Audience au Ve Congrès international de la famille. La dignité et les droits de la femme*, LA DOCUMENTATION CATHOLIQUE, No. 1797, 7 Dec. 1980, no. 2, at 1102) (author's translation).

13. *See* Snyder, *supra* note 11, at 5 (quoting MONIQUE DUMAIS, LES DROITS DES FEMMES 67 (Montreal: Editions Paulines & Médiaspaul, 1992)) (author's translation).

14. Maria A. Moraes Silva e Luciane dos Santos, Direitos Humanos: A Ausência das Mulheres [Human Rights: The Absence of Women] 9 (n.d.) (citing to N. Kyriakos, *Aspectos Éticos e Legais do Aborto no Brasil*, 37 REVISTA DA PROCURADORIA GERAL DO ESTADO DE SÃO PAULO 13–32 (June 1992)) (author's translation) (manuscript on file with author and editor).

15. Ávila, *supra* note 10, at 387 (author's translation).

16. Irene León, *La perspectiva latinoamericana [The Latin American Perspective]*, SERVIÇO INFORMATIVO 166, SEPARATA, 1 de febrero de 1993, at iii (author's translation).

17. *Id.* at v-vi (author's translation).

18. Ávila, *supra* note 10, at 390 (author's translation).

19. Leila de Andrade Linhares Barsted, *Legalização e descriminalização do aborto no Brasil: 10 anos de luta feminista [Legalization and Decriminalization of Abortion in Brazil: 10 Years of Feminist Struggle]*, 0 ESTUDOS FEMINISTAS 104, 108 (1992) (author's translation).

20. *See* Maria José Fontelas Rosado Nunes, *De Mulheres, Sexo e Igreja: Uma Pesquisa e Muitas Interrogações [Of Women, Sex, and the Church: An Inquiry and Many Questions]*, in ALTERNATIVAS ESCASSAS: SAÚDE, SEXUALIDADE E REPRODUÇÃO NA AMÉRICA LATINA 175, 177–78 (Albertina de Oliveira Costa e Tina Amado, orgs.) (series editora 34) (Rio de Janeiro: Albertina de Oliveira Costa e Tina Amado, PRODIR/F.C.C., 1994) (author's translation).

21. *Id.* at 177–78, 186–94 (author's translation).

22. *See* Decreto-Lei No. 2.848, de 7 de dezembro de 1940, art. 128, Codigo Penal.

23. *See* Courtney W. Howland, *The Challenge of Religious Fundamentalism to the Liberty and Equality Rights of Women: An Analysis under the United Nations Charter*, 35 COLUM. J. TRANSNAT'L L., 271, 280 (1997).

24. *Id.* (footnote omitted).

25. *See id.* at 277–79, 289–96.

26. *See id.* at 289–96; Geraldine Sharp, The Changing Nature of the Marriage Contract; The Control of Reproduction; and Patriarchy: in the Church of Pope John Paul II, Address Before the International Society for the Sociology of Religion, Laval University, Québec, Canada (June 1995) (manuscript on file with author and editor).

27. Maria Consuelo Mejía, Normas y Valores de la Iglesia Catolica en la Sexualidad y la Reproduccion: Nuevas Perspectivas [Norms and Values of the Catholic Church on Sexuality and Reproduction: New Perspectives], paper given at Seminario Nacional sobre Políticas Sociales, Sexualidad y Salud Reproductiva, Sala Alfonso Reyes, El Colégio de México, Nov. 20, 21, 1996, at 3 (quoting Marta Lamas, Desconstrucción simbólica y laicismo; dos requisitros Imprescindibles para la defensa de los derechos reproductivos, ponencia presentada en la V Reunión Nacional de Investigación Demográfica, El Colegio de México, junio de 1995, at 6) (author's translation) (manuscript on file with author and editor).

28. Ávila, *supra* note 10, at 389–90 (author's translation).

Chapter 27

Reclaiming the Religious Center from a Muslim Perspective: Theological Alternatives to Religious Fundamentalism

Ghazala Anwar

I. RELIGIOUS FUNDAMENTALISM

Religious fundamentalist groups, including Muslim groups, tend to have the following nine common features: they (1) assert that the group and eventually the whole society needs to be rescued from the secular society; (2) reject norms of universal human rights for the individual and display a lack of tolerance of others and the incapacity for self-criticism; (3) are committed to the authority of ancient scriptures; (4) hold religion to provide a total world view inseparable from politics, law, and culture; (5) rely on an idealized past; (6) are selective in drawing from an idealized past for religious traditions and orthodox practice; (7) center that idealized past in a patriarchal framework mandating separate gender spheres and a "pristine morality" emphasizing modesty and subordination in women; (8) reject outsiders and the concept of pluralism; and (9) are committed to activism and fighting for changed social, political, and legal order.[1]

Although there is a valid objection raised by many Muslim scholars regarding the use of the term "fundamentalism" in connection with Muslim ideological beliefs, preferring instead the term Islamism,[2] this chapter will use the two terms interchangeably. It is equally true both that the term "fundamentalism" in the context of Islam has been misused by the Western media to represent all Muslims, instead of a small minority amongst them, to the effect of fostering hostility and enmity between the Christian West and Muslims, and that Muslim Islamist groups do share basic features with fundamentalist groups from other major religious traditions.

II. THE REFORMERS OF ISLAM

In addition to the manifestation of different strands of fundamentalist/Islamist movements in the twentieth century, there have also been, and continue to be, many attempts by modernists and moderate intellectuals to reform the shari'ah (Islamic law) by making use of the concepts and tools available in *usul al-fiqh* (the inherited jurisprudence) and *usul al-tafsir* (hermeneutics).[3] The principles of *fiqh* most invoked are: *ijtihad* (creative personal intellectual grappling with specific texts), *ijma* (the consensus of scholars and, eventually, of the community), *maslaha* (the public interest), *darúra* (necessity), and *ada* (prevailing local custom). Hermeneutical tools used to draw distinctions between different categories of Qur'anic verses provide ample means to work out new compendia of laws articulated within the traditional juristic framework. This approach to reform, by adhering to familiar presuppositions and customary tools, staves off the intolerance, exclusivism, and supremacist tendencies of the Islamist movements—to a degree.

While respecting the creative potential inherent within the classical juristic and hermeneutical frameworks and the individual efforts at revising and reforming Islamic laws, I nonetheless have reservations about the efficacy of such methods to achieve the goals of articulating a basis for universal human rights, including civil rights and gender equity, from within an Islamic perspective. The reason such reformist attempts have limited efficacy in providing a model of an Islamic-practice alternative to the fundamentalist model is that they share some of the same basic premises with the Islamists. For example, reformers have in common with the Islamists at least five of the nine features used to define fundamentalism at the beginning of this chapter. First, although the various reformists do not express the need for rescue from the secular state, they nonetheless promote the absence of a secular state.[4] Thus, they fail to articulate a theological basis for a secular state, conceding ground to the Islamists on this crucial issue.[5] Second, the reformists too are committed to the authority of the Qur'an, and to some extent the hadith literature (the documented reports of the sayings and actions of the Prophet Muhammad that do not appear directly in the Qur'an), and their conceptualization of the two is identical with that of the Islamists.[6] Third, the reformists too idealize the earliest portion of Islamic history. Some reformists argue that although the acts of Muhammad and the earliest Muslim community were appropriate given their his-

torical circumstances, the contemporary Muslim community is not bound
to recreate the early Medinan state and society. Rather, reformists (including Muslim feminists) argue for the application of the ethical principles
that informed the creation of that society.[7] Such a concession—that these
idealized ethical principles must apply to contemporary times—seriously
hampers our capacity as Muslims to critique our own norms. Fourth, similar to Islamists, reformists too are selective in drawing from the past for religious traditions and orthodox practice.[8] For the most part, neither group
takes into consideration the texts that counter their own selected piece of
the tradition. Fifth, by relying on an idealized past as the authority to justify their arguments for reform, reformists tacitly consent to a patriarchal
framework. Such consent seriously hinders the possibility of a true, stable,
and gender-equitable model of Islam.

Muslim thinkers and activists who realize these limitations of the arguments of Muslim reformists thus decide to leave religion out completely
in their arguments for human rights. Such a "secession" from religion may
lack the capacity to speak to the hearts of the lay masses, including the un-
lettered ruralists, the urban working class, and Western-educated Muslims
seeking to reconnect to their spiritual roots.

III. DEVELOPING NEW PARADIGMS
FOR THE MUSLIM COMMUNITY

Under the traditional paradigm, inherited principles of jurisprudence and
hermeneutics presume that the Qur'an is the literal and explicit revealed
word of God, and that its layered ambiguities are open to wide, and even
unlimited, ranges of meaning. Obedience to God means literal obedience
to the words of the Qur'an. Because the Qur'an instructs unquestioning
obedience to Muhammad, then obedience to God must also entail reverence for, emulation of, and obedience to the Prophet.

Such uncritical reverence may lead to fanaticism. For example, brutal
fanaticism is currently being perpetrated in the form of blasphemy laws in
Pakistan, where religious minorities are being persecuted under the fabri-
cated charges of disrespect toward the Qur'an or the Prophet.[9]

In the face of such violations of justice, it becomes difficult for fair-
minded Muslims to identify not only with their fanatic co-religionists but
even with their own religion. In order to address effectively these various
issues of inequity within Islam we need to begin by redefining the nature
of revelation and the Prophet's authority, and to develop new paradigms
for community.

Fair-minded Muslims, whose sense of justice is deeply rooted in their
faith in God's justice and mercy, have become convinced that the only way

the name of God may be protected from such abuses is by establishing secular democracies that guarantee freedom of religion to all individuals and prohibit discrimination and persecution based on religion. Fundamentalists have been able to confuse and mislead the religious public by equating secularism with ungodliness. Yet it is clear to the faithful secularist that true godliness may thrive only in an environment where there is freedom of conscience and choice with regard to matters spiritual. In essence, for fairminded Muslims, it is a religious imperative to make a religious argument for a secular government. New paradigms require rethinking the Qur'an and the Sunnah (the sayings and exemplary customs and habits of the Prophet Muhammad drawn from the Qur'an and the hadith literature). This chapter contends that secularism and alternative understandings regarding the Qur'an and the Sunnah, whether spoken or unspoken, have always been a part of Muslim tradition and at the center of the soul of the *ummah* (all inclusive Muslim community), nurturing its spiritual life.

A. The Sunnah

On the official level, the Sunnah, as recorded in the hadith literature, was considered equal in authority to the Qur'an in the majority sect of Islam until the twentieth century. Fazlur Rahman's work, which applied historical critical method to the compendia of the hadith,[10] opened up the question of the authenticity of the hadith literature. Rahman stressed that the *Muhaddithin* (the classical Muslim hadith scholars) had developed and used the historical critical method to verify the authenticity of the reports circulating in the community that serve as the documentary records of the words and acts of the Prophet.[11] He asserted that the *Muhaddithin* failed to apply their own method as stringently as was required.[12] The care that they exhibited in verifying the chain of transmission of a particular report was not matched by the same care in examining its content.

The conclusions that Rahman reached regarding the authenticity of the hadith literature appear viable in the light of modern methods of historical textual criticism. It would appear that Rahman's primary impulse in undertaking a critique of the hadith literature was not scientific curiosity but rather theological concern—his cognition of the dissonance between the content of certain hadiths and the message of the Qur'an as he understood it. Rahman's use of the historical critical method is an expression of his deep faith in God as manifested in Islam. He was a modern *Muhaddith* who honored, and to an extent, completed the work of his precursors, and he did so in their spirit of intellectual integrity, commitment to truth, and allegiance to Islam. This is what makes his work relevant to the community of faith and conscience within Islam today. Yet, fundamentalist groups

in Pakistan labeled Rahman "munkar-i hadith" (destroyer of hadith literature), threatened his life, and forced him into exile.

For those Muslims who accept the conclusions of Rahman's work, the
hadith literature has been transformed from representing the actual word
or deed of the Prophet to representing the communal wisdom of the an-
cestral community mixed with the voices of those vying for political and
social goods. The hadith literature is thus another means to understanding
earlier Islamic centuries. Rahman's work also allows fair-minded Muslims
to continue to find the words of particular hadiths—those that ring true
and evoke a resonance in their hearts—as guiding lights in their personal
life.[13] Similarly, other hadiths that go against their ethical sensibility and
moral conscience no longer have a constricting diabolical character, and
may be recognized as serving the political exigencies of those who circulated them.[14] One may thus follow one's conscience, nurtured and developed by a remembrance of God, without being thwarted by what claims
to be the word or will of God.

B. The Qur'an

Although Rahman took a bold step in applying the historical critical
method to the hadith literature, he refrained from a similar critique of the
text of the Qur'an. In his extensive work on the study of the Qur'an, he
did not directly question the premise that the Qur'an was the literal and
explicit word of God. Rahman remained within the traditional framework
of building his theological views from Qur'anic texts. Although one of his
earlier works deals with classical philosophical views on the nature of revelation,[15] he never developed his own view on the nature of revelation. He
was a liberal modernist and a feminist, and tended to interpret the
Qur'anic verses on gender relations in a way that affirmed the dignity of
Muslim women.

Rahman, however, was critical of the piecemeal use of Qur'anic
verses without reference to their immediate and general context, and,
more important, without reference to their underlying ethical principles
or concerns.[16] He emphasized the need for extrapolating a system of
ethical principles that he assumed was underlying all of the Qur'anic
verses. This system of ethical principles would in turn serve as the basis
for both Islamic law and theology. Such a cogent system of Islamic law
and ethics would then replace the haphazard use of decontextualized
verses to support varying theological and legal positions according to
prevailing exigencies.

The beginnings of such a system of Qur'anic values may be discerned
in Rahman's final writings. In how God must approach his creatures and

creations, Rahman discusses one overarching principle: God's justice proceeds from his mercy and compassion.[17] In how humans must approach God and his creatures and creations, Rahman stressed *taqwa* (fear of God).[18] Extrapolating from Rahman's understanding of the Qur'an, God approaches humans in compassion, and humans must approach God in awe in the expectation of finding protection and profound peace if—and only if—they have treated their fellow creatures with compassion and justice.

The concern for human rights, including gender equity, of many sincere and devout Muslims may well derive from this principle of a mutuality of compassion and justice among persons. Yet despite their devout beliefs, such Muslims are confronted by arguments that the literal texts of the Qur'an do not support their sense of justice and concern for human rights. This dilemma underscores the ethical imperative that Rahman highlighted for developing a system of Qur'anic ethics that rejects and overrules the practice of atomistic use of the Qur'anic texts as unchangeable laws.

Muhammad Arkoún's work may be used to extend the kind of critique that Rahman applied to the hadith literature to the Qur'an. Unlike Rahman, who is a rational philosopher and ethical theologian, Arkoún is a philosophical anthropologist who respects the human need for theology but also seeks to understand revelation as a linguistic and cultural phenomenon prior to constructing a theology upon it.

Arkoún notes that several different terms are used to refer to different stages or facets of the phenomenon of revelation in the Qur'an.[19] Important among them are *umm-al-kitāb* (mother book or archetype of the book), which is a preverbal revelatory condition and distinguishable from *al-quran,* which are the oral recitations that circulated among the nascent Muslim community before they were written down.[20] *Al-quran,* organically related to the life of the first Muslim community, is different, in turn, from the *muṣḥaf,* the written, closed, official corpus (the document that is now referred to as the Qur'an). The *muṣḥaf* was assembled in the reign of the third caliph, 'Uthman, decades after the death of Muhammad and in a period of great political turmoil.[21] Before 'Uthman, there was not a standard, written version of the Qur'an. 'Uthman set up a committee and required all persons to bring all manuscripts or notes of the Qur'an to this committee, which then assembled the official Qur'an.[22] All previous copies and notes of the Qur'an were destroyed.[23]

As Arkoún notes, this phenomenon—the collection of the *muṣḥaf* under the authority of a state—marked a transition to the Qur'an being used to serve the interests of the state.[24] This transition was also marked by language functioning in a different way; written words served to control persons more than to empower them. The belief that all of the pages bound together as *muṣḥaf,* and only those pages, contain the very word of God means that the *muṣḥaf* is the one unifying document across Muslim communities through time. Initially, the *muṣḥaf* helped to consolidate an empire consisting of numerous culturally diverse and closed societies.[25] Thus, centralized state power could become the norm. The state was at once legitimized by being the holder and protector of the *muṣḥaf* and at the same time laid claim to having power over the meaning of the *muṣḥaf.* This role for the *muṣḥaf,* as set in history, serves as precedent today for existing states, particularly new states, which claim to use the *muṣḥaf* as the foundation for the state in order to bolster the state's legitimacy in the absence of democratic processes.

Arkoún also notes that the three aspects of revelation, *umm-al-kitāb, al-quran,* and the *muṣḥaf,* must be studied and analyzed as separate and distinct phenomenon.[26] The distinctions between these three aspects of revelation create space between the *revelation* and the *written word,* breaking the assumed identity between them.

With respect to revelation, Arkoún avers that its primary function is to reveal meanings, without reducing the mystery—the inexpressible character of that which is revealed. Furthermore, the function of revelation is to institute a relation of human being to God where the human being plays host to a power equipped with an infinite capacity to signify things, including the truth of being. The Sufis understand this phenomenon as the personal revelation of the Qur'an on the heart of the seeker.[27] Some passages of the *muṣḥaf* do indeed function in such a capacity. Of course, different passages have this potential at different moments for different individuals. Similar to certain hadiths, there may also be passages that do not have that effect, but rather violate our sense of justice, compassion, or self-respect.

Some portions of the Qur'an thus have the potential of revealing God to an individual, while other portions have the opposite potential. Like the hadith literature, the Qur'an is a composite of different types of passages: passages that are truly inspired and attempt to capture the experience of the divine impress on the human heart; passages that reflect the general communal wisdom or lack thereof of the first generations of Muslims; and passages that defend or justify the acts of the first Muslim male leadership to consolidate and expand their political base and cultural hegemony.

With respect to the *muṣḥaf,* Arkoún also advises that the relationship between the theologically or religiously oriented readings and the "purely scientific," nontheistic, and nonaxiological research be recognized and analyzed.[28]

What does Arkoún's analysis mean for fair-minded, devout Muslims? It may be argued that under Arkoún's analysis, it is clear that the written word, the *mushaf,* is twice removed from the pre-revelatory state, and may therefore be, and is intended to be, subject to historical critical analysis. Once the *mushaf* is open for such critical analysis, then it is implicit that it may not be taken as the literal word of God. This gives fair-minded, devout Muslims the space to reaffirm their sense of justice and belief in human rights, in accordance with Rahman's derived principle of a mutuality of mercy, compassion, and justice among persons. However, such Muslims may also be reasonably concerned that if the Qur'an is treated as an historical document, then no space remains for truth and religious life.

The entire Muslim religious culture is grounded in the belief that God did communicate with human beings. If we build on Arkoún's analysis, it is clear that the possibility of revelation—the foundational belief for Muslims—is maintained. However, in not taking the *mushaf* as the literal word of God, the concept of revelation is opened up for new understandings. Discussions of revelation such as Arkoún's open the way for maintaining the integrity of the Muslim *ummah* while at the same time maintaining the integrity of individual conscience and freedom of expression.

Another consequence of not taking the *mushaf* as the literal word of God is that states will no longer be able to rely on the *mushaf* as a tool to bolster the legitimacy of their nondemocratic governments. According to the theological arguments sketched above, the state has no obligation to guard the *mushaf,* but rather to guarantee freedom of speech and freedom of religion that afford a safe space for Muslims to critically study the *mushaf,* revelation, and other key elements of their religious tradition in their search for religious truth. There can be no integrity of faith and sincerity of religious expression under a religious state that engenders the opposite: cowardice instead of courage of conviction, religious hypocrisy, and self-serving and often inhumane use of religious symbols. Freedom of speech and freedom of religion are to be found in secular democratic governments. Such governments are not dependent on the *mushaf* for their legitimization and allow the space for Muslims seeking truth and justice to follow the call of their conscience.

C. The Prophet

Once the concept of revelation and the *mushaf* are opened for discussion, then it is possible to rethink the nature, function, and status of the Prophet. In the earliest extant biography of Muhammad by Ibn Is'haq, the mythical and the historical are intertwined.[29] Sufis developed their own mystical understanding of Muhammad as the primordial light dwelling with God that pre-existed all creation and was the reason for creation. The jurists developed a persona of Muhammad as lawgiver and statesman. In a similar vein, contemporary Muslim fundamentalists recreate the Prophet in their own image. The problem with all these various understandings of Muhammad for the fair-minded, devout Muslim who is concerned with universal human rights is that the Prophet is not understood to be an upholder of such rights.

A fair-minded Muslim is unable to have unqualified reverence for the Prophet as he is portrayed by the Qur'an, the hadith literature, or the biographies of his life if those texts are considered to be historically accurate. From an ethical point of view, there are serious problems regarding aspects of each of these portrayals.[30] But respect or affection for the Prophet could ensue from the fact that the community traces its heritage back to him. Over the centuries we have had, and have today, Muslims who would serve as better exemplars of faith and action than what we know of the Prophet from the Qur'an and his biographies. Some of these Muslim saints chose to pay homage to him because, with all his failings and imperfections, he opened up a discourse of faith that has engaged and continues to engage the religious imagination of thousands.

If revelation consists in humans' playing host to a power equipped with an infinite capacity to signify things, including the truth of being, then a Prophet is one who not only takes the risk (political, social, personal) of opening him/herself to this power, but also one who opens up this possibility for others by his/her example. Developing an approach to the Prophet as the model for this openness to revelation, rather than as a model for specific acts, would clear the way for articulating an Islamic theology that supports human rights. Instead of referring to one particular individual, prophethood could refer to a collective interactive bearing of witness by a community of faith whose receptivity, anticipation, and surrender evokes infinite possibilities of meaning. Such a changed conception of prophecy would enable Muslim women and men to develop an honest appreciation of Muhammad that does not compromise their own dignity and self-worth.

A rethinking of revelation and prophethood would also lead to a rethinking and new understanding of the central rituals, practices, and religious institutions. Such a rethinking would be conducive to the emergence of an egalitarian, nonsexist, and nonviolent Islam, a glimpse of which we catch in our encounters with a sufficient number of Muslims to sustain our faith in Islam as a viable option for those of us drawn to things religious.

NOTES

1. *See* Courtney W. Howland, *The Challenge of Religious Fundamentalism to the Liberty and Equality Rights of Women: An Analysis under the United Nations Charter,* 35 COLUM. J. TRANSNAT'L L. 271, 277–78 (1997).

2. *See, e.g.,* Riffat Hassan, *The Burgeoning of Islamic Fundamentalism: Toward an Understanding of the Phenomenon, in* THE FUNDAMENTALIST PHENOMENON: A VIEW FROM WITHIN; A RESPONSE FROM WITHOUT 151, 151–71 (Norman J. Cohen, ed.) (Grand Rapids, MI: William B. Eerdmans Publishing Co., 1990); Mir Maqsud Ali, *Resurgence of Islam: A Dream or a Reality?, in* ISLAM: A CONTEMPORARY PERSPECTIVE 33, 36 (Mohammad Ahmadullah Siddiqi, ed.) (Chicago/London/Delhi: NAAMPS Publications, 1994).

3. *See* Ghazala Anwar, *Muslim Feminist Discourses, in* FEMINIST THEOLOGY IN DIFFERENT CONTEXTS 53 (Elisabeth Schüssler Fiorenza & M. Shawn Copeland, eds.) (London: SCM Press and Maryknoll: Orbis Books, 1996).

4. *See, e.g.,* ABDULLAHI AHMED AN-NA 'IM, TOWARD AN ISLAMIC REFORMATION: CIVIL LIBERTIES, HUMAN RIGHTS, AND INTERNATIONAL LAW 10, 67–68 (Syracuse, N.Y.: Syracuse University Press, 1990).

5. Dr. Asghar Ali Engineer, activist and Islamic scholar, founded the Centre for Study of Society and Secularism, in Mumbai, India, which publishes the journal, *Indian Journal of Secularism.* Dr. Engineer, chief editor of the journal, is committed to secularism and yet, even in his liberal theological writings, he has not argued for a secular state as an Islamic imperative.

6. *See, e.g.,* Riffat Hassan, *An Islamic Perspective, in* WOMEN, RELIGION AND SEXUALITY 93, 93–96 (Jeanne Becher, ed.) (Trinity Press International, 1991) (1990).

7. *See, e.g.,* Azizah Y. al-Hibri, *Marriage Laws in Muslim Countries: A Comparative Study of Certain Egyptian, Syrian, Moroccan, and Tunisian Marriage Laws, in* 4 INT'L REV. COMP. PUB. POL'Y 227, 228 (Barbara Stark, ed.) (JAI Press Inc., 1992); FATIMA MERNISSI, THE VEIL AND THE MALE ELITE: A FEMINIST INTERPRETATION OF WOMEN'S RIGHTS IN ISLAM (Mary Jo Lakeland, trans.) (Reading, MA/Menlo Park, CA/New York/Ontario/Wokingham, UK/Amsterdam/Bonn/Sydney/Singapore/Tokyo/Madrid/San Juan/Paris/Seoul/Milan/Mexico City/Taipei: Addison-Wesley Publishing Company, 1991) (Editions Albin Michel S.A., 1987).

8. *See* Dr. Asghar Ali Engineer, *Islam and Transplantation of Organs,* 1 ISLAM AND MODERN AGE, June 1998, at 1–13 (discussing approaches of different theologians to transplants based on different text selections). For an example of a fundamentalist approach, see SAFIA IQBAL, WOMAN AND ISLAMIC LAW: REVISED EDITION 1991 (Shandar Market Chittli Qabar Delhi: Adam Publishers & Distributors, 1991).

9. *See* Sara Hossain, *The Jamaat's Proposed 'Blasphemy Law': Destroying Secular and Democratic Space, in* FATWAS AGAINST WOMEN IN BANGLADESH 110, 114–17 (Grabels, France: Women Living Under Muslim Laws, 1996).

10. *See* FAZLUR RAHMAN, ISLAMIC METHODOLOGY IN HISTORY ix-x, 27–85, 139–41 (Karachi: Central Institute of Islamic Research, 1965).

11. *Id.* at 27–85, 139–41.

12. *Id.* at 46, 70–76.

13. For example, the following hadith might serve as a guiding light: "[t]he reward of deeds depends upon the intentions and every person will get the reward according to what he has intended." Book of Revelation, Chapter: "How the divine inspirations started," in 1 THE TRANSLATION OF THE MEANINGS OF SAHIH AL-BUKHARI: ARABIC-ENGLISH 1 (Dr. Muhammad Muhsin Khan, trans.) (New Delhi: Kitab Bhavan, 5th ed., 1984) (hereinafter SAHIH AL-BUKHARI).

14. For example, the Qur'anic verse 4:34 states, "[T]hose women on whose part you fear insubordination (*nushuz*), admonish them, leave them alone in beds and beat them . . . ," and its corresponding hadith aids the political goal of subjugating women to men: "The Prophet said, '[n]one of you should flog his wife as he flogs a slave and then have sexual intercourse with her in the last part of the day.'" Book of Nikah (Wedlock), Chapter: 'Beat them (lightly)' 7 SAHIH AL-BUKHARI, *supra* note 13, at 100–01.

15. FAZLUR RAHMAN, PHILOSOPHY OF MULLA SADRA 184–88 (Sadr al-Din al-Shirazi) (Albany: State University of New York Press, 1975).

16. Fazlur Rahman, *Law and Ethics in Islam, in* ETHICS IN ISLAM 3, 11 (Richard G. Hovannissian, ed.) (Malibu, CA: Undena Publications, 1985) (hereinafter Rahman, *Law and Ethics*).

17. FAZLUR RAHMAN, MAJOR THEMES OF THE QUR'AN 1–16, 31, 69 (Minneapolis: Bibliotheca Islamica, 2d ed., 1989)

18. Rahman, *Law and Ethics, supra* note 16, at 13; Fazlur Rahman, *Some Key Ethical Concepts of the Qur'an,* 11 J. RELIGIOUS ETHICS 170, 176–82 (1983).

19. MOHAMMED ARKOÚN, RETHINKING ISLAM: COMMON QUESTIONS, UNCOMMON ANSWERS 30–34, 38 (Robert D. Lee, ed. & trans.) (Boulder/San Francisco/Oxford: Westview Press, 1994).

20. *Id.* at 37–38.

21. *Id.* at 30, 35, 38.

22. *See* PHILIP K. HITTI, HISTORY OF THE ARABS: FROM THE EARLIEST TIMES TO THE PRESENT 123 (London: Macmillan; New York: St. Martin's Press, 10th ed., 1970).

23. *See id.* at 123; JOHN BURTON, THE COLLECTION OF THE QUR'AN 105–13 (Cambridge/London/New York/Melbourne: Cambridge University Press, paperback, 1979).

24. ARKOÚN, *supra* note 19, at 36.

25. *Id.* at 36.

26. *Id.* at 37–39. For an analysis of the *mushaf* and a history of the collection of the Qur'an texts, see BURTON, *supra* note 23.

27. M.R. BAWA MUHAIYADDEEN, ISLAM & WORLD PEACE: EXPLANATIONS OF A SUFI 132–38 (Philadelphia, PA: The Fellowship Press, 1987).

28. ARKOÚN, *supra* note 19, at 39.

29. THE LIFE OF MUHAMMAD: A TRANSLATION OF ISḤĀQ'S SĪRAT RASŪL ALLĀH [D. 768] (A. Guillaume, ed. & trans.) (London: Oxford University Press, 1st ed., 1955).

30. For example, there are serious ethical issues raised by the presumption in the Qur'an and by the hadith (with respect to the Prophet) that women may be beaten. *See supra* note 14.

Contributors

MAHNAZ AFKHAMI

Mahnaz Afkhami is president of the Sisterhood Is Global Institute (SIGI) and executive director of the Foundation for Iranian Studies. She taught at the National University of Iran, where she chaired the English department. She was formerly Minister of State for Women's Affairs in Iran. Ms. Afkhami has written and lectured extensively on Muslim women's human rights, women and development, and women and leadership. Her many publications include: *Faith & Freedom: Women's Human Rights in the Muslim World* (ed.) (Syracuse: Syracuse University Press, 1995); and *In the Eye of the Storm: Women in Post-revolutionary Iran* (co-edited with Erika Friedl) (Syracuse: Syracuse University Press, 1994).

GHAZALA ANWAR

F.A. Kinnaird College; B.A. Kalamazoo College; M.A. Aligarh Muslim University; M.A. University of Chicago; Ph.D. Temple University

Ghazala Anwar is an associate professor in the religious studies department at the University of Christchurch, New Zealand. She started her education in Pakistan and completed it in the United States. As a scholar and teacher in Islamic studies, she specializes in Quranic Studies, hadith methodology, Islamic jurisprudence, Islamic humanities, Sufism, and women and Islam, and has published extensively in these areas.

CHRISTINE CHINKIN

LL.B., LL.M. University of London; LL.M. Yale University; Ph.D. University of Sydney

Christine Chinkin is professor of international law at the London School of Economics. She was formerly dean and professor of law at the University of Southampton in the United Kingdom. Professor Chinkin has taught international law on three continents and is one of the world's leading experts on public international law, human rights, especially women's rights, and dispute resolution. She has published extensively in all of these areas, and her many publications include *Third Parties in International Law* (Oxford: Clarendon Press/New York: Oxford University Press, 1993).

RADHIKA COOMARASWAMY

B.A. Yale University; J.D. Columbia University; Diploma, Parker School of International and Comparative Law; LL.M. Harvard University

Radhika Coomaraswamy is director of the International Centre for Ethnic Studies (ICES) in Colombo, Sri Lanka. Since 1994 she has also served as the United

Nations Special Rapporteur on Violence Against Women, investigating and reporting on such issues as domestic violence, Japanese military sexual slavery during
World War II, trafficking and prostitution in Eastern Europe, migrant workers in
Western Europe, and gendered aspects of violence during times of armed conflict
in Africa. She has written extensively in the areas of women, religion, and ethnicity.

MARIE-CLAIRE S.F.G. FOBLETS
LL.M., Ph.D. University of Leuven
Marie-Claire S.F.G. Foblets is professor of law and legal anthropology in the law
faculty of the Catholic University of Leuven in Leuven, Belgium, and at the Universities of Antwerp (U.I.A.) and Brussels (K.U.B.). She is also an associate professor at the University of Paris, Sorbonne. In addition, she is chair of the department
of social and cultural anthropology at the University of Leuven. Professor Foblets
has published extensively in several languages.

DEIRDRE FOTTRELL
*B.A., LL.B. University College Galway, National University of Ireland; M.A. Dublin
City University; LL.M. London School of Economics*
Deirdre Fottrell is lecturer in human rights law and director of the M.A. Programme
in Human Rights at the Institute of Commonwealth Studies at the University of
London. She holds degrees in law, English literature, and journalism. She has pub-
lished in the areas of children's rights and human rights in the Irish Republic.

LYNN P. FREEDMAN
B.A. Yale University; J.D. Harvard University; M.P.H. Columbia School of Public Health
Lynn Freedman is director of the Law and Policy Project at the Center for Population and Family Health at the Columbia School of Public Health in New York.
She is chair of the board of directors of Research, Action & Information Networks
for Bodily Integrity of Women (RAINB♀), and on the board of directors of
Baobab, Lagos, Nigeria, and on the board of the Reproductive Health Technolo-
gies Project. She has written extensively in the area of women's rights and reproductive health.

ASMA M. ABDEL HALIM
LL.B., LL.M. University of Khartoum; M.A. Ohio State University
Asma M. Abdel Halim is a fellow at the University of Michigan. She is also a technical advisor at USAID working in the Women in Development Office. Her degrees are in both common law and shari'ah (Islamic) law and she is currently
working on a project on the status of Sudanese women under the current Islamic
regime. She has published extensively in the area of women's human rights.

JOHN STRATTON HAWLEY
A.B. Amherst College; M.Div. Union Theological Seminary; Ph.D. Harvard University
John Stratton Hawley is professor of religion at Barnard College, Columbia Uni-
versity, and has frequently chaired this department. Until recently, he was director

of the National Resource Center for South Asia at Columbia, where he has also served as director of the Southern Asian Institute. He has published extensively, including several books in Indological studies, and has also edited several volumes, including *Fundamentalism and Gender* (New York: Oxford University Press, 1994).

MARIE-AIMÉE HÉLIE-LUCAS

Marie-Aimée Hélie-Lucas is an Algerian feminist of worldwide reputation who took part in the liberation struggle of Algeria. After Algeria achieved independence, she was put in charge of the policy of education and training in new industries and oil for three years. In 1984, she founded the international solidarity network, Women Living Under Muslim Laws (WLUML), for which she is the international coordinator. Since 1986 she has been editor of the WLUML journal, DOSSIERS, which provides information about the lives and struggles of women living in diverse Muslim communities and countries around the world. She has written and lectured extensively on women's issues and is widely published in both French and English.

COURTNEY W. HOWLAND

B.A. Barnard College, Columbia University; J.D. Yale University

Courtney W. Howland is visiting scholar in residence at the International Women's Human Rights Center at Georgetown University Law Center. Formerly, she was senior fellow at the International Rule of Law Center (IRLC) and scholar in residence at The George Washington University Law School. The 1998 conference on Religious Fundamentalisms and the Human Rights of Women grew out of her publication, *The Challenge of Religious Fundamentalism to the Liberty and Equality Rights of Women: An Analysis under the United Nations Charter,* 35 Columbia Journal of Transnational Law 271–377 (1997). She has also published in the areas of women's rights and the military.

PAULA E. HYMAN

B.J. Hebrew College of Boston; B.A. Radcliffe College; M.A., Ph.D. Columbia University

Paula E. Hyman is the Lucy Moses Professor of Modern Jewish History and chair of the Program in Judaic Studies at Yale University. She previously taught Jewish History at Columbia University. She also taught at the Jewish Theological Seminary of America and served there as Dean of the Seminary College of Jewish Studies. She was a founding member of Ezrat Nashim, one of the first American Jewish feminist groups. She has published extensively in the history of French Jewry and in Jewish women's history. Her many books include *Gender and Assimilation in Modern Jewish History: The Roles and Representation of Women* (Seattle: University of Washington Press, 1995).

RATNA KAPUR

B.A. University of New Delhi; B.A., M.A. Cambridge University; LL.M. Harvard University

Ratna Kapur is co-director of the Centre for Feminist Legal Research, New Delhi. She conducts training in the areas of feminist legal theory and practice, and women's rights in India and the Asia–Pacific region. Ms. Kapur has written extensively in the area of feminism and law. Her recent publications include *Subversive Sites: Feminist Engagements with Law in India* (New Delhi/Thousand Oaks/London: Sage Publications, 1996) (co-authored with Brenda Cossman).

FRANCES KISSLING

Frances Kissling is president and chief executive officer of Catholics for Free Choice (CFFC), located in Washington, D.C., with sister organizations in seven Latin American countries and a network extending throughout Europe, where CFFC is affiliated with the European Catholic Network. Ms. Kissling is a leader in the feminist religious and international reproductive health movements. She is co-founder of The Global Fund for Women; board member of the Sexuality Information and Education Council of the United States (SIECUS); and co-founder and advisor of The Religious Consultation on Population, Reproductive Health and Ethics. She has published extensively, including articles and opinion-editorial pieces in major newspapers and journals.

ANN ELIZABETH MAYER

B.A., M.A., Ph.D. University of Michigan; J.D. University of Pennsylvania; Certificate in Comparative and Islamic Law, School of Oriental and African Studies, University of London

Ann Elizabeth Mayer is associate professor of legal studies at the Wharton School of the University of Pennsylvania. She has researched in many countries, including Egypt, Kuwait, Libya, Morocco, Pakistan, the Sudan, and Tunisia, and has written extensively in the areas of Islamic law in contemporary Middle Eastern societies, human rights, women's rights, and comparative law. Her publications have been translated and published in Arabic, French, and Persian. Her numerous publications include *Islam and Human Rights: Tradition and Politics* (Boulder/San Francisco: Westview Press, 3d. ed., 1999).

AZAR NAFISI

Ph.D. University of Oklahoma

Azar Nafisi is currently visiting professor at the Foreign Policy Institute of Johns Hopkins University School of Advanced International Studies (SAIS), where she teaches in the areas of current cultural theories and the relation between aesthetics and politics. She taught English and Persian literature at Tehran University, Free Islamic University, and Allameh-Tabatbaii University. She left the Islamic Republic of Iran in 1997, and moved to the United States. She has written extensively on Western and Persian literature and culture, as well as on the rights of women. Her numerous publications include *Anti-Terra: A Critical Reading of Vladimir Nabakov's Novels* (Tehran: Tareh Now, 1994).

PAUL NEJELSKI

B.A., LL.B. Yale University; M.P.A. American University; Certificate in Theological Studies, Georgetown University

Paul Nejelski was an immigration judge with the U.S. Department of Justice from 1989 to 1998. He decided many important cases advancing women's rights in asylum cases. Judge Nejelski first joined the Department of Justice in 1964 as Assistant United States Attorney General for New Jersey. He later became chief of all immigration and nationality litigation in federal district and circuit courts as well as the first director of court research for the National Institute of Justice. From 1977–79, he was a Deputy Assistant Attorney General.

MARIA JOSÉ F. ROSADO NUNES

B.A. Faculdade de Filosofia, Ciências e Letras de Itajubá, Minas Gerais; M.S.S., Pontifícia Universidade Católica (PUC)/São Paolo and Université Catholique, Louvain-la-Neuve; Ph.D. École des Hautes Études, Paris

Maria José F. Rosado Nunes is graduate professor in religious sciences at Pontifícia Universidade Católica (PUC)/São Paolo and holds the Feminist Lecturer's Chair at the Universidade Metodista de São Paolo. She is a technical consultant to the Center for Women's Studies and Gender Relations (NEMGE) at the Universidade de São Paolo and is a director, and former vice-president, of the Institute for Religious Studies in Rio de Janeiro. In addition, she is coordinator for Brazil of Catholics for the Right to Decide. She was a member of the State Council of the Feminine Condition in São Paolo. She has published extensively on the Catholic position on abortion.

LUCINDA JOY PEACH

B.A. University of Massachusetts; M.A., Ph.D. Indiana University; J.D. New York University

Lucinda Joy Peach is assistant professor of philosophy and religion at American University, Washington, D.C. She teaches and researches in the area of ethics, especially applied and feminist ethics, law and religion, legal philosophy, and women's studies. She has written extensively on these topics and is a contributing author to *Women in American Culture: An Anthology* (Cambridge: Blackwell Publishers, 1998). Her recent publications regarding women and Buddhism include *Review of Rita M. Gross, Buddhism After Patriarchy,* Cyber Sangha 30–37 (Winter 1995).

FRANCES RADAY

LL.B. London School of Economics; Ph.D. Hebrew University of Jerusalem

Frances Raday is professor of law at Hebrew University of Jerusalem, where she holds the Lieberman Chair in Labour Law. She is chief editor of the Israel Law Review. She was chair of the Hebrew University's Lafer Center for Women's Studies from 1990 to 1996. Professor Raday has published extensively in several languages. She was co-author and chief editor of *Women's Status in Israeli Law and Society* (with C. Shalev and M. Kobi-Liban) (Tel Aviv: Shocken Publishing House, 1995) (in Hebrew), the first book on feminist legal theory published in Israel.

CECILE RICHARDS
B.A. Brown University
Cecile Richards is the founder and former executive director of the Texas Freedom Network (TFN) in Austin, Texas. The TFN is a nonprofit grassroots organization dedicated to providing an alternative to the religious political extremists in Texas, including the Christian Coalition. In addition, Ms. Richards formed a subgroup of TFN, Texas Faith Network, which includes ministers, priests and rabbis, and is a faith-based response to the religious right. Prior to founding the TFN, she spent ten years organizing low-wage service workers in Louisiana, Texas, and California, primarily with the Service Employees International Union. Ms. Richards has written articles for media journals and has been interviewed extensively by the media.

SUSAN D. ROSE
B.A. Dickinson College; M.A., Ph.D. Cornell University
Susan D. Rose is professor of sociology and chair of the sociology department at Dickinson College in Carlisle, Pennsylvania. She has written extensively in the area of Christian fundamentalism and is the author of numerous works on evangelicalism, fundamentalism, gender, education, sexuality, and violence. Her recent book, *Exporting the American Gospel: Global Christian Fundamentalism* (co-authored with Steve Brouwer and Paul Gifford) (New York/London: Routledge, 1996), is a comparative study of the growth of fundamentalism in Guatemala, the Philippines, South Korea, and Africa.

SUWANNA SATHA-ANAND
B.A. Chulalongkorn University; M.A., Ph.D. University of Hawaii
Suwanna Satha-Anand is associate professor of philosophy and former chair of the Philosophy department at the Chulalongkorn University, Bangkok, Thailand. Her research interests are in the fields of Buddhist philosophy, philosophy of women, and religions and social change. She has published extensively, and her recent books include: *Currents of Chinese Philosophy* (Bankok: Chulalongkorn University Press, 1996); and *Mahayana Buddhism and Buddhadasa's Philosophy* (Bangkok: Khrongkan Phoeiphrae Phoonngan Wichai, Fai Wichai, Chulalongkonmahawitthayalai, 1993).

MICHAEL SINGER
B.A., M.A. Cambridge University; Ph.D. King's College, University of London; J.D. Stanford University
Michael Singer is currently visiting senior research fellow at King's College, University of London. He was formerly executive director of the International Rule of Law Center, and a visiting professor of law at The George Washington University Law School. Dr. Singer has led several recent missions of legal experts for the Office for Democratic Institutions and Human Rights of the Organization for Security and Cooperation in Europe, to examine and report on democracy, human rights, and the rule of law in Albania and Belarus. He has published in the areas of human rights, immunities, and jurisdiction in international law.

BAHIA G. TAHZIB-LIE

LL.B., LL.M., Ph.D. Utrecht University; LL.M. University of Michigan
Bahia G. Tahzib-Lie is the human rights advisor at the Human Rights Department of the Netherlands Ministry of Foreign Affairs in The Hague. Dr. Tahzib-Lie has also served as a legal staff member at the Council of State, Legislation Department, The Hague, and has been lecturer in the fields of international law and international organizations in the law faculty of Utrecht University. She was researcher in the area of human rights at the Baha'i International Community United Nations Office, Geneva. Her numerous publications include *Freedom of Religion or Belief: Ensuring Effective International Legal Protection* (The Hague: Martinus Nijhoff, 1996).

GERALDINE VAN BUEREN

LL.B. University of Wales; LL.M. University of London
Geraldine Van Bueren is professor of international human rights law and director of the Programme on International Rights of the Child in the faculty of law of Queen Mary and Westfield College, University of London. She represented Amnesty International during the negotiations on the United Nations Convention on the Rights of the Child and also participated in the drafting of the United Nations Rules for the Protection of Juveniles Deprived of their Liberty and the United Nations High Commissioner for Refugees' Guidelines on Refugee Children. She has written extensively on children's rights issues, and her numerous publications include *The International Law on the Rights of the Child* (Dordecht/Boston/London: Martinus Nijhoff Publishers: Kluwer Academic Publishers, 1995).

SAKENA YACOOBI

B.A. University of the Pacific; M.A. Loma Linda University
Sakena Yacoobi is volunteer executive director of the Afghan Institute of Learning (an Afghan women's nongovernmental organization), which she founded in 1995 with two other women in Peshawar, Pakistan. She was born in Herat, Afghanistan, and received her college education in the United States. She was a professor of psychology, mathematics, and biology at D-Etre University in Detroit, Michigan, before becoming coordinator of the female education programs for the International Rescue Committee in Peshawar, Pakistan, in 1992 and the ACBAR delegate working on the education portion of the United Nations Rehabilitation Plan for Afghanistan.

NIRA YUVAL-DAVIS

B.A., M.A. Hebrew University of Jerusalem; Ph.D. Sussex University
Nira Yuval-Davis is professor and graduate course director in gender and ethnic studies at the University of Greenwich in London, the United Kingdom. She is a founding member of Women Against Fundamentalism based in London. She has

written extensively on the intersectionality of gender, race, ethnicity, class, citizenship, nationalism, and fundamentalism, both theoretically and in several historical contexts, especially Israel, the United Kingdom, and in Settler Societies. Her numerous publications include: *Gender And Nation* (London: Thousand Oaks/New Delhi: Sage Publications, 1997); and *Refusing Holy Orders: Women And Fundamentalism In The UK* (co-edited with Gita Sahgal) (London: Virago, 1992).